GAMSAT-Prep.com

The Gold Standard textbook is a critical component of a multimedia experience including live courses on campus, MP3s, smartphone apps, online videos and interactive programs, *Heaps* of Practice GAMSATs and a lot more.

GAMSAT-Prep.com

The only prep you need.™

Gold Standard Live GAMSAT Courses are held in the following cities:
Sydney • Melbourne • Dublin • London • Brisbane • Perth • Adelaide • Cork

GOLD STANDARD
MULTIMEDIA EDUCATION

* GAMSAT is administered by ACER which does not endorse this study guide.

THE GOLD STANDARD

GAMSAT

Editor and Author

Brett Ferdinand BSc MD-CM

Contributors

Lisa Ferdinand BA MA
Sean Pierre BSc MD
Kristin Finkenzeller BSc MD
Ibrahima Diouf BSc MSc PhD
Charles Haccoun BSc MD-CM
Timothy Ruger BA MA
Jeanne Tan Te

Illustrators

Harvie W. Gallatiera BSc
Daphne McCormack
Nanjing Design
• Ren Yi, Huang Bin
• Sun Chan, Li Xin

RuveneCo inc

Free Online Access Features*

Chapter Review Questions
Access to relevant, topical teaching videos from our GS Video Library
Organic Chemistry Summary (cross-referenced)
Physics Equation List (cross-referenced)

*One year of continuous access for the original owner of this textbook using the enclosed online access card.

Be sure to register at www.GAMSAT-prep.com by clicking on Register in the top right corner of the website. Once you login, click on GAMSAT Textbook Owners in the right column and follow directions. Please Note: benefits are for 1 year from the date of on-line registration, for the original book owner only and are not transferable; unauthorized access and use outside the Terms of Use posted on GAMSAT-prep.com may result in account deletion; if you are not the original owner, you can purchase your virtual access card separately at GAMSAT-prep.com.

Visit The Gold Standard's Education Center at www.gold-standard.com.

Copyright (c) 2017 RuveneCo (Worldwide), 1st Edition

ISBN 978-1-927338-39-1

Address all inquiries, comments, or suggestions to the publisher. For Terms of Use go to: www.GAMSAT-prep.com

The reviews on the back cover represent the opinions of individuals and do not necessarily reflect the opinions of the institutions they represent.

Gold Standard GAMSAT Product Contact Information

Distribution in Australia, NZ, Asia	**Distribution in Europe**	**Distribution in North America**
Woodslane Pty Ltd	Central Books	RuveneCo Publishing
10 Apollo Street Warriewood	99 Wallis Road	334 Cornelia Street # 559
NSW 2102 Australia	LONDON,	Plattsburgh, New York
ABN: 76 003 677 549	E9 5LN, United Kingdom	12901, USA
learn@gamsat-prep.com	orders@centralbooks.com	buy@gamsatbooks.com

RuveneCo Inc. is neither associated nor affiliated with the Australian Council for Educational Research (ACER) who has developed and administers the Graduate Medical School Admissions Test (GAMSAT) nor The University of Sydney. Printed in China.

This is not a typical 1st edition textbook.

The Gold Standard GAMSAT, the first GAMSAT textbook ever, had already gone through 5 editions with significant revisions. In the last edition, hundreds of new pages were added and it grew to just over 3 kilograms (the weight of a healthy baby!). Unfortunately, that met with some student complaints, it had become unwieldy - especially if the aim was to review a small section of the book on campus or at work. Meanwhile, we had plans to revise and expand the book yet again.

And so, with more content, more images and more practice questions, the 1 textbook has become 3. We hope that studying will now be more convenient!

Besides adding more content, we have added more online access. Previous editions had 10 hours of video access over the 1-year online access period. Throwing caution to the wind, for the first time ever, we have increased access to unlimited viewings of our hundreds of online videos during the 1-year access period.

Over 8 years, we have been teaching monthly GAMSAT webinars, science review GAMSAT courses on campuses in Australia, the UK and Ireland, as well as producing over 100 YouTube videos providing step-by-step worked solutions to the official (ACER's) practice materials for the GAMSAT. We have met the full range of GAMSAT students: 'young' and 'old', hoping for a career vs. having built one already, arts vs. science, experts vs. neophytes, etc. In all likelihood, we have heard your voice expressed, to one degree or the other, among the thousands of students that we have taught over the years. Each time, we grew and improved with that voice in mind.

We hope to impart to you our excitement about the awesome beauty of learning, and of sharing the mental manoeuvres of those who are still here, and others throughout history from Aristotle to Pythagoras, and from Freud to Newton.

Your formula for GAMSAT success comes in 3 parts: content review, practice problems, and full-length testing. We will guide you through the process.

Let's begin.

– B.F., MD

GAMSAT SCORE!

Good, we have your attention! We just want to be sure that you understand that not every student needs the same Section 3 (science) score in order to be admitted to medical school. Some science students must ace Section 3 to be admitted while some non-science students can gain admittance with an average Section 3 score because of an exceptional performance in the non-science sections. This book is for all students. This means that there may be some science chapters that might not be "worth it" for the non-science student. So we have colour-coded the importance of chapters in providing pertinent background information based on our experience.

HIGH   MEDIUM   LOW

Now you can use your own judgement based on how much time you have to study and our assessment of the **importance** of that chapter. Also, if you have no science background in any of the subjects then we highly recommend taking advantage of the hours of online video time that comes with this textbook. In addition, we suggest that all students complete the non-science problem sets in this textbook as well as the science chapter review questions with worked solutions that are online. Reviewing content only provides the background needed for science reasoning. In order to move to the next level, you must do problem sets followed by timed, full-length practice. Review, practice and full-length testing can help you obtain an exceptional GAMSAT score.

As of the publication date of this textbook, calculators are no longer permitted.

To further discuss any of the issues above: gamsat-prep.com/forum.

The Graduate Medical School Admissions Test (GAMSAT) is a paper-based test (no calculators are allowed) and consists of 2 essay writing tasks and 185 multiple-choice questions. This exam requires approximately 5.5 hours to complete and is comprised of 3 Sections. There is no break between Section I and II. There is a lunch break between Section II and III. The following are the three subtests of the GAMSAT exam:

1. **Section I: Reasoning in Humanities and Social Sciences - 75 questions; 100 min.**

   - Interpretation and understanding of ideas in socio-cultural context. Source materials: written passages, tabular or other visual format.

2. **Section II: Written Communication - 2 essays; 60 min.**

   - Ability to produce and develop ideas in writing. Task A essay: socio-cultural issues, more analytical; Task B more personal and social issues.

3. **Section III: Reasoning in Biological and Physical Sciences - 110 questions, 170 min.**

   - Chemistry (40%), Biology (40%), Physics (20%). First-year undergraduate level in Biology and Chemistry and Year 12/A-Level/Leaving Certificate course in Physics. Chemistry is equally divided into General and Organic.

> The overall GAMSAT score is calculated using the following formula*:
>
> Overall Score = (1 x Section I + 1 x Section II + 2 x Section III) / 4

* Note: the formula applies to all medical schools that require the GAMSAT in Australia, the UK and Ireland except for the University of Melbourne and University of Sydney which currently weigh all 3 sections equally. Please carefully review the admissions information for all of your target programmes.

Common formula for acceptance:

GPA + GAMSAT score + Interview = Medical School Admissions

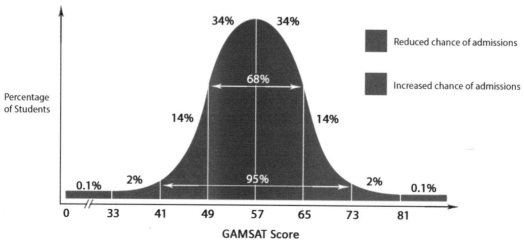

GAMSAT Score
Typical Overall GAMSAT Score Distribution (Approx)

The GAMSAT is challenging, get organised.

gamsat-prep.com/free-GAMSAT-study-schedule

1. How to study:

1. Study the Gold Standard (GS) textbook and videos to learn
2. Do GS Chapter review practice questions
3. Consolidate: create and review your personal summaries (= Gold Notes) daily

2. Once you have completed your studies:

1. Full-length practice test
2. Review mistakes, all solutions
3. Consolidate: review all your Gold Notes and create more
4. Repeat until you get beyond the score you need for your targeted medical/dental school

Recommended GAMSAT Communities:
- All countries (mainly Australia): pagingdr.net
- Mainly UK: thestudentroom.co.uk (Medicine Community Discussion)
- Mainly Ireland: boards.ie

Is there something in the Gold Standard that you did not understand? Don't get frustrated, get on-line: gamsat-prep.com/forum

GAMSAT Scores*

50% not science   50% science

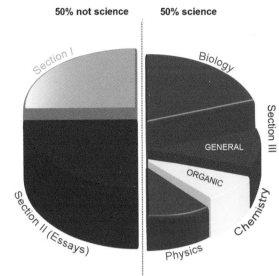

Section I
Biology
Section III
GENERAL
ORGANIC
Chemistry
Section II (Essays)
Physics

*see exceptions on previous page.

3. Full-length practice tests:

1. ACER practice exams
2. Gold Standard GAMSAT exams
3. Heaps of GAMSAT Practice: 10 full-length exams

4. How much time do you need?

On average, 3-6 hours per day for 3-6 months; depending on life experiences, 2 weeks may be enough and 8 months could be insufficient.

To make the content easier to retain, you can also find aspects of the Gold Standard programme in other formats such as:

Good luck with your studies!

Gold Standard Team

THE GOLD STANDARD
MULTIMEDIA EDUCATION

GAMSAT Section 3, Reasoning in Biological and Physical Sciences, is the longest of the 3 subtests on exam day (110 MCQs). 'Biological Sciences' refers to Organic Chemistry and Biology. 'Physical Sciences', which is the focus of this textbook, refers to Physics and General (Inorganic, not Organic) Chemistry. In our experience, most students with a non-science background (NSB) can successfully learn the assumed knowledge for GAMSAT independently, while a smaller number may need to enrol in a short tertiary-level science course.

Essentially, 20% of Section 3 is Physics and 20% is General Chemistry. The level of assumed knowledge is first year university Chemistry and A-Level/Leaving Certificate/Year 12 Physics. Before examining these 2 subsections, we need to revisit a graphic presented in the Section 1 segment of our GS GAMSAT Book 1, Bloom's taxonomy:

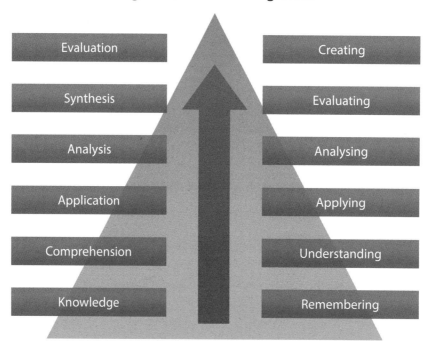

Figure 1: Bloom's original taxonomy on the left and revised taxonomy on the right (Anderson, Krathwohl 2002; Adapted from Tangient LLC 2014).

GAMSAT requires HOTS, not LOTS! Effective and efficient studying – with reasoning as the priority – trumps attempts to commit copious amounts of detail to memory.

For a typical secondary or tertiary-level exam, you could read all the chapters in the relevant book, commit as much to memory as possible, walk into the exam room, match the questions with your knowledge, and reply. Your training: study anytime, even the night before the exam since you might encounter something that is word-for-word on exam day, replicate what you read, and you can ace the exam, in fact, you are brilliant!

The GAMSAT: study all you want even the night before, extremely unlikely to be able to identify something word-for-word on exam day, no feeling of being brilliant (this is true even for many students who actually 'ace' the exam). The actual exam includes 2 atypical sensations: 1) you must learn a lot of new information *during* the exam; 2) the topics and questions almost seem random. In some ways, these atypical sensations emulate life as a doctor!

In summary, you have been trained to focus on 'knowledge' as a priority to succeed in university studies. Frankly, for some exams, 'understanding' is secondary. If you had both knowledge and understanding, you would likely ace any exam – except GAMSAT. We will continually try to adjust the way you study while you read chapters herein. Aim for HOTS.

Why is there so much GAMSAT Math content in this textbook?

GAMSAT is designed and administered by ACER. Here is ACER's quote about the structure and content of the exam:

"The purpose of GAMSAT is to assess the ability to understand and analyse material, to think critically about issues ... to read and think about a passage of writing, to interpret graphical displays of information, to use mathematical relationships and to apply reasoning skills to tables of data."

https://gamsat.acer.org/about-gamsat/structure-and-content (2017)

In their very first paragraph regarding the exam's structure and content, they embedded at least 3 phrases that link directly to GAMSAT Math: 'analyse', 'interpret graphical displays', and 'use mathematical relationships'. And maths is not a formal GAMSAT subject, shocking!

The first time we published GAMSAT books, the calculator was permitted, so we had no GAMSAT Math chapters. Then the calculator was banned for GAMSAT (which underlines the fact that you should avoid its use – even when you practice). We then added a section for GAMSAT Math. Due to its popularity among science and NSB students alike, it has finally become – beyond our expectations – the section of this book with more pages than either Physics or General Chemistry!

GAMSAT Math is the foundation for all GAMSAT Section 3, except perhaps GAMSAT Organic Chemistry. The other 3 sciences follow ACER's quote very closely. In our Book 3 on Biological Sciences, you will discover ACER's emphasis on geometric (spatial) reasoning which is unique to GAMSAT Organic Chemistry. The other 3 sciences have a laser-like focus on equation manipulation – with or without exponential or logarithmic relationships – and the interpretation and analysis of diagrams, graphs, tables and flow charts.

If you are a NSB candidate, please do not consider advancing in the sciences without fortifying the foundation by working through all the GAMSAT Math chapters. For students who already have adequate algebra skills, our GAMSAT Math chapters will begin at an excruciatingly (!!) basic level; however, we assure you that irrespective of your academic background, you will encounter problems across the GAMSAT Math (GM) chapters that will challenge you and improve your performance on the real exam. In particular, we have added new and unique content to – what may be the 2 chapters that will have the greatest effect on your GAMSAT score – GM Chapter 2: Scientific Measurement and Dimensional Analysis, and GM Chapter 3: Algebra and Graph Analysis.

What is Physics?

Physics is largely concerned with the nature and properties of matter (= *physic*al substances) and energy. This includes mechanics (= movement and forces), heat, light and other radiation, sound, electricity, magnetism, and the structure of atoms.

Physics is not just about sending rocket ships to the moon. Physics includes walking (gait), running, surfing, throwing, blood circulation, heart defibrillation, bungee jumping, vision, etc. In fact, all of the preceding have been publicly reported as past GAMSAT Physics topics on the real exam. From common every day events to the strange behaviour of tiny things (subatomic particles, PHY Chapter 12), all can be described by graphs and/or equations.

As Latin was the language of ancient Romans, Math is the language of Physics. In fact, there have been branches of Math that have been 'invented' simply to describe occurrences in the physical world.

What is General Chemistry?

General (or Inorganic, not Organic) Chemistry is principally concerned with atoms and molecules, how they interact, and how they transform into other atoms and molecules. The one basic force that underlies virtually all GAMSAT General Chemistry, *electrostatics*, boils down to the one catch phrase that almost everyone has heard before: 'opposites attract' and thus like charges repel. The latter is not an oversimplification, it is the true founding principle of Chemistry.

General Chemistry includes stoichiometry (the quantitative relationship between reactants and products), the infamous periodic table, the different phases of matter (gas, liquid, solid), acids & bases, heat changes in reactions (thermodynamics), how quickly reactions occur (rate processes), and the production of electricity from chemicals (electrochemistry).

You have always been a chemist. As a child, you likely experimented by mixing water with some solid or crystals (dirt, salt, sugar, whatever!) and observed solubility and precipitation (= 2 common GAMSAT topics; the latter relates to the inability to dissolve any more). As an adult, you took it much further: brewing coffee or tea; dissolving sugar (easier at high temperature rather than low temperature); noting the separation of oil and water; observing the phase changes of water – ice (solid), 'water' (liquid), steam (gas); acids (pH < 7) with their sour taste as opposed to bases (pH > 7); the in-house chemistry lab: the kitchen (adding energy to *denature* or change certain bonding patterns); the curious energy stored in batteries (electrochemistry) – just to name a few.

How do I study GAMSAT Physics and General Chemistry?

We do not believe that it would be an efficient use of your time to plan to read all chapters in this textbook multiple times, nor to attempt to read straight through from the beginning to the end in one go. Ideally, you would plan to read each chapter once while taking very brief notes (less than 1 page per chapter). Either before or after reading a chapter – where applicable – watch the online videos for that chapter while also taking very brief notes. Review your notes often according to your GAMSAT study schedule which you can modify from the one we created (gamsat-prep.com/free-GAMSAT-study-schedule).

Afterwards, we have 3 levels of practice questions:

1) Basic, understanding questions to ensure that you have read the chapter; if you have a NSB, if you do not know the answer, it would be better to treat these questions as 'open-book' questions rather than just looking at the solutions;

2) Reasoning, application questions which are designed to get you using HOTS (!!);

3) Full-length practice tests which span the depth and breadth of a simulation of the real exam. Be warned: We do not replicate real exam questions, we replicate real exam reasoning.

For GAMSAT Sciences, "Study, practice, then full-length testing" should be your mantra for success!

A word about your online access card . . .

The GS Online Access Cards have saved thousands of trees and have reduced the cost of this book to you. It is not just the hundreds of online MCQs that you get access to with your personal identification number (PIN), it is the fact that we do not have to limit the length of our worked solutions because of printing cost restrictions. It permits this textbook to sell for less than most with the same production value.

Additionally, your PIN now provides more online video access than we have ever provided. Most students find that our Gold Standard videos at gamsat-prep.com and YouTube are very helpful for GAMSAT preparation. If, however, you do not find that your understanding is advancing efficiently, you could try other free video resources such as Khan Academy or the Physics/Chemistry Crash Course on YouTube. Since ACER does not provide an official syllabus, consider using our Gold Standard GAMSAT Index as a guide so that you avoid non-GAMSAT content.

Cross-references!

Wherever possible, we will identify another chapter, section or subsection of the book where you can find more information regarding a particular topic. For the most part, each book is self-contained but there are some exceptional cases where we cross-reference between different GS books. The following table contains a summary of the abbreviations used throughout the following chapters.

Cross-references in the Gold Standard (GS) books, videos, apps, etc.

Abbreviation	Subject	Gold Standard (GS) Book
GM	GAMSAT Math	GS Physical Sciences, Book 2
CHM	General Chemistry	GS Physical Sciences, Book 2
PHY	Physics	GS Physical Sciences, Book 2
ORG	Organic Chemistry	GS Biological Sciences, Book 3
BIO	Biology	GS Biological Sciences, Book 3
RHSS	Reasoning in Humanities & Social Sciences	GS Section 1 & 2, Book 1
WC	Written Communication	GS Section 1 & 2, Book 1

For example, CHM 2.4 means that you will find more information by looking at the GS Physical Sciences textbook, Chapter 2 General Chemistry, in the section 2.4. After a few chapters, you will find the system to be quite straightforward and, often, helpful.

Note: Despite the many new additions throughout this textbook, it remains 99% error-free. Should you have any doubts, join us at gamsat-prep.com/forum.

Good luck!

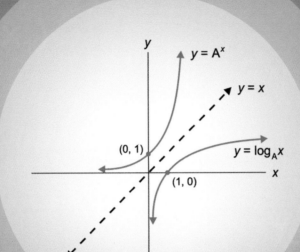

GAMSAT MATH

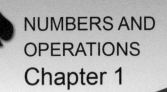

NUMBERS AND OPERATIONS
Chapter 1

Memorize	Understand	Not Required
* Properties of Real Numbers * Order of Operations * Rules on Zero * Important Fraction-Decimal Conversions * Properties of Exponents * Common squares and cubes of integers	* Integer, Rational, and Real Numbers * Basic Operations and Definitions * Fractions, Mixed Numbers, Decimals and Percentages * Root and Exponent Manipulations * Ratios and Proportions	* Advanced-level math * Memorizing mathematical terms

GAMSAT-Prep.com

Introduction

Math is not specifically a section of the GAMSAT but basic, secondary school math is necessary for most GAMSAT Physical Sciences (i.e. Physics and General Chemistry), and a surprising amount of GAMSAT Biological Sciences (particularly logs and graph analysis in Biology). Thus GAMSAT Section 3 preparation must begin with math.

There will never be a GAMSAT question where you would need to know mathematical terms in order to get the right answer (i.e. terms such as 'rational numbers' or 'integers' or 'associative laws', etc.). However, if we are to have an understanding of 'GAMSAT Math' then, for some students, we will need to start with the basics. If the math is too basic for you, either skim through until it gets to your level, or at least complete the practice questions within chapters and at the end of the chapters to ensure that you are up to speed. As for your entire Section 3 review, please take very brief notes ('Gold Notes') and review them frequently according to your GAMSAT study schedule.

Additional Resources

Free Online Forum

Special Guest

1.1 Integers, Rational Numbers, and the Number Line

1.1.1 Integers

Integers are whole numbers without any decimal or fractional portions. They can be any number from negative to positive infinity including zero.

> **EXAMPLES** −2, −1, 0, 1, 2, 3 etc.

1.1.2 Rational Numbers

Rational numbers are numbers that can be written as fractions of integers. "Rational" even contains the word "ratio" in it, so if you like, you can simply remember that these are ratio numbers.

EXAMPLES

$$\frac{1}{2}$$

$$-5 \left(-5 = \frac{-5}{1} \right)$$

$$1.875 \left(1.875 = \frac{15}{8} \right)$$

> **NOTE**
>
> Every integer is also a rational number, but not every rational number is an integer. You can write them as fractions simply by dividing by 1.

Make sure you are extra careful when ratios and fractions are involved because they are notorious for causing mistakes.

Irrational numbers are numbers that cannot be written as fractions of integers. Irrational numbers are normally numbers that have a decimal number that goes on forever with no repeating digits.

EXAMPLES

$$\sqrt{2} = 1.4142135623730950...$$

$$Pi = \pi = 3.14159265358979...$$

$$e = 2.718281828459045...$$

For GAMSAT Math, it is expected that you have memorized pi to 3.14 and you will work faster during the exam if you recognize root 2 as 1.4 and root 3 as 1.7.

We will discuss the number e in context (natural logs) in Chapter 3.

1.1.3 Real Numbers and the Number Line

Real numbers are all numbers that can be represented on the number line. These include both rational and irrational numbers.

EXAMPLES

$$0, -\frac{1}{3}, \sqrt{2}, \text{ etc.}$$

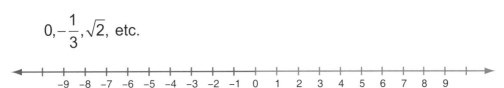

The **number line** is an infinite straight line on which every point corresponds to a real number. As you move up the line to the right, the numbers get larger, and down the line to the left, the numbers get smaller.

Absolute value refers to how far a real number is from zero on the number line and it is indicated by a bar "|" placed on either side of a number or expression. For GAMSAT purposes, "absolute value" means to remove any negative sign in front of a number, thus the number must be positive (or zero). Thus |−3| = 3, and |8| = 8, and |−4×8| = 32. {This simple concept is needed for: ACER's current *GAMSAT Practice Questions* "Red" booklet, Section 3, Unit 12, Question 33.}

1.2 Basic Arithmetic

1.2.1 Basic Operations

An **operation** is a procedure that is applied to numbers. The fundamental operations of arithmetic are addition, subtraction, multiplication, and division.

A **sum** is the number obtained by adding numbers.

EXAMPLE

The sum of 7 and 2 is 9 since $2 + 7 = 9$.

A **difference** is the number obtained by subtracting numbers.

EXAMPLE

In the equation $7 - 2 = 5$, 5 is the difference of 7 and 2.

A **product** is the number obtained by multiplying numbers.

EXAMPLE

The product of 7 and 2 is 14 since $7 \times 2 = 14$.

A **quotient** is the number obtained by dividing numbers.

> Unlike a sum or a product, difference and quotient can result in different numbers depending on the order of the numbers in the expression:
>
> $$10 - 2 = 8 \text{ while } 2 - 10 = -8$$
> $$20 \div 5 = 4 \text{ while } 5 \div 20 = 0.25$$

The sum and difference of positive numbers are obtained by simple addition and subtraction, respectively. The same is true when adding negative numbers, except that the sum takes on the negative sign.

EXAMPLES

$$(-3) + (-9) = -12$$

$$(-5) + (-12) + (-44) = -61$$

On the other hand, when adding two integers with unlike signs, you need to ignore the signs first, and then subtract the smaller number from the larger number. Then follow the sign of the larger number in the result.

EXAMPLES

$$(-6) + 5 = 6 - 5 = -1$$

$$7 + (-10) = 10 - 7 = -3$$

When subtracting two numbers of unlike signs, start by changing the minus sign into its reciprocal, which is the plus sign. Next reverse the sign of the second

EXAMPLE

In the equation $8 \div 2 = 4$, 4 is the quotient of 8 and 2.

number. This will make the signs of the two integers the same. Now follow the rules for adding integers with like signs.

EXAMPLES

$$(-6) - 5 = (-6) + (-5) = -11$$

$$7 - (-10) = 7 + 10 = 17$$

Multiplication and division of integers are governed by the same rules: If the numbers have like signs, the product or quotient is positive. If the numbers have unlike signs, the answer is negative.

EXAMPLES

$$5 \times 6 = 30$$
$$-5 \times -3 = 15$$
$$81 \div 9 = 9$$
$$-20 \div -4 = 5$$
$$7 \times -4 = -28$$
$$-9 \times 6 = -54$$
$$-15 \div 3 = -5$$
$$16 \div -2 = -8$$

An **expression** is a grouping of numbers and mathematical operations.

EXAMPLE

$2 + (3 \times 4) \times 5$ is a mathematical expression.

An **equation** is a mathematical sentence consisting of two expressions joined by an equals sign. When evaluated properly, the two expressions must be equivalent.

EXAMPLE

$2 \times (1+3) = \dfrac{16}{2}$ is an equation

since the expressions on both sides of the equals sign are equivalent to 8.

> **NOTE**
>
> Whenever you see simple calculations in these chapters, take the time to make sure that you are able to make the presented calculations quickly and efficiently. We know that you have learnt all of these skills before, we just want to firmly rebuild your foundation for more complex, speed-driven, GAMSAT-level math.

1.2.1.1 Summary of Properties of Positive and Negative Integers

Positive + Positive = Positive

$$5 + 4 = 9$$

Negative + Negative = Negative

$$(-6) + (-2) = -8$$

Positive + Negative = Sign of the highest number and then subtract

$$(-5) + 4 = -1$$
$$(-8) + 10 = 2$$

Negative − Positive = Negative

$$(-7) - 10 = -17$$

Positive − Negative = Positive + Positive = Positive

$$6 - (-4) = 6 + 4 = 10$$

Negative − Negative = Negative + Positive = Sign of the highest number and then subtract

$$(-8) - (-7) = (-8) + 7 = -1$$

Negative × Negative = Positive

$$(-2) \times (-5) = 10$$

Positive/Positive = Positive

$$8/2 = 4$$

Negative × Positive = Negative

$$(-9) \times 3 = -27$$

Positive/Negative = Negative

$$64/(-8) = -8$$

1.2.2 Properties of the Real Numbers

Whenever you are working within the real numbers, these properties hold true. It isn't necessary to memorize the name of each property, but you must be able to apply them all.

Symmetric Property of Equality: The right and left hand sides of an equation are interchangeable, so if $a = b$, then $b = a$.

Transitive Property of Equality: If $a = b$ and $b = c$, then $a = c$. This means that if you have two numbers both equal to one other number, those two numbers are also equal.

Commutative Property of Addition: When adding numbers, switching the position of the numbers will not change the outcome, so $a + b = b + a$.

Associative Property of Addition: When adding more than two numbers, it doesn't matter what order you do the addition in, so $(a + b) + c = a + (b + c)$.

Commutative Property of Multiplication: When multiplying numbers, switching the position of the numbers will not change the outcome, so $a \times b = b \times a$.

Associative Property of Multiplication: When multiplying more than two numbers, it doesn't matter what order you do the multiplication in, so $(a \times b) \times c = a \times (b \times c)$.

Identity Property of Addition: When zero is added or subtracted to any number, the answer is the number itself, so $10b - 0 = 10b$.

Identity Property of Multiplication: When a number is multiplied or divided by 1, the answer is the number itself, so $6a \times 1 = 6a$.

Distributive Property of Multiplication: When multiplying a factor on a group of numbers that are being added or subtracted, the factor may be distributed by multiplying it by each number in the group, so $a (b - c) = ab - ac$.

> Subtraction and division do not follow associative laws.

1.2.3 Order of Operations

Knowing the order of operations is fundamental to evaluating numerical expressions. If you follow it properly, you will always come up with the correct answer! Here it is in list form, to be followed from the top down:

Parentheses
Exponents (including square roots)
Multiplication
Division
Addition
Subtraction

This forms the simple acronym **PEMDAS**, which is a great way to keep the operations straight. Alternatively, some people find it easier to remember the phrase "**P**lease **E**xcuse **M**y **D**ear **A**unt **S**ally."

If you don't like either of these techniques, feel free to come up with your own. It's important to have this clear because, as simple as it may seem, being able to carry out the order of operations quickly is crucial.

Using PEMDAS, let's evaluate this expression composed only of integers.

$$2^2 + [(3 + 2) \times 2 - 9]$$

First, evaluate the expression contained in the inner set of parentheses.

$$= 2^2 + [(5) \times 2 - 9]$$

You can then choose to strictly follow the PEMDAS order by evaluating the exponent next. Alternatively, you can perform the operations within the square brackets, working your way outward, for a more organized procedure as follows:

First, perform the multiplication.

$$= 2^2 + (10 - 9)$$

Then, perform the subtraction.

$$= 2^2 + 1$$

Now evaluate the exponent.

$$= 4 + 1$$

Finally, evaluate the remaining expression.

$$= 5$$

NOTE

- Multiplication and division have the same rank. It is generally recommended to do them in order from left to right as they appear in the expression, but you can also do them in whatever order that makes most sense to you.

- The same goes for addition and subtraction. Execute them from left to right, or in the order that feels most comfortable.

- When you encounter nested parentheses, evaluate the innermost ones first then work your way outward.

NOTE

Don't like PEMDAS? BODMAS is equally helpful! BODMAS stands for "B"rackets, "O"f or "O"rder, "D"ivision, "M"ultiplication, "A"ddition and "S"ubtraction. As long as you have the order correct, the means to help you remember can be whatever is easiest for you.

1.3 Rules on Zero

1.3.1 Addition and Subtraction with Zero

Zero is a unique number, and it has special properties when it comes to operations.

Zero is known as the **additive identity** of the real numbers since whenever it is added to (or subtracted from) a number, that number does not change.

Let's examine a simple expression.

$$(3 + 2) - 4$$

We can add or subtract zero anywhere within the expression and the value will not change:

$$(3 - 0 + 2) - 4 + 0$$
$$= (3 + 2) - 4$$

The addition or subtraction of the two zeros has no effect whatsoever on the outcome.

1.3.2 Multiplication and Division with Zero

When adding zero in an expression, it is easy to come up with a practical picture of what the operation represents; you begin with a collection of things and add zero more things to them. When multiplying and dividing with zero, however, such a conceptualization is more difficult. The idea of using zero in this manner is far more abstract.

Fortunately, you don't need to wrestle with trying to picture what multiplication or division with zero looks like. You can simply remember these easy rules:

Multiplying by Zero: The result of multiplying any quantity by zero is *always* equal to zero.

Remember that by the commutative property of multiplication, $a \times b = b \times a$, so

if we let $b = 0$, then we have $a \times 0 = 0 \times a$. This means that instead of trying to imagine multiplying a number by zero, you can reverse the thought and consider multiplying zero by a number instead. This second statement is more natural to visualize. You start with nothing, and then no matter how many times you duplicate that nothing, you still end up with nothing.

EXAMPLE

$3 \times 0 = 0$

$123.79 \times 0 = 0$

$$\left[1.2 + \left(37 - \sqrt{5} \right) \times 2.331 \right] \times 0 = 0$$

In the last example, there is no need to go through the order of operations and evaluate the expression inside the parentheses. Because you can see immediately that the entire parenthetical expression is being multiplied by zero, you know that the end result will be zero.

Zero Divided by a Number: The result of dividing zero by any quantity is *always* equal to zero. As with multiplication by zero, if you start with nothing and then take a portion of that nothing, you still end up with nothing.

EXAMPLE

$$0 \div 3 = 0$$

$$0 \div 123.79 = 0$$

$$0 \div \left[1.2 + \left(37 - \sqrt{5} \right) \times 2.331 \right] = 0$$

Just like with the multiplication by zero example, you do not need to evaluate the parenthetical expression in order to know that the solution is zero.

Dividing by Zero: Dividing any nonzero quantity by zero results in a solution that is not defined and is therefore undefined.

You should never have to deal with this case on the GAMSAT. If you end up with division by zero in a calculation, you have probably made a mistake. Similarly, you should never end up with zero divided by zero (an undefined quantity). If you do, you should go back and check your work.

1.4 Fractions, Decimals, and Percentages

1.4.1 Fractions

A **fraction** is the quotient of two numbers. It represents parts of a whole and may be seen as a proportion. The number on top is the *numerator*, and the one on the bottom is the *denominator*. Another way of understanding fractions is to consider one as the number of parts present (*numerator*) and the amount of parts it takes to make up a whole (*denominator*). These values can be divided by each other, and this fraction is the quotient.

EXAMPLE

$$\frac{2}{7}$$

In this fraction, 2 is the numerator and 7, the denominator.

Remember, all rational numbers (including integers) can be written as fractions.

1.4.2 Manipulating Fractions

A. Fraction Multiplication

To multiply fractions, simply multiply the numerators together (this will be the new numerator) and then multiply the denominators together (this will be the new denominator).

EXAMPLE

$$\frac{2}{3} \times \frac{4}{5}$$

Multiply the numerators and denominators separately.

$$= \frac{(2 \times 4)}{(3 \times 5)}$$

$$= \frac{8}{15}$$

B. Fraction Division

A **reciprocal** is the number obtained by switching the numerator with the denominator of a fraction. For example, the reciprocal of $\frac{2}{3}$ is $\frac{3}{2}$.

To divide a number by a fraction, multiply that number by the reciprocal of the fraction. {"*Dividing fractions is easy as pie, flip the second fraction then multiply.*"}

EXAMPLE

$$3/(4/3) = 3 \div \frac{4}{3}$$

Switch the numerator and the denominator in the fraction and multiply. Re-

member that 3 is really 3 ÷ 1 so the new denominator would be the product of 1 × 4.

$$= \frac{3}{1} \times \frac{3}{4}$$

$$= \frac{9}{4}$$

Note: 3/(4/3) is not the same as (3/4)/3. Using the rule for fraction division, (3/4)/3 = 3/4 × 1/3 = 3/12 = 1/4.

C. Fraction Addition and Subtraction

With fractions, addition and subtraction are not so easy. You can only add or subtract fractions from each other if they have the same denominator. If they satisfy this condition, then to add or subtract, you do so with the numerators only and leave the denominator unchanged.

EXAMPLE

$$\frac{1}{5} + \frac{3}{5}$$

Both fractions have the same denominator, so add the numerators.

$$= \frac{1 + 3}{5}$$

$$= \frac{4}{5}$$

EXAMPLE

$$\frac{3}{5} - \frac{1}{5}$$

Both fractions have the same denominator, so subtract the numerators.

$$= \frac{3 - 1}{5}$$

$$= \frac{2}{5}$$

What if the denominators of two fractions you are adding or subtracting are not the same? In this case, you must find the Lowest Common Denominator (LCD), the smallest number that is divisible by both of the original denominators.

Ideally, you would like to find the smallest common denominator because smaller numbers in fractions are always easier to work with. But this is not always easy to do, and usually it isn't worth the extra time it will take to do the necessary calculation. The simplest way to find a common denominator is to multiply each fraction by a new fraction in which the numerator and denominator are both the same as the denominator of the other fraction.

EXAMPLE

$$\frac{2}{3} + \frac{2}{7}$$

Don't be confused by the fact that the numerators are the same. We still need to find a common denominator because the denominators are different.

$$= \left(\frac{2}{3} \times \frac{7}{7}\right) + \left(\frac{2}{7} \times \frac{3}{3}\right)$$

$$= \frac{14}{21} + \frac{6}{21}$$

Now that we have the same denominator, we can add the numerators.

$$= \frac{20}{21}$$

This method of finding common denominators utilizes the fact that any number multiplied by 1 is still the same number. The new fractions we introduce are always made of equivalent numerators and denominators, which make the fraction equal to 1, so the values of the original fractions do not change.

D. Comparing Fractions

Another method with which you should be familiar when manipulating fractions is comparing their values (i.e., which of the given fractions is greater than or lesser than the other) when they have different denominators. We will show you three ways to do this.

When you are confronted with only two fractions, finding their common denominator makes the task of evaluating the values easier.

1. Similar to the preceding discussion on adding or subtracting fractions that have different denominators, the fastest way to come up with a common denominator is to multiply both the numerator and denominator of each fraction by the other's denominator.

Let's say you are given the two fractions:

$$\frac{4}{5} \text{ and } \frac{3}{7}$$

Multiply the first fraction by 7 over 7 and the second fraction by 5 over 5. (The 7 comes from the fraction $\frac{3}{7}$ while 5 from $\frac{4}{5}$.)

$$\frac{4}{5} \times \frac{7}{7} = \frac{28}{35}$$

$$\frac{3}{7} \times \frac{5}{5} = \frac{15}{35}$$

With both fractions having 35 as the common denominator, you can now clearly see that 28 must be greater than 15. Therefore, $\frac{4}{5}$ is greater than $\frac{3}{7}$.

2. Another way to go about this is through cross-multiplication. Using the same fractions as examples, you first multiply the numerator of the first fraction by the denominator of the second fraction. The product will then serve as the new numerator of the first fraction.

$$\frac{4}{5} \searrow \frac{3}{7} \Rightarrow 4 \times 7 = 28$$

Next, multiply the denominators of the two fractions. The product will now serve as the new denominator of the first fraction.

$$\frac{4}{5} \to \frac{3}{7} \Rightarrow 5 \times 7 = 35$$

The resulting new fraction would be $\frac{28}{35}$.

Now, let's work on the second fraction. To get its new numerator, this time, multiply the numerator of the second fraction by the denominator of the first fraction. Then multiply the denominators of both fractions.

$$\frac{4}{5} \swarrow \frac{3}{7} \Rightarrow 3 \times 5 = 15$$

$$\frac{4}{5} \leftarrow \frac{3}{7} \Rightarrow 7 \times 5 = 35$$

The second fraction will now become $\frac{15}{35}$. Thus comparing the first and second fractions, we get the same result as we had in the first method.

Because $\frac{28}{35}$ is greater than $\frac{15}{35}$, therefore $\frac{4}{5}$ is greater than $\frac{3}{7}$.

Both procedures follow the same basic principles and prove to be efficient when dealing with two given fractions. But what if you were given three or four fractions (since the GAMSAT is multiple choice, this will happen from time to time)?

3. A much simpler way is to convert each fraction to decimals, and then compare the decimals. All you have to do is divide the numerator of the fraction by its own denominator. With a little practice, you can actually train your brain to work fast with arithmetic.

Now let's say a third fraction is introduced to our previous examples: $\frac{4}{5}, \frac{3}{7}, \frac{9}{13}$. Working on the first fraction, simply divide 4 by 5; on the second fraction, 3 by 7; and on the last, 9 by 13 (you should try this yourself to ensure that you can perform these basic calculations quickly and correctly).

$$\frac{4}{5} = 4 \div 5 = 0.8$$

$$\frac{3}{7} = 3 \div 7 = 0.43$$

$$\frac{9}{13} = 9 \div 13 = 0.69$$

Comparing the three fractions in their decimal forms, 0.43 ($\frac{3}{7}$) is the smallest, 0.69 ($\frac{9}{13}$) is the next, and the largest is 0.8 ($\frac{4}{5}$).

NOTE

For the GAMSAT, decimals should be the recourse of last resort. When needed, try to complete calculations using fractions which will improve your speed.

E. Reduction and Cancelling

To make calculations easier, you should always avoid working with unnecessarily large numbers. To reduce fractions, you can cancel out any common factors in the numerator and denominator.

EXAMPLE

$$\frac{20}{28}$$

First, factor both the numerator and denominator.

$$= \frac{(4 \times 5)}{(4 \times 7)}$$

Since both have a factor of four, we can cancel.

$$= \frac{5}{7}$$

When multiplying fractions, it is possible to cross-cancel like factors before performing the operation. If there are any common factors between the numerator of the first fraction and the denominator of the second fraction, you can cancel them. Likewise, if there are common factors between the numerator of the second and the denominator of the first, cancel them as well.

EXAMPLE

$$\frac{5}{9} \times \frac{6}{25}$$

First, factor the numerators and denominators.

$$= \frac{5}{(3 \times 3)} \times \frac{(2 \times 3)}{(5 \times 5)}$$

Now, we see that we can cross-cancel 5s and 3s.

$$= \frac{1}{3} \times \frac{2}{5}$$

$$= \frac{2}{15}$$

F. Mixed Numbers

You may encounter numbers on the GAMSAT that have both an integer part and a fraction part. These are called mixed numbers.

EXAMPLE

$$3\frac{1}{2}$$

Mixed numbers should be thought of as addition between the integer and the fraction.

EXAMPLE

$$3\frac{1}{2} = 3 + \frac{1}{2}$$

Now in order to convert a mixed number back to a fraction, all you have to do is consider the integer to be the fraction of itself over 1 and perform fraction addition.

EXAMPLE

$$3\frac{1}{2}$$

$$= \frac{3}{1} + \frac{1}{2}$$

Obtain a common denominator.

$$= \left(\frac{3}{1}\right)\left(\frac{2}{2}\right) + \frac{1}{2}$$

$$= \frac{6}{2} + \frac{1}{2}$$

$$= \frac{7}{2}$$

To add or subtract mixed numbers, you can deal with the integer and fraction portions separately. {*Notice above that parentheses (brackets) side by side is shorthand for multiplication.*}

EXAMPLE

$$3\frac{1}{2} - 2\frac{1}{2}$$

$$= (3-2) + \left(\frac{1}{2} - \frac{1}{2}\right)$$

$$= 1$$

NOTE

To convert a mixed number to a fraction, keep the denominator of the fraction while multiplying the integer part of the mixed number by the denominator. Then add to the numerator of the mixed number.

EXAMPLE

$$6\frac{2}{5} = \frac{(6 \times 5) + 2}{5} = \frac{30 + 2}{5} = \frac{32}{5}$$

G. Fractions: Summary

Multiplying $\left(\dfrac{a}{b}\right)\left(\dfrac{c}{d}\right) = \dfrac{ac}{bd}$

Addition $\dfrac{a}{b}+\dfrac{c}{d} = \dfrac{ad+bc}{bd}$

Dividing $\dfrac{\left(a/b\right)}{\left(c/d\right)} = \dfrac{ad}{bc}$

Subtraction $\dfrac{a}{b}-\dfrac{c}{d} = \dfrac{ad-bc}{bd}$

1.4.3 Decimals and Percentages

There are two other ways to represent non-integer numbers that you will encounter on the GAMSAT: As decimals and as percentages.

A. Decimals

Decimal numbers can be recognized by the decimal point (a period) that they contain. Whatever digits are to the left of the decimal point represent a whole number, the integer portion of the number. The digits to the right of the decimal point are the decimal portion.

EXAMPLE

12.34

The integer portion of the number is 12, and .34 is the fractional portion.

The value of the decimal portion of a number operates on a place-value system just like the integer portion. The first digit to the right of the decimal point is the number of tenths (1/10 is one tenth), two digits over is the number of hundredths (1/100 is one hundredth), three digits over is the number of thousandths, then ten-thousandths, etc.

For example, in the decimal 0.56789:

- the 5 is in the tenths position;
- the 6 is in the hundredths position;
- the 7 is in the thousandths position;
- the 8 is in the ten thousandths position;
- the 9 is in the one hundred thousandths position.

Thus, to convert a decimal into a fraction, just drop the decimal point and divide by the power of ten of the last decimal digit. To convert a fraction to a decimal, simply perform the long division of the numerator divided by the denominator.

EXAMPLE

$$0.34 = \dfrac{34}{100}$$

B. Operations with Decimals

Addition and Subtraction: Adding and subtracting decimals is the same as with integers. The only difference is that you need to take care to line up the decimal point properly. Just like with integers, you should only add or subtract digits in the same place with each other.

EXAMPLE

Add 3.33 to 23.6.

$$23.60$$
$$+\ 03.33$$

Notice how we have carried the decimal point down in the same place. Also, to illustrate the addition more clearly, we have added zeros to hold the empty places. Now perform the addition as if there were no decimal points.

$$23.60$$
$$+\ 03.33$$
$$\overline{26.93}$$

Multiplication: You can multiply numbers with decimals just as you would with integers, but placing the decimal point in the solution is a little tricky. To decide where the decimal point goes, first count the number of significant digits after the decimal points in each of the numbers being multiplied. Add these numbers together to obtain the total number of decimal digits. Now, count that number of digits in from the right of the solution and place the decimal point in front of the number at which you end.

EXAMPLE

Multiply 3.03 by 1.2.

$$3.03$$
$$\times\ 1.20$$

We have written in a zero as a place-holder at the end of the second number, but be careful not to include it in your decimal count. Only count up to the final nonzero digit in each number (the 0 in the first number counts because it comes before the 3). Thus our decimal digit count is $2 + 1 = 3$, and we will place our decimal point in the solution 3 digits in from the right; but first, perform the multiplication while ignoring the decimal.

$$3.03$$
$$\times\ 1.20$$
$$\overline{606}$$
$$+\ 3030$$
$$\overline{3636}$$

Now, insert the decimal point to obtain the final solution.

$$= 3.636$$

When counting significant digits, remember to consider the following:

1. all zeros between nonzero digits

EXAMPLE

0.45078 → 5 significant figures

2. all zeros in front of a nonzero number

EXAMPLE

0.0056 → 4 significant figures

3. ignore all zeros after a nonzero digit

EXAMPLE

0.2500 → 2 significant figures

> **NOTE**
>
> Unfortunately, this last math rule is not so simple because in science labs, significant figures (= significant digits = sig figs) represent the accuracy of measurement. The good news is that if there were ever a question on the GAMSAT involving significant figures, they would clarify which rule to apply before asking questions.

Division: We can use our knowledge of the equivalence of fractions to change a decimal division problem into a more familiar integer division problem. Simply multiply each number by the power of ten corresponding to the smallest significant digit out of the two decimal numbers being divided, and then, perform the division with the integers obtained.

This operation is acceptable because it amounts to multiplying a fraction by 1.

EXAMPLE

Divide 4.4 by 1.6

$$\frac{4.4}{1.6}$$

Since the smallest decimal digit in either number is in the tenth place, we multiply the top and bottom by 10.

$$= \frac{4.4}{1.6} \times \frac{10}{10}$$

$$= \frac{44}{16}$$

$$= \frac{11}{4}$$

If you like, you can convert this back to a decimal.

$$= 2.75$$

Rounding Decimals: Rounding decimals to the nearest place value is just like rounding an integer. Look at the digit one place further to the right of the place to which you are rounding. If that digit is 5 or greater, add 1 to the previous digit and drop all the subsequent digits. If it is 4 or less, leave the previous digit alone and simply drop the subsequent digits.

Consider the number 5.3618:

(a) Round to the nearest tenth.

$$= 5.4$$

Since the digit after the tenth place is a 6, we add 1 tenth and drop every digit after the tenth place.

(b) Round to the nearest hundredth.

$$= 5.36$$

Since the digit after the hundredth place is a 1, we do not change any digits. Just drop every digit after the hundredth place.

Fraction-Decimal Conversions to Know: Having these common conversions between fractions and decimals memorized will help you save valuable time on the test.

Fraction	Decimal
1/2	.5
1/3	~ .33
1/4	.25
1/5	.2
1/6	~.167
1/8	.125
1/10	.1

C. Percentages

Percentages are used to describe fractions of other numbers. One percent (written 1%) simply means 1 hundredth. This is easy to remember since "percent" can literally be broken down into "per" and "cent", and we all know that one cent is a hundredth of both a dollar and a euro.

We can use this conversion to hundredths when evaluating expressions containing percents of numbers, but a percentage has no real meaning until it is used to modify another value. For example, if you see 67% in a problem you should always ask "67% of what?"

EXAMPLE

What is 25% of 40?

$$= .25 \times 40$$
$$= 10$$

To find what percentage a certain part of a value is of the whole value, you can use what is known as the **percentage formula**:

Percent = (Part/Whole) × 100

EXAMPLE

What percentage of 50 is 23?

$$Percentage = (23/50) \times 100$$
$$= (46/100) \times 100$$
$$= 46\%$$

Combining percentages requires some nuance (i.e. 'it depends on the question' thus there are several possibilities). Although GAMSAT scores are not percentages, since they are scaled scores out of 100, they can be used as an analogy.

To calculate your *average* (GM 6.2.1) GAMSAT score, you would add the scaled score for each of the 3 sections and divide by 3, thus (S1 + S2 + S3)/3. To get a weighted score, since most medical programmes weight Section 3 twice: (S1 + S2 + 2 x S3)/4. However, no programme weights each question equally: (total correct)/(total number of questions). We will calculate average percentages when we look at ternary nomograms (GM 3.9).

1.5 Roots and Exponents

1.5.1 Properties of Exponents

An exponent is simply shorthand for multiplying that number of identical factors. So 4^3 is the same as $(4)(4)(4) = 64$, three identical factors of 4. Thus x^2 (i.e. 'x squared') is two factors of x, $(x)(x)$, while x^3 (i.e. 'x cubed') is three factors of x, $(x)(x)(x)$.

To multiply exponential values with the same base, keep the base the same and add the exponents.

EXAMPLE

$$a^2 \times a^3 = a^{2+3} = a^5$$

To divide exponential values with the same base, keep the base the same and subtract the exponent of the denominator from the exponent of the numerator.

EXAMPLE

$$\frac{x^5}{x^3} = x^{5-3} = x^2$$

To multiply exponential values with different bases but the same exponent, keep the exponent the same and multiply the bases.

EXAMPLE

$$2^x \times 3^x = (2 \times 3)^x = 6^x$$

To divide exponential values with different bases but the same exponent, keep the exponent the same and divide the bases.

EXAMPLE

$$\frac{6^x}{2^x} = \left(\frac{6}{2}\right)^x = 3^x$$

To raise an exponential value to another power, keep the base the same and multiply the exponents.

EXAMPLE

$$(x^3)^4 = x^{(3 \times 4)} = x^{12}$$

Even though all of the preceding examples use only positive integer exponents, these properties hold true for all three of the types described in section 1.5.3.

1.5.2 Scientific Notation

Scientific notation, also called exponential notation, is a convenient method of writing very large (or very small) numbers. Instead of writing too many zeroes on either side of a decimal, you can express a number as a product of a power of ten and a number between 1 and 10. For example, the number 8,765,000,000 can be expressed as 8.765 x 10^9.

The first number 8.765 is called the coefficient. The second number should always have a base of ten with an exponent equal to the number of zeroes in the original numbers. Moving the decimal point to the left makes a positive exponent while moving to the right makes a negative exponent.

In multiplying numbers in scientific notation, the general rule is as follows:

$$(a \times 10^x)(b \times 10^y) = ab \times 10^{x+y}$$

EXAMPLE

To multiply 2.0×10^4 and 10×10^2

{Whenever possible, when you see a practice question like the one above, consider using a sheet of paper or Post-It note to cover the worked solution while you try to answer the question yourself.}

(i) Find the product of the coefficients first.

$2.0 \times 10 = 20$

(ii) Add the exponents.

$4 + 2 = 6$

(iii) Construct the result.

20×10^6

(iv) Make sure that the coefficient has only one digit to the left of the decimal point. This will also adjust the number of the exponent depending on the number of places moved.

2.0×10^7

Dividing numbers in scientific notation follows this general rule:

$$\frac{(a \times 10^x)}{(b \times 10^y)} = \frac{a}{b} \times 10^{x-y}$$

Going back to our preceding example, let's divide 2.0×10^4 and 10×10^2 this time:

(i) Divide the coefficients.

$2.0 \div 10 = 0.2$

(ii) Subtract the exponents.

$4 - 2 = 2$

(iii)   Construct the result and adjust the values to their simplest forms.

$$0.2 \times 10^2 = 2 \times 10 = 20$$

In adding and subtracting numbers written in scientific notation, you need to ensure that all exponents are identical. You would need to adjust the decimal place of one of the numbers so that its exponent becomes equivalent to the other number.

EXAMPLE

Add 34.5×10^{-5} and 6.7×10^{-4}

(i)   Choose the number that you want to adjust so that its exponent is equivalent to the other number. Let's pick 34.5 and change it into a number with 10^{-4} as its base-exponent term.

$$3.45 \times 10^{-4} + 6.7 \times 10^{-4}$$

(ii)   Add the coefficients together:

$$3.45 + 6.7 = 10.15$$

(iii)   The exponents are now the same, in this case 10^{-4}, so all you have to do is plug it in:

$$10.15 \times 10^{-4}$$

(iv)   Adjust the end result so that the coefficient is a number between 1 and 10:

$$1.015 \times 10^{-3}$$

The same procedure basically applies to subtraction.

NOTE

Notice in the examples in this section, when you lower the power from the coefficient (i.e. by moving the decimal to the left), you must add to the exponent, and vice-versa.

1.5.3 Types of Exponents

Positive Integer Exponents: This is the type of exponent you will encounter most often. Raising a base number b to a positive integer exponent x is equivalent to making x copies of b and multiplying them together.

EXAMPLE

$$2^4 = 2 \times 2 \times 2 \times 2 = 16$$

Fractional Exponents: Fractional exponents are also known as roots. Let x be the fraction. To raise a base number b to the x power we make use of the fifth property of exponents in section 1.5.1.

We can write $b^{\frac{n}{d}}$ as $\left(b^{\frac{1}{d}}\right)^n$. The value $b^{\frac{1}{d}}$ is known as the d-th root of b. So the base b raised to the x power is the same as the d-th root of b raised to the n power.

EXAMPLE

$$8^{\frac{2}{3}}$$

$$= \left(8^{\frac{1}{3}}\right)^2$$

The expression inside the parentheses is the cube root of 8. Since $2 \times 2 \times 2 = 8$, the cube root of 8 is 2.

$$= 2^2$$
$$= 4$$

Consider the following: What is the cube root of 125, and separately, what is the cube root of -125? The number 5 multiplied by itself 3 times equals 125. Similarly, the number -5 multiplied by itself 3 times equals -125. Thus the answers are 5 and -5, respectively.

Negative Exponents: The value of a base raised to a negative power is equal to the reciprocal of the base, raised to a positive exponent of the same value. For any exponential value b^{-x}, b^{-x} is equivalent to $\dfrac{1}{\left(b^x\right)}$.

EXAMPLE

$$3^{-2}$$

Take the reciprocal and invert the sign of the exponent.

$$= \frac{1}{(3^2)}$$

$$= \frac{1}{(3 \times 3)}$$

$$= \frac{1}{9}$$

1.5.4 Zero and Exponents

Raising a Number to the Zero: Any number raised to the zero power is equal to 1.

We can see that this follows the rules of exponents (see section 1.5), because $a^0 = a^1 \times a^{-1} = a/a = 1$.

> **NOTE**
>
> The quantity 0^0 (read as zero to the zero power) is 1.

EXAMPLES

$$3^0 = 1$$
$$123.79^0 = 1$$
$$\left[1.2 + \left(37 - \sqrt{5}\right) \times 2.331\right]^0 = 1$$

As with multiplication and division, you should not waste time evaluating the parenthetical expression.

1.5.5 Summary of the Rules for Exponents

$$a^0 = 1 \qquad\qquad a^1 = a$$

$$a^n \, a^m = a^{n+m} \qquad\qquad a^n/a^m = a^{n-m}$$

$$(a^n)^m = a^{nm} \qquad\qquad a^{\frac{1}{n}} = \sqrt[n]{a}$$

1.5.6 Recognizing Number Patterns

It is possible to save a lot of time during the real GAMSAT by avoiding unnecessary calculations by the recognition of certain patterns. One helpful way to achieve this is by knowing at least the following relationships that are typically memorized in primary school math class (see table below).

Test makers choose their numbers carefully. The moment you see 1.44 on the GAMSAT, there would be a high likelihood that taking the square root, which gives 1.2, would be required (because, of course, the square root of 144 is 12, the square root of 1.44 must be 1.2). Likewise, the square root of 1.7, being an approximation of 1.69, must be 1.3 (the square root of 169 being 13).

EXAMPLE 1

If you have not done your Physics review yet, don't worry, we will discuss simple harmonic motion later (SHM; PHY 7.2.3). Please try the following practice questions before looking at the worked solutions. For now, just focus on the math. If you have done your Physics review, in the small angle approximation, the motion of a simple pendulum is approximated by the following equation:

$$T = 2\pi\sqrt{\frac{\ell}{g}}$$

where T is the period of a mass attached to a pendulum of length ℓ with gravitational acceleration g.

x	1	2	3	4	5	6	7	8	9	10	11	12	13	14	15	20
x^2	1	4	9	16	25	36	49	64	81	100	121	144	169	196	225	400
x^3	1	8	27	64	125	-	-	-	-	1000	-	-	-	-	-	-

Table 1: Common squares and cubes that are helpful to know. Applying the rules of exponents (GM 1.5.3, 1.5.5), $5^2 = 25$, $5^3 = 125$; square root of 121 $= (121)^{1/2} = \sqrt[2]{121} = \sqrt{121} = 11$; cube (= 3rd) root of 64 $= (64)^{1/3} = \sqrt[3]{64} = 4$. These basic manipulations are commonly required for the real exam.

Again, please ignore Physics for now. If the length of the pendulum increases by 70%, by what percentage will the period increase?

    A. 30%
    B. 40%
    C. 50%
    D. 70%

If the length increases by 70%, that is the same as saying 1.70(ℓ), 1.70 is similar to 1.69 and since we know that square root 1.69 is 1.3 (because 13 squared is 169), this means that the original square root of ℓ has increased by 30%.

$$T = 2\pi\sqrt{\frac{\ell}{g}}$$

$$T = 2\pi\sqrt{\frac{(1.69)\ell}{g}}$$

$$T = 1.30\left[2\pi\sqrt{\frac{\ell}{g}}\right]$$

Translation: the original equation is 1.30 times higher which means 30% greater. Answer: **A**.

EXAMPLE 2

If the pendulum is in an environment with 1/50th of Earth's gravity, what would be the change in the period?

    A. It would be 15 times the original.
    B. It would be 10 times the original.
    C. It would be 7 times the original.
    D. It would be 1/10th times the original.

$$T = 2\pi\sqrt{\frac{\ell}{g}}$$

By observing that gravity will change and a square root is imminent (as well as the fact that the answer choices are not very 'tight' or close together), let's estimate 50 as 49 which has a simple square root:

$$T = 2\pi\sqrt{\frac{\ell}{g/49}}$$

A denominator in a denominator is the same as a numerator (in other words, if you divide by a fraction, it is the same as multiplying by the inverse; *see* GM 1.4.2B):

$$T = 2\pi\sqrt{\frac{(49)\ell}{g}}$$

Of course, the square root of 49 is 7:

$$T = 7\left[2\pi\sqrt{\frac{\ell}{g}}\right]$$

Translation: the original equation is 7 times greater. Answer: **C**. Note that the actual square root of 50 is approximately 7.1 so our estimate is valid considering the answer choices. Note: The preceding manipulations – often using equations that you are not expected to have seen before – are commonly required for the real exam.

> **NOTE**
>
> Try to complete all the chapter review warm-up exercises as quickly as possible and, of course, without the use of a calculator.

1.6 Ratio and Proportion

1.6.1 What is a Ratio?

A **ratio** is the relation between two numbers. There are multiple ways they can be written, but ratios can always be denoted as fractions.

These are all ways to represent the same ratio:

$$3 \text{ to } 4 = 3:4 = \frac{3}{4} = 3/4$$

If a ratio is written out in words, the first quantity stated should generally be placed in the numerator of the equivalent fraction and the second quantity in the denominator. Just make sure you keep track of which value corresponds to which category.

1.6.2 Solving Proportions

A **proportion** is a statement of equality between two or more ratios.

Solving for an unknown variable is the most common type of proportion problem. If you have just a ratio on either side of an equation, you can rewrite the equation as the numerator of the first times the denominator of the second equal to the denominator of the first times the numerator of the second. This allows you to find the missing information more easily.

EXAMPLE

Solve for x in the following equation.

$$\frac{2}{3} = \frac{5}{x}$$

Cross multiply to eliminate fractions.

$$2 \times x = 3 \times 5$$
$$2x = 15$$
$$x = \frac{15}{2} = 7\frac{1}{2}$$

This means that the ratio 2 to 3 is equivalent to the ratio 5 to $7\frac{1}{2}$.

Unless it is stated, a proportion does not describe a specific number of things. It can only give you information about quantities in terms of other quantities. But if it is explicitly stated what one of the two quantities is, the other quantity can be determined using the proportion.

GOLD STANDARD WARM-UP EXERCISES

CHAPTER 1: Numbers and Operations

1. What is the approximate value of

   $$0.125 + \sqrt{\frac{1}{9}}?$$

   A. 0.40
   B. 0.46
   C. 0.50
   D. 0.45

2. 0.8 is to 0.9 as 80 is to:
   A. 9
   B. 100
   C. 8
   D. 90

3. If you invest in Bank A, you will receive 19% interest on the amount you invest. If you invest in Bank B, you will receive 21% interest. The maximum amount you can invest in Bank A is $6,430, and the maximum amount you can invest in Bank B is $5,897. How much more interest will you earn if you invest the maximum amount in Bank B than if you invest the maximum amount in Bank A?
   A. $16.67
   B. $16.30
   C. $101.27
   D. $111.93

4. Board C is 3/4 as long as Board B. Board B is 4/5 as long as Board A. What is the sum of the lengths of all three Boards if Board A is 100 m long?
   A. 255 m
   B. 225 m
   C. 240 m
   D. 235 m

5. The proportion of the yellow marbles in a jar of yellow and green jars is 7 out of 9. If there are 999 marbles in the jar, how many of these are yellow?
   A. 111
   B. 777
   C. 2
   D. 222

6. If 0.25 months is equal to one week, what fraction of a month is equal to one day?
   A. 1/7
   B. 4/7
   C. 1/30
   D. 1/28

7. Which of the following is 6.4% of 1,000?
   A. $64^{\frac{3}{4}}$
   B. $256^{\frac{3}{4}}$
   C. $\left(\frac{64}{100}\right)^{2}$
   D. 6.4 / 100

8. $2 + \left[71 - 8 \left(\dfrac{6}{2} \right)^2 \right]$ is what percent of $\sqrt{2500}$?

   A. 50%
   B. 1%
   C. 44%
   D. 2%

9. Which is the largest?
   A. 0.636
   B. 0.136
   C. 0.46
   D. 0.163

10. Determine the sum of 9, -5, and 6.
    A. 20
    B. − 20
    C. − 10
    D. 10

11. Determine the value of 1.5 x 10^7 divided by 3.0 x 10^4.
    A. 5.0 x 10^3
    B. 5.0 x 10^2
    C. 5.0 x 10^{-2}
    D. 0.5 x 10^{-3}

12. Determine the value of 1.5 x 10^7 subtracted by 3.0 x 10^4.
    A. 1.497 x 10^7
    B. - 1.5 x 10^3
    C. 1.2 x 10^3
    D. 1.47 x 10^7

13. Determine the value of $|(-3)(6)|$.
    A. 3
    B. -3
    C. 18
    D. -18

14. Determine the value of $-|2-5|$.
    A. 3
    B. -3
    C. 7
    D. -10

15. Try to complete the following calculation in under 30 seconds: Determine the value of .333 x .125. {Reminder: all calculations in this book should be performed without the use of a calculator.}
    A. 0.02
    B. 0.03
    C. 0.04
    D. 0.05

NOTE

No matter what your previous experience has been, please keep in mind: Math skills improve with practice. Each GAMSAT Math chapter has practice questions. Gold Standard has over 1000 chapter-review practice questions in the Physical and Biological sciences – hundreds of which require math skills to one degree or the other. You will be exposed repeatedly to all of the common math manipulations required for the real exam. Persistent effort will eventually meet reward.

GS ANSWER KEY

CHAPTER 1

		Cross-Reference				Cross-Reference
1.	B	GM 1.2.3, 1.4.3		9.	A	GM 1.4.3
2.	D	GM 1.6.2		10.	D	GM 1.2.1
3.	A	GM 1.4.3		11.	B	GM 1.5.2
4.	C	GM 1.4.2		12.	A	GM 1.5.1, 1.5.2
5.	B	GM 1.6.2		13.	C	GM 1.2.1.1, 1.1.3
6.	D	GM 1.6.1		14.	B	GM 1.2.1.1, 1.1.3
7.	B	GM 1.2.3, 1.4.3, 1.5.2		15.	C	GM 1.4.3
8.	D	GM 1.2.3, 1.4.3				

* Worked solutions can be found at the end of the GAMSAT Math chapters. If something is still not clear, go to the forum at GAMSAT-prep.com.

SCIENTIFIC MEASUREMENT AND DIMENSIONAL ANALYSIS
Chapter 2

Memorize	Understand	Not Required
Conversions between units in the SI system SI units	* SI prefixes * How to convert between units * Dimensional analysis	* Memorizing conversion factors between different systems of units.

GAMSAT-Prep.com

Introduction

It is extremely important to know the SI system of measurement for the GAMSAT. The metric system is very much related to the SI system. The British system, though familiar, does not need to be memorized for the GAMSAT (related questions would only be asked if relevant conversion factors were provided). 'Dimensional analysis' is a technique whereby simply paying attention to units and applying the basic algebra we covered in GM Chapter 1, you will be able to solve several real exam questions in GAMSAT Physics, Chemistry and Biology – even without previous knowledge in those subjects.

Additional Resources

Free Online Forum

Special Guest

2.1 Systems of Measurement

2.1.1 British Units (Imperial System of Measurement)

You are probably already familiar with several of these units of measurement, but we recommend reviewing them at least once.

A. Length: These units are used to describe things like the length of physical objects, the displacement of a physical object, the distance something has traveled or will travel, etc. Area and volume are also measured as the square and cube (respectively) of these units.

Inches	The *inch* is the smallest measurement of length in the British System.
Feet	There are 12 inches in every foot. 1 ft. = 12 in.
Yards	There are 3 feet in every yard. 1 yd. = 3 ft.
Miles	The *mile* is the largest unit of length in the British System. There are 5,280 feet in every mile. 1 mi. = 5,280 ft.

B. Time: These units describe the passage of time.

Seconds	The *second* is the smallest unit of time in the British System.
Minutes	There are 60 seconds in every minute. 1 min. = 60 s.
Hours	There are 60 minutes in every hour. 1 h. = 60 min.
Days	There are 24 hours in every day. 1 day = 24 h.
Years	The *year* is the largest unit of time in the British System. There are 365 days in every year. 1 yr. = 365 days

C. Mass/Weight: These terms are not technically the same and we will discuss the differences in Physics. The following units describe the amount of matter in an object.

Ounces	The *ounce* is the smallest unit of mass in the British System.
Pounds	There are 16 ounces (oz.) in every pound (lb.). 1 lb. = 16 oz.
Tons	The *ton* is the largest unit of mass in the British System. There are 2,000 lbs. in an American ton, and 2,240 lbs. in a British tonne. Neither should be committed to memory.

2.1.2 Metric Units

Measuring with Powers of 10: Unlike the British System, the Metric System has only one unit for each category of measurement. In order to describe quantities that are much larger or much smaller than one of the base units, a prefix is chosen from a variety of options and added to the front of the unit. This changes the value of the unit by some power of 10, which is determined by what the prefix is. The following are the most common of these prefixes (with the representative symbols in brackets):

Milli (m)   One thousandth (10^{-3}) of the base unit

Centi (c)   One hundredth (10^{-2}) of the base unit

Deci (d)   One tenth (10^{-1}) of the base unit

Deca (da)   Ten (10^{1}) times the base unit

Kilo (k)   One thousand (10^{3}) times the base unit

There is a mnemonic that may be used to identify these prefixes:

King	Kilometer	Kilo
Henry	Hectometer	Hecto (h)
Died	Decameter	Deca
Unexpectedly	Unit Base	Unit
Drinking	Decimeter	Deci
Chocolate	Centimeter	Centi
Milk	Milimeter	Milli

As you go down, you divide by 10 and as you go up, you multiply by 10 in order to convert between the units.

EXAMPLE

How many meters is 1 kilometer?

$$1 \text{ km} = 1{,}000 \text{ m}$$

From general knowledge, we know that kilo means one thousand. This means there are 1,000 meters in a kilometer. But just in case you get confused, you can also use the clue from the mnemonic. Now we know that Kilo is three slots upward from the Unit base. Hence we multiply 3 times by 10: 10 x 10 x 10 = 1000.

An even less confusing way to figure out how to do the metric conversions quickly and accurately, is to use a metric conversion line. This is quite handy with any of the common units such as the *meter, liter,* and *grams.*

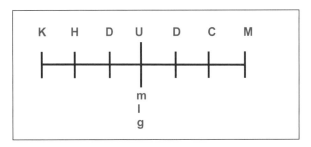

Figure GM 2.1: The Metric Conversion Line. The letters on top of the metric line stands for the "King Henry" mnemonic. On the other hand, the letters below the metric line - **m, l, g** – stand for the unit bases, **m**eter, **l**iter, or **g**ram, respectively.

To use this device, draw out the metric line as shown in Fig GM 2.1. From the centermost point **U**, the prefixes going to the left represent those that are larger than the base unit (kilo, hecto). These also correspond to the decimal places that you will be moving from the numerical value of the unit to be converted. Those going to the right are for the ones smaller than the unit (deci, centi, milli).

EXAMPLE

How much is 36 liters in milliliters?

Step 1: Place your pen on the given unit, in this case L (liter). Then count the number of places it takes you to reach the unit being asked in the problem (milliliter).

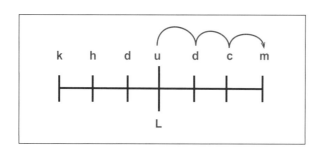

Fig GM 2.2: Converting liter to milliliter using the metric conversion line.

Step 2: Because it took you three places going to the right to move from the liter to the milliliter units, you also need to add three places from the decimal point of the number 36.0.

36 L = 36,000 ml

Now, let's try converting centimeter to kilometer: What is 6.3 cm in km?

1.   Place your pen on the **c** (centi) point in the metric line.

2.   Moving from **c** to **k** (kilo) takes five places going to the left. This also means moving five places from the decimal point of the number 6.3.
6.3 cm = .000063 km

Using this method definitely makes doing the metric conversions so much faster than the fraction method!

There are other prefixes that are often used scientifically:

Tera (T) 10^{12} times the base unit
Giga (G) 10^{9} times the base unit
Mega (M) 10^{6} times the base unit
Micro (μ) 10^{-6} of the base unit
Nano (n) 10^{-9} of the base unit
Pico (p) 10^{-12} of the base unit

A. Length: As with British length units, these are used to measure anything that has to do with length, displacement, distance, etc. Area and volume are also measured as the square and cube (respectively) of these units.

Meters	The *meter* is the basic unit of length in the Metric System.
Other Common Forms	millimeter, centimeter, kilometer

B. Time: These are units that quantify the passage of time.

Seconds	Just as in the British System, the *second* is the basic unit of time in the Metric System. Minutes, hours, and the other British units are not technically part of the Metric System, but they are often used anyway in problems involving metric units.
Other Common Forms	millisecond

C. Mass: These are units that describe the amount of matter in an object.

Grams	The *gram* is the basic metric unit of mass.
Other Common Forms	milligram, kilogram

2.1.3 SI Units

SI units is the **International System of Units** (abbreviated **SI** from the French *Le Système International d'Unités*) and is a modern form of the metric system. SI units are used to standardize all the scientific calculations that are done anywhere in the world. Throughout this book, and during the real exam, you will see the application of base SI units and the units derived from the base SI units.

> **NOTE**
>
> Typically, because of Chemistry, students think that the liter (L) is an SI unit. It is not. The cubic meter is the SI unit for volume. It is important that you know that 1 L = 1000 cubic centimeters (= cc or mL) = 1 cubic decimeter.

Table 1: SI Base Units

Base quantity	Name	Symbol
	SI base unit	
length	meter	m
mass	kilogram	kg
time	second	s
electric current	ampere	A
thermodynamic temperature	kelvin	K
amount of substance	mole	mol

Table 2: Examples of SI Derived Units

	SI derived unit	
area	square meter	m^2
volume	cubic meter	m^3
speed, velocity	meter per second	m/s
acceleration	meter per second squared	m/s^2

Table 3: SI Derived Units with Special Names and Symbols

				SI base unit
frequency	hertz	Hz	-	s^{-1}
force	newton	N	-	$m \cdot kg \cdot s^{-2}$
pressure, stress	pascal	Pa	N/m^2	$m^{-1} \cdot kg \cdot s^{-2}$
energy, work, quantity of heat	joule	J	$N \cdot m$	$m^2 \cdot kg \cdot s^{-2}$
power	watt	W	J/s	$m^2 \cdot kg \cdot s^{-3}$
electric charge, quantity of electricity	coulomb	C	-	$s \cdot A$
electric potential difference, electromotive force	volt	V	W/A	$m^2 \cdot kg \cdot s^{-3} \cdot A^{-1}$

> **NOTE**
>
> We will see all the units from these 3 tables in the Physics and Chemistry chapters.
>
> Do not try to memorize the last 2 columns in Table 3. However, if this is your second time reviewing this page, you should be able to derive all the units displayed in the last 2 columns of Table 3. In fact, the derivation of units through dimensional analysis is a regular type of GAMSAT question. You will be tested on this point with the online chapter review practice questions in Physics and Chemistry that are included with this textbook.

Table 4: Important SI prefixes for GAMSAT, A closer look

Prefix Name	Symbol	Base 10	Decimal	English Word
tera	T	10^{12}	1000000000000	trillion
giga	G	10^{9}	1000000000	billion
mega	M	10^{6}	1000000	million
kilo	k	10^{3}	1000	thousand
hecto	h	10^{2}	100	hundred
deca	da	10^{1}	10	ten
BASE UNIT	-	10^{0}	1	one
deci	d	10^{-1}	0.1	tenth
centi	c	10^{-2}	0.01	hundredth
milli	m	10^{-3}	0.001	thousandth
micro	μ	10^{-6}	0.000001	millionth
nano	n	10^{-9}	0.000000001	billionth
pico	p	10^{-12}	0.000000000001	trillionth

There exists more SI prefixes than those presented in Table 4 but, if needed, additional prefixes will be defined during the exam. However, Table 4 is considered 'assumed knowledge' and therefore must be memorized.

As we have seen in GM 2.1.2, each prefix name has a symbol (Table 4) that is used in combination with the symbols for units of measure (Tables 1-3). For example, the symbol for *kilo*- is 'k', and is used to produce 'km', 'kg', and 'kW', which are the SI symbols for kilometer, kilogram, and kilowatt, respectively. Even if you do not have a science background, you have likely heard of many SI prefixes because of your use of computers (a *byte* is a unit of digital memory): very small files like the text of an email = kilobytes, larger files like a good quality digital image = megabytes, storage space on a smartphone = gigabytes, but storage space on a computer is increasingly measured in terabytes.

The following practice questions do not require previous knowledge in Physics. For 'beginners', please feel free to consult Tables 1-4 to assist in solving the questions.

NOTE

As mentioned in Chapter 1, whenever possible, consider using a sheet of paper or Post-It note to cover the worked solution while you try to answer the question yourself. You will benefit from doing so for most of the practice questions in this chapter and subsequent chapters.

EXAMPLE 1

The power (P) of an electrical appliance can be calculated from the current (I) that flows through it and the potential difference (V) across it, such that P = IV (PHY 10.2).

Determine the power if the potential difference is 5 mV and the current is 5 mA.

A. 25 μW
B. 25 MW
C. 2.5×10^{-3} W
D. 2.5×10^{-3} mW

P = IV = 5 mA × 5 mV
  = 5×10^{-3} A × 5×10^{-3} V

P = 25×10^{-6} A•V = 25 μW

- the latter is equivalent to 25×10^{-6} W = 25×10^{-3} mW, NOT 2.5×10^{-3} mW.
- Ref. Tables 1-4; PHY 10.2. Answer: A.

Note that the preceding question and those to follow have no science assumed knowledge other than the understanding of SI units. Also note that if the base units have prefixes, all but one of the prefixes must be expanded to their numeric multiplier, except when combining values with identical units (i.e. 'you can add apples to apples but you can't add apples to oranges').

Consider the following (if you are stuck, please consult any of the preceding tables – 1 to 4 – to try to work out the answer before looking at the worked solution).

EXAMPLE 2

What is the sum of 5.00 mV and 10 μV?

A. 15 μV
B. 5.1 mV
C. 5.01 mV
D. 5.001 mV

The common base unit is the volt (V, see Table 3).

We must ensure that the prefixes are the same in order to perform the addition (or subtraction if that had been the case). Thus 5.00 mV + 10 μV = 5.00 mV + 0.01 mV = 5.01 mV. Answer C.

When units are presented as exponents, for example, in square and cubic forms, the multiplication prefix must be considered part of the unit, and thus included as part of the exponent.

Consider the following cases:

- 1 km^2 means one square kilometer, or the area of a square of 1000 m by 1000 m and not 1000 square meters.

- 2 Mm^3 means two cubic megameters, or the volume of two cubes of 1 000 000 m by 1 000 000 m by 1 000 000 m or 2×10^{18} m^3, and not 2 000 000 cubic meters (2×10^6 m^3).

EXAMPLE 3

Which of the following is NOT equivalent?

A. $3 \text{ MW} = 3 \times 1\,000\,000 \text{ W}$
B. $9 \text{ km}^2 = 9 \times 10^6 \text{ m}^2$
C. $5 \text{ cm} = 5 \times 0.01 \text{ m}$
D. Each option above represents an equivalence.

- $3 \text{ MW} = 3 \times 10^6 \text{ W} = 3 \times 1\,000\,000 \text{ W}$ $= 3\,000\,000 \text{ W}$
- $9 \text{ km}^2 = 9 \times (10^3 \text{ m})^2 = 9 \times (10^3)^2 \times \text{m}^2$ $= 9 \times 10^6 \text{ m}^2 = 9 \times 1\,000\,000 \text{ m}^2$ $= 9\,000\,000 \text{ m}^2$
- $5 \text{ cm} = 5 \times 10^{-2} \text{ m} = 5 \times 0.01 \text{ m}$ $= 0.05 \text{ m}$
- Answer: D.

2.2 Mathematics of Conversions (Dimensional Analysis)

2.2.1 Dimensional Analysis with Numeric Calculations

Basically, a **dimension** is a measurement of length in one direction. Examples include width, depth and height. A line has one dimension, a square has two dimensions (2D), and a cube has three dimensions (3D). In Physics, 'dimensions' can also refer to any physical measurement such as length, time, mass, etc.

Dimensional analysis is a powerful technique – frequently helpful for the real GAMSAT – that permits the solving of problems across the sciences simply by carefully analysing and manipulating units.

The Process: In order to convert a quantity from one type of unit to another type of unit, all you have to do is set up and execute multiplication between ratios. Each conversion from the preceding sections is actually a ratio.

Let's look at the conversion from feet to inches.

"There are 12 inches in 1 foot."

This can be rewritten as a ratio in two ways:

"12 inches to 1 foot" or "1 foot to 12 inches."

$$= \frac{12 \text{ in}}{1 \text{ ft}} \text{ or } \frac{1 \text{ ft}}{12 \text{ in}}$$

When you are performing a conversion, you should treat the units like numbers. This means that when you have a fraction with a certain unit on top and the same unit on bottom, you can cancel out the units leaving just the numbers.

You can multiply a quantity by any of your memorized conversions, and its value will remain the same as long as all of the units, but one, cancel out.

EXAMPLE 1

Given that there are 2.54 cm in an inch, how many inches are there in 3 feet?

First, determine which conversion will help. Of course we have been provided a conversion directly between feet and inches, so that is what we'll use and we'll ignore the distractor (cm).

Next, determine which of the two possible conversion ratios we should use. The goal is to be able to cancel out the original units (in this case, feet), so we want to use whichever ratio has the original units in the denominator (in this case, inches/feet).

$$3 \text{ ft} = 3 \text{ ft} \times \frac{12 \text{ in}}{1 \text{ ft}}$$

Now perform the unit cancellation.

$$= 3 \times \frac{12 \text{ in}}{1}$$
$$= 36 \text{ in}$$

In many instances, you will not have a direct conversion. All you have to do in such a case is multiply by a string of ratios instead of just one.

EXAMPLE 2

How many inches are there in 5.08 meters? {Try the conversion yourself before looking at the solution. You may go back to the previous Example - or section - to find an appropriate conversion factor.}

We cannot convert meters directly into inches, but we can convert meters to centimeters and then centimeters into inches. We can set up both these conversions at the same time and evaluate.

$$5.08 \text{ m} = 5.08 \text{ m} \times \frac{100 \text{ cm}}{1 \text{ m}} \times \frac{1 \text{ in}}{2.54 \text{ cm}}$$

Next, cancel the units.

$$= 5.08 \times \frac{100}{1} \times \frac{1 \text{ in}}{2.54}$$

$$= \frac{508 \text{ in}}{2.54}$$

$$= 200 \text{ in}$$

NOTE

Make sure you check and see that all of your units cancel properly! A lot of unnecessary errors can be avoided simply by paying attention to the units. "Dimensional analysis" is the formal term given to these types of calculations that are solved while keeping an eye on the relations based on units. The solutions to many problems on the real GAMSAT are dependent on dimensional analysis.

The following are 2 typical GAMSAT-level dimensional analysis practice questions.

EXAMPLE 3

Consider the following diagram.

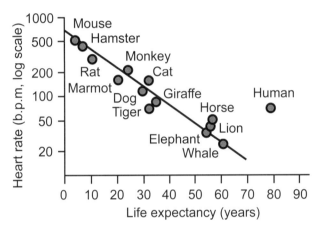

Figure 1: Heart rate in beats per minute (b.p.m.) on a log scale vs. life expectancy in years for various mammals.

Estimate the average number of heart beats over a lifetime for a person.

A. 2.9×10^{11}
B. 2.9×10^{9}
C. 2.9×10^{7}
D. 2.9×10^{5}

This question is asking for the number of heart beats per lifetime for a human being. If we can determine the rate of heart beats per minute from Figure 1, we could scale that quantity up to an hour, then a year, then a lifetime by estimating the average lifespan - also from Figure 1.

You can easily estimate your heart rate by counting your pulse while watching a clock for a minute for comparison, but this question refers to Figure 1.

The heart rate for 'Human' on the graph is approximately 60-70 b.p.m. (= beats per minute as explained by the caption below the graph). Because the answers are far enough apart, which commonly occurs during the real exam, whether you estimate 60 or 70 (or even 80), you will approximate the same answer. We will examine the log scale in GM 3.8 at which point you will better understand why the heart rate is most likely less than 75 b.p.m. From Figure 1, we can estimate life expectancy of a person as 80 years/lifetime.

Putting all of the preceding together, we get:

$$\frac{70 \text{ beats}}{1 \text{ minute}} \cdot \frac{60 \text{ minutes}}{1 \text{ hour}} \cdot \frac{24 \text{ hours}}{1 \text{ day}} \cdot \frac{365 \text{ days}}{1 \text{ year}} \cdot \frac{80 \text{ years}}{1 \text{ lifetime}}$$

What happened to the units?

$$\frac{70 \text{ beats}}{1 \text{ minute}} \cdot \frac{60 \text{ minutes}}{1 \text{ hour}} \cdot \frac{24 \text{ hours}}{1 \text{ day}} \cdot \frac{365 \text{ days}}{1 \text{ year}} \cdot \frac{80 \text{ years}}{1 \text{ lifetime}}$$

As a result of the cancellations, the final units must be beats/lifetime, or in other words, heart beats over a lifetime.

We have completed the dimensional analysis, so what about the math?

Keeping in mind that the math needs to be done quickly and efficiently by hand, we should seek ways to simplify the calculation. Fortunately, in terms of the order of operations (GM 1.2.3), we can perform the multiplications in any order that we want. In other words, we can choose to combine terms which create relatively simple answers.

For example: 70 x 60 is 4200 which is approximately 4000 (notice that we are rounding down to simplify the calculation, GM 1.4.3B; if we get an opportunity to round another calculation upward, it might restore a bit of balance). The 365 does not seem to be clearly simplified; however, 24 x 80 is approximately 25 x 80 which is 2000 (not only is it simpler than immediately using the 365, but it has the added advantage that we rounded upwards a small amount).

Thus, without performing any longhand calculations – only through observation – we have converted 4 factors to 4000 x 2000 = 8 000 000 = 8×10^6. Now we are left with $365 \times 8 \times 10^6$. If you have not already done it, you should complete 365 x 8 as a quick exercise.

Now we have $2920 \times 10^6 = 2.9 \times 10^9$, which is approximately 2.9 billion heart beats in a lifetime. If you did the calculation with a calculator (which is not permissible for the real exam), the result would still be approximately 2.9 billion heart beats per lifetime. Answer B.

With experience, you will not have to calculate 365 x 8 to get the correct answer. Once you had determined $365 \times 8 \times 10^6$, without having done any longhand calculation, you could have observed that 365 is somewhere between 3×10^2 and 4×10^2. Thus $365 \times 8 \times 10^6$ = between 3 and 4 $\times 10^2 \times 8 \times 10^6$ = between 24 and 32×10^8 = between 2.4 and 3.2×10^9. Answer B.

By observing how precise (or imprecise) the answer choices are, you will be able to gauge to what degree you can estimate in order to save time. Because suitable approximating is such a valuable skill for the time-pressured GAMSAT Section 3, we will be highlighting where it applies in the worked solutions for GAMSAT Math and subsequent online chapter review questions in the sciences.

NOTE

On the real exam, sometimes there could be a question that is missing some data because ACER believes that you should be able to estimate the missing information within a reasonable error margin, as examples: the rate of growth of a part of your body, change in height or weight over time, your heart rate, etc. After all, if Example 3 did not have Figure 1, most people would guess that a resting heart rate is between 60 and 100 b.p.m. Even if a person chose a number between 30 and 200, it would not matter because the answer choices are 100 times apart, so they would still approximate the same answer. Expect that you could be asked the unexpected but that you are equipped with the tools to answer correctly.

2.2.2 Dimensional Analysis with Variables

There will be occasions on the real exam where you will need to apply dimensional analysis but there will not be any SI units, nor SI prefixes, nor numbers! This becomes a disciplined exercise to ensure that you understand how variables can be manipulated using basic math.

EXAMPLE 4

Consider the Law of Gravitation where the force of gravity F is:

$$F = G(m_1 m_2 / r^2)$$

- F is the force between the masses;
- G is the gravitational constant;
- m_1 is the first mass;
- m_2 is the second mass;
- r is the distance between the centers of the masses.

{We will discuss the preceding Physics equation in PHY 2.4. If you have no background in Physics, please carefully consult Tables 1-3, GM 2.1.3, in order to remind yourself of the units for the various variables that are presented in this problem. Aside from a basic comfort with SI units, there is no assumed knowledge necessary to solve this question.}

The dimension of a physical quantity can be expressed as a product of the basic physical dimensions of mass (M), length (L) and time (T). For example, the dimension of the physical quantity speed or velocity (meters/second = m/s) is length/time (L/T).

Which of the following represents the gravitational constant G in the fundamental dimensions of mass (M), length (L) and time (T)?

A. $M^{-1}L^3T^{-2}$
B. $M^2L^3T^{-2}$
C. $M^{-1}L^{-3}T^{-2}$
D. $M^2L^3T^2$

This is a classic example of dimensional analysis. First, you should know that the unit of force is a newton which is also a kg•m/s^2 (see Tables 1-3, GM 2.1.3; in PHY 2.2, we will see the very important Newton's Law where F = ma so the units of F must be mass 'm' in kg multiplied by acceleration 'a' which is m/s^2). Of course, according to the preamble for the question, the 2 m's in the Law of Gravitation represent masses (M) and the 'r' represents a distance or length (L). So we get:

$$F = G(m_1 m_2 / r^2)$$

Now transferring to the fundamental quantities except for G:

$$MLT^{-2} = GM^2L^{-2}$$

In order to isolate G (our unknown), divide both sides by M^2L^{-2}:

$$MLT^{-2} / M^2L^{-2} = G$$

Remove the common M (GM 1.4.2):

$$LT^{-2} / ML^{-2} = G$$

Since the answer choices have no symbol for division, we can remove the denominator by following the rules for exponents (GM 1.5.1, 1.5.3, 1.5.5):

$$LT^{-2}M^{-1}L^2 = G$$

Thus: $G = M^{-1}L^3T^{-2}$

Answer A. Note that in SI units, which is the other way you could be asked the same question on the exam, the preceding final answer is the same as $m^3kg^{-1}s^{-2}$ (Table 1, GM 2.1.3).

Of course, if it is your first time completing such a problem, it may seem quite challenging. Ideally, you will see this type of problem dozens of times before you sit the GAMSAT so that dimensional analysis, in its many forms, will become routine. Regarding the step where we isolated G: we will be doing many more practice questions isolating variables in the next chapter.

GOLD STANDARD WARM-UP EXERCISES

CHAPTER 2: Scientific Measurement and Dimensional Analysis

1. How many millimeters are there in 75 meters?

   A.   750 mm
   B.   75 mm
   C.   7,500 mm
   D.   75,000 mm

2. Which of the following is the shortest distance?

   A.   10 m
   B.   1,000 mm
   C.   10 cm
   D.   0.1 km

3. A triathlon has three legs. The first leg is a 12 km run. The second leg is a 10 km swim. The third leg is a 15 km bike ride. How long is the total triathlon in meters?

   A.   37,000 m
   B.   3,700 m
   C.   1,000 m
   D.   37 m

4. If a paperclip has a mass of one gram and a staple has a mass of 0.05 g, how many staples have a mass equivalent to the mass of one paperclip?

   A.   10
   B.   100
   C.   20
   D.   25

5. Which of the following is the number of minutes equivalent to $17\frac{5}{6}$ hours?

   A.   1,080
   B.   1,056
   C.   1,050
   D.   1,070

6. The three children in a family weigh 67 lbs., 1 oz., 93 lbs., 2 oz., and 18 lbs., 5 oz. What is the total weight of all three children? {You may go back to section 2.1 to find an appropriate conversion factor.}

   A.   178.8 lbs.
   B.   178.5 lbs.
   C.   178.08 lbs.
   D.   179.8 lbs.

7. A lawyer charges clients $20.50 per hour to file paperwork, $55 per hour for time in court, and $30 per hour for consultations. How much will it cost for a 90-minute consultation, $\frac{8}{6}$ hours time filing paperwork, and 1 hour in court?

   A. $110.28
   B. $100.75
   C. $88.25
   D. $127.33

8. If a car moving at a constant speed travels 20 centimeters in 1 second, approximately how many feet will it travel in 25% of a minute? {You may go back to section 2.1 to find an appropriate conversion factor.}

 A. 10
 B. 15
 C. 12
 D. 9

9. The Dounreay Nuclear Power Station has been in operation for quite some time. Over the last six years, they have turned out a total of two megawatt-years of energy. Assuming that operations were continuous over a six year period at a constant rate, what was its power in watts (W)?

 A. 3.3×10^5 W
 B. 6.6×10^5 W
 C. 3.3×10^2 W
 D. 6.6×10^2 W

10. The dimension of a physical quantity can be expressed as a product of the basic physical dimensions of mass (M), length (L) and time (T). For example, the dimension of the physical quantity speed or velocity (meters/second = m/s) is length/time (L/T).

 Given that $F = at^{-1} + bt^2$ where F is the force and t is the time, then the dimensions of a and b must be, respectively (note: this is a challenging question but it is at the level of the real GAMSAT. You can look at the table in section 2.1 to guide you to the dimensions that should apply to the force F but that would not be given to you on the real exam. Don't worry if you could not do this problem. We will revisit this question type in our online Physics practice problems and in the practice exam at the back of the book.):

 A. LT^{-2}, T^{-2}
 B. T, T^{-2}
 C. LT^{-1}, T^{-2}
 D. MLT^{-1}, MLT^{-4}

NOTE

If you have completed and reviewed all of the practice questions with worked solutions in GAMSAT Math Chapter 2, consider logging into your GAMSAT-prep.com account, clicking on Videos, Physics, and then the following virtual-classroom video: Dimensional Analysis, Reviewing and Manipulating Equations. If necessary, you can have Tables 1-3 in GM 2.1.3 open to consult during the video. Good luck!

GS ANSWER KEY

CHAPTER 2

Cross-Reference

1. D GM 2.1, 2.2
2. C GM 2.1.2
3. A GM 2.2
4. C GM 2.1
5. D GM 2.1, 2.2

Cross-Reference

6.   B GM 2.1, 2.2
7.   D GM 2.1.1, 2.2
8.   A GM 2.1, 2.2; dimensional analysis
9.   A GM 2.1, 2.2; dimensional analysis
10. D GM 2.2; dimensional analysis

⋆ Worked solutions can be found at the end of the GAMSAT Math chapters. If something is still not clear, go to the forum at GAMSAT-prep.com.

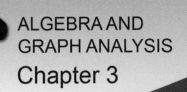

ALGEBRA AND GRAPH ANALYSIS
Chapter 3

Memorize	Understand	Not Required
• The #1 Rule of Algebra • Slope-Intercept Form for linear equations • Rules of logarithms • Gold Standard 5-step Graph Analysis Technique	* Basic equations and methods of problem solving * Simplifying equations * Solving one or more linear equations * Rules and graphs: logs and exponents * Graph analysis, slopes, area under curves * 2D (x, y) and 3D (x, y, z) graphs, nomograms	* Multiplying polynomials * Inequalities * Memorizing math expressions like "Cartesian Coordinates" * Memorizing equations for graphs other than the linear equation

GAMSAT-Prep.com

Introduction

Somewhere between 10% and 30% of GAMSAT Section 3 multiple-choice questions involve the manipulation of algebraic equations. Mastering these manipulations at a basic, secondary school level is all that is required. Additionally, many questions involve graph analysis and the manipulation of logs/exponents without the use of a calculator. Keep in mind that besides the GAMSAT Math chapter review questions, all the other science chapters have online chapter review questions where you will also practice the math reviewed in these math chapters. Also, for those of you looking for more practice, you can find hours of GAMSAT Graph Analysis videos in the Videos section of GAMSAT-prep.com.

Additional Resources

Free Online Forum

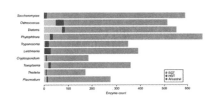

GAMSAT-prep.com Videos

Special Guest

3.1 Equation Solving and Functions

3.1.1 Algebraic Equations

Before we jump into more complicated algebra, let's review the basics.

A. Terms

Variable: A variable is a symbol - usually in the form of a small letter - that represents a number. It can take on any range of values.

Most problems that are strictly algebraic in nature will provide you with an equation (or equations) containing one or more unknown variables. Based on the information given, the values of the variables will most likely be fixed. Your job is to solve for those values.

Constant: A constant is a fixed value. A constant can be a number on its own, or sometimes it is represented by a letter such as a, b, k, π, e, etc. In the chapters to come, you will discover that there are many constants in nature.

Polynomial: A polynomial is an expression (usually part of a function or an equation) that is composed of the sum or difference of some number of terms. Please note that some of the terms can be negative. The **order** of a polynomial is equal to the largest exponent to which a variable is raised in one of the terms.

EXAMPLE $3x^2 + x + 5$

This expression is a polynomial. The variable here is x, and the order of the polynomial is 2 because that is the largest exponent to which x is raised.

B. Preserving Equality

The #1 Rule of Algebra: Whatever you do to one side of an equation, you *must* do to the other side also!

The equals sign implies equality between two different expressions. When you are given an equation, the equality established must be considered to be always true for that problem (unless you are told otherwise). So if you change one side of the equation and you do not also change the other side in the same way, you fundamentally alter the terms of the equation. The equation will no longer be true.

EXAMPLE

Consider this equation:

$$2x + 3 = 5$$

The following manipulation violates the above rule:

$$(2x + 3) - 3 = 5$$

Here, we have subtracted three from one side but not the other, so the equality no longer holds.

This manipulation, however, does not violate the rule:

$$(2x + 3) - 3 = 5 - 3$$

Here, we have subtracted three from both sides, so the equality still holds true.

C. Solving Basic Equations

We can use the rule of algebra described in Part B to help solve algebraic equations for an unknown variable. Keep in mind that addition and subtraction,

---

NOTE

If two sides of an equation are equal, you can add or subtract the same amount to/from both sides, and they will still be equal.

EXAMPLE

$a = b$

$a + c = b + c$

$a - c = b - c$

The same rule applies to multiplication and division.

EXAMPLE

$a = b$

$ac = bc$

$a \div c = b \div c$

---

along with multiplication and division, are inverse operations: They undo each other. First decide the operation that has been applied and then use the inverse operation to undo this (make sure to apply the operation to both sides of the equation). The idea is to isolate the variable on one side of the equation. Then, whatever is left on the other side of the equation is the value of the variable.

EXAMPLE

Solve: $2x + 3 = 5$

$2x + 3 - 3 = 5 - 3$

$2x = 2$

Subtracting 3, however, has not isolated the variable x. Hence, we need to continue undoing by dividing 2 on both sides.

$2x \div 2 = 2 \div 2$

$x = 1$

Here's a little more complicated equation for you to try: $2x + 2/3 = 3x - 2$

Objective: isolate the variable in order to provide a solution to the equation. When you have an equation with the variable on both sides, choose whichever you think will be easier to focus on. In this case, we will isolate x on the right. First, subtract $2x$ from both sides.

$$(2x + 2/3) - 2x = (3x - 2) - 2x$$

$\Rightarrow 2/3 = x - 2$

Next, add 2 to both sides to isolate x.

$(2/3) + 2 = (x - 2) + 2$
$\Rightarrow 8/3 = x$

3.1.2 Addition and Subtraction of Polynomials

When adding or subtracting polynomials, the general rules for exponents are applied and like terms are grouped together. You can think of it as similar to collecting the same things together.

EXAMPLE

$4x^3y + 5z^2 + 5xy^4 + 3z^2$

$= 4x^3y + 5xy^4 + (5+3)z^2$
$= 4x^3y + 5xy^4 + 8z^2$

By grouping the similar terms, seeing which terms may be added or subtracted becomes easier.

3.1.3 Simplifying Algebraic Expressions

Algebraic expressions can be factored or simplified using standard formulae:

$$a(b + c) = ab + ac$$
$$(a + b)(a - b) = a^2 - b^2$$
$$(a + b)(a + b) = (a + b)^2 = a^2 + 2ab + b^2$$
$$(a - b)(a - b) = (a - b)^2 = a^2 - 2ab + b^2$$
$$(a + b)(c + d) = ac + ad + bc + bd$$

3.2 Simplifying Equations

In order to make solving algebraic equations easy and quick, you should simplify terms whenever possible. The following are the most common and important ways of doing so.

3.2.1 Combining Terms

This is the most basic thing you can do to simplify an equation. If there are multiple terms being added or subtracted in your equation that contain the same variables, you can combine them.

EXAMPLE

Simplify the equation: $3x + 4xy - 2 = xy + 1$

Notice that there are two terms we can combine that contain xy and two terms we can combine that are just constants.

$$(3x + 4xy - 2) - xy = (xy + 1) - xy$$
$$\Rightarrow 3x \quad 3xy - 2 = 1$$

$$(3x + 3xy - 2) + 2 = 1 + 2$$
$$\Rightarrow 3x + 3xy = 3$$

$$\Rightarrow \left(\frac{3x + 3xy}{3}\right) = \frac{3}{3}$$
$$\Rightarrow x + xy = 1$$

Always make sure to look for like terms to combine when you are solving an algebra problem.

3.2.2 Variables in Denominators

When you are trying to manipulate an equation, having variables in the denominators of fractions can make things difficult. In order to get rid of such denominators entirely, simply multiply the entire equation by the quantity in the denominator. This will probably cause other terms to become more complicated, but you will no longer have the problem of a variable denominator.

EXAMPLE

Simplify the expression: $\frac{3}{2x} + 5x = 4$.

The problem denominator is $2x$, so we multiply both sides by $2x$.

$$(\frac{3}{2x} + 5x)2x = (4)2x$$
$$\Rightarrow 3 + 10x^2 = 8x$$

When there are different denominators containing variables, cross multiply the denominator to cancel out. Try the following example.

EXAMPLE

$$\frac{5}{(x+3)} = \frac{2}{x} - \frac{1}{3x}$$

Multiply 3x on both sides:

$$\frac{5}{(x+3)}(3x) = \frac{2}{x} - \frac{1}{3x}(3x)$$

$$\frac{15x}{(x+3)} = 6 - 1$$

Multiply (x+3) on both sides:

$$\frac{15x}{(x+3)}(x+3) = 5(x+3)$$

$$15x = 5x + 15$$

$$15x - 5x = 5x + 15 - 5x$$

$$10x = 15$$

$$x = \frac{15}{10} = \frac{3}{2}$$

3.2.3 Factoring

If every term of a polynomial is divisible by the same quantity, that quantity can be factored out. This means that we can express the polynomial as the product of that quantity times a new, smaller polynomial.

EXAMPLE

Factor the following expression:

$$2x^3 - 4x^2 + 4x$$

Every term in this polynomial is divisible by $2x$, so we can factor it out of each term. The simplified expression, then, is

$$2x(x^2 - 2x + 2).$$

To verify that you have properly factored an expression, multiply out your solution. If you get back to where you started, you've done it correctly.

3.3 Linear Equations

3.3.1 Linearity

Linear equation is an equation between two (or three) variables that gives a straight line when plotted on a graph (GM 3.5.1). In a linear equation, there can neither be variables raised to exponents nor variables multiplied together.

(a) $3x + 2y = z + 5$

This equation is linear.

(b) $3x^2 - 2xy = 1$

This equation is not linear. The terms $3x^2$ and $2xy$ cannot appear in a linear equation.

The reason such equations are called "linear" is that they can be represented on a Cartesian graph as a straight line. "Cartesian" is the basic coordinate system composed of an x axis and a y axis (and sometimes z axis as well) which we will review shortly.

3.3.2 Solving Linear Equations with Multiple Variables

In the previous sections we have only considered equations with single variables. In some cases though, GAMSAT problems will require you to deal with a second variable.

A. Isolating a Variable

When you have a single equation with two variables, you will not be able to solve for specific values. What you can do is solve for one variable in terms of the other. To do this, pick a variable to isolate on one side of the equation and move all other terms to the other side.

EXAMPLE

Solve the following for y: $4y - 3x = 2y + x - 6$.

Let's isolate y on the left side:

$$(4y - 3x) + 3x - 2y = (2y + x - 6) + 3x - 2y$$

$$\frac{(2y)}{2} = \frac{(4x - 6)}{2}$$

$$y = 2x - 3$$

Now we know the value of y, but only in relation to the value of x. If we are now given some value for x, we can simply plug it in to our solution and obtain y. For example, if $x = 1$ then $y = 2 - 3 = -1$.

B. Solving Systems of Equations

How do you know if you will be able to solve for specific values in an equation or not? The general rule is that if you have the same number of unique equations as variables (or more equations), you will be able find a specific value for every variable. So for the example in Part A, since we have two variables and only one equation, in order to solve for the variables, we would need one more unique equation.

In order for an equation to be unique, it must not be algebraically derived from another equation.

EXAMPLE

$$300 = 30x - 10y$$
$$30 = 3x - y$$

From the above example, the two equations describe the same line and therefore are not unique since they are scalar multiples of each other.

There are two strategies you should know for solving a system of equations:

I. **Substitution.** This strategy can be used every time, although, it will not always be the fastest way to come up with a solution. You begin with one equation and isolate a variable as in Part A. Next, wherever the isolated variable appears in the second equation, replace it with the expression this variable is equal to. This effectively eliminates that variable from the second equation.

If you only have two equations, all you need are two steps. Once you have followed the procedure above, you can solve for the second variable in the second equation and substitute that value back into the first equation to find the value of the first variable. If you have more than two variables and equations, you will need to continue this process of isolation and substitution until you reach the last equation.

EXAMPLE

Solve the following system of equations for x and y.

$$4y - 3x = 2y + x - 6$$
$$3x + y = 12$$

We have already isolated y in the first equation, so the first step is done. The new system is as follows:

$$y = 2x - 3$$
$$3x + y = 12$$

Next, we substitute $2x - 3$ for y in the second equation.

$$3x + (2x - 3) = 12$$
$$\Rightarrow 5x - 3 = 12$$
$$\Rightarrow 5x = 15$$
$$\Rightarrow x = 3$$

Now, we have a value for x, but we still need a value for y. Substitute 3 for x in the y-isolated equation.

$$y = 2(3) - 3$$
$$y = 3$$

So our solution to this system of equations is $x = 3$, $y = 3$.

II. **Equation Addition or Subtraction.** You will not always be able to apply this strategy, but in some cases, it will save you from having to do all of the time-consuming substitutions of Strategy I. The basic idea of equation addition or subtraction is exactly what you would expect: Addition or subtraction of equations directly to each other.

Say you have two equations, A and B. Because both sides of any equation are by definition equal, you can add, say, the left side of equation A to the left side of equation B and the right side of equation A to the right side of equation B without changing anything. In performing this addition, you are doing the same thing to both sides of equation B.

The purpose of performing such an addition is to try and get a variable to cancel out completely. If you can accomplish this, you can solve for the other variable easily (assuming you only have two variables, of course). Before adding the equations together, you can manipulate either of them however you like (as long as you maintain equality) in order to set up the cancellation of a variable.

If the only way to cancel out a variable is by subtracting the equation, this may be done as well.

EXAMPLE

Use equation addition or subtraction to solve the following for x and y.

$$2x - 2y = 1$$
$$4x + 5y = 11$$

If we multiply the first equation by two, we will have $4x$ present in each equation. Then if we subtract, the $4x$ in each equation will cancel.

$$
\begin{array}{r}
4x - 4y = 2 \\
- (4x + 5y = 11) \\
\hline
0x - 9y = -9 \\
\Rightarrow y = 1
\end{array}
$$

Now, we can substitute this value of y into whichever equation looks simpler to solve for x (either one will work though).

$$2x - 2(1) = 1$$
$$\Rightarrow 2x = 3$$
$$\Rightarrow x = \frac{3}{2}$$

So our solution to this system of equations is $y = 1$, $x = \frac{3}{2}$.

NOTE

A 'classic' GAMSAT-style question requires an understanding of Strategy II to solve Hess' Law problems (CHM 8.3).

3.4 Graphing Linear Functions

3.4.1 Linear Equations and Functions

Every linear equation can be rewritten as a linear function. To do so, simply isolate one of the variables as in GM 3.1.1C. This variable is now a function of the variables on the other side of the equation.

EXAMPLE

Rewrite the equation $3y - 2x = 6$ as a function of x.

$$3y - 2x = 6$$
$$\Rightarrow 3y = 2x + 6$$
$$\Rightarrow y = \frac{2}{3}x + 2$$

Now that we have isolated y, it is actually a function of x. For every input of x, we get a unique output of y. If you like, you can rewrite y as $f(x)$.

$$f(x) = \frac{2}{3}x + 2$$

3.4.2 Cartesian Coordinates in 2D

The Cartesian coordinate system is the most commonly used system for graphing. A Cartesian graph in two dimensions has two axes: The x-axis is the horizontal one, and the y-axis is the vertical one. The independent variable is always along the x-axis and the dependent variable is along the y-axis. The independent variable is controlled and the output depends on the independent variable.

The further right you go on the x-axis, the larger the numbers get; and on the y-axis, the numbers get larger the further up you go. A point on the graph is specified as an ordered pair of an x value and a y value like this: (x, y). This point exists x units from the origin (the point $(0, 0)$ where the axes cross) along the x-axis, and y units from the origin along the y-axis.

EXAMPLE

A *grid* is a network of lines that cross each other to form a series of squares or rectangles. Find the point $(3, -1)$ on the 8x8-grid Cartesian graph shown. To plot this point, simply count three units to the right along the x-axis and one unit down along the y-axis.

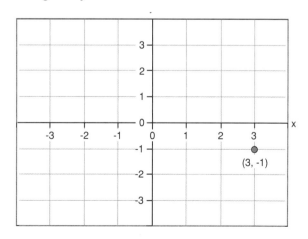

In order to graph a straight line in Cartesian coordinates, all you need to know is two points. Every set of two points has only one unique line that passes through both of them.

To find two points from a linear equation, simply choose two values to plug in for one of the variables. It is best to pick values that will make your calculations easier, such as 0 and 1. Plugging in each of these values, we can solve for y and obtain two points.

EXAMPLE

Graph the line defined by $2x + y = 3$.

3.4.4 Slope-Intercept Form

There are two pieces of information that are very useful in the graphing of a linear equation: The slope of the line and its y-intercept.

Slope refers to the steepness of a line. It is the ratio (slope = rise/run) of the number of units along the y-axis to the number of units along the x-axis between two points.

EXAMPLE

$$y = 5x + 3 \text{ and } y = 5x + 10$$

The preceding 2 equations would be parallel to each other since both slopes (m) = 5.

$$y = 3x + 6 \text{ and } y = -\frac{1}{3x} + 3$$

First, let's plug in $x = 0$ and $x = 1$ to find two points on the line.

$$2(0) + y = 3$$
$$\Rightarrow y = 3$$
$$2(1) + y = 3$$
$$\Rightarrow y = 1$$

Now, we have two points: (0, 3) and (1, 1). To graph the line, all we have to do is plot these points on a graph and draw a straight line between them.

These two equations are perpendicular. The line of the first equation has a positive slope and the perpendicular line has a decreasing slope and therefore both slopes have opposite signs. In fact, the general rule is that when slopes are negative reciprocals of each other, the 2 lines in question must be perpendicular to each other.

The y-**intercept** of a line is the y-coordinate of the point at which the line crosses the y-axis. The value of x where the line intersects, is always zero and its coordinates will be (0, y).

One of the standard forms of a linear equation is the slope-intercept form, from which the slope and the y-intercept of the line are immediately obvious. This form resembles $y = mx + b$. Here m and b are constants such that m is the slope of the line and b is the y-intercept.

EXAMPLE

Rewrite the following equation in slope-intercept form: $2y + 5x = 8$.

$$\Rightarrow 2y = -5x + 8$$

$$\Rightarrow y = -\frac{5}{2}x + 4$$

This is now in slope-intercept form. In this case, the slope m is $-5/2$ and the y-intercept is 4.

Slope-intercept form is also useful for constructing the equation of a line from other information. If you are given the slope and the intercept, obviously you can simply plug them in to $y = mx + b$ to get the equation. It is also very simple to obtain the slope and intercept if you know two points on the line, (x_1, y_1) and (x_2, y_2). The slope can be obtained directly from this information:

Slope = rise/run = $(y_2 - y_1)/(x_2 - x_1)$

Once the slope m is obtained, you only need to solve for b. To do so, plug in one of the points as well as m into the slope-intercept equation. You can then solve for b.

EXAMPLE

Find the equation for the line passing through (1, 1) and (2, 3).

First, determine the slope.

$$m = \frac{(3-1)}{(2-1)} = 2$$

Now plug m and a point into the slope-intercept equation to find b.

$$y = mx + b$$
$$\Rightarrow 1 = 2(1) + b$$
$$\Rightarrow -1 = b$$

Plugging in all of this information, we now have a complete equation.

$$y = 2x - 1$$

3.5 Basic Graphs

3.5.1 The Graph of a Linear Equation

Given any two points (x_1, y_1) and (x_2, y_2) on the line, we have:

$$y_1 = ax_1 + b$$

and

$$y_2 = ax_2 + b.$$

Subtracting the upper equation from the lower one and dividing through by $x_2 - x_1$ gives the value of the slope,

$$a = (y_2 - y_1)/(x_2 - x_1)$$

$$= \Delta y/\Delta x = \text{rise/run}$$

NOTE

Often on the real GAMSAT, you will need to either calculate the slope of a line or the area under a graph or line, or both.

Lines that have positive slopes, slant "up hill" (as viewed from left to right), like the graph on this page. Lines that have negative slopes, slant "down hill" (as viewed from left to right). Lines that are horizontal have no slope (= a slope of zero; *see* PHY 1.4.1).

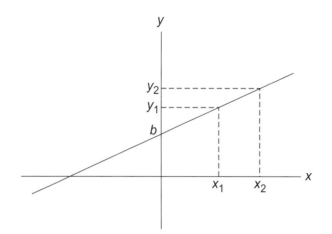

NOTE

Don't get attached to variables in equations. Only focus on the meaning of the equation. Among and within different textbooks and exams, different variables may be used in the same equations (*a* or *m* for slope; S or d or *x* for displacement, and many others). Some exam questions are designed to catch students who try to memorize without understanding equations.

3.5.2 Illustrations of Common Graphs

For the graphs in this section (GM 3.5.2), please consider replacing *x* by 0, 1 and 2 (or other values) to ensure that the graph behaves in a way that makes sense to you. In the following graph, note that the red and blue lines have the same slope (gradient); the red and green lines have the same *y*-intercept:

For any real number *x*, there exists a unique real number called the multiplicative inverse or *reciprocal* of *x* denoted $1/x$ or x^{-1} such that $x(1/x) = 1$. The graph of the reciprocal $1/x$ for any *x* is:

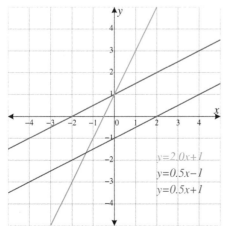

$y=2.0x+1$
$y=0.5x-1$
$y=0.5x+1$

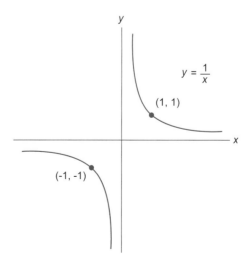

A quadratic equation (e.g. CHM 6.6.1) is a polynomial (GM 3.1.1) in which the highest-order term is 'to the power of 2'. For example, $y = ax^2$. A quadratic equation describes a parabola which is approximately U-shaped:

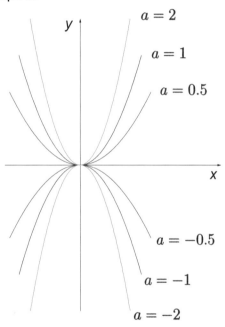

Interestingly, there are important graphs and shapes, including a parabola, that can be obtained by taking a simple cone and cutting it at various angles. This only requires a bit of imagination:

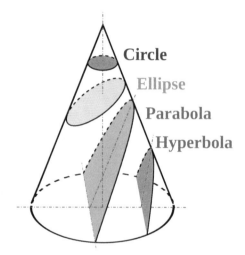

For GAMSAT purposes, it would not be helpful to commit the equation of any graph to memory – aside, of course, for the equation that describes a straight line.

3.5.3 Common Graphs Found in Other Sections or Chapters

There are classic curves which are represented or approximated in the science text as follows: Sigmoidal curve (CHM 6.9.1, BIO 7.5.1), sinusoidal curve (GM 5.2.3, PHY 7.1), hyperbolic curves (CHM 9.7 Fig III.A.9.3, BIO 1.1.2), exponential rise (GM 3.8, CHM 9.8.1) and decay (PHY 10.4, CHM 9.2). Another type of graph that you will likely see during the real GAMSAT is where one or both axes are logarithmic (so called semi-log and log-log graphs, respectively; GM 3.8 + CHM 4.3.3, CHM 6.9.1/2).

If you were to plot a set of experimental data, often one can draw a line or curve which can "best fit" the data. The preceding defines a *regression* line or curve (GM 6.3.1).

One purpose of the regression graph is to predict what would likely occur outside of the experimental data. The skill to extend a graph by inferring unknown values from trends in the known data is *extrapolation*.

3.5.4 Tangential Slope and Area under a Curve

During the real GAMSAT, you will very likely need to calculate a slope based on a curve (i.e. the slope of the straight line must just glance the curve at a specific point = *tangential*), and/or you will need to calculate the area under a curve (depending on the presentation, you would estimate the answer by either counting boxes below the graph or by multiplying some part of the x axis by some part of the y axis; the question could be in Physics, Chemistry or Biology). In neither instance will you be told which you should calculate, but rather you must learn, as part of basic graph analysis performed in this chapter, when one or the other applies (usually dimensional analysis is the key; GM 2.2).

As long as you pay attention to the units (dimensional analysis), then you do not have to memorize these common facts: velocity is the slope of a displacement vs. time graph (PHY 1.3); acceleration is the slope and displacement is the area under the curve of a velocity vs. time graph (PHY 1.4.1); the change in momentum (= impulse) is the area under a force vs. time graph (PHY 4.3); work is the area under the force vs. displacement graph (PHY 7.2.1).

Do not worry about the Physics for now. Just focus on the math. Let's examine a velocity vs. time graph of a bullet fired from a gun (side note: notice that the curve resembles ½ of an upside-down parabola). The y axis is velocity which is in the SI

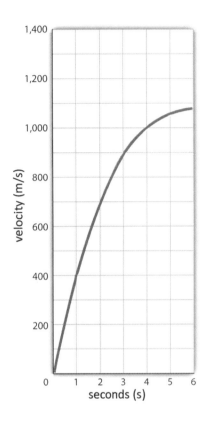

units of meters/second (m/s). The x axis is time in the SI units of seconds (s). Here are 2 questions that you can try to work out before looking at the solutions:

EXAMPLES

(1) Given that acceleration is in units of m/s², calculate the instantaneous acceleration at time = 3 seconds.

(2) Given that displacement is in the units of meters (m), calculate the displacement of the bullet in the first 2 seconds of being fired.

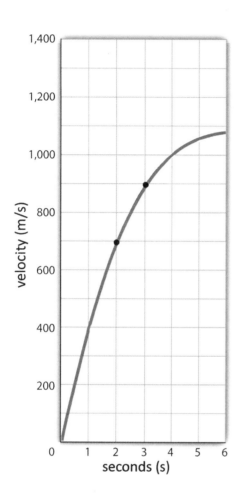

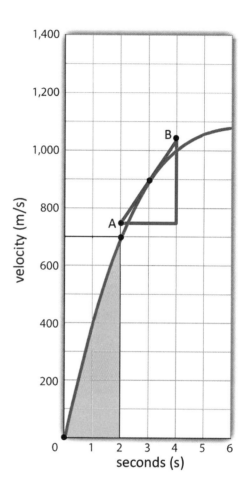

Hints if required:

(1) **Hint:** try to calculate the slope of a straight line off the curve at 3 seconds. Why does the slope solve the problem? Take a look at the units. A slope is the change of y divided by the change of x. In terms of units, this would make m/s/s = m/s^2 = acceleration.

(2) **Hint:** determine the area of the curve below that segment of the graph (i.e. the first 2 seconds). One way to do so is to calculate the area of one box and then estimate how many boxes are below the curve. Why the area? Again, the units: the area of a square or rectangle is one side times the other side. For a graph, it is x times y. So here is what happens to the units: m/s x s = m = meters which is displacement.

ANSWERS

(1) To calculate the slope at a point, the line that you draw needs to be tangential to the curve as described previously (see the preceding graphs). The line can be as long or as short as you want (basically, you choose the length to make the calculation as easy as possible).

We chose a change in x (i.e. from points A to B as seen from the x axis) which is easy to calculate = 2 seconds (i.e. 4 − 2 = 2). The change in y (i.e. from points A to B as seen from the y axis) is also easy = 300 m/s (1050 − 750 = 300). The slope is the change in y divided by the change in x so: (300 m/s)/(2 s) = 150 m/s^2.

Notice that point A in the graph is our point (x_1, y_1) and point B is (x_2, y_2); *see* GM 3.5.1. While sitting the GAMSAT, you may need to assess a slope by laying down a pen or pencil on the exam paper followed by a reasonable estimate of the data points.

(2) As explained in the "hint", we are trying to calculate the area under the curve in the first 2 seconds. If you put your pen in the line (0, 0) to (2, 700), you will notice that your pen approximates the green line (do not use a ruler because they are not permitted during the GAMSAT!).

In other words, if we were to imagine a rectangle that includes the points (0, 0) to (2, 700), then the area under the curve seems to be about ½ that value. Because a rectangle is simply one side times the other, we can multiply 2 seconds x 700 m/s = 1400 meters. The area below the green graph is about ½ that or 700 meters, which is thus the displacement.

Of course, it depends on the multiple choice answers. Careful observation will show you that the area under the curve is slightly more than 700 m.

An alternative way to calculate the area in blue would be to calculate the area of one single small box from the graph: 100 m/s times 1 s = 100 meters. If you carefully count the boxes in the blue shaded area (which you can see better from the graph on the left), you will be able to count about 7 complete boxes (i.e. approx. 700 m; of course, sometimes you need to add 2 incomplete boxes to make one full box).

Yet another alternative may have been the first choice of those with a science background: estimate the area in blue as a triangle (which we will discuss in GM 4.2.2) which is 1/2(base)(height) = 1/2(2)(700) = 700 m.

3.5.5 Breaking Axes and Error Bars

Among the many reasons that an axis could be broken would be if the missing part of the graph is not key to understanding the trend, and/or when the trend is obvious which allows more data to be shown in a smaller graph.

The following represents 3 different symbols for a broken axis.

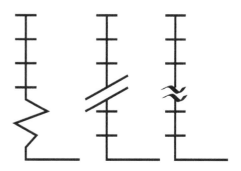

EXAMPLE 1

Consider the following diagram. The break in the *x* axis does not change the scale; however, the break in the *y* axis clearly permits the scale to jump from 0 to 0.5 in a way that is remarkably different from the rest of the *y* axis.

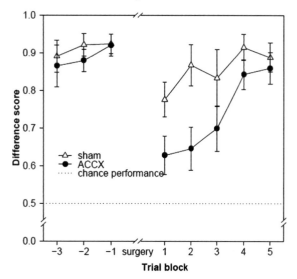

Error bars show the variability of data and indicate the error or *uncertainty* in a measurement. Error bars often represent one standard deviation of uncertainty (GM 6.3.2), or a particular confidence interval (e.g., a 95% chance that the actual data point falls within the extremes of the error bar). From the preceding graph, it can be seen that the error bars for the measurements for Trial block 3 are longer than for Trial block 1, meaning the latter has an average (*mean*) value that is more representative of the data (= more reliable). Also notice that only 2 trials (Trial block 1 and 2) have non-overlapping error bars. This means that in all of the other trials, because of the overlap, the difference between the data points of the sham versus ACCX trials may not be statistically significant.

Thus, even though you are not provided any details, the graph informs us that ACCX (whatever that means) has a statistically significant post-surgical 'difference score' within the first two trial blocks as compared to the sham group. Of course, 'sham' implies 'fake' and in science that implies a group (= *control* group; BIO 2.5) that is exposed to the same conditions as the experimental group, except that the control group does not receive the treatment (e.g. no ACCX).

Mathematically, we can describe a data point's error as 'plus or minus' the point seen in the graph. For example, for ACCX trial block 3, the data point is approximately 0.7 with a range given by the error bar of about 0.64 to 0.76. Thus the point can be described as 0.7 plus or minus 0.06 (i.e. 0.7 ± 0.06).

Let us consider another example of a broken axis but in this case the data is presented using rectangular bars of different heights (= a *histogram*, AKA bar graph or chart). Please note that the following histogram is presented with error bars and is using a linear scale (i.e. it is not logarithmic which we will explore in GM 3.7).

EXAMPLE 2

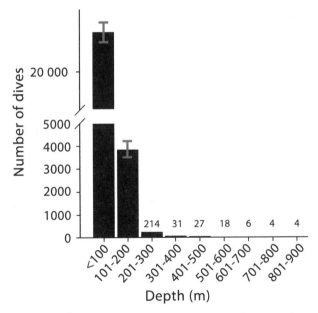

Figure 1 Depth ranges with respective number of dives of leatherback turtles under investigation. Adapted from Hays, Journal of Experimental Biology 2008 211: 2566-2575; doi: 10.1242/jeb.020065.

According to Figure 1, as compared to dives between 100 and 200 meters, dives below 100 meters occur:

A. more than twice as often but less than three times as often.

B. less than 15 000 dives more often.

C. between 15 000 and 20 000 dives more often.

D. over 20 000 dives more often.

Note that glancing at the histogram, without taking into account the broken *y* axis, could lead one to be misled into thinking that answer choice A is correct.

Using the distance on the *y* axis from 0 to 2000 as a guide, we can see that the first bar diagram seems to end approximately 2000 dives above 20 000 (i.e. 22 000; we can only make this conclusion because the increments are linear).

During the real exam, students sometimes use their ID card (for example, driver's license) to 'measure' distances since rulers are not permitted. We suggest having a long, straight pencil (NOT ergodynamic) which could be helpful for this purpose among others (e.g. slopes off of curves, and of course, writing essays!).

The second bar diagram seems to be between 3500 and 4000, which we can approximate as 3750. Thus we can estimate the difference as 22 000 − 3750 = 18 250 dives, thus answer choice C is correct.

The error bars are just an added distraction since they do not come into play here (i.e. they do not overlap). Had they overlapped, we could have no confidence that any difference between the 2 dives exists – even if there appeared to be a difference in the heights of the histograms.

3.6 Cartesian Coordinates in 3D

The GAMSAT will sometimes present 3D (3 dimensional) graphs to see if you are capable of a basic analysis.

EXAMPLE 1

Consider the following illustration of a 3D Cartesian coordinate system. Notice the origin *O* and the 3 axis lines *X*, *Y* and *Z*, oriented as shown by the arrows. The tick marks on the axes are one length unit apart. Look carefully at the black dot. What coordinate (x, y, z) would you give to identify the position of that dot? (2,2,3)? (3,2,4)? (4,3,2)? (2,4,3)? (2,3,4)? The black dot represents a point with coordinates x = 2, y = 3, and z = 4, or (2,3,4).

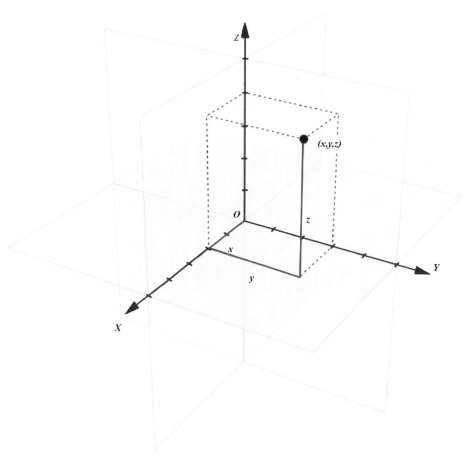

Figure IV.3.1: Three-dimensional Cartesian coordinate system. (Stolfi)

EXAMPLE 2

We will be looking at phase diagrams in General Chemistry Chapter 4. For now, we'll ignore the chemistry and just focus on graph analysis. So as an exercise to read 3D graphs, comment on the relative magnitudes of temperature and pressure for the SOLID (only) portion of the curve in Figure IV.3.2.

First, you must see the graph as a 3-dimensional object. This particular graph looks like a wooden block with parts of 4 sides gouged out, as well as part of the middle. The 3 arrows in the graph indicate increasing magnitudes in the directions of the arrows. Notice that the pressure for solids could be either high or low. However, the specific volume is always relatively low as is the temperature in the region where the graph shows only solid (of course, it makes sense that something that is solid takes up less volume than the gaseous state; also, because of our experience with water - for example, ice and steam - we expect solids to be at low temperatures and gas to be at high temperatures with liquid somewhere in between).

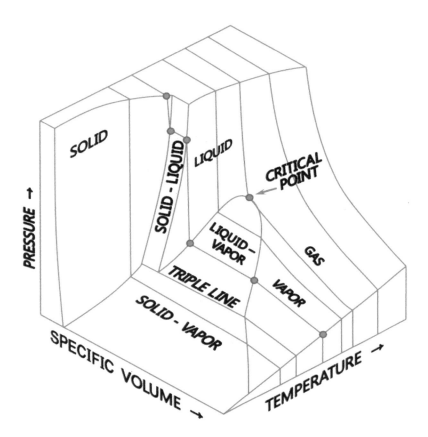

Figure IV.3.2: Pressure-volume-temperature diagram for a pure substance. (Lee/Padleckas)

In conclusion, the relative magnitude of the temperature for the SOLID (only) portion of the curve is low while the pressure can range from high to low.

EXAMPLE 3

In Figure IV.3.2, which of the following can be relatively high at the solid-vapor equilibrium: pressure, temperature or specific volume?

Notice the pressure is always low at the solid-vapor equilibrium (i.e. the part of the graph that says SOLID-VAPOR near the bottom). Temperature also seems to be relatively low at the SOLID-VAPOR part of the graph. However, the volume can be either high or low and thus the volume would be the correct answer.

Just as an aside, the line on the surface called a **triple line** is where solid, liquid and vapor can all coexist in equilibrium.

> **NOTE**
>
> When you start to complete GS Biology chapter review questions and practice tests online, you will find more questions based on 3D diagrams and log curves.

EXAMPLE 4

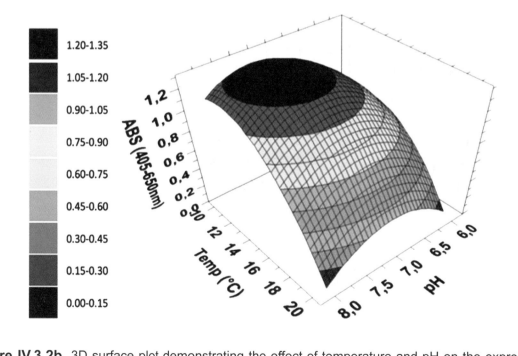

Figure IV.3.2b 3D surface plot demonstrating the effect of temperature and pH on the expression of the TS1-218 protein; the latter is positively correlated with spectrophotometric absorbance (ABS); in yeast cells monitored by ELISA. Jafari R., *Microb. Cell Fact.*, 2011.

We will continue to try many GAMSAT-level practice questions. As for the real exam, as long as your focus remains 'understanding, reasoning and data interpretation', you can answer the questions without a science background (of course, assuming that you have reviewed all previous GAMSAT Math sections and chapters). However, you must become accustomed to reading scientific material that is beyond the assumed knowledge for GAMSAT but with the confidence that the actual questions will be founded on basic, introductory-level concepts.

QUESTION 1

According to the data presented in Figure IV.3.2b, approximately what pH and temperature is best for TS1-218 expression?

- A. 7.5, 9.5 °C
- B. 7.5, 14 °C
- C. 6.5, 11 °C
- D. 7.0, 11 °C

QUESTION 2

Which of the following is most consistent with the peak absorbance in Figure IV.3.2b?

- A. Less than 1.2
- B. Exactly 1.2
- C. Above 1.2
- D. None of the above

EXPLANATION

You should develop a standard way to approach all GAMSAT graphs. Here is our Gold Standard 5-step Graph Analysis Technique

which you can modify to your liking (we also use this technique during our YouTube videos providing the worked solutions to ACER's GAMSAT practice materials). With experience, it should take you about 30 seconds:

Step 1) Quickly read the labels for all axes (i.e. ABS, Temp, pH) and, most importantly, the caption below the graph, if present. "3D surface plot" suggests that although it is a 3D diagram, we only need to be concerned with the surface of the graph (e.g. it seems to be shaped like a segment of an egg but we only need to be concerned with the eggshell); the rest of the caption can be reasonably interpreted to mean that pH and temperature affects TS1-218 expression which increases with increasing ABS. Thus high ABS = high TS1-218 expression (though the preceding could be inferred, for more about positive correlation: GM 6.3.1). {Note: Sometimes ACER will not have a caption for a diagram, if there is none, make one up! Taking 5-10 seconds to consider your own description of a diagram can focus your mind on the 'big picture'.}

As part of your routine for reading the labels for a graph, you must consider any *key* if present. A key or *legend* is an explanatory list of symbols and/or categories used in a graph, map or table. The key for Figure IV.3.2b is to the left of the graph and clearly shows that the darkest shading at the top refers to values of 1.20-1.35 which means that for the second question, answer choice C is correct. Had you chosen otherwise, it is likely because you did not identify the key and/or fully appreciate the 3D aspect of the diagram. You can tell by the 3 axes that we must be looking at the "top of the eggshell" from the top down, and at an angle.

In other words, you can't just read the ABS value (1.2) from the top of the curve because we are not looking at the graph head-on.

Step 2) Always double check the units (e.g. nm, °C, pH) and the graph's intervals. The latter can be the source of many trick questions, so always check the regularity of the actual distance between the lines on each axis; the unit distance between those lines; as well as the point of origin for each axis to identify cases where the axis begins at a number other than zero.

The intervals for our particular 3D graph are linear (we will later see that pH is logarithmic and so trick questions are still possible but we will not explore that issue for now). Notice that from pH 6 to 8, each major interval is regular at 0.5 pH units. Also note that the surface graph has a grid (GM 3.4.2), and although you do not have to be too precise, you can count - more or less - 30 lines by 30 lines for the grid. That means that to correspond to a pH of 7 (half way between 6 and 8), you would follow a line at approximately 15 on the grid (half of 30, which is due to the graph's visual symmetry; note: you could be off by 3 grid lines - higher or lower - and you would still get the correct answer which is D).

We have placed red asterisks on the 3D graph for you to follow a line from pH 7.0 to the imaginary (approx.) apex of the diagram.

Thus pH has determined that the answer for the first question must be D. The temperature does not need to be precisely calculated but it appears that the Temp axis ranges from about 9 to 21, or about 12

degrees; 30 lines/12 degrees, about 2.5 lines per degree so 11 degrees is about 5 3D-grid lines from the back of the graph, counting along the axis for Temp (side note: we discuss this graph in the Gold Standard Graph Analysis, Part 2 video).

We have already answered both questions, but we will continue with the GS 5-step Graph Analysis Technique which you may need for other types of questions.

Step 3) Recheck the axes to ensure there is not a second labelling system (note that the second graph in GM 3.9 has 2 different labels for the same x-axis), nor any broken axes (i.e. GM 3.5.5).

Step 4) Double check for logarithmic or exponential changes (GM 3.7; yes, it's that important!).

Step 5) Depending on the question type (i.e. GM 3.5.4), assess what the slope or area under the curve would give. This stage may require the equation of a line (GM 3.5.1) and/or dimensional analysis (GM 2.2).

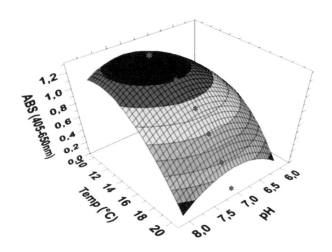

3.7 Logarithms

3.7.1 Log Rules and Logarithmic Scales

A logarithm (i.e. log) is simply the opposite of expressing exponents (GM 1.5). Using a logarithm answers the question: "How many of one number do we multiply to get another number?"

For example: How many 5s must we multiply to get 125? Answer: 5 × 5 × 5 = 125 (GM 1.5.6), so we had to multiply 3 of the 5s to get 125. Now we can say that the log of 125 with base 5 is 3: $\log_5(125) = 3$.

Just as we have already reviewed various rules for exponents (GM 1.5.1-1.5.5), we will shortly learn basic log rules which will permit manipulations for more complex logs, and we will see that the rules can also be applied to the preceding example thus: $\log_5(125) = \log_5(5)^3 = 3\log_5(5) = 3$.

Like many aspects of math, riding a bike is a good analogy: familiarity will have you applying log rules effortlessly. Logarithmic and exponential scales are found widely in medicine as well as, of course, the basic sciences that we are reviewing.

The rules of logarithms are also discussed in context, for example, Acids and Bases in General Chemistry (CHM 6.5.1). These basic log rules also apply to the "natural logarithm" which is the logarithm to the base e, where "e" is an irrational constant approximately equal to 2.71... (GM 1.1.2). The natural logarithm is usually written as $\ln x$ or $\log_e x$.

Table 1: Common values for the log base 10 (note the trends)

x	Exponential form	$\log_{10}(x)$
0.0001	10^{-4}	-4
0.001	10^{-3}	-3
0.01	10^{-2}	-2
0.1	10^{-1}	-1
1	10^{0}	0
10	10^{1}	1
100	10^{2}	2
1000	10^{3}	3
10000	10^{4}	4

In general, the power of logarithms is to reduce wide-ranging numbers to quantities with a far smaller range. For example, the graphs commonly seen in this text, including the preceding 2-dimensional graphs, are drawn to a unit or *arithmetic scale*. In other words, each unit on the x and y axes represents exactly *one* unit. This scale can be adjusted to accommodate rapidly changing curves. For example, in a unit scale the numbers 1 (= 10^0), 10 (= 10^1), 100 (= 10^2), and 1000 (= 10^3), are all far apart with varying intervals. Using a <u>logarithmic scale</u>, the sparse values suddenly become separated by one unit: Log 10^0 = 0, log 10^1 = 1, log 10^2 = 2, log 10^3 = 3, and so on.

In practice, logarithmic scales are often used to convert a rapidly changing curve (e.g. an exponential curve) into a straight line (see Fig IV.3.4 in GM 3.8). It is called a *semi-log* scale when either the x axis *or* the y axis is logarithmic. It is called a *log-log* scale when both the x axis *and* the y axis are logarithmic. Note: if not specified otherwise, when you just see "log" with no base, then it is considered to be the "common log" which means log base 10.

Here are the rules you must know:

1) $\log_a a = 1$
2) $\log_a M^k = k \log_a M$
3) $\log_a(MN) = \log_a M + \log_a N$
4) $\log_a(M/N) = \log_a M - \log_a N$
5) $10^{\log_{10} M} = M$
6) $\log_a(1) = 0$, given "a" is greater than zero.

EXAMPLE 1

Given:

$$pH = -\log_{10}[H^+]$$

Let us calculate the pH of 0.001 H^+ (for now, ignore the chemistry, focus only on the math):

$[H^+]$ = 0.001
using the #1 Rule of Algebra (GM 3.1.1):
$-\log[H^+] = -\log(0.001)$
pH = $-\log(10^{-3})$
pH = 3 log 10   (log rule #2)
pH = 3   (rule #1, a = 10)

EXAMPLE 2

What is log (1 000 000)?
log (1 000 000) = log 10^6 = 6

EXAMPLE 3

What is log (1/100)?
log (1/100) = log 10^{-2} = -2

EXAMPLE 4

Given that ln2 = 0.69, what is $ln2e^3$?

Try to solve the problem while keeping in mind: (1) ln is the natural logarithm, meaning that it is log to the base e; (2) our 3rd rule of logarithms permits you separate factors.

$ln2e^3 = ln2 + lne^3 = 0.69 + 3 = 3.69$

Notice that if you have the base of the log and the base of the number with the exponent the same, then the answer is simply the exponent. Thus

$Log(1000) = log10^3 = lne^3 = 3$.

GAMSAT log problems come in the form of pH, pKa, pKb, rate law, Nernst equation, semi-log graphs, log-log graphs, decibels/sound intensity (PHY 8.3), Gibbs free energy (CHM 9.10), just to name a few! The relevant equations are usually provided. In other words, the 'science' reduces to a basic math problem.

EXAMPLE 5

Approximate log(200).

Because the number 200 is between 100 and 1000 (but clearly closer to 100), and since log(100) = 2 and log(1000) = 3, log(200) must be a number between 2 and 3 but closer to the number 2. Such an approximation is sufficient for a multiple choice exam. {Incidentally, log(200) happens to be approximately 2.3.}

3.8 Exponential and Logarithmic Curves

The exponential and logarithmic functions are *inverse functions*. That is, their graphs can be reflected about the $y = x$ line which you can see in Figure IV.3.3.

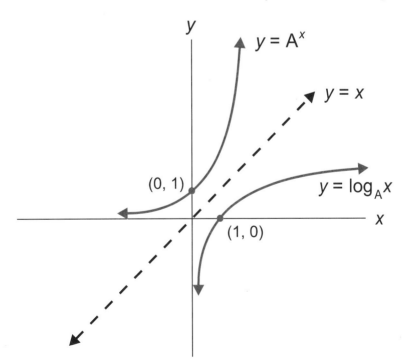

Figure IV.3.3: Exponential and Logarithmic Graphs, A > 1. Notice that when a positive number is raised to the power of 0, then the result is 1 [i.e. the point (0, 1); see also GM 1.5.4, 1.5.5 for rules of exponents]. Also note that log(1) = ln (1) = 0 [i.e. the point (1, 0) on the generic logarithmic curve].

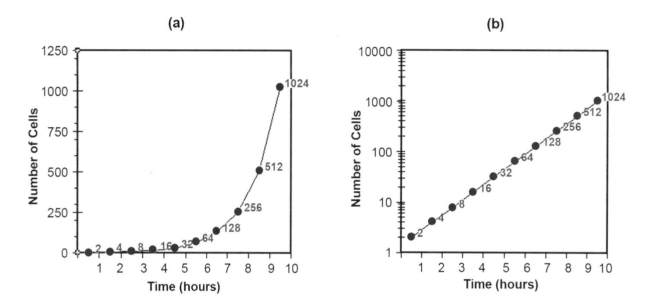

Figure IV.3.4: Growth curves of cells dividing mitotically. (a) An exponential curve with a linear scale for the x and y axis. (b) A logarithmic scale on the y axis converts the data rising exponentially into a linear graph. This is referred to as a semi-log graph or semi-log plot (GM 3.7.1). Notice that it is observation or analysis that leads to the conclusion as to what type of graph is being assessed as neither graph is labelled "exponential" nor "logarithm" anywhere.

Let's revisit one of the key reasons for using logarithms: when the data points vary from low numbers to very high numbers, sometimes a log helps to better demonstrate all the data points on one graph. Consider Figure IV.3.4: two growth curves that both represent the same data of bacteria doubling over time (2^n = 2, 2^2, 2^3, 2^4, 2^5, 2^6, 2^7, 2^8, 2^9, 2^{10} which is 1024; BIO 2.2).

Notice that in the first graph, the y axis increases in a linear fashion: the difference between each major marking is 250 cells and it starts at zero. The problem however is that the first 4 or 5 points on the exponential curve are not really distinguishable. They are all such small

relative numbers making the first ½ of the curve quite flat before it increases rapidly. It is that rapid rise that we recognize visually as an exponential increase (even though, of course, it is the entire curve which is exponential, being 2 to the power of n).

On the other hand, the second graph uses a logarithmic scale on the *y* axis (i.e. each number is 10 times the preceding number and equally spaced; the 4th number does not represent 4 times some number, rather, it represents 10 to the power of 4 times which is 10 000 times larger); suddenly the exponential curve is converted to a manageable, more clear, linear relationship where small and large

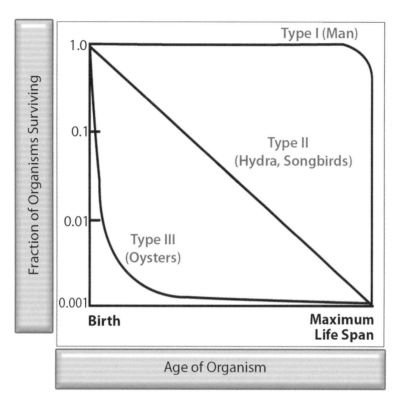

Figure IV.3.5: Type I, II and III survivorship curves scaled to a maximum life span for each species.

data points are easily visible on one graph. Notice that if you took the log of the 5 numbers along the *y* axis, you would get the quite regular result of 0, 1, 2, 3 and 4 (recall that log 10000 = log10^4 = 4). Incidentally, because the *x* axis increases in a linear fashion, the preceding is a semi-log graph.

Thus a graph that has a scale that is logarithmic on one axis but is linear on the other axis is semi-log. The term for the graph is unimportant for the GAMSAT but recognizing that you are dealing with such a graph is often critical to answering the

questions properly. We will now explore another semi-log graph (Figure IV.3.5) and we will work through some log-log graphs online (Biology chapter review questions).

Spend a few moments considering Figure IV.3.5.

QUESTION 1

Based on the diagram provided, is it true that approximately ½ of songbirds would be expected to survive ½ of their maximum lifespan? {Please consider your answer before turning the page.}

QUESTION 2

One perspective regarding the biological success of a species would be to equate success with the absolute number of individual organisms belonging to the species in question. Given this perspective, if oysters, songbirds and humans are all equally successful, based on the diagram, which of the three likely produces the least number of organisms (i.e. the least number of offspring per organism)?

EXPLANATION 1

NO! Not even close!! First, let's get a sense of the scales. We must assume that the x axis is linear because no other information is provided. However, the y axis is clearly logarithmic. It looks like it is regular (in a linear sense) but when you look at the numbers, they are increasing logarithmically. Each marking on the y axis is 10 times the previous marking. After 3 markings, 1000 times or 10^3. If you take the log of the 4 numbers on the y axis, you would get the very regular numbers of -3, -2, -1 and 0.

Now let's look at ½ of the maximum life span (so ½ of the length of the x axis). When you look at the Type II line at that point (signifying songbirds and hydra; it's not important that you know what hydra means) and look across to the y axis, you get a point ½ way between 0.01 and 0.1. Even if we imagine the higher of the 2 numbers, 0.1, that is only 1/10th of the

surviving organisms (0.1 = 1/10 = 10%). And because the lower number is 1/100th (= 1%) of the surviving organisms, the actual result is between the two which is far lower than ½ of surviving organisms (i.e. 50%). This is a common question type that can appear in any of the GAMSAT science subtopics. If you do not understand the scale, you will get the wrong answer.

EXPLANATION 2

Presumably, for the next generation to exist, the current generation must survive long enough to reproduce. The survivorship curve with the most extreme change between birth and a presumed age of reproductive ability would be the Type III survivorship curve. Let's see what we can infer from the shapes of that curve.

Most individuals in populations with Type III survivorship must produce many thousands of individuals, most of whom, according to the diagram, die right away. Once

---

NOTE

Notice that neither Figure IV.3.4 (b) nor Figure IV.3.5 had a clear origin of (0, 0). Though not important here, sometimes questions are designed to test whether you observed that the origin was other than (0, 0) and that you took it into account when necessary. We will see some questions like that in Biology.

this initial period is over, survivorship is relatively constant. Examples of this would likely include fish, marine larvae, and of course oysters. Relatively little effort or parental care is likely invested in each individual.

Type I survivorship includes humans, likely, we could reason, in developed countries. As a result of environment and the re-

sources invested in each individual, there is a high survivorship throughout the life cycle. Most individuals, according to the graph, die of old age. If Type III must produce a lot of individuals to survive the 'die off' and still be successful, then Type I requires relatively few offspring to be successful because the survivorship is better than the other two groups. Thus the answer is: humans.

EXAMPLE

Consider the following diagram.

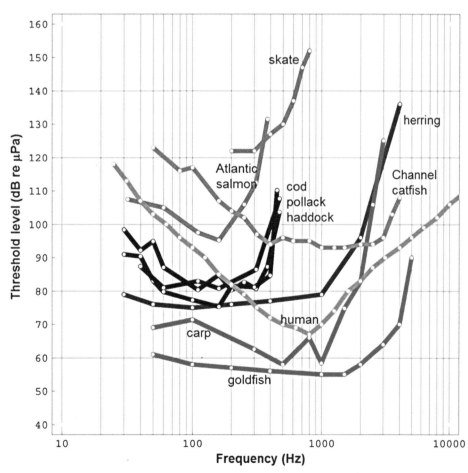

Figure IV.3.6 Audiogram curves showing the faintest sounds – as sound pressure recorded as decibels (dB) – that can be heard at each frequency, underwater. Amundsen and Landrø, GEOexPro Vol. 8, No. 3; 2011.

We will now proceed with some GAMSAT-level multiple-choice questions based on the logarithmic scale (Fig. IV.3.6).

QUESTION 1

According to the diagram, which of the following best approximates the human underwater minimum sound pressure and corresponding frequency, respectively?

    A.   67 dB, 0.8 kHz
    B.   67 dB, 1000 Hz
    C.   66 dB, 9.8×10^2 Hz
    D.   66 dB, 9.9×10^2 Hz

QUESTION 2

Hearing range describes the range of frequencies, from lowest to highest, that can be heard by humans or other animals. According to the diagram, which of the following has the greatest hearing range?

    A.   Herring
    B.   Carp
    C.   Channel catfish
    D.   Goldfish

QUESTION 3

According to the diagram, how many species are likely to hear a sound of 90 dB and 3000 Hz?

    A.   1
    B.   2
    C.   3
    D.   More than 3

EXPLANATION

The caption links the expression "sound pressure" to dBs which can be read along the y axis.

The minimum sound pressure value for the 'human' graph seems to be between 65 and 70 dB, though it is not possible to be overly accurate (yes, ambiguity is embedded in the question). However, we can be very precise about the frequency at that sound pressure: It is clearly and exactly 800 Hz [if you are unsure as to how to read the logarithmic scale, go back to the beginning of this section, GM 3.8, and examine the y axis of Figure IV.3.4, graph (b); also re-examine our discussion for Figure IV.3.5; and finally, consider labelling Figure IV.3.6 yourself so that between 100 and 1000 along the x axis, you add the following numbers below the vertical lines: 200, 300, 400, 500, 600, 700, 800, 900]. It is very important for GAMSAT purposes that you also remember your SI unit prefixes (GM 2.1.2, 2.1.3). 800 Hz = 0.8 kiloHz = 0.8 kHz, thus A is the correct answer for the first question. The other 3 answer choices are all above 900 Hz which is clearly incorrect.

For Question 2, as defined, the expression 'range' is generally understood to mean the difference between the highest and lowest number (side note: we will discuss statistical measures for the GAMSAT in Math Chapter 6).

If the scale were linear, then the easiest way to determine the widest frequency range would simply be to inspect each curve to see which is the widest (from left to right), and then 'herring' would be the winner! However, the x axis is logarithmic so such simplifications do not apply. By far, 'goldfish' has the greatest range (answer choice D is correct) because it begins at a number far higher than the rest:

A. Herring: 4000 – 30 = 3970 Hz
B. Carp: 3000 – 50 = 2950 Hz
C. Channel catfish: 4000 – 50 = 3950 Hz
D. Goldfish: 5000 – 50 = 4950 Hz

For Question 3, label the graph in increments of 1000 between labels 1000 Hz

and 10000 Hz so you have no doubt as to where the vertical line for 3000 Hz lies. To meet this line, using a straight pencil from 90 dB, you should intersect a point which is just above (or at) the 'human' graph. Thus the sound in question (90 dB and 3000 Hz) is at - or above - the threshold for human, and far above the threshold for 'goldfish'. The answer is B.

3.9 Nomograms: The Art of Unusual Graphs

A **nomogram** is a diagram representing the relations between three or more changing variables using several scales. Each scale is arranged so that the value of one variable can be found by simple geometry, for example, by drawing a straight line intersecting the other scales at the appropriate values.

Most students, with or without a science background, have little to no experience with nomograms which is exactly why ACER loves them! In addition, there is such a wide variety of what may be loosely called 'nomograms' that it assures ACER that in the long run, almost all students will be confronted with a nomogram which they would see for the first time in the exam room.

EXAMPLE 1

Consider the following nomogram. Using a straight pencil as a guide, you can join a point from the water temperature on the upper scale to the dissolved oxygen reading (ppm) on the bottom scale. You

can then read the percentage oxygen saturation from the point at which your pencil crosses the middle scale. For example, at 7 °C and 12 ppm of dissolved oxygen, the result is approximately 100% saturation (note: ACER typically provides an example to get you oriented).

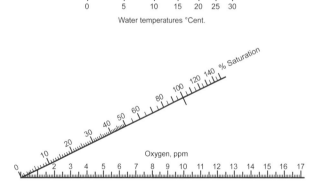

Nomogram for dissolved oxygen saturation.
Ref. Environments in Profile, an aquatic perspective,
W Kaill and J Frey, Canfield Press, 1973.

What is the % saturation for 1.5 ppm of dissolved oxygen at a water temperature of 18 °C?

A. Less than 10%   C. 20%
B. 15%   D. More than 20%

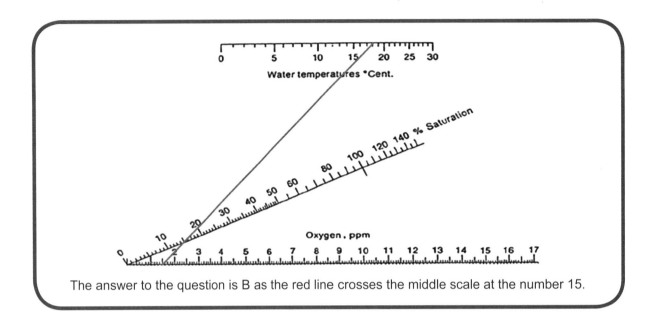

The answer to the question is B as the red line crosses the middle scale at the number 15.

Side note: Although there is no assumed knowledge for the preceding question, the nomogram teaches an important point about gases dissolved in water which comes up frequently on the real exam. Hopefully, after you study General Chemistry, you will understand why the same concentration of oxygen (in this case, ppm) results in lower saturation in water at lower temperatures. Consequently, more gas can "fit" in water when the temperature is low (like a can of Coke or champagne, the gas bubbles are lost faster at higher temperatures).

> **NOTE**
>
> Please avoid trying to think: 'I will memorize this or that graph for the exam'. The better long-term strategy would be: 'I need to have a reliable method to approach novel graphs so when I see one, I will have the confidence to break it down (and hopefully have some fun along the way!)'.

EXAMPLE 2

Nomograms can appear to be more complex than the preceding straight lines as will be illustrated next. The many graphs to follow will have associated GAMSAT-level practice questions which do not have any assumed science knowledge (as is often the case with real GAMSAT Section 3 graph analysis questions).

The following represents normal values for arterial blood in humans: pH 7.4, bicarbonate 24 mmol/L, pCO_2 40 mmHg.

Consider Figure IV.3.7.

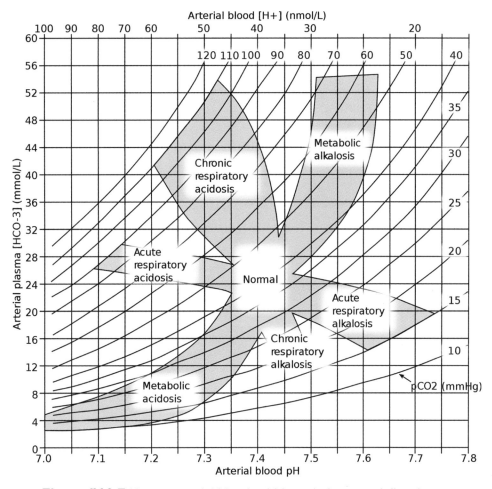

Figure IV.3.7 Human arterial blood acid-base balance and disorders

QUESTION 1

According to Figure IV.3.7, an arterial blood pH of 7.5 with a pCO_2 of 25, corresponds best with which of the following?

A. Metabolic alkalosis
B. Acute respiratory alkalosis
C. Chronic respiratory alkalosis
D. Chronic respiratory acidosis

QUESTION 2

Consider a patient with metabolic alkalosis. Based on Figure IV.3.7, which of the following would be most consistent with returning the patient back to normal?

A. Increase in arterial [H+], decrease arterial bicarbonate
B. Increase arterial pH, increase arterial bicarbonate
C. Decrease pCO_2, decrease arterial [H+]
D. Increase pCO_2, decrease arterial bicarbonate

EXPLANATION

For Question 1, you must begin with the example provided in the preamble and trace the lines of pH 7.4, bicarbonate 24 mmol/L, and the curved line of pCO_2 40 mmHg which all intersect in the graph at one point – basically, in the middle of 'Normal'.

Notice that the bottom right corner of the diagram points to a curved line which says pCO_2 (mmHg) to suggest that all the curved lines represent pCO_2.

Now our attention turns towards the two lines in the question: pH of 7.5 with a pCO_2 of 25 which just manage to intersect at 'Acute respiratory alkalosis'. The answer is B for Question 1.

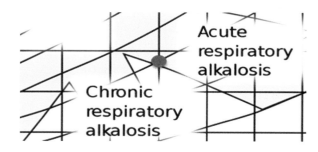

For Question 2, note that 'metabolic alkalosis' is in the top right portion of the graph. 'Normal' is, comparatively, down and to the left of 'metabolic alkalosis'. Looking at the *y* axis to the left, we can see that going down means that we would have a decrease in arterial bicarbonate. Now be careful to notice that the *x* axis at the top of the graph has arterial [H^+] decreasing from left to right, which means that moving to the left results in an increase in arterial [H^+]. The answer is A for Question 2.

Even though we have not formally reviewed General Chemistry, having already seen the equation for pH (GM 3.7.1; pH = $-\log_{10}[H^+]$), because of the negative sign, when pH rises, you can deduce that [H^+] must decrease, and vice versa. This point is confirmed by the nomogram (Fig. IV.3.7) and is the source of over a dozen questions among ACER's GAMSAT practice materials. We will review the pH scale next in CHM 6.5.

EXAMPLE 3

Ternary (AKA trilinear, triangular) graphs or plots, tephigrams (commonly used in weather analysis and forecasting), and some thermodynamic diagrams can be loosely defined as nomograms. The ternary graph is encountered the most frequently.

The following is the most widely-used scale for a ternary graph. From time to time, return to this common scale to confirm your understanding.

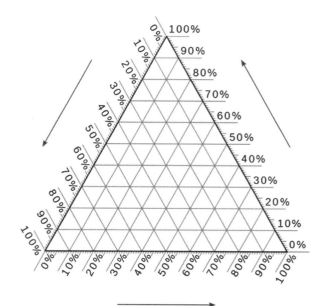

Now we will learn how to read a ternary graph with the following 3 variables: organic matter, clay and sand.

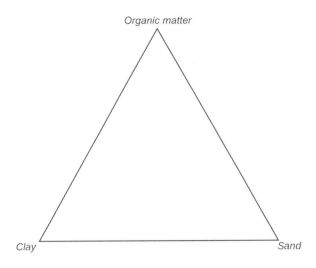

As a general rule, the percentage of one component is given by a line that is parallel with the line between the other 2 components. For example, consider the diagram below. Notice that the percentage of 'Organic matter' is represented by a line that is parallel to the Clay-Sand line.

Notice that the percentage of 'Clay' in the following diagram is represented by a line that is parallel to the Organic matter-Sand line. The caption in the diagram reads: "One coordinate only tells us the one proportion: at any point along these lines, the proportion of Clay is the percentage given, but we don't know the proportions of Organic matter or Sand."

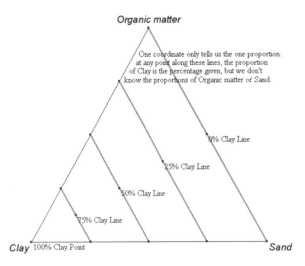

Notice in the following diagram that the percentage of 'Sand' is represented by a line that is parallel to the Clay-Organic matter line.

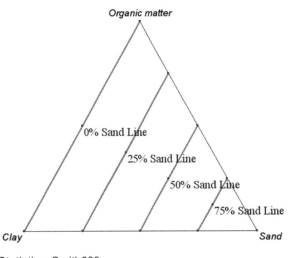

Ref.: Wikipedia Commons Statistics, Smith609

As long as you know that a ternary graph is based on 100%, you should be able to read it without any percentages showing (this will ensure that you will not fall for any tricks like leaving out key numbers on any or all 3 axes).

As you progress through this section on nomograms, you will likely find some challenging questions. Please take the time that you need to solve the problem.

EXAMPLE 4

Consider the following ternary graph. Note: similar to the previous ternary graphs, the maximum possible for any single component is 100%.

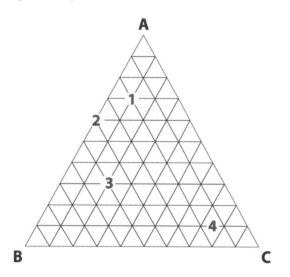

Which of the following correctly corresponds to the label provided in the preceding ternary diagram?

A. 1. 80% A | 10% B | 10% C
B. 2. 60% A | 30% B | 10% C
C. 3. 20% A | 60% B | 20% C
D. 4. 10% A | 15% B | 75% C

Notice that the 3 components can always be added up to a sum total of 100% since that is the scale provided in the question (i.e. A + B + C = 100%). If you are unsure, go back to the first diagram which we described as the "most widely-used scale for a ternary graph." If it is still not clear, you may login to your gamsat-prep.com account, click on Videos, and look for GAMSAT Graph Analysis Recorded Webinar Part 3, and of course we also have the gamsat-prep.com/forum.

Here are the actual percentages which reveal that only answer choice D is correct:

1. 70% A | 20% B | 10% C
2. 60% A | 40% B | 0% C
3. 30% A | 50% B | 20% C
4. 10% A | 15% B | 75% C

EXAMPLE 5

Coloured gold metal may include silver and copper in various proportions, producing white, yellow, green and red golds. Pure 100% gold is 24 karat (K) by definition, so all coloured golds are less than this, with the common ones being 18K (75%), 14K (58%), and 9K (38%).

Consider the following ternary plot showing different colours of Ag-Au-Cu alloys.

We suggest using a pencil to determine your answers – as you would do for the real exam – since you may change your mind and wish to erase and restart.

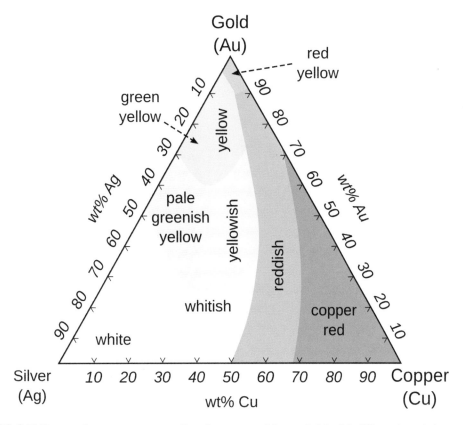

Figure IV.3.8 Trilinear diagram representing the percent by weight of 3 different metals and the resultant appearance of the mixture (= *metal alloy*). en.wikipedia.org/wiki/Colored_gold Ref: Metallos

QUESTION 1

Based on the information provided, choose the correct statement.

A. Pure gold is 'yellow' gold.
B. Increasing copper in the alloy increases the chance of a possible greenish appearance.
C. "Yellowish" gold is present when ½ of the mixture is gold, while silver and copper are equal.
D. Pure silver added to 'pale greenish yellow' gold can produce 'yellow' gold.

QUESTION 2

Equal amounts by weight of 14K and 9K gold are mixed together. According to Figure IV.3.8, which of the following is the likely result of the appearance of the mixture if it contains 10% copper?

A. Pale greenish yellow
B. Yellow
C Yellowish
D. Whitish

EXPLANATION 1

For the first question:

A. Pure gold, according to the preamble before the diagram, is 100% gold which is clearly labelled 'red yellow' in the diagram as opposed to simply 'yellow'.

B. Increasing copper increases the chance of a red appearance (in fact, the corner where copper is highest is labelled "copper red". The 'pale greenish yellow' appearance is possible only when copper is 0-30%.

C. Converting the words to math: gold must be 50%, and thus silver and copper must be 25% each. Drawing the appropriate lines confirms that answer choice C is correct.

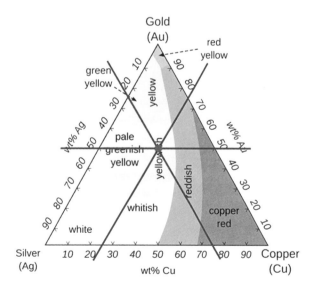

D. To add pure silver is to increase the silver % which means to go from 'pale greenish yellow' to 'whitish' or 'white' rather than the opposite direction to 'yellow'.

EXPLANATION 2

For the second question:

14K (58% gold according to the preamble) and 9K (38% gold) are combined thus we have (58 + 38)/2 = 48% gold (combining percentages: GM 1.4.3C). We can use the 2 lines (48% gold and 10% copper) to determine that the answer is 'pale greenish yellow' and to confirm the concentration of the 3rd component (100 − 48 − 10 = 42% silver). Answer choice A is correct.

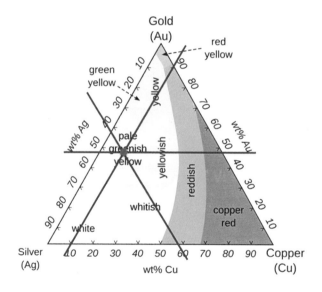

EXAMPLE 6

A piper plot is often used to visualise the chemistry of a rock, soil, or water sample. There are 3 components: a ternary (or triangular) diagram in the lower left representing cations, a ternary diagram in the lower right representing anions, and a diamond plot (or 'rhomboid') in the middle representing a combination of the two. Note that following a line parallel to the outer axis of each ternary diagram, and projecting each point in the ternary diagrams upward until they intersect will create one associated point in the diamond plot. These three points represent one sample. For example, for potable groundwater, the sample labelled 'A' in Figure IV.3.9, we can make the following approximations from the combined (diamond) plot: Ca + Mg = 23%; SO_4 + Cl = 98%.

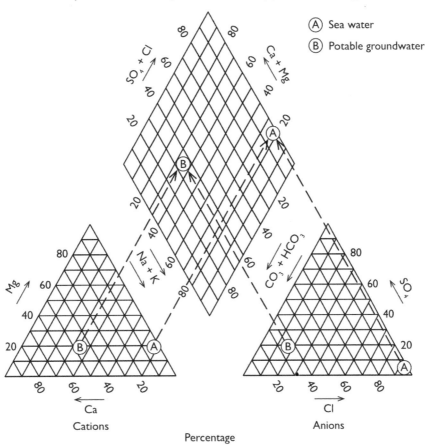

Figure IV.3.9 Chemical analyses of water represented as percentages of total equivalents per liter on the diagram developed by Hill (1940) and Piper (1944).

QUESTION 1

According to Figure IV.3.9, the percent concentration of which of the following is most consistent with the percent concentration of K?

A. Na
B. Mg + Ca
C. 100 – (Mg + Ca + Na)
D. Cannot be determined by the information provided.

QUESTION 2

There are 4 general categories of groundwater based on the dominant ions: 1) Ca-SO_4; 2) Ca-HCO_3; 3) Na-HCO_3; 4) Na-Cl. Using these 4 numbered categories, which of the following is most consistent with sea water and potable groundwater in Figure IV.3.9, respectively?

A. 4, 2   C. 1, 1
B. 2, 3   D. 3, 4

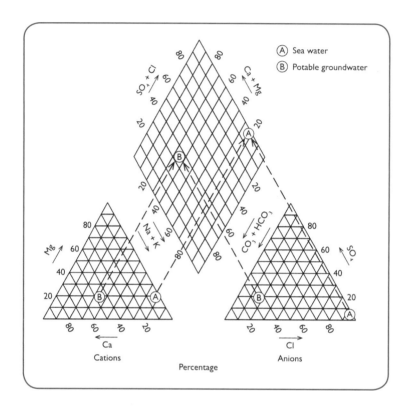

EXPLANATION 1

If you had trouble reading the ternary graph, consider going back to the scale and examples that we have already seen. Then consider completing the labelling of the diagrams: for example, in the ternary graph in the bottom left of Fig. IV.3.9, write '100% Mg' at the top (that is where it is 100%), write '100% Ca' in the bottom left of the triangle and '100% Na + K' in the bottom right, this may help orient you (of course, additional labelling may not occur on the real exam so you should do it manually if needed).

Side note: notice that the samples labelled A and B have the same concentration of one of the ions! Which one? Consider looking back at the diagram.

We have established a couple of times that the components of the trilinear diagram must add to the maximum value – which is 100% – according to the diagram and caption. So, for the cations we have:

$$Mg + Ca + Na + K = 100$$
$$K = 100 - Mg - Ca - Na$$
$$= 100 - (Mg + Ca + Na)$$

Thus the correct answer for the first question is C.

For our "Side note" question, samples A and B both have 20% Mg.

EXPLANATION 2

For the second question, the diagram's key indicates that the samples labelled A and B represent sea water and potable groundwater, respectively. The diamond plot's dashed lines provide a clear statement: Each sample is composed of both cations and anions. There is no assumed science knowledge.

We are told in the question stem that the categories are based on dominant ions. So, let us determine the balance of ions in each sample and then choose the dominant (foremost) cations and anions.

Using the technique we have practiced:

- From the ternary graph in the bottom left corner, approx. (± 3%): A = Mg: 20%, Ca: 5%, Na + K: 75%; B = Mg: 20%, Ca: 45%, Na + K: 35%.
- From the ternary graph in the bottom right corner, approx. (± 3%): A = SO_4: 5%, Cl: 90%, CO_3 + HCO_3: 5%; B = SO_4: 20%, Cl: 15%, CO_3 + HCO_3: 65%.

Dominant (highest percentage) for A: Na + K and Cl, which resembles category 4 (notice that K – alone – is never dominant among the categories). Dominant (highest percentage) for B: Ca and CO_3 + HCO_3, which resembles category 2 (notice that CO_3 – alone – is never dominant among the categories). Thus the correct answer is A and the other 3 answer choices present at least one of the samples with an ion with minimum concentration thus the process of elimination would also confirm that only one answer is possible.

The following image shows the names of the various ions which we will learn in GS GAMSAT General Chemistry Chapter 5,

Solution Chemistry. At that time, you can return to Fig. IV.3.9 and insert the missing superscripts (i.e. the charges for each species) since each component in the diagram is either a positively-charged cation or a negatively-charged anion.

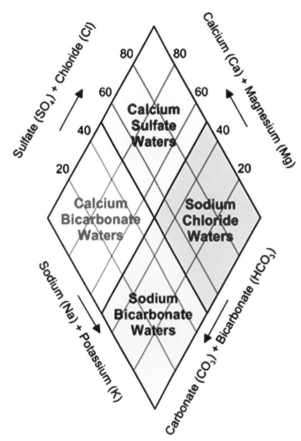

Golden Software LLC Interpretation of the diamond plot (modified from inside.mines.edu/~epoeter/_GW/18WaterChem2/WaterChem2pdf.pdf).

If it is still not clear, you may login to your gamsat-prep.com account, click on Lessons, General Chemistry, Chapter 5: Solution Chemistry, GAMSAT Section 3 PBL: Ions and The Piper Plot; of course, we also have gamsat-prep.com/forum.

GOLD STANDARD WARM-UP EXERCISES

CHAPTER 3: Algebra and Graph Analysis

1. If $y = \dfrac{12}{4x^3 - 6x + 5}$, then if x = 2 then y equals:

   A. 12/17
   B. 12/49
   C. 12/9
   D. 12/25

2. $13xy^2z$ is to $39y$ as $9xyz^6$ is to:

   A. $3z^5$
   B. $27z$
   C. $9y$
   D. $27z^5$

3. At what point do the lines y = 2x − 1 and 6x − 5y = −3 intersect?

   A. (2, 3)
   B. (0.5, 0)
   C. (−1,−3)
   D. (−0.5, −2)

4. Loubha has a total of $.85. If she has two less dimes than nickels, how many dimes and nickels does she have? {Note that: One dollar ($1) is composed of 100 cents; a dime is a 10-cent piece and a nickel is a 5-cent piece.}

   A. 5 nickels, 7 dimes
   B. 6 nickels, 4 dimes
   C. 4 nickels, 2 dimes
   D. 7 nickels, 5 dimes

5. If $2.5 \times 10^3(3 \times 10^x) = 0.075$, then x equals:

   A. −3
   B. −5
   C. 0
   D. −4

6. A plank of wood is leaning against the left side of a house with vertical walls. Both are on level ground. If the plank touches the ground 7 feet away from the base of the house, and touches the house at a point 5 feet above the ground, at what slope is the plank lying?

   A. −5/7
   B. 7/5
   C. −7/5
   D. 5/7

7. If $n + n = k + k + k$ and $n + k = 5$, then $n = ?$

   A. 9
   B. 6
   C. 5
   D. 3

8. Let x = 4 and y = 8. Evaluate the expression: $((y^{-2/3})^{1/2}) / (x^{-1/2})$.

   A. 8
   B. 4
   C. 1
   D. 1/2

9. Evaluate the expression: $\log_6(24)$ + $\log_6(9)$.

    A. 3
    B. 2
    C. 1
    D. 1/2

10. Solve for x: $\log_{10}(70) = x + \log_{10}(7)$.

    A. 0
    B. 1
    C. 2
    D. 3

11. Simplify the expression: $x(\log_b(y))$ + $y(\log_b(y))$.

    A. $\log_b(y^{x-y})$
    B. $\log_b(y^{x+y})$
    C. $\log_b(y^{xy})$
    D. $\log_b(xy^{xy})$

12. Evaluate the expression: $\ln(e^3)\log_3(27)$ + $\ln(1)\ln(e)$.

    A. e
    B. 3
    C. 6
    D. 9

13. Which equation matches the graph below?

    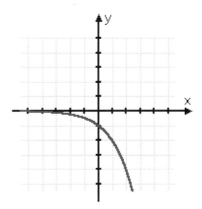

    A. $y = 2^x - 1$
    B. $y = -(2^x) + 1$
    C. $y = 2^x$
    D. $y = -(2^x)$

14. Which equation matches the graph below?

    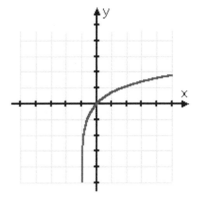

    A. $y = \ln(x)$
    B. $y = -\ln(x - 1)$
    C. $y = -\ln(x + 1)$
    D. $y = \ln(x + 1)$

15. pH is measured on a logarithmic scale given by the equation pH = $-\log_{10}(H)$. Given that H is positive but less than 1, as H decreases, the slope of the graph of pH vs H:

   A. decreases.

   B. increases.

   C. remains constant.

   D. sometimes decreases, sometimes increases.

Dear GAMSAT Math,

Please stop asking me to find your x.

She's not coming back and I don't know y either.

gamsat-prep.com

GS ANSWER KEY

CHAPTER 3

Cross-Reference

1. D   GM 3.1.4
2. D   GM 3.3.2, 3.3.3
3. A   GM 3.4.2A, 3.4.2B
4. D   GM 3.4.2B
5. B   GM 3.3.1
6. D   GM 3.5.4
7. D   GM 3.3.1, 3.4.2A, 3.4.2B
8. C   GM 1.5

Cross-Reference

9. A   GM 3.7
10. B   GM 3.7
11. B   GM 1.5, 3.7
12. D   GM 1.5, 3.7
13. D   GM 3.7, 3.8
14. D   GM 3.7, 3.8
15. B   GM 3.7, 3.8

* Worked solutions can be found at the end of the GAMSAT Math chapters. If something is still not clear, go to the forum at GAMSAT-prep.com.

Memorize	Understand	Not Required
The Pythagorean Theorem Perimeter, Area, and Volume Formulas Properties of Triangles	* Points in Cartesian Coordinates * Parallel and Perpendicular Lines * Similar Polygons * Types of Triangles and Angles * Problems with Figures and Solids	* Vertices, cones, volumes of complex solids

GAMSAT-Prep.com

Introduction

Geometry is a very visual branch of mathematics dealing with lines and shapes and relations in space, so drawing and labelling pictures can be extremely helpful when you are confronted with certain GAMSAT physics problems. But don't forget about algebra! More often than not, these problems are simply algebraic equations in disguise.

Additional Resources

Free Online Forum

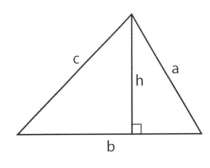

Special Guest

4.1 Points, Lines and Angles

4.1.1 Points and Distance

Knowing your way around the Cartesian coordinate systems begins with understanding the relationships between simple points. As discussed in section 3.5, points on a graph are represented as an ordered pair of an x and y coordinate, (x, y).

A. Addition and Subtraction of Points

To add or subtract two points, simply add or subtract the two x values to obtain the new x value and add or subtract the two y values to obtain the new y value.

EXAMPLE

Add the points (2, 3) and (1, -5).

$$(2, 3) + (1, -5)$$
$$= (2 + 1, 3 - 5)$$
$$= (3, -2)$$

Graphically, addition of points is easy to visualize. All you are doing when you add two points is treating the first point as the new origin. You then plot the second point in terms of this new origin to find the sum of the two points.

You can add more than two points in the same way. Just add all of the x values together, and then add all of the y values together.

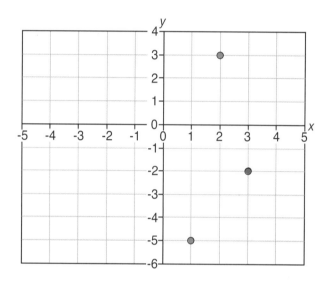

B. Distance between Points

Finding the distance between two points requires the use of the Pythagorean Theorem. This theorem is probably the most important tool you have for solving geometric problems.

Pythagorean Theorem: $x^2 + y^2 = z^2$

This theorem describes the relationship between the lengths of the sides of a right triangle. The lengths x and y correspond to the two legs of the triangle adjacent to the right angle, and the length z corresponds to the hypotenuse of the triangle.

In order to find the distance between two points (x_1, y_1) and (x_2, y_2), consider there to be a line segment connecting them. This line segment (with length z equivalent to the distance between the points) can be thought of as the hypotenuse of a right triangle. The other two sides extend from the points: One is parallel to the x-axis; the other, to the y-axis (with lengths x and y, respectively).

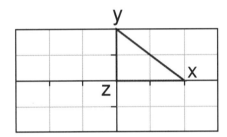

To find the distance between the two points, simply apply the Pythagorean Theorem.

$$x = (x_2 - x_1)$$
$$y = (y_2 - y_1)$$
$$z = \sqrt{(x^2 + y^2)}$$

Plugging in the point coordinates will yield z, the distance between the two points.

EXAMPLE

Find the distance between the points (5, 0) and (2, -4).

$$x = (2 - 5) = -3$$
$$y = (-4 - 0) = -4$$
$$z = \sqrt{(-3^2 + -4^2)}$$
$$= \sqrt{(9 + 16)} = \sqrt{25} = 5$$

So the distance between the points is $z = 5$.

4.1.2 Line Segments

A. Segmentation Problems

These problems are a kind of geometry-algebra hybrid. You are given a line segment that has been subdivided into smaller segments, and some information is provided. You are then asked to deduce some of the missing information.

In a segmentation problem, some of the information you are given may be geometric, and some may be algebraic. There is not, however, a clear algebraic equation to solve. You will need to logically determine the steps needed to reach a solution.

EXAMPLE

The line segment QT of length $4x + 6$ is shown in the figure that follows. Point S is the midpoint of QT and segment RS has length $x - 1$. What is the length of line segment QR?

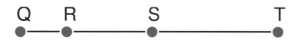

First, determine what information you know. The length of QT and RS are given. Also, since we have a midpoint for QT, the length of QS and ST are simply half of the length of QT.

Now, determine an algebraic relationship regarding the length of QR, which is what we are looking for. We can see that the length of QR is simply QS with the RS segment removed.

$$QR = QS - RS$$

Plugging in our information, we get the following:

$$QR = \frac{(4x+6)}{2} - (x-1)$$
$$= 2x + 3 - x + 1$$
$$= x + 4$$

Before you start working out a solution, it can be extremely helpful to list the information you are given. This will help you understand and organize the problem, both in your own mind and on the page.

B. Segments in the Plane

In segmentation problems, you only have to deal with one dimension. However, line segments can also turn up in problems dealing with a two dimensional Cartesian graph.

To determine the length of a line segment in a plane, simply find the distance between its endpoints using the Pythagorean Theorem (see section 4.1.1).

Any line segment in a plane corresponds to a single linear equation. This can be determined as in chapter 3 from any two points on the line segment. Knowing this linear equation can help you find other points on the line segment.

4.1.3 Angles

An **angle** is formed by the intersection of two lines.

In problems that are not trigonometric, angles are almost always measured in degrees. A full circle makes 360°.

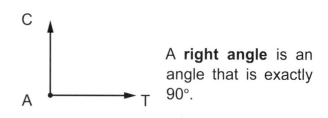

A **right angle** is an angle that is exactly 90°.

An **obtuse angle** is an angle that is greater than 90°.

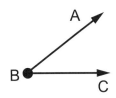

An **acute angle** is an angle that is less than 90°.

A **straight angle** is an angle that is exactly 180°.

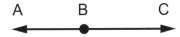

A **vertical angle** is the angle opposite of each other that is formed by two intersecting lines. The two angles across from each other are equal in measure. The following example shows that angles 1 and 3 are vertical angles and equal to each other. Same are angles 2 and 4. At the same time, adjacent vertical angles 1 and 4 or 2 and 3 are also supplementary angles and will form 180°.

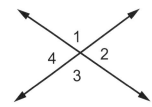

Complementary angles are two angles that add up to 90°. The example that follows shows that angles A and B add up to 90°.

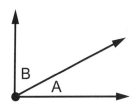

Supplementary angles are two angles that add up to 180°. This example shows that angles A and B add up to 180°.

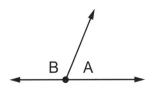

A. Angles and Lines in the Plane

If two lines are **parallel**, they have the same slope. Such lines will never intersect, and so they will never form angles with one another.

If two lines are **perpendicular**, their intersection forms only 90° angles. If the slope of a given line is a/b, then the slope of any perpendicular line is $-b/a$.

EXAMPLE

Consider the line defined by $y = 2x + 3$.

(a) Give the equation for a parallel line:

$$y = 2x + 2.$$

Any line that still has a slope of 2 will suffice. So, in slope-intercept form, any line of the form $y = 2x + a$ will be a parallel line.

(b) Give the equation for the perpendicular line that intersects the given line at the *y*-axis.

In this case, there is only one solution since the line can only intersect the *y*-axis once. The solution will be a line with the same *y*-intercept (which is 3) and the negative reciprocal slope (which is -½): rule from GM 3.4.4.

$$y = -\frac{1}{2}x + 3$$

The standard kind of angle-line problem deals with a setup of two parallel lines that are cut by a transversal, like the one in the following diagram (this type of geometry may present in Physics Chapter 11: Light and Geometric Optics).

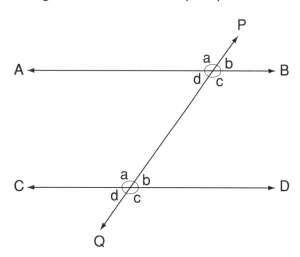

The trick with these problems is to realize that there are only ever two values for the angles.

First, think of the two areas of intersection as exact duplicates of each other.

The upper left angles are equivalent, as are the upper right, the lower left, and the lower right. Using just this information, you automatically know the value of the twin of any angle that is given to you.

Also, angles that are opposite each other are equivalent. So the lower left angle is the same as the upper right and vice versa.

The other fact you can use to determine unknown angles is that the angle along a straight line is 180°. When you are given an angle *a*, you can find supplement *b* by subtracting 180° - *a*.

EXAMPLE

In the figure that follows, if angle *a* is 35°, what is the value of angle *b*?

Angle *b* is the twin of the supplement of *a*, so *b* is equal to 180° - *a*.

$$b = 180° - 35° = 145°$$

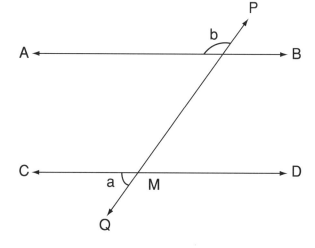

B. Properties of Parallel Line Angles

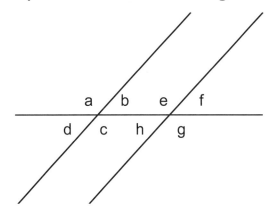

When two parallel lines are cut by a transversal line:

1. both pairs of acute angles as well as obtuse angles are equal: $a = e, b = f, d = h, c = g$.

2. alternate interior angles are equal in measure as well: $c = e, b = h$.

C. Interior Angles of a Polygon

Sometimes you may be dealing with a shape that you are not familiar with and that you do not know the total of all interior angles. A polygon is a flat (i.e. plane) figure with at least three straight sides and angles. If the polygon has x sides, the sum, S, is the total of all interior angles for that polygon. For a polygon with x sides, the sum may be calculated by the following formula:

$$S = (x - 2)(180°)$$

EXAMPLE

A triangle has 3 sides, therefore,

$$S = (3 - 2) \times 180°$$
$$S = 180°$$

A rectangle has 4 sides,

$$S = (4 - 2) \times 180°$$
$$S = 360°.$$

Given the total angles for a polygon, you can determine each interior angle of a polygon by dividing the sum of the polygon by the number of sides.

EXAMPLE

A rectangle has a sum of 360°. Given that x = 4, 360° ÷ 4 = 90°. Therefore, each angle in a rectangle is 90°.

> **NOTE**
>
> Though not common, these question types are usually related to projectile motion, inclined planes and optics which will be explored in Physics.

4.2 2D Figures

Make sure you know how to find the area, perimeter, side lengths, and angles of all the figures in this section. There are all kinds of ways to combine different shapes into the same problem; but if you can deal with them all individually, you'll be able to break down any problem thrown your way!

4.2.1 Rectangles and Squares

A **rectangle** is a figure with four straight sides and four right angles. In rectangles, opposite sides always have the same length, as do the two diagonals that can be drawn from corner to corner.

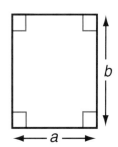

Perimeter: The perimeter of a rectangle is equal to the sum of its sides.

$$\text{Perimeter} = a + b + a + b = 2a + 2b$$

Area: The area of a rectangle is equal to the product of its length and width.

$$\text{Area} = \text{Length} \times \text{Width} = a \times b$$

A **square** is a rectangle with all four sides of the same length, so $a = b$.

The perimeter of a square is

$$P = a + a + a + a = 4a.$$

The area of a square is

$$A = a \times a = a^2.$$

4.2.2 Types of Triangles

While there are a wide variety of types of triangles, every one shares these properties:

(i) The sum of the interior angles of a triangle is always equal to 180°. In the following figure, a, b, and c are interior angles.

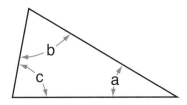

$$3x - 10 = 25 + x + 15$$
$$2x = 10 + 25 + 15$$
$$2x = 50$$
$$x = 25$$

(ii) The sum of the exterior angles of a triangle is always equal to 360°. The following figure shows *d, e,* and *f* to be exterior angles.

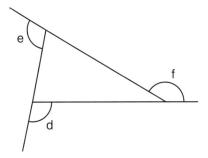

(iii) The value of an exterior angle is equal to the sum of the opposite two interior angles.

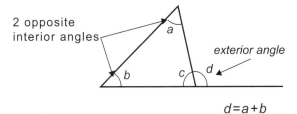

$$d = a + b$$

EXAMPLE

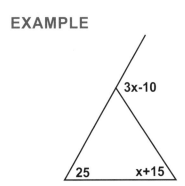

(iv) The perimeter of a triangle is equal to the sum of its sides.

(v) The area of a triangle is always half the product of the base and the height.

$$\text{Area} = \frac{1}{2} \text{Base} \times \text{Height}$$

You can pick any side of the triangle to function as the base, and the height will be the line perpendicular to that side that runs between it and the opposite vertex (i.e. highest point).

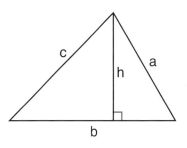

NOTE

If you ever see a triangular shaped graph during the GAMSAT, check the units of one axis multiplied by the other. If the units match the answer choices of any of the questions then you are likely 1/2 way to getting the correct answer without even having read the question yet! As an example, see the 2nd question and the 2nd graph (blue shaded area) in GM 3.5.4.

A. Right Triangles

A **right triangle** is a triangle that contains a right angle. The other two angles in a right triangle add up to 90°.

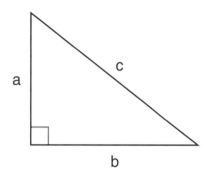

The two short legs of a right triangle (the legs that come together to form the right angle) and the hypotenuse (the side opposite the right angle) are related by the Pythagorean Theorem:

$$a^2 + b^2 = c^2$$

To find a missing side of the triangle, plug the values you have into the Pythagorean Theorem and solve algebraically.

The two legs of a right triangle are its base and height. So to find the area, compute as shown.

> **NOTE**
>
> The area of a triangle, the Pythagorean Theorem and its special ratios appear regularly on the real GAMSAT.

$$\text{Area} = \frac{1}{2}(a \times b)$$

Special Cases: There are a few cases of right triangles you should know. First, the ratios of side lengths 3:4:5 and 5:12:13 are often used. Identifying that a triangle corresponds to one of these cases can save you precious time since you will not have to solve the Pythagorean Theorem.

There are also two special ratios of interior angles for right triangles: 30°-60°-90° and 45°-45°-90°. The sides of a 30°-60°-90° triangle have the ratio $1:\sqrt{3}:2$ and the sides of a 45°-45°-90° triangle have the ratio $1:1:\sqrt{2}$.

B. Isosceles Triangles

An **isosceles triangle** is a triangle that has two equal sides. The angles that sit opposite the equal sides are also equal.

For an isosceles triangle, use the odd side as the base and draw the height line to the odd vertex. This line will bisect the side, so it is simple to determine the height using the Pythagorean Theorem on one of the new right triangles formed.

Pythagorean Theorem

Knowing any two sides of a right triangle lets you find the third side by using the Pythagorean formula: $a^2 + b^2 = c^2$.

3-4-5 triangle: if a right triangle has two legs with a ratio of 3:4, or a leg to a hypotenuse ratio of either 3:5 or 4:5, then it is a 3-4-5 triangle.

5-12-13 triangle: if a right triangle has two legs with a ratio of 5:12, or a leg to a hypotenuse ratio of either 5:13 or 12:13, then it is a 5-12-13 triangle.

45°-45°-90° triangle: if a right triangle has two angles that are both 45°, then the ratio of the three legs is $1:1:\sqrt{2}$.

30°-60°-90° triangle: if a right triangle has two angles of 30° and 60°, then the ratio of the three legs is $1:\sqrt{3}:2$.

Confirm for yourself that the ratio of sides in the 4 preceding triangles actually fulfill the Pythagorean Theorem.

C. Equilateral Triangles

An **equilateral triangle** is a triangle with all three sides equal. All three interior angles are also equal, so they are all 60°.

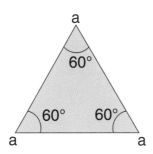

Drawing a height line from any vertex will divide the triangle into two 30°-60°-90° triangles, so you can easily solve for the area.

D. Scalene Triangles

A **scalene triangle** is any triangle that has no equal sides and no equal angles. To find the value for the height of this kind of triangle requires the use of trigonometric functions (see Chapter 5).

E. Similar Triangles

Two triangles are **similar** if they have the same values for interior angles. This means that ratios of corresponding sides will be equal. Similar triangles are triangles with the same shape that are scaled to different sizes.

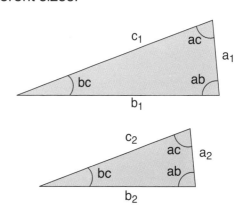

To solve for values in a triangle from information given about a similar triangle, you will need to use ratios. The ratios of corresponding sides are always equal, for example $\frac{a_1}{a_2} = \frac{b_1}{b_2}$. Also, the ratio of two sides in the same triangle is equal to the corresponding ratio in the similar triangle, for example $\frac{a_1}{b_1} = \frac{a_2}{b_2}$.

4.2.3 Circles

A **circle** is a figure in which every point is the same distance from the center. This distance from the center to the edge is known as the **radius** (*r*). The length of any straight line drawn from a point on the circle, through the center, and out to another point on the circle is known as the **diameter** (*d*). The diameter is twice the radius.

$$d = 2 \times r \quad \text{or} \quad r = \frac{1}{2}d$$

There are no angles in a circle.

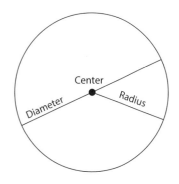

Circumference: The circumference of a circle is the total distance around a circle. It is equal to pi times the diameter.

$$\text{Circumference} = \pi \times d = 2\pi \times r$$

Area: The area of a circle is equal to pi times the square of the radius.

$$\text{Area} = \pi \times r^2 = \frac{1}{4}\pi \times d^2$$

Length: Length of an arc is defined as a piece of circumference formed by an angle of *n* degrees measured as the arc's central angle in a circle of radius *r*.

$$L = \frac{n^\circ}{360^\circ} \times 2\pi r$$

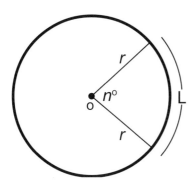

$$\text{Area (sector)} = \frac{1}{2}r^2\theta \ \text{(in radians)}$$

$$\text{Area (sector)} = \frac{n^\circ}{360^\circ} \times \pi r^2 \ \text{(in degrees)}$$

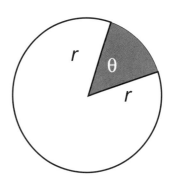

Area of a sector: The area of a sector is a portion of the circle formed by an angle of *n* degree measured as the sector's central angle in a circle of radius *r*.

4.2.4 Trapezoids and Parallelograms

A. Trapezoids

A **trapezoid** is a four-sided figure with one pair of parallel sides and one pair of non-parallel sides.

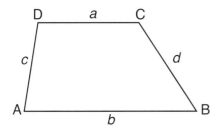

Usually the easiest way to solve trapezoid problems is to drop vertical lines down from the vertices on the smaller of the two parallel lines. This splits the figure into two

right triangles on the ends and a rectangle in the middle. Then, to find information about the trapezoid, you can solve for the information (side length, area, angles, etc.) of these other shapes.

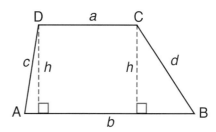

1. The area of a trapezoid is calculated as

$$\frac{a+b}{2}h$$

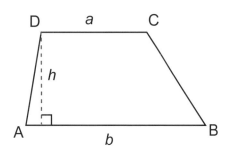

2. The upper and lower base angles are supplementary angles (i.e., they add up to 180°).

$$\text{Angle A} + \text{Angle D} = 180°$$
$$\text{Angle B} + \text{Angle C} = 180°$$

> **NOTE**
>
> "Really, will the GAMSAT ever specifically ask for the area of a trapezoid?" No! But they may occasionally present a graph that is shaped like a trapezoid and the question requires you to calculate the area under the graph or 'curve' (i.e. the area of the trapezoid).

Sometimes it can be useful to draw a line from vertex to vertex and construct a triangle that way, but this usually only makes sense if the resulting triangle is special (i.e. isosceles).

Isosceles Trapezoids: Just like isosceles triangles, **isosceles trapezoids** are trapezoids with two equal sides. The sides that are equal are the parallel sides that form angles with the base of the trapezoid. Similarly, if the left and right sides are of the same lengths, these angles are the same as well.

In this isosceles trapezoid, ABCD means that Angle A = Angle B, Angle D = Angle C, and Diagonal AC = Diagonal BD.

The perimeter = $a + b + 2c$

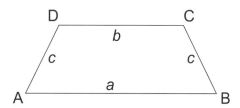

B. Parallelograms

A **parallelogram** is a quadrilateral that has two sets of parallel sides. A square, for example, is a special kind of parallelogram, as is a rhombus (which has four sides of equal length but, unlike a square, has two different pairs of angle values).

Area: The area of a parallelogram is simply the base times the height.

> Area = (Base) × (Height)

The height of a parallelogram can be found by dropping a vertical from a vertex to the opposite side and evaluating the resulting right triangle.

The sum of all the angles in a parallelogram is 360°. Opposite angles are equivalent, and adjacent angles add up to 180°.

4.3 3D Solids

In three dimensions, it does not always make sense to talk about perimeters. Shapes with defined edges (such as boxes and pyramids) still have them, but rounded shapes (such as spheres) do not. Instead, we are generally concerned with the values of surface area and volume.

4.3.1 Boxes

Boxes are the three-dimensional extension of rectangles. Every angle in a box is 90°, and every box has six rectangular faces, twelve edges, and eight vertices. Opposite (and parallel) faces are always of the same length, height, and width, as are opposite (and parallel) edges. None of the equations in these sections (4.3.1, 4.3.2, 4.3.3) should be memorized. Hopefully, most of the equations will make sense to you in some way.

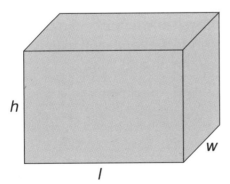

Perimeter: The perimeter of a box is the sum of its edges. There are, however, only three different lengths and four edges corresponding to each one. So to find the perimeter, we can simply take the sum of four times each the width, length, and height.

$$\text{Perimeter} = 4l + 4w + 4h = 4(l + w + h)$$

Surface Area: The surface area of a box is the sum of the area of each of its faces. Since there is one duplicate of each unique face, we only need to find three products, double them, and add them together.

$$\text{Surface Area} = 2lw + 2wh + 2lh$$
$$= 2(lw + wh + lh)$$

Volume: Calculating the volume of a box can be visualized as taking the surface of any of its rectangular faces and dragging it through space, like you were blowing a box-shaped bubble. So you start with the product of a width times a height, and then you multiply that by a length.

$$\text{Volume} = l \times w \times h$$

4.3.2 Spheres

The definition of a sphere is basically identical to that of a circle, except that it is applied in three dimensions rather than two: It is a collection of points in three dimensions that are all of the same distance from a particular center point. Again, we call this distance the radius, and twice the radius is the diameter. A sphere has no vertices or edges, so it has no circumference.

Surface Area:

$$\text{Surface Area} = 4\pi \times r^2$$

Volume:

$$\text{Volume} = (4/3)\pi \times r^3$$

4.3.3 Cylinders

Spheres may be the 3D equivalent of circles, but if you start with a circle and extend it into the third dimension, you obtain the tube shape known as a cylinder. Cylinders have two parallel circular faces, and their edges are connected by a smooth, edgeless surface.

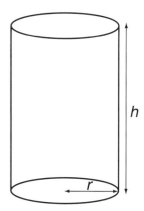

Surface Area: The surface area of a cylinder is composed of three parts: The two circular faces and the connecting portion. To find the total area of a cylinder, add the areas of these two parts. We already know how to calculate area for circles; and for the connecting surface, all we need to do is extend the circumference of one of the circles into three dimensions. So, multiply the circumference by the height of the cylinder.

$$\text{Surface Area} = 2(\pi \times r^2) + (2\pi \times r) \times h$$

Volume: The volume of a cylinder is equal to the area of one of its bases (circle) multiplied by the height.

$$\text{Volume} = (\pi \times r^2) \times h$$

NOTE

Notice that a cylinder approximates a pipe (Physics) or a small part of a blood vessel (Biology).

GOLD STANDARD WARM-UP EXERCISES

CHAPTER 4: Geometry

1. The area of a circle is 144π. What is its circumference?
   A. 6π
   B. 24π
   C. 72π
   D. 12π

2. The points (2,-3) and (2,5) are the endpoints of a diameter of a circle. What is the radius of the circle?
   A. 64
   B. 4π
   C. 8
   D. 4

3. A and B are similar 45°-45°-90° triangles. If B has an area of 12 square meters, and A has three times the area of B, what is the length of A's hypotenuse?
   A. $\sqrt{72}$ m
   B. 36 m
   C. 72 m
   D. 12 m

4. Leslie drives from Highway 1 to the parallel Highway 2 using the road that crosses them, as in the given figure below. Leslie misses the turn onto Highway 1 at point Q and drives 2 km further, to point P. Driving in a straight line from point P to get back to Highway 1, how much further will Leslie travel?

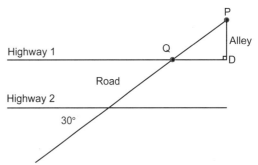

   A. 1/2 km
   B. $\sqrt{3}$ km
   C. 1 km
   D. 2 km

5. A circle is inscribed in a square with a diagonal of length 5. What is the area of the circle?
   A. $\dfrac{25}{8}\pi$
   B. $\dfrac{25}{2}\pi$
   C. $\dfrac{25}{16}\pi$
   D. $\dfrac{25}{4}\pi$

6. A circle is drawn inside a larger circle so that they have the same center. If the smaller circle has 25% the area of the larger circle, which of the following is the ratio of the radius of the small circle to that of the larger circle?

   A. $\dfrac{1}{8}$

   B. $\dfrac{3}{4}$

   C. $\dfrac{1}{4}$

   D. $\dfrac{1}{2}$

7. A circle passes through the point (0,0) and the point (10,0). Which of the following could NOT be a third point on the circle?

   A (1, -3)
   B (2, 4)
   C (7, 4)
   D (5, 0)

8. Consider a box with length l, width w and height h, if the thickness of the cardboard is t, how much empty space is inside this cardboard box?

   A. l x w x h
   B. (l - t) x (w - t) x (h - t)
   C. (l + t) x (w + t) x (h + t)
   D. (l - 2t) x (w - 2t) x (h - 2t)

GS ANSWER KEY

CHAPTER 4

Cross-Reference

1. B   GM 4.2, 4.2.3
2. D   GM 4.2, 4.2.3
3. D   GM 4.2, 4.2.2
4. C   GM 4.1, 4.1.3

Cross-Reference

5. A   GM 4.2, 4.2.1, 4.2.3
6. D   GM 4.2, 4.2.3
7. D   GM 4.1, 4.1.1, 4.2.3
8. D   GM 4.3.1; deduce

★ Worked solutions can be found at the end of the GAMSAT Math chapters. If something is still not clear, go to the forum at GAMSAT-prep.com.

TRIGONOMETRY
Chapter 5

Memorize	Understand	Not Required
* Formulas for Sine, Cosine, and Tangent * Important Values of Sine and Cosine	* Graphing Sine, Cosine, and Tangent * The Unit Circle * Degrees vs. Radians * Inverse Trigonometric Functions	* Memorizing the unit circle

GAMSAT-Prep.com

Introduction

Trigonometry is the most conceptually advanced branch of mathematics with which you will need to be familiar for the GAMSAT test. But don't let that scare you. Basically, everything in this section boils down to right triangles, and after Chapter 5, you will be a triangle pro!

Additional Resources

Free Online Forum

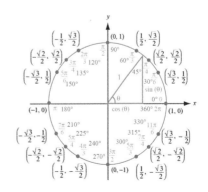

Special Guest

5.1 Basic Trigonometric Functions

The trigonometric functions describe the relationship between the angles and sides of right triangles. The angle in question is generally denoted by θ, the Greek letter theta, but you will never see the right angle used as θ.

We call the leg connecting to the corner of θ: the *adjacent side* ("b" in the diagram); and the leg that does not touch: the *opposite side* ("a" in the diagram). The edge across from the right angle is called the *hypotenuse* ("c" in the diagram).

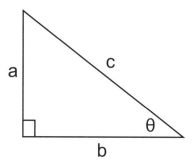

5.1.1 Sine

A lot of people like to use the mnemonic device "SOH-CAH-TOA" to remember how to evaluate the three basic trigonometric functions: Sine, cosine, and tangent. The first three letters, "SOH," refer to the first letter of each word in the following equation.

$$\text{Sine} = \frac{\text{Opposite}}{\text{Hypotenuse}}$$

Sine of an angle θ is written sin(θ). So to calculate this value, simply divide the length of the opposite side by the length of the hypotenuse.

EXAMPLE

What is sin(θ) in the following triangle?

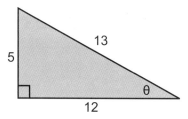

The opposite side has length 5, and the hypotenuse has length 13, so

$$\sin(\theta) = \frac{5}{13}$$

5.1.2 Cosine

The second set of three letters in SOH-CAH-TOA refers to the equation for the cosine of an angle.

$$\text{Cosine} = \frac{\text{Adjacent}}{\text{Hypotenuse}}$$

The abbreviation for the cosine of an angle is $\cos(\theta)$.

EXAMPLE

In the 5–12–13 triangle in Section 5.1.1, what is $\cos(\theta)$?

Dividing the adjacent side by the hypotenuse, we obtain the following solution:

$$\cos(\theta) = \frac{12}{13}$$

5.1.3 Tangent

The final three letters in SOH-CAH-TOA refer to the equation for finding the tangent of an angle.

$$\text{Tangent} = \frac{\text{Opposite}}{\text{Adjacent}}$$

You can also find the tangent of an angle if you know the value for sine and cosine. Notice that the hypotenuse cancels out if you divide sine and cosine.

$$\text{Tangent} = \frac{\text{Sine}}{\text{Cosine}}$$

You can also manipulate this equation to express sine or cosine in terms of the tangent.

EXAMPLE

In the 5–12–13 triangle in Section 5.1.1, what is $\tan(\theta)$?

Dividing the opposite side by the adjacent side, we obtain:

$$\tan(\theta) = \frac{5}{12}$$

5.1.4 Secant, Cosecant, and Cotangent

These three functions are far less commonly used than sine, cosine, and tangent, but you should still be familiar with them. They are not very hard to remember because they are just the reciprocals of the main three functions.

$$\text{Cosecant} = \frac{1}{\text{Sine}}$$

$$= \frac{\text{Hypotenuse}}{\text{Opposite}}$$

$$\text{Secant} = \frac{1}{\text{Cosine}}$$

$$= \frac{\text{Hypotenuse}}{\text{Adjacent}}$$

$$\text{Cotangent} = \frac{1}{\text{Tangent}}$$

$$= \frac{\text{Adjacent}}{\text{Opposite}}$$

The abbreviations for these functions are sec, csc, and cot, respectively. Unlike sine, cosine and tangent, you do not need to memorize these unusual functions.

5.2 The Unit Circle

5.2.1 Trig Functions on a Circle

As you can see from the equations in Section 5.1, the trigonometric functions are ratios of side lengths. This means that every angle has a value for each of the functions that *does not* depend on the scale of the triangle.

In Section 5.1 we looked at examples with a 5–12–13 triangle. Our solutions were as follows:

$$\sin(\theta) = \frac{5}{13}$$

$$\cos(\theta) = \frac{12}{13}$$

$$\tan(\theta) = \frac{5}{12}$$

Let's compare these results with the trigonometric functions for the similar triangle 10, 24, 26, which clearly has longer sides but the same angle θ:

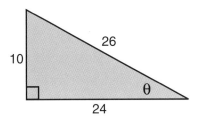

$$\sin(\theta) = \frac{10}{26} = \frac{5}{13}$$

$$\cos(\theta) = \frac{24}{26} = \frac{12}{13}$$

$$\tan(\theta) = \frac{10}{24} = \frac{5}{12}$$

As you can see, the trigonometric values for the angle remain the same.

Also, the absolute value of sine and cosine is never greater than 1 for any angle. This makes perfect sense because the hypotenuse of a triangle is always its longest side, and for sine and cosine, the hypotenuse is in the denominator.

If we plot the graph of sine and cosine for θ from 0° to 360° in Cartesian Coordinates with $x = \cos(\theta)$ and $y = \sin(\theta)$, we

obtain a circle of radius 1. This is known as the **unit circle**, as shown in the succeeding picture. The angle formed at the vertex of the x-axis is equal to θ.

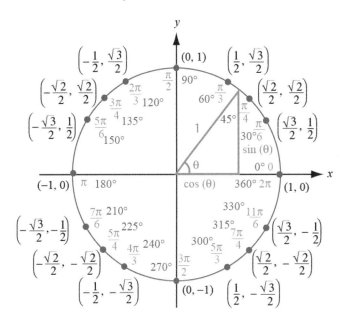

When simply dealing with right triangle figures, we never use negative numbers because negative length does not make sense. With the unit circle, though, legs of the triangle can be in negative space on the Cartesian plane. This can result in negative values for sine and cosine. You do not need to memorize the results of the unit circle.

5.2.2 Degrees and Radians

Up until this point, we have measured angles using degrees. When dealing with trigonometric functions, however, it is often more convenient to use the unit-less

measurement of **radians**. There are 2π radians in 360°, so one trip around the unit circle is an increase in θ by 2π radians.

$$2\pi \text{ radians} = 360°$$

This translates to 1 radian $= \dfrac{360}{2\pi}$, but you will usually be working with radians in multiples of π, so it is not necessary to memorize this.

Here is a list of important angles (in degrees and radians) and their sine and cosine values that can be deduced from the unit circle:

Degrees	Radians	Sine	Cosine
0°	0	0	1
30°	$\dfrac{\pi}{6}$	$\dfrac{1}{2}$	$\dfrac{(\sqrt{3})}{2}$
45°	$\dfrac{\pi}{4}$	$\dfrac{1}{\sqrt{2}}$	$\dfrac{1}{\sqrt{2}}$
60°	$\dfrac{\pi}{3}$	$\dfrac{(\sqrt{3})}{2}$	$\dfrac{1}{2}$
90°	$\dfrac{\pi}{2}$	1	0

Note that $\dfrac{1}{\sqrt{2}}$ is the same as $\dfrac{\sqrt{2}}{2}$.

These major angles repeat for each quadrant of the unit circle, but the signs of the sine and cosine values change. Moving counterclockwise around the circle and beginning with the upper right, the quadrants are labelled I, II, III, and IV.

Quadrant	Sine	Cosine
I	+	+
II	+	−
III	−	−
IV	−	+

NOTE

How many degrees are there in $\dfrac{3(\pi)}{4}$ radians?

Because 2π radians = 360°, this makes $1(\pi)$ radian = 180°.

Solution:

1π radian = 180°

$$\dfrac{3\pi}{4} = \dfrac{3\pi}{4} \times \dfrac{180°}{\pi}$$

$$= 135°$$

How many radians are there in 270°?

Solution:

1π radian = 180°

$$270° \times \dfrac{\pi}{180°} = \dfrac{3\pi}{2}$$

5.2.3 Graphing Trig Functions

Looking at the unit circle, it is very apparent that the trigonometric functions are **periodic**. This means that they continue to repeat the same cycle infinitely. After you go once around the circle, a full 360°, you end up right back at the beginning and begin to cycle through again. It is due to this *periodicity* that these functions are used to describe periodic motion (e.g. a pendulum or swing in motion, etc.) which we will explore in Physics Chapter 7.

A. Sine

As you can see from the table in 5.2.2, the sine function increases for the first 90°. For the next 90° it decreases while staying positive, then it continues to decrease into the negatives, and finally for the last 90°, it increases from −1 back to 0. From this information, we can picture the general shape of the graph, and we know that the period of the function is a full 360° or 2π radians.

The graph itself looks like this:

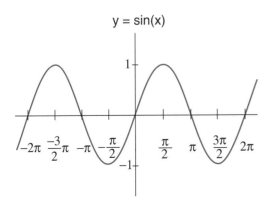

$y = \sin(x)$

As you can see in the graph, the sine function reaches a maximum at $\frac{\pi}{2} + 2\pi \times n$, has an x-intercept at $\pi \times n$, and a minimum at $\frac{3\pi}{2} + 2\pi \times n$ where n is any integer.

B. Cosine

The cosine function is identical to the sine function, except that it is shifted along the x-axis by half a period. So rather than starting at 0 and increasing, it starts at one and decreases. The period is still 2π radians.

The graph looks like this:

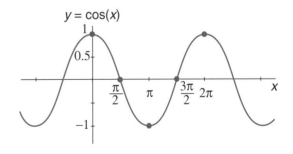

$y = \cos(x)$

Just like with the sine function, you can see where the maxima, minima, and intercepts of the cosine function are from the graph. It reaches a maximum at $2\pi \times n$, an x-intercept at $\frac{\pi}{2} + \pi \times n$, and a minimum at $2\pi \times n + \pi$ where n is any integer.

C. Tangent

The graph of the tangent function differs from sine and cosine graphs in a few important ways. First of all, the tangent function repeats itself every π radian instead of every 2π. So it is π-periodic rather than 2π-periodic. Also, it has vertical **asymptotes**, vertical lines that the function approaches but never crosses, at $(n)\left(\dfrac{\pi}{2}\right)$ for every odd integer n. The value of the tangent goes infinity as it approaches an asymptote from left to right; and negative infinity as it approaches from right to left.

> **NOTE**
>
> We will see the application of sine curves when we discuss Wave Characteristics and Periodic Motion in Physics Chapter 7.

Remember, the tangent function is the ratio of the sine function to the cosine function, so the asymptotes occur when the cosine of an angle is equal to zero, where $\cos(x) = 0$, because division by zero is undefined. 0/0 is never possible for the tangent function, so it is irrelevant.

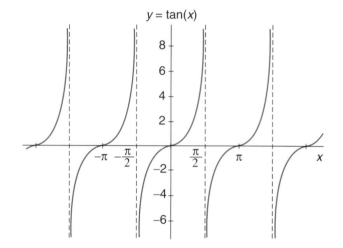

5.3 Trigonometric Problems

5.3.1 Inverse Trig Functions

We have discussed the formulas for finding the value of trigonometric functions for different angles, but how can you find the value of an angle if all you know is the value of one of the functions? This is where the inverse trigonometric functions come into play.

The **inverse** of a trigonometric function takes an input value x and outputs an angle. The value of the inverse trigono-metric function of x is equal to the angle. To represent an inverse function, we write -1 in superscript like we would an exponent. But remember, this is not actually an exponent.

Inverse sine is represented as $\sin^{-1}$ and it is defined as such:

$$\sin(\sin^{-1}(x)) = x$$

So, $\sin(\theta) = x$ and $\sin^{-1}(x) = \theta$.

Now that we have inverse functions in our toolbox, we can begin to solve algebraic problems that contain trigonometric functions.

Solve the following equation for x.

$$\pi - \tan 2x = \left(\frac{4}{3}\right)\pi$$

$$\Rightarrow -\tan 2x = \left(\frac{1}{3}\right)\pi$$

$$\Rightarrow \tan 2x = \frac{-\pi}{3}$$

$$\Rightarrow 2x = \tan^{-1}\left(\frac{-\pi}{3}\right)$$

$$\Rightarrow x = \left(\frac{1}{2}\right)\tan^{-1}\left(\frac{-\pi}{3}\right)$$

GAMSAT-Prep.com
THE GOLD STANDARD

GOLD STANDARD WARM-UP EXERCISES
CHAPTER 5: Trigonometry

> **NOTE**
>
> All these questions are "open book" practice questions. Please feel free to find information in this chapter to help you solve these problems. This type of practice helps to improve your deductive reasoning. Of course, please do not use a calculator.

1. What percentage of the unit circle is represented by the angle $8\pi/5$?
   A. 1.6%
   B. 80%
   C. 0.25%
   D. 160%

2. Which of the following is the value of $-\cos(\pi/2)$?
   A. 0
   B. −1
   C. 1
   D. $1/\sqrt{2}$

3. The tangent of one of the acute angles in a right triangle is 3/2. If the leg opposite this angle has a length of 12, what is the length of the hypotenuse?
   A. 8
   B. $6\sqrt{13}$
   C. $4\sqrt{13}$
   D. 18

4. Given that the sine of an acute angle is equal to the cosine of its complement, and vice versa, the value of $\cos(\pi/6)$ equals the value of which of the following? (note: for complementary angles, *see* GM 4.1.3)

   A. $\sin(\pi/2)$
   B. $\sin(\pi/4)$
   C. $\sin(\pi/6)$
   D. $\sin(\pi/3)$

GS ANSWER KEY

CHAPTER 5

Cross-Reference

1. B GM 5.2, 5.2.1
2. A GM 5.5

Cross-Reference

3. C GM 5.1, 5.1.3, 5.3, 5.3.3
4. D GM 4.1.3, 5.2, 5.2.3

* Worked solutions can be found at the end of the GAMSAT Math chapters. If something is still not clear, go to the forum at GAMSAT-prep.com.

PROBABILITY AND STATISTICS
Chapter 6

Memorize	**Understand**	**Not Required**
* Formula for Average * Formula for Probability	* Determining Probabilities * Combining Probabilities of Multiple Events * Mode, Median, Variance, Standard Deviation and its Corresponding Graph * Correlation Coefficient * Regression lines ("lines of best fit")	* Permutations and combinations * Formulae for standard deviation and variance

GAMSAT-Prep.com

Introduction

Often research passages are presented as stimulus material for GAMSAT questions so a basic understanding of probability and statistics is useful. From the standpoint of performing calculations, probability and statistics are relatively minor subjects for the GAMSAT. This section will help you keep things straight such as when to multiply and when to add probabilities – simple questions that can often be the most confusing probabilities.

Additional Resources

Free Online Forum

$0 < r < +1$

Special Guest

6.1 Probability

6.1.1 What is Probability?

Probability is a measure of the likelihood that something will happen.

In mathematics, probability is represented as a ratio of two numbers. The second number - the denominator - corresponds to the total number of possible outcomes the situation can have. The first number - the numerator - corresponds to the number of ways the particular outcome in question can occur.

$$\text{Probability} = \frac{(\text{number of ways the outcome can occur})}{(\text{number of possible outcomes})}$$

Let's look at a simple example.

Let's consider the flipping of a coin. Of course, we know that there are only two possible outcomes of a coin flip, heads or tails. So the total number of outcomes is 2, which will be our denominator.

Say we want to find the probability that a flipped coin will be heads. There is only one way this outcome can come about, so the numerator will be 1. Therefore, the probability of flipping heads is 1 in 2:

$$\text{Probability of Heads} = \frac{1}{2}$$

It is important to note that the quantity in the numerator of a probability ratio is a subset of the quantity in the denominator. The number of ways an outcome can occur is always less than or equal to the total number of outcomes. This means that a probability will never be more than 1, since 1 would mean the outcome is the *only* possibility. Also, the sum of the probabilities of all possible outcomes will always be 1.

Let's look at a slightly more complicated example.

Say you have a typical six-sided die with the sides labelled 1 through 6. If you roll the die once, what is the probability that the number will not be divisible by 3?

Let's begin by finding the total number of outcomes. Be careful here. The only outcomes we wish to determine the probability of are rolls of numbers divisible by 3, but the total number of possible outcomes is not affected by this restriction. There are still 6 in total, one for each number it is possible to roll.

Now we want to know how many ways out of these 6 we can roll a number that is not divisible by 3. Well, the only two numbers that are divisible by 3 that are possibilities are 3 and 6. So 1, 2, 4, and 5 are not. This means that there are 4 ways for the outcome to occur.

$$\text{Probability} = \frac{4}{6}$$

$$\text{Probability} = \frac{2}{3}$$

Reducing fractions is usually fine when working with probability; just know that if you do, the numerator and denominator will not necessarily correspond to the number of possibilities anymore.

The simplest way to complicate a probability problem is to allow for multiple correct outcomes. To find the total probability, simply add the individual probabilities for each correct outcome. For the above example, the total probability is actually the sum of the probabilities of rolling 1, 2, 4, and 5.

6.1.2 Combining Probabilities

What if you are asked to find the probability that multiple events will occur?

The solution to such a problem will still be a ratio in which the numbers represent the same quantities as before. The new difficulty is figuring out how many different outcome possibilities there are. Luckily, there is an easy way to calculate this. All you have to do is find the probability of each individual event and then multiply them together.

Why does this work? Think about it this way: For each possible outcome of the first event, there is still every possible outcome for the second. So the total number of possibilities will be the number of outcomes in the first times the number of outcomes in the second.

EXAMPLE

Let's go back to the flipping coin! If you flip it twice, what is the probability that the first flip will turn up heads and the second tails?

When dealing with multiple events, always focus on one event at a time before combining. So start with the first flip. We know that the probability it will be heads is ½. Now for the second flip, the probability it will be tails is also ½.

Now to find the probability that both of the events will occur, we multiply the individual probabilities:

$$\text{Probability} = \frac{1}{2} \times \frac{1}{2}$$
$$= \frac{1}{4}$$

Let's look at another coin flip example.

EXAMPLE

If you flip a coin twice, what is the probability that it will come up heads exactly one time?

This question seems almost identical to the previous example, but be careful! The difference is that the phrasing of this question does not specify particular outcomes for the individual events.

Let's solve this in two ways:

(i) Let's combine both events into one. To find the total number of possible outcomes, multiply the totals of each event, so there are 2 × 2 = 4 possibilities. Now count the number of ways we can flip heads once. Well, we could have heads on the first flip and tails on the second, so that is 1, or we could have tails then heads, so that is 2. Therefore, the probability of flipping heads exactly once is 2 to 4.

$$Probability = \frac{2}{4}$$

(ii) Now let's treat the events separately. Ask yourself: What are the odds that an outcome of the first event will be compatible with flipping heads once? The answer is $\frac{2}{2}$ since we can still achieve the overall desired outcome with the second flip no

matter what the first flip is.

Now what are the odds that an outcome of the second event will be compatible with flipping heads once? Since you already have a first flip determined, there is only one outcome for the second flip that will give the desired result. If the first flip was heads we need a tails flip, and if the first flip was tails we need a heads flip. So the odds for the second flip are ½ .

$$Probability = \frac{2}{2} \times \frac{1}{2}$$
$$= \frac{2}{4}$$

There are all kinds of confusing ways probability problems can be written. You have to be extra careful to break them down and determine exactly what is being asked because the test writers love to try and trick you. Double and triple-check that you have the setup right for probability problems because it is so easy to accidentally overlook something.

> **NOTE**
>
> When you want to know the probability of event A or B, the probabilities must be added. If you want to know the probability of events A and B, the probabilities must be multiplied.

6.2 Statistics

6.2.1 Averages

When given a collection of numbers, the **average** is the sum of the numbers divided by the total number of numbers.

$$\text{Average} = \frac{(\text{sum of numbers})}{(\text{number of numbers})}$$

EXAMPLE

What is the average of the set {4, 7, 6, 7}?

Add up the numbers and, since there are 4 of them, divide by 4.

$$\text{Average} = \frac{(4+7+6+7)}{4}$$
$$= \frac{24}{4}$$
$$= 6$$

The average may or may not actually appear in the set of numbers, but it is a common way to think of the typical value for the set.

6.2.2 Mode, Median, Mean

Here are a few other statistics terms you should know:

The **mode** of a set of values is the number that appears the most times. Mode can be bimodal or multimodal. Simply stated, bimodal means that two numbers are repeated the most while multimodal indicates two or more numbers are repeated the most.

The **median** of a set of values is the number that appears exactly in the center of the distribution. This means there are an equal number of values greater than and less than the median.

Arithmetic mean is just another name for the average of a set of numbers. The terms are interchangeable.

EXAMPLE

Find the mode, median, and mean of the following set: {3, 5, 11, 3, 8}.

Let's begin with the mode. All we need to do is see which value or values repeat the most times. In this case, the only one that repeats is 3.

Mode = 3

To find the median we always need to first arrange the set in numerical order.

{3, 3, 5, 8, 11}

Now the median is whichever number lies in the exact center.

Median = 5

Since the mean is the same as the average, we add the values and divide by 5.

$$\text{Mean} = \frac{(3+3+5+8+11)}{5}$$
$$= \frac{30}{5}$$
$$= 6$$

NOTE

If a set has an even number of values, there will be no value exactly in the center. In this case, the median is the average of the two values that straddle the center.

Example

Given: 3, 4, 5, 6, 6, 8, 9, 10, 10, 12

The median is the average of the two middle data: $\frac{(6+8)}{2} = 7$

6.3 More Tools for Probability and Statistics

6.3.1 The Correlation Coefficient

The correlation coefficient r indicates whether two sets of data are associated or *correlated*. The value of r ranges from -1.0 to 1.0. The larger the absolute value of r, the stronger the association. Given two sets of data X and Y, a positive value for r indicates that as X increases, Y increases. A negative value for r indicates that as X increases, Y decreases.

Imagine that the weight (*X*) and height (*Y*) of everyone in the entire country was determined. There would be a strong positive correlation between a person's weight and their height. In general, as weight increases, height increases (*in a population*). However, the correlation would not be perfect (i.e. r < 1.0). After all, there would be some people who are very tall but very thin, and others who would be very short but overweight. We might find that *r* = 0.7. This would suggest there is a strong positive association between weight and height, but it is not a perfect association.

If two sets of data are correlated, does that mean that one *causes* the other? Not necessarily; simply because weight and height are correlated does not mean that if you gained weight you will necessarily gain height! Thus association does not imply causality.

Note that a correlation greater than 0.8 is generally described as strong, whereas a correlation that is less than 0.5 is generally described as weak. However, the interpretation and use of these values can vary based upon the "type" of data being examined. For example, a study based on chemical or biological data may require a stronger correlation than a study using social science data. You will regularly see regression lines with well-correlated data in ACER's practice materials and during the real GAMSAT.

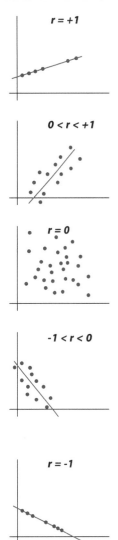

Varying values of the correlation coefficient (r) based on data plotted for two variables (= scatter diagrams). In red is the line of "best fit" (= *regression line*). One purpose of the regression line is to predict what would likely occur outside of the experimental data (meaning, you can extrapolate beyond what is shown).

6.3.2 The Standard Deviation

When given a set of data, it is often useful to know the average value, *the mean*, and the *range* of values. As previously discussed, the mean is simply the sum of the data values divided by the number of data values. The range is the numerical difference between the largest value and the smallest value.

Another useful measurement is the *standard deviation*. The standard deviation indicates the dispersion of values around the mean. Given a bell-shaped distribution of data (e.g., the height and weight of a population, the GPA of undergraduate students, etc.), each standard deviation (SD) includes a given percentage of data. For example, the mean +/– 1 SD includes approximately 68% of the data values, the mean +/– 2 SD includes 95% of the data values, and the mean +/– 3 SD includes 99.7% of the data values.

> **NOTE**
>
> To see a Normal Curve displaying GAMSAT score results, go to www. GAMSAT-prep.com/GAMSAT-scores.

For example, imagine that you read that the mean GPA required for admission to Belcurve University's Dental School is 3.5 with a standard deviation of 0.2 (SD = 0.2). Thus approximately 68% of the students admitted have a GPA of 3.5 +/– 0.2, which means between 3.3 and 3.7. We can also conclude that approximately 95% of the students admitted have a GPA of 3.5 +/– 2(0.2), which means between 3.1 and 3.9. Therefore the standard deviation becomes a useful measure of the dispersion of values around the mean 3.5.

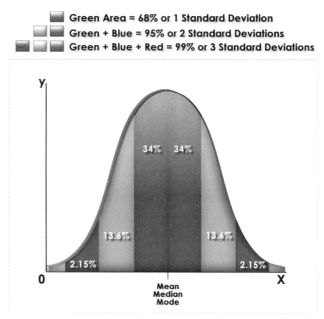

Figure 6.1: The Normal Curve (also referred to as: the Normal Distribution Curve).

6.3.3 Variance

Variance is another measure of how far a set of numbers is spread out or, in other words, how far numbers are from the mean. Thus variance is calculated as the average of the squared differences from the mean.

There are three steps to calculate the variance:

1. Determine the mean (the simple average of all the numbers)
2. For each number: subtract the mean and square the result (the squared difference)
3. Determine the average of those squared differences

The variance is also defined as the square of the standard deviation. Thus unlike standard deviation, the variance has units that are the square of the units of the variable itself.

For example, a variable measured in meters will have a variance measured in meters squared.

You are unlikely to need to calculate the standard deviation nor the variance. But having a basic understanding of these statistical measures can help when reading passages or analysing graphs (e.g., with error bars; GM 3.5.5) during the GAMSAT.

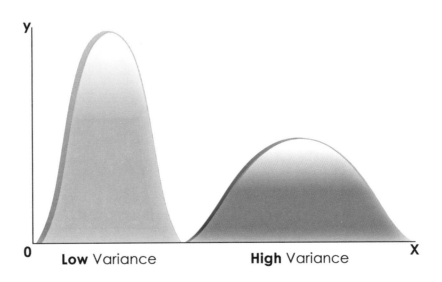

Figure 6.2: Variance.

6.3.4 Simple Probability Revisited

Let's apply a formula to simple probability. If a phenomenon or experiment has n equally likely outcomes, s of which are called successes, then the probability P of success is given by $P = \dfrac{s}{n}$.

EXAMPLE

- if "heads" in a coin toss is considered a success, then
$$P(\text{success}) = \frac{1}{2};$$

- if a card is drawn from a deck and diamonds are considered successes, then
$$P(\text{success}) = \frac{13}{52}.$$ It follows that $P(\text{success}) = 1 - P(\text{failure})$.

> **NOTE**
>
> Any of the 4 GAMSAT sciences may require the use of simple probability but it most often presents itself in Genetics (Biology Chapter 15).

GOLD STANDARD WARM-UP EXERCISES

CHAPTER 6: Probability and Statistics

1. A jar contains 4 red marbles and 6 blue marbles. What is the probability that a marble chosen at random will be red?

   A. 4/6
   B. 4/10
   C. 2/6
   D. 6/10

2. A box contains 6 yellow balls and 4 green balls. Two balls are chosen at random without replacement. What is the probability that the first ball is yellow and the second ball is green?

   A. 5/12
   B. 1/10
   C. 6/25
   D. 4/15

3. An English teacher wants to prepare a class reading list that includes 1 philosophy book, 1 work of historical fiction, and 1 biography. She has 3 philosophy books, 2 works of historical fiction, and 4 biographies to choose from. How many different combinations of books can she put together for her list?

   A. 32
   B. 288
   C. 9
   D. 24

4. A medical training survey shows that the distribution of the residents' annual income is a bell curve. 2,516 residents are within one standard deviation of the average annual income. How many residents were in the survey's sample?

   A. 3,700
   B. 2,648
   C. 2,524
   D. 2,523

5. The average time it takes 3 students to complete a test is 35 minutes. If 1 student takes 41 minutes to complete the test and another takes 37 minutes, how many minutes does the third student take to complete the test?

   A. 4
   B. 38
   C. 27
   D. 39

6. A small library receives a shipment of grey books, blue books, black books, and brown books. If the librarian decides to shelve all the books of one color on Monday, all of the books of another color on Tuesday, and the rest of the books on Wednesday, in how many different ways can the book shelving be completed?

A. 3

B. 4

C. 8

D. 12

7. When you roll a die, what is the probability to first get a 3 and then a 1 or a 2?

A. 1/6

B. 1/8

C. 1/32

D. 1/18

GS ANSWER KEY

CHAPTER 6

Cross-Reference

1.   B   GM 6.1.1
2.   D   GM 6.1, 6.1.2
3.   D   GM 6.3, 6.3.4
4.   A   GM 6.3.2

Cross-Reference

5.   C   GM 6.2, 6.2.1
6.   D   GM 6.3.4
7.   D   GM 6.1, 6.1.2

★ Worked solutions can be found at the end of the GAMSAT Math chapters. If something is still not clear, go to the forum at GAMSAT-prep.com.

CHAPTER REVIEW SOLUTIONS GAMSAT MATH

Question 1   B

See: GM 1.2.3, 1.4.3

According to the rules of order of operations, we work with the square root first: $0.125 + \sqrt{\frac{1}{9}} = 0.125 + \frac{1}{3}$. Since the answers are in decimal form, this problem is easiest to solve if all values are in decimal form. From the list of fraction-to-decimal conversions, $\frac{1}{3} \approx 0.33$, and so, $0.125 + \frac{1}{3} \approx 0.125 + 0.33 = 0.455$. All of the answers have only two decimal places, so we must round this answer off to the hundredths decimal place. The digit in the thousandths decimal place is a 5, and so the digit in the hundredths decimal place increases by 1 to become 6. 0.455 therefore rounds off to 0.46.

Quick Solution:

$$0.125 + \sqrt{\frac{1}{9}} = 0.125 + \frac{1}{3} \approx 0.125 + 0.333$$

$$= 0.458 \approx 0.46.$$

Question 2   D

See: GM 1.6.2

This is a proportion problem, so there will be two equivalent ratios. We construct the first ratio as $\frac{0.8}{0.9}$ and the second as $\frac{80}{x}$. If we set them equal, we get $\frac{0.8}{0.9} = \frac{80}{x}$, and cross-multiplication gives us $0.8x = (0.9)(80)$, or $0.8x = 72$. Therefore, $x = \frac{72}{0.8} = 90$.

> **Quick Solution:** 80 differs from 0.8 by a factor of 100. This means that the answer must be related to 0.9 by the same factor: $x = 100(0.9) = 90$

Question 3   A

See: GM 1.4.3

The interest earned by investing $5,897 in Bank B is 21% of $5,897, or $(0.21)(\$5,897) = \$1238.37$. The interest earned by investing $6,430 in Bank A is 19% of $6,430, or $(0.19)(\$6,430) = \$1221.70$. Subtracting the smaller from the larger, we get $1238.37 - \$1221.70 = \$16.67$.

Though you won't be asked about interest for the GAMSAT, the words will be different but the math will be the same. Also, you must be quick and precise with your calculations.

Question 4   C

See: GM 1.4.2

We must work backwards to find the lengths of boards B and C. Board B is 4/5 as long as Board A, which is $\frac{4}{5}(100m) = 80m$. Board C is 3/4 as long as this, which is $\frac{3}{4}(80m) = 60m$. To find the sum of these lengths, we add the three values: 100m + 80m + 60m = 240m.

Question 5   B

See: GM 1.6.2

This is a proportion problem in which the following are given: The proportion of the yellow marbles in the jar of yellow and green marbles is 7 out of 9. This makes the ratio of the number of yellow marbles to green marbles 7:2. The total number of marbles is 999. Therefore, the number of yellow marbles = (7/9) × 999 = 777 marbles.

Question 6   D

See: GM 1.6.1

This is a ratio problem involving different units. The given ratio is 0.25 months per week. We need to re-write this as a fraction: 0.25 months per week $= \frac{25}{100}$ months/week $= \frac{1}{4}$ months/week. This ratio tells us that there are four weeks in one month. We can express the number of months corresponding to one day using an intermediate relationship. There are 7 days in one week, which we can express with the ratio $\frac{1}{7}$ weeks/day. To express the number of months per day, we must multiply the first ratio by the second: $(\frac{1}{4}$ months/week$)(\frac{1}{7}$ weeks/day$) = \frac{1}{28}$ months/day. Notice that the weeks units cancel so that the only units left are months and days. If we had used a ratio expressing the number of days per week (the reciprocal of weeks per day), $\frac{7}{1}$ days/week, this cancellation would not occur and the final answer would not have the correct units of months per day.

> **Quick Solution:** To convert a ratio that expresses a relationship between months and weeks to one that expresses a relationship between months and days, multiply it by a ratio that expresses a relationship between weeks and days:
>
> $$(\frac{1}{4}$ months/week$)(\frac{1}{7}$ weeks/day$) = \frac{1}{28}$ months/day.$$

We will link the process to solve the problem above to 'dimensional analysis' in Chapter 2 (GM 2.2).

Question 7   B

See: GM 1.2.3, 1.4.3, 1.5.2

The first step in this problem is to find the value of 6.4% of 1,000. We convert the percentage to a decimal (0.064) and multiply by one thousand: 0.064(1,000) = 64. Next, we find which of the answer choices is equal to this value. Choice A is obviously incorrect because 64 taken to any power besides 1 does not equal 64. The order of operations tells us that we must perform the calculation inside the parentheses first in choice C, which is a decimal (0.64). Squaring this value does not give us 64. Choice D begins with a small number (6.4) and divides it by a much larger number, so we know that the answer will be even smaller, and therefore not equal to 64. The correct choice is B. To check this, note that $256^{3/4} = (256^{1/4})^3 = (4)^3$ (because $4 \times 4 \times 4 \times 4 = 256$) and $(4)^3 = 64$.

Question 8   D

See: GM 1.2.3, 1.4.3

First, simplify the expressions according to the rules of the order of operations:

$$2 + \left[71 - 8\left(\frac{6}{2}\right)^2\right] = 2 + (71 - 8(3)^2)$$

$$= 2 + (71 - 8(9))$$
$$= 2 + (71 - 72)$$
$$= 2 + (-1) = 1$$

and $\sqrt{2500} = 50$. So, we need to find the percentage of 50 that is constituted by 1. Using the formula

Percent = Part/Whole × 100

$$\frac{1}{50} \times 100 = 0.02 \times 100 = 2,$$

we see that the answer is 2%.

Question 9   A

See: GM 1.4.3

The tenths decimal place is the largest occupied in each number. Comparing the digits in this decimal place, it is clear that the .6 in .636 is the largest.

Question 10   D

See: GM 1.2.1

Following the rule of adding like and unlike signs:

= 9 + −5 + 6
= 4 + 6
= 10

Question 11   B

See: GM 1.5.2

Dividing the coefficients 1.5 and 3.0 gives an answer of 0.5. Then the correct exponent value is determined by subtracting the exponents involved, which are 7 and 4. The final answer in scientific notation is $0.5 \times 10^3 = 5.0 \times 10^2$.

Question 12   A

See: GM 1.5.1, 1.5.2

Convert so that both numbers have the same power of 10, then and only then can subtraction (or addition) be accomplished.

1.5 x 10⁷ = 1500 x 10⁴

1500 x 10⁴ - 3.0 x 10⁴ =

1497 x 10⁴ = 1.497 x 10⁷

Question 13   C

See: GM 1.2.1.1, 1.1.3

Vertical bars mean 'absolute value'. First we calculate what is within the vertical bars, then to take the absolute value, we convert to a positive number.

$$|(-3)(6)| = |-18| = 18$$

Question 14   B

See: GM 1.2.1.1, 1.1.3

Vertical bars mean 'absolute value'. First we calculate what is within the vertical bars, then to take the absolute value, we convert to a positive number. Note that there is a negative symbol *outside* the vertical lines which will ensure that the answer becomes negative.

$$-|2-5| = -|-3| = -|3| = -3$$

{Recall: 2−5 = −3, |−3| = 3, and then the first minus gets you −3}

Question 15   C

See: GM 1.4.3

It is usually easier to calculate using fractions than decimals. You should instantly recognize .333 as 1/3 and .125 as 1/8 (GM 1.4.3).

1/3 x 1/8 = 1/24 which is approximately 1/25 = 4/100 = 0.04.

You may be surprised at how often the test makers for the GAMSAT choose numbers to give you the option to work faster with fractions.

Question 1   D

See: GM 2.1, 2.2

Construct a ratio comparing millimeters to meters using the definition of the prefix "milli." Remember that we want to convert from meters to millimeters, so the denominator of the fraction we use for this ratio must contain the units of meters:

$\dfrac{1000\,\text{mm}}{1\,\text{m}}$. Now multiply this ratio and the given value:

$$75\,\text{m}\left(\dfrac{1000\,\text{mm}}{1\,\text{m}}\right) \;=\; 75{,}000\,\text{mm}.$$

Question 2   C

See: GM 2.1.2

Start with any of the choices and compare it to the rest:

$$0.1\,\text{km} \;=\; 100\,\text{m} \;>\; 10\,\text{m}$$

$$0.1\,\text{km} \;>\; 10\,\text{m}$$

$$10\,\text{cm} \;<\; 10\,\text{m}$$

$$1000\,\text{mm} \;=\; 1\,\text{m} \;>\; 10\,\text{cm}$$

Question 3   A

See: GM 2.2

The total length of the triathlon is 12 km + 10 km + 15 km = 37 km. Express the ratio of kilometers to meters as a fraction,

with kilometers in the denominator to cancel the units of 37 km:

$\dfrac{1000\,\text{m}}{1\,\text{km}}$. Now multiply: $37\,\text{km}\left(\dfrac{1000\,\text{m}}{1\,\text{km}}\right) \;=\; 37{,}000\,\text{m}.$

Question 4   C

See: GM 2.1

Construct an equation that expresses an unknown number of staples, times the weight of each, equals the weight of one paper-clip:

$$0.05x \;=\; 1$$

$$x \;=\; \dfrac{1}{0.05} \;=\; 20$$

Question 5   D

See: GM 2.1, 2.2

Convert the mixed number to an improper fraction (which you should be able to 'do in your head' because 17 times 6 can be broken down to 10 times 6 = 60 PLUS 7 times 6 = 42 so SUBTOTAL = 102 PLUS 5 for a TOTAL = 107):

$$17\tfrac{5}{6} \;=\; \dfrac{107}{6}$$

Convert using the fact that 60 minutes equals 1 hour (notice that the number 6 cancels so the problem is reduced to 107 times 10 = 1070):

$$\left(\dfrac{107}{6}\,\text{hours}\right)\left(\dfrac{60\,\text{minute}}{1\,\text{hour}}\right) \;=\; 1070\,\text{minutes}$$

Question 6   B

See: GM 2.1, 2.2

Add like units:

$$67\text{ lbs.} + 93\text{ lbs.} + 18\text{ lbs.} \;=\; 178\text{ lbs.}$$

$$1\text{ oz.} + 2\text{oz.} + 5\text{oz.} \;=\; 8\text{oz.}$$

Convert to pounds the part of the total weight that is in ounces and add to the rest of the weight:

$$(8\,\text{oz.})\left(\dfrac{1\text{ lbs.}}{16\text{ 0z.}}\right) \;=\; 0.5\text{ lbs.}$$

$$178\text{ lbs.} \;+\; 0.5\text{ lbs.} \;=\; 178.5\text{ lbs.}$$

Question 7   D

See: GM 2.1.1, 2.2

Given that the charges are:

$20.50 per hour to file paper,
$55 per hour for time in court,
$30 per hour for consultations,

a 90-minute consultation = $30 + $15 = $45.
8 /6   hours = 80 minutes time filing paper work = $20.50 + $6.83 = $27.33

Since 20 minutes = $6.83

1 hour in court = $55

Total charges = $45 + $27.33 + $55 = $127.33

Notice that the first and third charge add to $100 making the calculation trivial.

Question 8   A

See: GM 2.1, 2.2; dimensional analysis

Multiply by all ratios necessary to convert centimeters to feet (via inches) and seconds to minutes, and divide by 4 to calculate the speed for only 25% of a minute:

$$\left(20\text{ cm/sec.}\right)\left(\dfrac{1}{2.54}\text{ in./cm}\right)$$

$$\left(\dfrac{1}{12}\text{ ft./in.}\right)(60\text{ sec./min.})\left(\dfrac{1}{4}\right) \;\approx\; 10\text{ ft./min.}$$

Question 9   A

See: GM 2.1, 2.2; dimensional analysis

This problem is strictly a matter of dimensional analysis.
In the SI system, "mega" means 10^6
1 Megawatt = 10^3 kW = 10^6 W
Therefore, power in watts = (Total number of watt-years)/(Number of years)
Notice that the equation is constructed to allow "years" to cancel (i.e. it is in the numerator and in the denominator).
2×10^6 watt-years/6 years = 0.33×10^6 W = 3.3×10^5 W

Question 10   D

See: GM 2.2; dimensional analysis

We will explore force in Physics. Force is in units called 'newtons' which is mass times acceleration, thus a newton is equivalent to a $kg(m/s^2)$ [see section 2.1] and since kg is M (mass), m is L (length) and s is T (time), we get that the force is dimensionally equivalent to ML/T^2. Now the terms added on

the right side of the equation must also be dimensionally equal to ML/T^2. Let's first solve for 'a' (note: most of the steps that we will show are really mental manipulations but we'll show the steps in case you are not used to it):

$$ML/T^2 = at^{-1} = aT^{-1} = a/T$$

To isolate 'a', multiply through by T:

$$(T)ML/T^2 = (T)a/T$$

Cancel T:

$$ML/T = a = MLT^{-1}$$

Now we solve for 'b':

$$ML/T^2 = bt^2 = bT^2$$

To isolate 'b', divide both sides by T^2:

$$ML/T^2/T^2 = ML/T^4 = b$$

Question 1   D

See: GM 3.1.4

Substitute 2 for x in the function:

$$y = \frac{12}{4(2)^3 - 6(2) + 5}$$
$$= \frac{12}{4(8) - 12 + 5}$$
$$= \frac{12}{32 - 12 + 5} = \frac{12}{25}$$

Question 2   D

See: GM 3.3.2, 3.3.3

Create a ratio with the first two values and simplify:

$$\frac{13xy^2z}{39y} = \frac{xyz}{3}$$

The unknown ratio must also be equal to this value. Let k represent the variable and cross-multiply:

$$\frac{9xyz^6}{k} = \frac{xyz}{3}$$
$$3(9xyz^6) = (xyz)k$$
$$\frac{27xyz^6}{xyz} = k$$
$$27z^5 = k$$

Question 3   A

See: GM 3.4.2A, 3.4.2B

Substitute the first equation into the second, replacing y:

$$\begin{aligned}
6x - 5y &= -3 \\
6x - 5(2x - 1) &= -3 \\
6x - 10x + 5 &= -3 \\
-4x + 5 &= -3 \\
-4x &= -8 \\
x &= 2
\end{aligned}$$

Substitute this value back into either equation to find y:

$$\begin{aligned}
y &= 2x - 1 \\
y &= 2(2) - 1 \\
y &= 3
\end{aligned}$$

Question 4   D

See: GM 3.4.2B

We will need to write equations that correspond to the sentences. Let d represent the number of dimes, and n represent the number of nickels. Since there are two less dimes than nickels,

$$d = n - 2.$$

The amount of money a group of coins is worth is equal to the value of the coins times the number of coins. The total value of Loubha's nickels is $0.05n$ and the total value of her dimes is $0.10d$. These add up to all of the money she has:

$$\$0.05n + \$0.10d = \$0.85.$$

Substitute the first equation into the second for *n*:

$$\$0.05n + \$0.10(n - 2) = \$0.85$$
$$\$0.05n + \$0.10n - \$0.20 = \$0.85$$
$$\$0.15n = \$0.85 + \$0.20$$
$$\$0.15n = \$1.05$$

$$n = \$1.05 / \$0.15$$
$$n = 7$$

There are 7 nickels. We can plug this into either of the two original equations, but the first is easiest to use:

$$d = n - 2$$
$$d = 7 - 2$$
$$d = 5$$

NOTE: In this particular problem, the fastest way is to just try the different answers until one fits the requirements. We have shown the work in case it was a different question type then you would still know the approach.

Question 5   B
See: GM 3.3.1
Simplify the expression:

$$(2.5 \times 10^3)(3 \times 10^x) = 0.075$$
$$(2.5 \times 3)(10^3 \times 10^x) = 0.075$$
$$(7.5)(10^{3+x}) = 0.075$$

Divide both sides of the equation 7.5, or simply note that 0.075 is one-hundredth $\left(\frac{1}{100}\right) = 10^{-2}$ of 7.5:

$$10^{3+x} = 10^{-2}$$
$$3 + x = -2$$
$$x = -5$$

Question 6   D
See: GM 3.5.4
If we think of the plank as a straight line in a coordinate system, we can use the points at which its ends are located to find its slope. The origin can be anywhere we choose, and the base of the house's left wall is a good choice. This point of the house must be located at (0, 0), and so the base of the plank, 7 feet to the left, is located at (−7, 0). The point at which the plank touches the left wall is 5 feet above the origin, at (0, 5). The slope of the plank is therefore

$$m = \frac{0 - 5}{-7 - 0} = \frac{-5}{-7} = \frac{5}{7}$$

Question 7   D
See: GM 3.3.1, 3.4.2A, 3.4.2B
It is given that $2n = 3k$, which implies that $\frac{2}{3}n = k$. $n + k = 5$ can therefore be rewritten:

$$n + \frac{2}{3}n = 5$$
$$\frac{5}{3}n = 5$$
$$n = 3$$

Question 8   C
See: GM 1.5
First combine the exponents where possible, and rearrange so they are all positive:

$$((y^{-2/3})^{1/2}) / (x^{-1/2})$$
$$= (y^{-1/3}) / (x^{-1/2})$$
$$= (x^{1/2}) / (y^{1/3})$$

Now plug in x=4 and y=8. Notice that $4=2^2$ and $8=2^3$.

$$= (4^{1/2}) / (8^{1/3})$$
$$= (2^{(2)1/2}) / (2^{(3)1/3})$$
$$= 2^1 / 2^1$$
$$= 1.$$

Question 9   A
See: GM 3.7
When adding logarithms of the same base, combine them by multiplying the numbers in parentheses (note: an asterisk - or dot • - can be used as a multiplication symbol). In this case:

$$\log_6(24) + \log_6(9)$$
$$= \log_6(24*9)$$
$$= \log_6(216)$$
$$= \log_6(6^3)$$

Now remember, a logarithm is an exponent. The question it poses is, "the base raised to what power is equal to the number in the parentheses?" So 6 raised to what power is equal to 6^3? The answer is, of course, 3.

Question 10   B
See: GM 3.7
First isolate the x terms on one side and all other terms on the other side of the equation.

$$\log_{10}(70) = x + \log_{10}(7)$$
$$\log_{10}(70) - \log_{10}(7) = x$$

Now combine the logarithms. When subtracting logarithms of the same base, combine them by dividing the numbers in parentheses.

$\log_{10}(70/7) = x$

$\log_{10}(10) = x$

$1 = x.$

Question 11   B

See: GM 1.5, 3.7

A coefficient multiplied by a logarithm can by brought inside the parentheses as an exponent.

$$x(\log_b(y)) + y(\log_b(y))$$
$$= \log_b(y^x) + \log_b(y^y)$$
$$= \log_b(y^x y^y)$$
$$= \log_b(y^{x+y}).$$

Question 12   D

See: GM 1.5, 3.7

The natural log has base e. Note that a logarithm of 1, no matter what the base, is equal to 0. And a log of its own base is equal to 1. So:

$$\ln(e^3)\log_3(27) + \ln(1)\ln(e)$$
$$= \ln(e^3)\log_3(27) + 0*1$$
$$= 3\log_3(27)$$
$$= 3(3)$$
$$= 9.$$

Question 13   D

See: GM 3.5, 3.7, 3.8

There are some useful pieces of information to notice that will help you answer this problem.

- What is the x and/or y intercept, if there is one?

- Where is the vertical asymptote? [Note: an 'asymptote' refers to a line that keeps approaching a given curve but does not meet the curve at any finite distance (GM 5.2.3C).] And does the curve approach positive or negative infinity?

In this case there is no x intercept, but the y intercept is at the point (0, -1). Plugging x = 0 into the given equations we can rule out all options except $y = -(2^x)$, so that is the solution.

Question 14   D

See: GM 3.7, 3.8

There are some useful pieces of information to notice that will help you answer this type of problem.

- What is the x and/or y intercept, if there is one?

- Where is the vertical asymptote? And does the curve approach positive or negative infinity?

The x and y intercept of this graph are the same, at (0, 0). Plugging in y = 0 to the given equations we can eliminate all but y = ln (x+1) and y = -ln (x+1). Next find the vertical asymptote. It appears to be located at x = -1, and the curve approaches negative infinity. When x is small, -ln (x+1) is positive, so it cannot be the solution. Thus the graph represents y = ln (x+1).

Question 15   B

See: GM 3.7, 3.8

You can think of pH and H as corresponding to y and x respectively. So the graph you are considering is $y = -\log_{10}(x)$, the logarithm graph reflected about the x-axis. So the slopes along the curve are the opposite of the positive logarithm graph. Therefore when we decrease the value of x (moving right to left along the axis) the slope increases. If you are unsure of your solution, plug in test points to check. To see a positive log graph: GM 3.8.

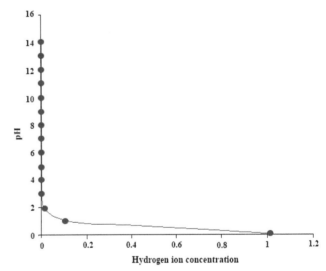

Question 1   B

See: GM 4.2, 4.2.3

Using the given information to write an equation, we have:

$$\pi r^2 = 144\pi$$

We need the value of the radius to find the circumference, so we solve for r:

$$r^2 = \frac{144\pi}{\pi}$$
$$r = \sqrt{144}$$
$$r = 12$$

The formula for the circumference of a circle gives us:

$$2\pi r = 2\pi(12) = 24\pi$$

Question 2   D

See: GM 4.2, 4.2.3

The length of the radius is half of the length of the diameter, which is $d = \sqrt{(2-2)^2 + (-3-5)^2} = \sqrt{0+64} = 8$ units long. The radius is therefore equal to 4.

Question 3   D

See: GM 4.2, 4.2.2

Triangle A has an area of $\frac{bh}{2} = 3(12m^2) = 36m^2$ which means that its base times its height is equal to 72 square feet. The base and height of all 45°–45°–90° triangles are the same, so (b × h)/2 = (b × b)/2 = 36. Solving for b gives us b = $\sqrt{72}$. Using the Pythagorean Theorem, we can solve for the hypotenuse. $h^2 = (\sqrt{72})^2 + (\sqrt{72})^2 = 144$, therefore h = $\sqrt{144} = 12$.

Question 4   C

See: GM 4.1, 4.1.3

The angle PQD has a measure equal to that of the given angle, 30 degrees, because the highways are parallel and the road forms a transversal across them. The hypotenuse of the right triangle PQD is 2 km long, and the alley, which forms the leg of the triangle that is opposite angle PQD, has a length of

$$(2 \text{ km}) \sin(30°) = 1 \text{ km}$$

Don't worry if you did not know or remember how to solve a problem with the sine function. As long as you understand the set up for the solution, that's fine for now. We will discuss trigonometric functions in the next GAMSAT Math chapter and again in Physics Chapter 1.

Question 5   A

See: GM 4.2, 4.2.1, 4.2.3

The relationship between the length of a side *s* and the length of the diagonal d of a square is (i.e. because the diagonal cuts the square into 45-45-90 triangles and remembering the ratio of that triangle's sides):

$$d = s\sqrt{2}$$

The length of a side of the given square is therefore

$$s = \frac{d}{\sqrt{2}} = \frac{5}{\sqrt{2}}$$

This is always the length of the diagonal of the inscribed circle, which has a radius of length $\frac{5}{\sqrt{2}} \div 2 = \frac{5}{2\sqrt{2}}$. The area of the circle is therefore

$$\pi\left(\frac{5}{2\sqrt{2}}\right)^2 = \frac{25\pi}{8}$$

Question 6   D

See: GM 4.2, 4.2.3

Represent the areas of the large and small circle by πr_L^2 and πr_S^2, respectively. 25% is equivalent to $\frac{1}{4}$, so

$$\pi r_S^2 = \frac{1}{4}(\pi r_L^2)$$

$$r_S^2 = \frac{1}{4}r_L^2$$

$$\sqrt{r_S^2} = \sqrt{\frac{1}{4}r_L^2}$$

$$r_S = \frac{1}{2}r_L$$

and the ratio of the radii is $\dfrac{r_S}{r_L} = \dfrac{\frac{1}{2}r_L}{r_L} = \dfrac{1}{2}$.

Question 7   D

See: GM 4.1, 4.1.1, 4.2.3

$(0,0)$, $(10,0)$, and any given point except $(5,0)$ can be connected by an arc, which can form part of a circle. $(0,0)$, $(10,0)$, and $(5,0)$ can only be connected by a line, which can never form part of a circle.

Question 8   D

See: GM 4.3.1; deduce

Because it is cube-like, we need to multiply 3 different sides together in order to get the volume. Consider that if you were to just multiply the 3 sides together, you would get a volume which includes the actual cardboard (i.e. calculating the volume that way would get a result which is somewhat greater than the actual volume INSIDE the box). However, if we were to examine the length for example, the space available inside the box would be less than the length of the box because of the thickness at BOTH ends.

Thus the inside measurements are reduced by the thickness of each side:

- The inside length will be l-2t
- The inside width will be w-2t
- The inside height will be h-2t

Thus the space (volume) inside the box = (l - 2t) x (w - 2t) x (h - 2t)

This style of reasoning including the development of an equation (during the exam!) that you have never seen before is a common though infrequent part of the real GAMSAT.

Note: Answer choice A is a reasonable approximation but answer choice D is the best answer among the choice provided. Part of the challenge of multiple choice exams is getting in the habit of identifying the best among options.

Question 1   B

See: GM 5.2, 5.2.1
A circle covers a total of 2π radians, and

$$\frac{\frac{8\pi}{5}}{2\pi} = \frac{4}{5}$$

which is equivalent to 80%.

Question 2   A

See: GM 5.5

$$-\cos\left(\frac{\pi}{2}\right) = \cos\left(\frac{\pi}{2}\right) = 0$$

Question 3   C

See: GM 5.1, 5.1.3, 5.3, 5.3.3
In a right triangle, the tangent of an angle represents the ratio of sides $\dfrac{opposite}{adjacent}$, so the given values form the proportion

$\dfrac{3}{2} = \dfrac{12}{x}$, where x is the side adjacent the angle in question. Cross-multiplication gives us $3x = 24$, or $x = 8$, and we can fnd the length of the hypotenuse using the Pythagorean Theorem:

$$12^2 + 8^2 = c^2$$
$$144 + 64 = c^2$$
$$\sqrt{208} = c$$
$$\sqrt{4 \times 4 \times 13} = c$$
$$4\sqrt{13} = c$$

Question 4   D

See: GM 4.1.3, 5.2, 5.2.3
The cosine of an angle is equal to the sine of its complement.
$\dfrac{\pi}{6}$, or $\left(\dfrac{\pi}{6}\right)\left(\dfrac{180°}{\pi}\right) = 30°$, is the complement of $\dfrac{\pi}{3} = 60°$.

Question 1   B

See: GM 6.1.1
There are four red marbles, and a total of 4 red + 6 blue = 10 marbles, so the probability is $\dfrac{4}{10}$.

Question 2   D

See: GM 6.1, 6.1.2
With a total of 10 balls and 6 yellow balls, the probability that the first ball is yellow is $\dfrac{6}{10} = \dfrac{3}{5}$. After the first ball is chosen, there are 9 left, of which 4 are green. The probability of choosing a green ball at this point is therefore $\dfrac{4}{9}$. The total probability is $\left(\dfrac{3}{5}\right)\left(\dfrac{4}{9}\right) = \dfrac{4}{15}$

Question 3   D

See: GM 6.3, 6.3.4
Multiply all possible choices: $3 \times 2 \times 4 = 24$

Question 4   A

See: GM 6.3.2
The 2516 residents represent 68% of the total number of residents x:

$$2516 = 0.68x = (2/3)x \text{ (approx.)}$$
$$x = 2516/(2/3) = (2516 \times 3)/2 = 7548/2 = 3774$$

Question 5   C

See: GM 6.2, 6.2.1
If the third student takes x minutes to complete the test:

$$\frac{41 + 37 + x}{3} = 35$$
$$78 + x = 105$$
$$x = 27$$

Question 6   D

See: GM 6.3.4
There are 4 different book colors, so there are 4 different choices for books to shelve on Monday. There are only 3 choices on Tuesday. On Wednesday, the rest of the books will be shelved, so there is only 1 choice. This gives a total of $4 \times 3 \times 1 = 12$ different ways to shelve the books.

Question 7   D

See: GM 6.1, 6.1.2
A die has a total of 6 possible sides. There is only one side that displays a 3, so the probability of rolling a 3 is $\frac{1}{6}$. Similarly, the probability of rolling any other number is also $\frac{1}{6}$. The probability of rolling a 1 or a 2 is the sum of their individual probabilities: $\frac{1}{6} + \frac{1}{6} = \frac{1}{3}$. Because this probability is independent of the probability of first rolling a 3, we multiply the results to get the total probability: $\left(\frac{1}{6}\right)\left(\frac{1}{3}\right) = \frac{1}{18}$.

$= P2 + \rho gh2 + 1/2\ \rho v22$

$= P2 + \rho gh2 + 1/2\ \rho v22$

$= P2 + \rho gh2 + 1/2\ \rho v22$

$v = \sqrt{600} = \sqrt{6(100)} = 10\sqrt{6} = 24\ m/s$

$Ek = 1/2$

$v = \sqrt{600} = \sqrt{6(100)} = 10\sqrt{6} = 24\ m/s$

$Ek = 1/2\ mv2.$

$P1 + \rho gh1 + 1/2\ \rho v12$

$P1 + \rho gh1 + 1/2\ \rho v12$

$Y = \dfrac{(F/A)}{(\Delta l/l)} = \dfrac{F \times l}{A\,\Delta l}$

$ET = Ek + Ep = 1/2mv2 + mgh$

$) = \sqrt{2} = 14 m/s$

$ET = Ek + Ep = 1/2mv2 + mgh$

$v = \sqrt{2(300) - 2(}$

$= P2 + \rho gh2 + 1/2\ \rho v22$

$v = \sqrt{2(300) - 2(10)20} = \sqrt{2(100)} = \sqrt{2} = 14$

GAMSAT-prep.com

PHYSICS
PART III.B: PHYSICAL SCIENCES

IMPORTANT: The beginning of each science chapter provides guidelines as to what you should Memorize, Understand and what is Not Required. These are guides to get you a top score without getting lost in the details. Our guides have been determined from an analysis of all ACER materials plus student surveys. Additionally, the original owner of this book gets a full year access to many online features described in the Preface and Introduction including an online Forum where each chapter can be discussed.

Memorize	Understand	Not Required*
Trigonometric functions: definitions Pythagorean theorem Define: displacement, velocity, acceleration Equations: acceleration, kinematics	* Scalar vs. vector * Add, subtract, resolve vectors * Determine common values of functions * Conversion of the angle to other units * Displacement, velocity, acceleration (avg. and instant.) including graphs	* Knowledge beyond introductory-level (A-level/Leaving Certificate/Year 12) course * Any derivatives with or without vectors * Complex vector systems

GAMSAT-Prep.com

Introduction

Translational motion is the movement of an object (or particle) through space without turning (rotation). Displacement, velocity and acceleration are key vectors — specified by magnitude and direction — often used to describe translational motion. Being able to manipulate and resolve vectors is critical for problem solving in GAMSAT Physics.

Whether science or non-science background: (1) please complete the GAMSAT Math chapters prior to starting Physics; (2) closely consider information underlined, in italics, in red boxes or highlighted in yellow; (3) go to your online access account and consider: watching videos, printing our GAMSAT Physics Equation List or making your own, and irrespective of your initial comfort level, try some online practice questions because they will begin with the basics and then work up to challenge you.

Additional Resources

Free Online Q&A + Forum

GAMSAT-prep.com Videos

Flashcards

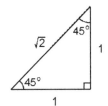

Special Guest

1.1 Scalars and Vectors

Scalars, such as <u>speed</u>, have magnitude only and are specified by a number with a unit (55 miles/hour). Scalars obey the rules of ordinary algebra (i.e. GM Chap. 2 and 3). *Vectors*, like <u>velocity</u>, have both magnitude **and** direction (100 km/hour, west). Vectors are represented by arrows where: i) the length of the arrow indicates the magnitude of the vector, and ii) the arrowhead indicates the direction of the vector. Vectors obey the special rules of vector algebra. Thus vectors can be moved in space but their orientation must be kept the same.

Addition of Vectors: Two vectors **a** and **b** can be added geometrically by drawing them to a common scale and placing them head to tail. The vector connecting the tail of **a** to the head of **b** is the sum or <u>resultant</u> vector **r**.

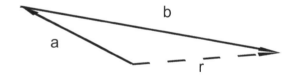

Figure III.B.1.1: The vector sum a + b = r.

Subtraction of Vectors: To subtract the vector **b** from **a**, reverse the direction of **b** then add to **a**.

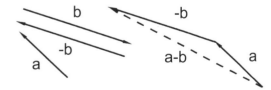

Figure III.B.1.2: The vector difference
a - b = a + (-b).

Resolution of Vectors: Perpendicular projections of a vector can be made on a coordinate axis. Thus the vector **a** can be *resolved* into its x-component (a_x) and its y-component (a_y).

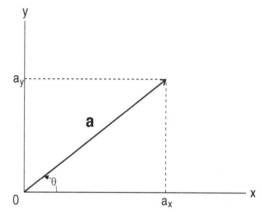

Figure III.B.1.3: The resolution of a vector into its scalar components in a coordinate system.

Analytically, the resolution of vector **a** is as follows:

$$a_x = \mathbf{a}\ cos\ \theta \quad \text{and} \quad a_y = \mathbf{a}\ sin\ \theta$$

Conversely, given the components, we can reconstruct vector **a**:

$$\mathbf{a} = \sqrt{a_x^2 + a_y^2} \quad \text{and} \quad tan\ \theta = a_y / a_x$$

If you have not used vectors before, please go online and try the first few PHY Chapter 1 practice questions before you continue.

We will now foreshadow the scalar and vector quantities that we will be exploring over the 12 Physics chapters. You may already have a sense as to the logic of the classification but, if not, after you have completed Physics, please return to this section to confirm.

Examples of Scalar Quantities
distance, speed, time, temperature, mass, area, volume, energy, entropy, electric charge

Examples of Vector Quantities
displacement, velocity, acceleration, force, momentum, gravitational field, electrical field

1.1.1 Trigonometric Functions

The power in trigonometric functions lies in their ability to relate an angle to the ratio of scalar components or *sides* of a triangle. These functions may be defined as follows:

$$sin\ \theta = opp/hyp = y/r$$

$$cos\ \theta = adj/hyp = x/r$$

[*opp* = *the length of the side opposite* angle θ, *adj* = the length of the side *adjacent* to angle θ, *hyp* = the length of the *hypotenuse*]

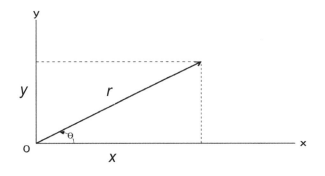

Thus sine (*rsin* θ) gives the *y*-component and cosine (*rcos* θ) gives the x-component of vector r. The tangent function (*tan* θ) and two important trigonometric identities relate sine and cosine:

$$tan\ \theta = sin\ \theta/cos\ \theta = opp/adj = y/x$$

$$sin^2\ \theta + cos^2\ \theta = 1$$

and

$$sin\ 2\theta = 2\ sin\ \theta\ cos\ \theta$$

Other functions of very little importance for GAMSAT physics include: cotangent (*cot* θ = *x/y*), secant (*sec* θ = *r/x*) and cosecant (*csc* θ = *r/y*).

The Pythagorean Theorem relates the sides of the right angle triangle according to the following:

$$r^2 = x^2 + y^2.$$

1.1.2 Common Values of Trigonometric Functions

There are special angles which produce standard values of the trigonometric functions. Several of the values are derived from the unit circle (GM 5.2) and can be resolved using the following triangles (consider practicing to confirm):

θ	$sin\ \theta$	$cos\ \theta$	$tan\ \theta$
$0°$	0	1	0
$30°$	$1/2$	$\sqrt{3}/2$	$1/\sqrt{3}$
$45°$	$1/\sqrt{2}$	$1/\sqrt{2}$	1
$60°$	$\sqrt{3}/2$	$1/2$	$\sqrt{3}$
$90°$	1	0	∞
$180°$	0	-1	0

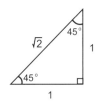 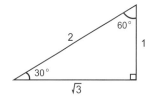

Table III.B.1.1:
Common values of trigonometric functions.
The angle θ may be given in radians (R) where $2\pi^R = 360° = 1$ revolution. Recall $\sqrt{3} \approx 1.7$, $\sqrt{2} \approx 1.4$.

Note that $1° = 60$ arcminutes, 1 arcminute = 60 arcseconds. These conversions do not need to be memorized because they would be given on the exam if needed.

Each trigonometric function (i.e. sine) contains an inverse function (i.e. sin^{-1}), where if $sin\ \theta = x$, $\theta = sin^{-1} x$. Thus $cos\ 60° = 1/2$, and $60° = cos^{-1}(1/2)$. Some texts denote the inverse function with "arc" as a prefix. Thus $arcsec\ (2) = sec^{-1}(2)$.

1.2 Distance and Displacement

Distance is the amount of separation between two points in space. It has a magnitude but no direction. It is a scalar quantity and is always positive.

Displacement of an object between two points is the difference between the final position and the initial position of the object in a given referential system. Thus, a displacement has an origin, a direction and a magnitude. It is a vector.

The sign of the coordinates of the vector displacement depends on the system under study and the chosen referential system. The sign will be positive (+) if the system is moving towards the positive axis of the referential system and negative (-) if not.

The units of distance and displacement are expressed in length units such as *feet (ft), meters (m), miles* and *kilometers (km)*. The International System of Units (SI), the standard for the GAMSAT and science in general, uses the meter for length (*see* GM 2.1.3).

Speed is the rate of change of distance with respect to time. It is a scalar quantity, it has a magnitude but no direction, like distance, and it is always positive.

Velocity is the rate of change of displacement with respect to time. It is a vector, and like the displacement, it has a direction and a magnitude.   Its value depends on the position of the object. The sign of the coordinates of the vector velocity is the same as that of the displacement.

The instantaneous velocity of a system at a given time is the slope of the graph of the displacement of that system vs. time at that time.The magnitude of the velocity decreases if the vector velocity and the vector acceleration have opposite directions.

The units of speed and velocity are expressed in length divided by time such as *feet/sec., meters/sec. (m/s)* and *miles/hour.*

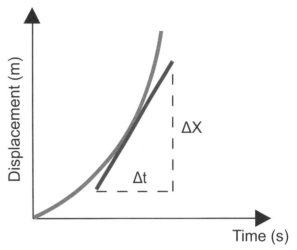

Figure III.B.1.4: Displacement vs. time. The capital letter X denotes displacement as opposed to referring to the x-axis (small letter x) which is time.

Dimensional Analysis: remember from GAMSAT Math (GM 3.5.1) that a slope is "rise over run" meaning it is the change in the y-axis divided by the change in the x-axis. So, when we consider the units in the graph above, we get m/s for the slope which is velocity in SI units (compare with the graph analysis of the velocity vs. time graph in GM 3.5.4).

1.4 Acceleration

Acceleration (a) is the rate of change of the velocity (v) with respect to time (t):

$$a = v/t$$

Like the velocity, it is a vector and it has a direction and a magnitude.

The sign of the vector acceleration depends on the net force applied to the system and the chosen referential system. The units of acceleration are expressed as velocity divided by time such as meters/sec^2 (m/s^2; SI units). The term for negative acceleration is deceleration.

1.4.1 Average and Instantaneous Acceleration

The average acceleration a_v between two instants t and t′ = t + Δt, measures the result of the increase in the speed divided by the time difference,

$$a_v = \frac{v' - v}{\Delta t}$$

The instantaneous acceleration can be determined either by calculating the **slope** (*see* GM 3.5.4) of a velocity vs. time graph at any time, or by taking the limit when Δt approaches zero of the preceding expression.

$$a_v = \lim_{\Delta t \to 0} \frac{v' - v}{\Delta t}$$

Math involving "limits" does not exist on the GAMSAT. So let's discuss what this definition is describing in informal terms. The limit is the value of the change in velocity over the change in time as the time approaches 0. It's like saying that the change in velocity is happening in an instant. This allows us to talk about the acceleration in that incredibly fast moment: the instantaneous acceleration which can be determined graphically.

Consider the following events illustrated in the graph (Fig. III.B.1.4): your car starts at rest (0 velocity and time = 0); you steadily accelerate out of the parking lot (the change in velocity increases over time = acceleration); you are driving down the street at constant velocity (change in velocity = 0 and thus acceleration is 0 divided by the change in time which means: a = 0); you see a cat dart across the street safely which made you slow down temporarily (change in velocity is negative thus negative acceleration which, by definition, is deceleration); you now enter the on-ramp for the highway so your velocity is now increasing at a faster and faster rate (increasing acceleration). You can examine the instantaneous acceleration at any one point (or instant) during the period that your acceleration is increasing.

To determine the displacement (*not* distance), take the area under the graph or curve. To calculate area: a rectangle is base (b) times height (h); a triangle is ½b × h; and for a curve, they can use graph paper and expect you would count the boxes under the curve to estimate the area (GM 3.5.4, Question 2).

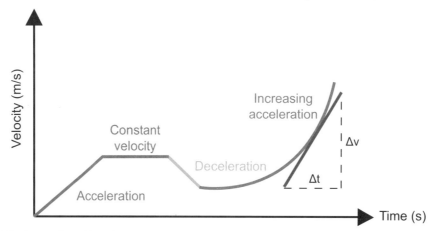

Figure III.B.1.4: Velocity vs. time. Note that at constant velocity, the slope and thus the acceleration are both equal to zero.

1.5 Uniformly Accelerated Motion

The magnitude and direction of the acceleration of a system are solely determined by the exterior forces acting upon the system. If the magnitude of these forces is constant, the magnitude of the acceleration will be constant and the resulting motion is a *uniformly accelerated motion*. The initial displacement, the velocity and the acceleration at any given time contribute to the over-all displacement of the system:

$x = x_0$ – displacement due to the initial displacement x_0.

$x = v_0 t$ – displacement due to the initial velocity v_0 at time t.

$x = \frac{1}{2}at^2$ – displacement due to the acceleration at time t.

The total displacement of the uniformly-accelerated motion is given by the following formula:

$$x = x_0 + v_0 t + \frac{1}{2}at^2$$

The translational motion is the motion of the center of gravity (PHY 2.1) of a system through space, illustrated by the above equation.

1.6 Equations of Kinematics

Kinematics is the study of objects in motion with respect to space and time. There are three related equations which must be memorized. The first is above (PHY 1.5), the others are:

$$v = v_0 + at \quad \text{and}$$
$$v^2 = v_0^2 + 2ax$$

where v is the final velocity; we will put these equations to use in PHY 2.6.

Reminder: Chapter review questions are available online for the original owner of this textbook. Doing practice questions will help clarify concepts and ensure that you study in a targeted way. First, register at gamsat-prep.com, then login and click on GAMSAT Textbook Owners in the right column so you can use your Online Access Card to have access to the Lessons section.

No science background? Consider watching the relevant videos at gamsat-prep.com and you have support at gamsat-prep.com/forum. Don't forget to check the Index at the beginning of this book to see which chapters are **HIGH**, **MEDIUM** and **LOW** relative importance for the GAMSAT.

Your online access continues for one full year from your online registration.

FORCE, MOTION, AND GRAVITATION
Chapter 2

Memorize	Understand	Not Required*
efine with units: weight, mass ewton's laws, Law of Gravitation quation for uniformly accelerated motion	* Mass, weight, center of gravity * Newton's laws * Law of Gravitation, free fall motion * Projectile motion equations and calculations	* Knowledge beyond introductory-level (A-level/Leaving Certificate/Year 12) course * Memorizing values for K, G

GAMSAT-Prep.com

Introduction ▮▮▮▮

Force is a vector (often a push or pull) that can cause a mass to change velocity thus motion. Forces can be due to gravity, magnetism or anything that causes a mass to accelerate. Nuclear forces (strong) are far greater than electrostatic forces (opposite charges attract), which in turn are far greater than gravitational forces (one of the weakest forces in nature).

Additional Resources

| Free Online Q&A + Forum | GAMSAT-prep.com Videos | Flashcards | Special Guest |

2.1 Mass, Center of Mass, Weight

The mass (m) of an object is its measure of inertia. It is the measure of the capacity of that object to remain motionless or to move with a constant velocity if the sum of the forces acting upon it is zero. This definition of inertia is derived from Newton's First Law.

The *center of mass* of an object is a point whose motion can be described like the motion of a particle through space. The center of mass of an object always has the simplest motion of all the points of that object.

The center of gravity (COG) is also the center of mass seen as the center of application of all the gravitational forces acting on the object. For example, for a uniform plank hanging horizontally, the COG is at half the length of the plank.

The COG can be determined experimentally by suspending an object by a string at different points and noting that the direction of the string passes through the COG.

The intersection of the projected lines in the different suspensions is the COG.

An object is in *stable equilibrium* if the COG is as low as possible and any change in orientation will lead to an elevation of the COG. An object is in *unstable equilibrium* if the COG is high relative to the support point or surface and any change in orientation will lead to a lowering of the COG.

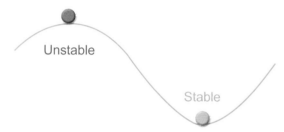

The *weight* is a force (i.e. newtons, pounds). It is a vector unlike the *mass* which is a scalar (i.e. kilograms, slugs). The weight is proportional to the mass. It is the product of the mass by the vector gravitational acceleration g.

$$W = m \times g$$

2.2 Newton's Second Law

Newton's Second Law, also called the fundamental dynamic relation, states that the sum of all the exterior forces acting upon the center of mass of a system is equal to the product of the mass of the system by the acceleration of its center of mass.

Therefore, if there is a net force, the object must accelerate. It is a vectorial equality which asserts that <u>a net force against an object *must* result in acceleration</u>:

$$\Sigma F = m \times a$$

It is important to note that for a system in complex motion, Newton's Second Law can only determine the acceleration of the center of mass. It does not give any indication about the motion of the other parts of the system.

Whereas, for a system in translational motion, Newton's Second Law gives the acceleration of the system.

In your daily life, you would already have the sense that objects with a greater mass (m) require a greater force (F) to get it to move with increasing speed (a). If you maintain a net force on an object, it will not only move, it must accelerate. We will be exploring more consequences of Newton's Second Law both in this and later chapters.

2.3 Newton's Third Law

For every action there is an equal and opposite reaction. If one object exerts a force, F, on a second object, the second object exerts a force, F', on the first object. F and F' have opposite direction but the same magnitude.

One conclusion would be that forces are found in pairs. Consider the time you sit in a chair. Your body exerts a force downward (mg) and that chair needs to exert an equal force upward (the normal force N) or

the chair will collapse. There is symmetry. Acting forces encounter other forces in the opposite direction. Consider shooting a cannonball. When the explosion fires the cannonball through the air, the cannon is pushed backward. The force pushing the ball out is equal to the force pushing the cannon back, but the effect on the cannon is less noticeable because it has a much larger mass and it may be restrained. Similarly, a gun experiences a "kick" backwards when a bullet is fired forward.

2.4 The Law of Gravitation

The Law of Gravitation states that there is a force of attraction existing between any two bodies of masses m_1 and m_2. The force is proportional to the product of the masses and inversely proportional to the square of the distance between them (we explored a GAMSAT-level practice question based on the Law of Gravitation in GM 2.2.1).

$$F = K_G(m_1m_2/r^2)$$

r is the distance between the bodies; K_G is the universal constant of gravitation, and its value depends on the units being used.

2.5 Free Fall Motion

The free fall motion of an object is the upward or downward vertical motion of that object with reference to the earth.

The motion is always uniformly accelerated with the acceleration g: vertical, directed towards the center of the earth and the magnitude is considered constant during the free fall motion.

Also, during the free fall motion, the air resistance is considered negligible. The equation of the motion can easily be derived from Newton's Second Law.

$$\Sigma F = ma$$

Where ΣF represents all the forces acting on the object, m is the mass of the object and a is the acceleration of the center of mass of the object. Hence, a can be replaced by g since $a = g$ by definition. In the free fall motion, the only force acting on the object is the gravitational force, which gives the following equality:

$$K_G m_{object} \frac{M_{earth}}{r^2_{earth}} = m_{object}\, g$$

dividing both sides by m_{object} we get :

$$g = K_G \frac{M_{earth}}{r^2_{earth}}$$

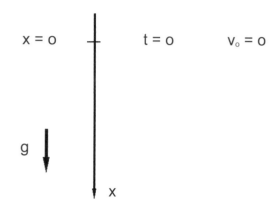

Figure III.B.2.1: Free fall motion.

The values of g are: 32 ft/s^2 (Imperial units), 980 cm/s^2 (CGS units), or 9.8 m/s^2 (**SI** units). The equation for uniformly accelerated motion is applicable by replacing a by g:

$$x = x_0 + v_0 t + 1/2\, gt^2$$

$$v = gt$$

$$a = g$$

Before doing any calculation, the reference point and a positive direction must be chosen. In the free fall of an actual object, the value of g is modified by the buoyancy of air and resistance of air. This results in a *drag force* which depends on the location on earth, shape and size of the object, and the velocity of the object (as free fall velocity increases, the drag force increases). When the drag force reaches the force of gravity, the object reaches a final velocity called the terminal velocity and continues to fall at that velocity.

The projectile motion is the motion of any object fired or launched at some angle α from the horizontal (Figure III.B.2.2). The motion defines a parabola (*see* GM 3.5.2) in the plane *O-x-y* that contains the initial (*original*) vector velocity v_o.

The motion can be decomposed into two distinct motions: a vertical (*x*) component, affected by *g*, and a horizontal (*y*) component, independent of *g*. Algebra and trigonometry help to resolve vectors into their *x* and *y* components, which simplifies the problem (PHY 2.6.1).

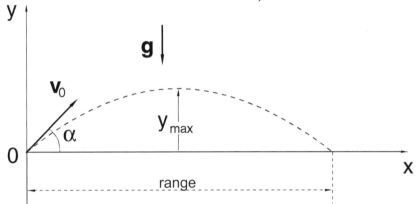

Figure III.B.2.2: Projectile motion.

Vertical component (free fall)
- initial speed : $V_{oy} = V_o \sin α$
- displacement at time *t*: $y = V_{oy}t + 1/2gt^2$
- speed at any time *t*: $V_y = V_{oy} + gt$

Horizontal component (linear with constant speed)
- initial speed : $V_{ox} = V_o \cos α$
- displacement at any time *t*: $x = V_{ox}t$
- speed at any time t: $V_x = V_{ox}$ (speed is constant)

Initial velocity

- magnitude: $|V_o| = \sqrt{V_{ox}^2 + V_{oy}^2}$

- direction: *alpha*: $\tan α = V_{oy}/V_{ox}$

- important points to consider:
1)   Neglecting air resistance, there is no acceleration in the horizontal direction: V_x is constant.
2) V_y is zero at Y_{max}, then $V_y = 0 = V_{oy} + gt_{up}$ or $-V_{oy} = gt_{up}$ can be solved for t.

3)   Also, by eliminating the variables y and t in the equations, we can get the following equality :

$$x = \frac{V_o^2 \sin 2α}{g}$$

The horizontal distance from the origin to where the object strikes the ground (= *the range*) is maximum for a given V_o when $\sin 2α = 1$, hence for $2α = (π/2)^R$ => $α = (π/4)^R$ or $α = 45$ degrees.

2.6.1 Projectile Motion Problem (Imperial units)

In the Rugby World Cup, a player kicks the ball at an angle of 30° from the horizontal with an initial speed of 75 ft/s. Assume that the ball moves in a vertical plane and that air resistance is negligible.

Given information:
- acceleration due to gravity: 32 ft/s^2
- there are 3 feet in 1 yard
- feel free to return to PHY 1.1.2 to find the solution to any function you believe would help solve this problem.

(a) *Find the time at which the ball reaches the highest point of its trajectory.*
{*key: height refers to the y-component; we can define gravity as a negative vector since it is directed downwards*}

V_y is zero at Y_{max} (= *the highest point*), thus:

$V_y = 0$, $V_o = 75$ ft/s, α = 30°, $g = -32$ ft/s^2

$V_y = V_o \sin α + g t_{up}$

Isolate t_{up}:

$t_{up} = \dfrac{V_y - V_o \sin α}{g} = \dfrac{-75(\sin 30°)}{-32}$

$= 1.2$ seconds

(b) *How high does the ball go?*

$Y_{max} = V_o (\sin α) t_{up} + 1/2 g t_{up}^2$

$Y_{max} = 75(\sin 30°)1.2 + 1/2(-32)(1.2)^2 =$ 22 feet

(c) *How long is the ball in the air and what is its range?*
{*key: time is the same for x- and y-components, range = x-component*}

Once the ball strikes the ground its vertical displacement y = 0, thus:

$y = 0 = V_o (\sin α) t + 1/2 g t^2$

Divide through by t then isolate:

$t = 2V_o(\sin α)/g = 2.4$ seconds.

Since t = $2t_{up}$, we can conclude that the time required for the ball to go up to Y_{max} is the same as the time required to come back down: 1.2 seconds in either direction.

The range $x = V_o(\cos α)t$

$x = 75(\cos 30°)2.4 ≈ 150$ feet

or

$x ≈ 150$ ft (1 yd/ 3 ft) = 50 yards

{*Had the player kicked the ball at 45° from the horizontal he would have maximized his range. He should be benched for not having done his physics!*}

(d) *What is the velocity of the ball as it strikes the ground?*

{*key: velocity* is the resultant vector of V_x and V_y - the final velocities in the x and y directions}

$$V_x = V_o\cos \alpha = 75(\cos 30°) = 65 \text{ ft/s}$$

$$V_y = V_o\sin \alpha + gt$$

$$= 75(\sin 30°) + (-32)(2.4) = -39 \text{ ft/s}$$

$$V = \sqrt{V^2_x + V^2_y} = \sqrt{(65)^2 + (-39)^2}$$

$$= \sqrt{(13 \times 5)^2 + (13 \times -3)^2}$$

$$V = 13\sqrt{(5)^2 + (-3)^2} = 13\sqrt{34}$$

To estimate $\sqrt{34}$ we must first recognize that the answer must be at least 5 ($5^2 = 25$) but closer to 6 ($6^2 = 36$). Try squaring 5.7, 5.8, 5.9. Squaring 5.8 is the closest estimate (= *33.6*), thus

$$V = 13(5.8) = 75 \text{ ft/s.}$$

Please note:
- With no air resistance and a symmetric problem (the ball is launched and returns to the same vertical point), the initial and final speeds are the same (75 ft/s).
- Usually ACER will use SI units in GAMSAT problems, but many problems on the real GAMSAT are solved using dimensional analysis, with or without SI units.
- Please be sure you can do all the preceding calculations efficiently. To learn more about SI units, *see* GM 2.1.3.

Go online to GAMSAT-prep.com for free chapter review Q&A and forum.

Memorize	Understand	Not Required*
* Centripetal force and acceleration * Circumference and area of a circle	* Equations: f_{max}, μ. * Static vs. kinetic friction * Resolving vectors * Uniform circular motion * Solve pulley system, free body diagram	* Knowledge beyond introductory-level (A-level/Leaving Certificate/Year 12) course * Memorizing values of μ

GAMSAT-Prep.com

Introduction ▮▮▮▮

Particle dynamics is concerned with the physics of motion. Among other topics, particle dynamics includes Newton's laws, frictional forces, and problems dealing with incline planes, uniform circular motion and pulley systems.

Additional Resources

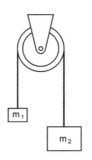

Free Online Q&A + Forum   GAMSAT-prep.com Videos   Flashcards   Special Guest

3.1 Overview

For the GAMSAT, particle dynamics is concerned with the physics of motion. Among other topics, particle dynamics inclu-des Newton's laws, frictional forces, and problems dealing with incline planes, uniform circular motion and pulley systems.

3.2 Frictional Forces

Frictional forces are nonconservative (mechanical energy is not conserved) and are caused by molecular adhesion between tangential surfaces but are independent of the area of contact of the surfaces. Frictional forces always oppose the motion. The maximal frictional force has the following expression: $f_{max} = \mu N$, where μ is the coefficient of friction and N is the normal force to the surface on which the object rests, it is the reaction of that surface against the weight of the object. Thus N always acts perpendicular to the surface.

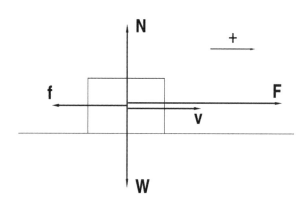

Figure III.B.3.1: Frictional force f and force normal N.

Static friction is when the object is not moving, and it must be overcome for motion to begin. The coefficient of static friction μ_s is given as :

$$\mu_s = \tan \alpha$$

where α is the angle at which the object first begins to move on an inclined plane as the angle is increased from 0 degrees to α degrees (*see Figure III.B.3.2*). There is also a coefficient of kinetic friction, μ_k, which exists when surfaces are in motion; $\mu_k < \mu_s$ always.

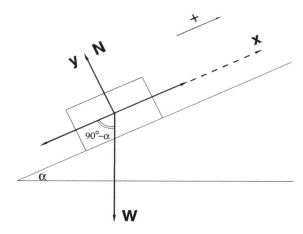

Figure III.B.3.2:
Analysis of motion on an incline. To understand the relationship of the angles in the diagram, *see* Geometry GM 4.1.3.

The weight (W) due to gravity (g) may be sufficient to cause motion if friction is overcome. The reference axes are usually chosen as shown such that one (the x) is along the surface of the incline.

Note that W is directed downward and N is directed upward but *perpendicular* to the surface of the incline (i.e. in the positive *y* direction).

3.2.1 Incline Plane Problem with Friction (SI units)

A 50 kilogram block is on an incline of 45°. The coefficient of sliding (= *kinetic*) friction between the block and the plane is 0.10. Take *g* as 9.8 m/s².

Determine the acceleration of the block. {key: *motion* is along the plane, so only the *x*-components of the force is relevant to the acceleration}

Begin with Newton's Second Law:

$$F = m \times a$$

thus

$$F_x = f_k - W\sin\alpha = \mu_k N - W\sin\alpha = m \times a$$

The force normal (*N*) can be determined by summing the forces in the y direction where the acceleration is zero:

$$F_y = N - W\cos\alpha = m \times a = 0$$

Therefore,

$$N = W\cos\alpha$$

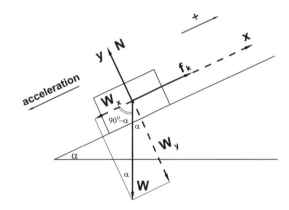

Figure III.B.3.3: Resolving the weight W into its x-component (W sinα) and its y-component (W cosα).

Solving for a and combining our first and last equations we get (*recall: W = mg*):

$$a = (\mu_k W\cos\alpha - W\sin\alpha)/m$$
$$= mg(\mu_k\cos\alpha - \sin\alpha)/m = g(\mu_k\cos\alpha - \sin\alpha)$$

Substituting the values:

$$a = 9.8 \text{ m/s}^2(0.10\cos45° - \sin45°) = -6.2 \text{ m/s}^2$$

• Thus the block accelerates at 6.2 m/s² *down* the plane. Also note that the *mass* of the block is irrelevant.

3.3 Uniform Circular Motion

In Chapter 1 we saw that acceleration is due to a change in velocity (PHY 1.4). For a particle moving in a circle at constant speed (= *uniform circular motion*), the velocity vector changes continuously in <u>direction</u> but the <u>magnitude</u> remains the same.

The velocity is always tangent to the circle and since it is always changing (i.e. *direction*) it creates an acceleration directed radially inward called the *centripetal* acceleration (a_c). The magnitude of the acceleration a_c is given by v^2/r where r is the radius of the circle.

Every accelerated particle must have a force acting on it according to Newton's Second Law. Thus we can calculate the *centripetal* force,

$$F_c = ma_c = mv^2/r.$$

The centripetal force can be produced in many ways: a taut string which is holding a ball at the end that is spinning in a circle (Fig. III.B.3.4a); a radially directed frictional force like when a car drives around a curve on an unbanked road; a contact force exerted by another body like driving around a curve on a banked road (Fig. III.B.3.4b, c) or like the wall of an amusement park rotor.

Any particle moving in a circle with *non-uniform* speed will experience both centripetal <u>and</u> tangential forces and accelerations. {Reminder: the circumference of a circle is $2\pi r$ and the area is πr^2, GM 4.2.3}

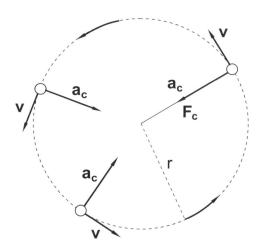

Figure III.B.3.4a: Uniform Circular Motion.

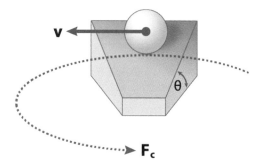

Figure III.B.3.4b: A ball in uniform circular motion on a banked curve at angle θ from the horizontal, analogous to driving on a banked, slippery road. The ball will slide to the center unless it travels fast enough (e.g. roulette).

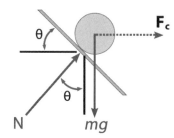

Figure III.B.3.4c: The net force on the ball due to vector addition of the normal force N exerted by the road and vertical force mg due to gravity must equal the centripetal force F_c to continue to travel the circular path.

3.4 Pulley Systems

Consider two unequal masses connected by a string which passes over a frictionless, massless pulley (*see* Figure III.B.3.5). Let us determine the following parameters: i) the tension T in the string which is a force and ii) the acceleration of the masses given that m_2 is greater than m_1.

Always begin by drawing vector or *free-body* diagrams of a problem. The position of each mass will lie at the origin O of their respective axes. Now we assign positivity or negativity to the directions of motion. We can arbitrarily define the upward direction as positive. Thus if the acceleration of m_1 is a then the acceleration of m_2 must be $-a$.

Using Newton's Second Law we can derive the equation of motion for m_1:

$$F = T - m_1 g = m_1 a$$

and for m_2:

$$F = T - m_2 g = - m_2 a$$

Subtracting one equation from the other eliminates T then we can solve for a:

$$a = \frac{m_2 - m_1}{m_2 + m_1} g$$

Solve for a using the equations of motion, equate the formulas, then we can solve for T:

$$T = \frac{2\, m_1 m_2}{m_1 + m_2} g$$

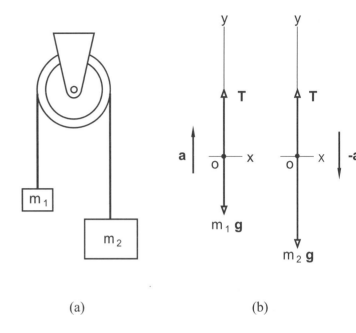

(a)   (b)

Figure III.B.3.5: A Pulley System. (a) Two unequal masses suspended by a string from a pulley (= Atwood's machine). (b) Free-body diagrams for m_1 and m_2.

Consider solving the problem yourself given $g = 10$ m/s^2 and where m_2 is 3.0 kg ($W_2 = m_2 g$ = 30 N) and m_1 is 1.0 kg ($W_1 = m_1 g = 10$ N):

$$a = \frac{3.0 - 1.0}{3.0 + 1.0} g = g/2 = 5 \text{ m/s}^2$$

and

$$T = \frac{2\,(1.0)\,(3.0)}{1.0 + 3.0} (10) = 15 \text{ N}$$

• Note that T is always between the weight of mass m_1 and that of m_2. The reason is that T must exceed $m_1 g$ to give m_1 an upward acceleration, and $m_2 g$ must exceed T to give m_2 a downward acceleration.

Go online to GAMSAT-prep.com for free chapter review Q&A and forum.

EQUILIBRIUM
Chapter 4

Memorize	Understand	Not Required*
* Definitions and equations to solve torque problems * Newton's First Law, inertia * Equations for momentum, impulse	* Solve torque, collision problems * Choosing an appropriate pivot point * Create vector diagrams * Elastic vs. inelastic vs. conservation of E. * Solve momentum problem	* Knowledge beyond introductory-level (A-level/Leaving Certificate/Year 12) course * Complex torque or collision problems * Torque as a function of time * Machine torque

GAMSAT-Prep.com

Introduction ▌▌▌▌

Equilibrium exists when a mass is at rest or moves with constant velocity. Translational (straight line) and rotational (turning) equilibria can be resolved using linear forces, torque forces, Newton's first law and inertia. Momentum is a vector that can be used to solve problems involving elastic (bouncy) or inelastic (sticky) collisions.

Additional Resources

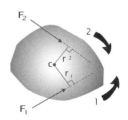

Free Online Q&A + Forum   GAMSAT-prep.com Videos   Flashcards   Special Guest

4.1 Translational, Rotational and Complex Motion

When a force acts upon an object, the object will undergo translational, rotational or complex (translational and rotational) motion.

Rotational motion of an object about an axis is the rotation of that object around that axis caused by perpendicular forces to that axis. The effective force causing rotation about an axis is the torque (L).

The torque is like a *turning force*. Consider a hinged door. If you were to apply a force F at the pivot point (*the hinge*), the door would not turn ($L=0$). If you apply the *same* force further and further from the pivot point, the turning force multiplies and the acceleration of the door increases. Thus the torque can be defined as the force applied multiplied by the perpendicular distance from the pivot point (= *lever or moment arm* = r).

$$L = (\text{force}) \times (\text{lever arm})$$

Thus according to Figure III.B.4.1:

$$L_1 = F_1 \times r_1 = \text{counterclockwise torque (1)} = \text{positive}$$

and

$$L_2 = F_2 \times r_2 = \text{clockwise torque (2)} = \text{negative.}$$

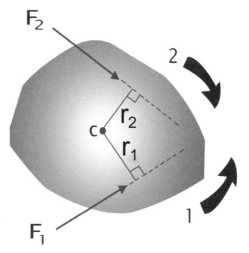

Figure III.B.4.1: Rotational Motion.

Positivity and negativity are arbitrary designations of the two opposite directions of motion. To determine the direction of rotation caused by the torque, imagine the direction the object would rotate if the force is pushing its moment arm at right angles. The net torques acting upon an object is obtained by summing the counterclockwise (+) and the clockwise (-) torques. An object is at equilibrium when the net forces and the net torques acting upon the object is zero. Thus, the object is either motionless or moving at a constant velocity due to its internal inertia.

The conditions of equilibrium are:

For translational equilibrium:

$$\Sigma F_x = 0 \text{ and } \Sigma F_y = 0$$

For rotational equilibrium:

$$\Sigma L = 0$$

In terms of translational equilibrium, the meaning of the equations can be summarized as: all upward forces equal all downward forces (y axis), all forces to the left equal all forces to the right (x axis), all forces towards you equals all forces away from you (z axis, $\sum F_z = 0$; the latter is possible, but not likely to be found as a GAMSAT question).

In terms of rotational equilibrium, if the torques sum to zero about one point in an object, they will sum to zero about any point in the object. If the point chosen as reference (= *pivot point or fulcrum*) includes the line of action of one of the forces, that force need not be included in calculating torques.

4.1.1 Torque Problem (SI units)

A 70 kg person sits 50 cm from the edge of a non-uniform plank which weighs 100 N and is 2.0 m long (*see Figure III.B.4.2*). The weight supported by point *B* is 250 N. Find the center of gravity (COG) of the plank.

{key: draw a vector diagram then choose an unknown value as the pivot point i.e. point A; see section 2.1 for a definition of COG}

(a)

(b)

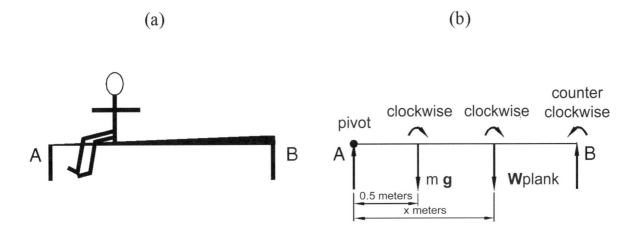

Figure III.B.4.2: Torque Problem.
(a) A person sitting on a non-uniform bench which is composed of a plank with two supports A and B. (b) Vector diagram with point A as the reference point. The torque force at point A is zero since its distance from itself is zero.

The counterclockwise torque (CCW) is given by the force at point B multiplied by its distance from the reference point A:

$$CCW = F_B r_B = 250(2.0) = 500 \text{ Nm}$$

The clockwise torques (CW) are given by the force exerted by the person (= the weight mg) multiplied by the distance from the pivot point ($r = 50$ cm $= 0.5$ m) *and* the force exerted by the plank (= the weight) multiplied by the distance from the pivot point where the weight of the plank acts (= COG):

$$CW = mgr + W(COG)$$
$$= 70(10)0.5 + 100(COG)$$
$$= 350 + 100(COG)$$

Gravity was estimated as 10 m/s². Now we have:

$$\Sigma L = CCW - CW = 500 - 350 - 100(COG) = 0$$

Isolate *COG*

$$COG = 150/100 = 1.5 \text{ m from point } A.$$

• Note that had the plank been uniform its COG would be at its center which is 1.0 m from either end.

• Had the problem requested the weight supported at point A, it would be easy to determine since $\Sigma F_y = 0$. If we define upward forces as positive, we get:

$$\Sigma F_y = F_A + F_B - mg - W_{plank} = 0$$

Isolate F_A

$$F_A = 70(10) + 100 - 250 = 550 \text{ N}.$$

4.2 Newton's First Law

Newton's First Law states that objects in motion or at rest tend to remain as such unless acted upon by an outside force. That is, objects have inertia (resistance to motion). For translational motion, the mass (m) is a measure of inertia.

For rotational motion, a quantity derived from the mass called the moment of inertia (I) is the measure of inertia. In general $I = \Sigma mr^2$ where r is the distance from the axis of rotation. However, the exact formulation depends on the structure of the object.

The momentum (M) is a <u>vector</u> quantity. The momentum of an object is the product of its mass and its velocity.

$$M = m\,v$$

Linear momentum is a measure of the tendency of an object to maintain motion in a straight line. The greater the momentum (M), the greater the tendency of the object to remain moving along a straight line in the same direction. The momentum (M) is also a measure of the force needed to stop or change the direction of the object.

The <u>impulse</u> I is a measure of the change of the momentum of an object. It is the product of the force applied by the time during which the force was applied to change the momentum.

$$I = F\,\Delta t = \Delta M$$

where F is the acting force and Δt is the elapsed time during which the force was acting. *The <u>momentum is also conserved just like energy</u>*. The total linear momentum of a system is constant when the <u>resultant external force acting on the system is zero</u>.

4.4 Collisions

During motion, objects can collide. There are two kinds of collisions: *elastic* and *inelastic*. During an elastic collision (objects rebound off each other), there is a conservation of momentum and conservation of kinetic energy. Whereas, during an inelastic collision (objects stick together), there is conservation of momentum but not conservation of kinetic energy. Kinetic energy is lost as heat or sound, so total energy is conserved.

Examples of elastic collisions include 2 rubber balls colliding, particle collisions in ideal gases, and the slingshot type gravitational interactions between satellites and planets popularized in science fiction movies. Examples of inelastic collisions include 2 cars colliding at high speed becoming stuck together and a ballistic pendulum

which can be a huge chunk of wood used to measure the speed of a moving object (i.e. bullet) which becomes completely embedded in the wood. If, however, the bullet were to emerge from the wood block, then it would be an elastic collision since the objects did not stick together.

Imagine two spheres with masses m_1 and m_2 and the velocity components before the collision v_{1i} and v_{2i} and after the collision v_{1f} and v_{2f}. If the momentum and the velocity are in the same directions, and we define that direction as positive, from the conservation of momentum we obtain:

$$m_1 v_{1i} + m_2 v_{2i} = m_1 v_{1f} + m_2 v_{2f}.$$

If the directions are not the same then each momentum must be resolved into x- and y-components as necessary.

- In the explosion of an object at rest, the total momentum of all the fragments must sum to zero because of the conservation of momentum and because the original momentum was zero.

- If one object collides with a second identical object that is at rest, there is a total transfer of kinetic energy, that is the first object comes to rest and the second object moves off with the momentum of the first one.

4.4.1 Collision Problem (CGS units)

A bullet of mass 10 g and a speed of 5.0×10^4 cm/s strikes a 700 g wooden block at rest on a very smooth surface. The bullet emerges with its speed reduced to 3.5×10^4 cm/s.

Find the resulting speed of the block. {CGS uses centimeters, grams, and seconds as units; the CGS unit of force is a dyne}.

Let m_1 = the mass of the bullet (10 g), v_{1i} = the speed of the bullet before the collision (5.0×10^4 cm/s), m_2 = the mass of the wooden block (700 g), v_{2i} = the speed of the block before the collision (0 cm/s), v_{1f} = the speed of the bullet after the collision (3.5×10^4 cm/s), and v_{2f} = the speed of the block after the collision (unknown), now we have:

$$m_1v_{1i} + m_2v_{2i} = m_1v_{1f} + m_2v_{2f}$$

Solving for v_{2f}

$$v_{2f} = (m_1v_{1i} - m_1v_{1f})/m_2$$
$$= (5.0 \times 10^5 - 3.5 \times 10^5)/(700)$$
$$= 2.1 \times 10^2 \text{ cm/s}.$$

- Note: the least precise figures that we are given in the problem contain at least two digits or significant figures. Thus our answer can not be more precise than two significant figures. The exponent 10^x is not considered when counting significant figures unless you are told that the measurement was more precise than is evident {For more on significant figures see GM 1.4.3, 1.5.2 and PHY 8.5.1}.

- Note: Sometimes, during the exam, you will want to convert to SI units (i.e. meters, kilograms, etc.; GM 2.1-2-3); however, depending on the answer choices and the nature of the equation or any constants, it may be faster to avoid any conversions. Experience with practice questions will enable you to decide efficiently.

Go online to GAMSAT-prep.com for free chapter review Q&A and forum.

Memorize	Understand	Not Required*
Define, equation, units: work Equations and units: potential energy Equations and units: kinetic energy, power	* Path independence of work done in a g field * Work-Energy Theorem * Conservation of E.; conservative forces * Solving Conservation of E. problems	* Knowledge beyond introductory-level (A-level/Leaving Certificate/Year 12) course

GAMSAT-Prep.com

Introduction ▮▮▮▮

Work and energy are used to describe how bodies or masses interact with the environment or other bodies or masses. Conservation of energy, work and power describe the forms of energy and the changes between these forms.

Additional Resources

Free Online Q&A + Forum   GAMSAT-prep.com Videos   Flashcards   Special Guest

* The real GAMSAT may have advanced level information presented (ie. in a passage) but previous knowledge of said information
is not required to answer the questions that would follow. Practice ACER and GS practice GAMSATs can help you clarify this point.

5.1 Work

The work of a force *F* on an object is the product of the force by the distance travelled by the object where the force is in the direction of the displacement.

• *Units*: both work and energy are measured in joules where 1 *joule (J)* = 1 *N* × 1 *m*. {Imperial units: the *foot-pound*, CGS units: the *dyne-centimeter* or *erg*}

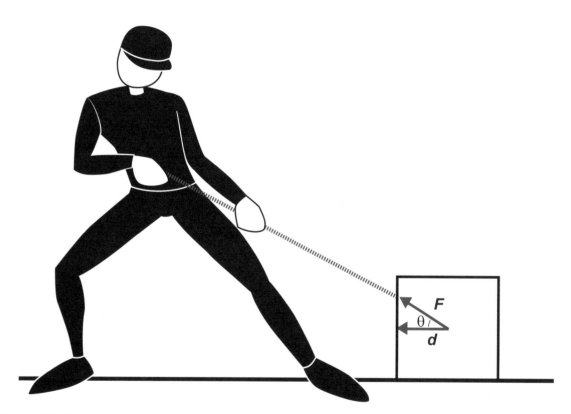

Figure III.B.5.1: Work. The displacement depends on the final and initial positions of the object. The angle θ is necessary to determine the component of a constant force F in the same direction of the displacement. Note that if F acts perpendicular to the displacement then the work *W = F d cos(90°) = 0*.

5.2 Energy

We usually speak of mechanical, electrical, chemical, potential, kinetic, sound, atomic and nuclear energy, to name a few. In fact, these different kinds of energy are different forms or manifestations of the same energy. Energy is a scalar. It is defined as a physical quantity <u>capable of producing work</u>.

1) Definition of kinetic energy

Kinetic energy (E_k) is the energy of motion which can produce work. It is proportional to the mass of the object and its velocity:

$$E_k = 1/2\ mv^2.$$

2) The Work-Energy Theorem

A net force is the sum of interior and exterior forces acting upon the system. The variation of the kinetic energy of a system is equal to the work of the net force applied to the system:

$$W \text{ (of the resultant force)} = \Delta E_k.$$

Consequently, if the speed of a particle is constant, $\Delta E_k = 0$, then the work done by the resultant force must be zero. For example, in uniform circular motion the speed of the particle remains constant thus the centripetal force does no work on the particle. A force at right angles to the direction of motion merely changes the direction of the velocity but not its magnitude.

5.4 Potential Energy

Potential energy (E_p) is referred to as potential because it is accumulated by the system that contained it. It varies with the configuration of the system, i.e., when distances between particles of the system vary, the interactions between these particles vary. The variation of the potential energy is equal to the work performed by the interior forces caused by the interaction between the particles of the system. The following are examples of potential energy:

a) potential energy (= electric potential = E_p) derived from the Coulomb force (r is the distance between point charges q_1 and q_2, PHY 9.1.4):

$$E_p = k\ q_1 q_2 / r$$

b) potential energy derived from the universal attraction force (r is the distance between the COG of masses m_1 and m_2):

$$E_p = G\ m_1 m_2 / r$$

c) potential energy derived from the gravitational force (h is the height):

$$E_p = mgh$$

d) potential energy derived from the elastic force (i.e. a compressed spring):

$$E_p = kx^2/2.$$

{k = the spring constant, x = displacement, cf. PHY 7.2.1}

5.5 Conservation of Energy

a) *Definition*

The mechanical energy (E_T) of a system is equal to the sum of its kinetic energy and its potential energy:

$$E_T = E_k + E_p.$$

b) *Theorem of mechanical energy*

The variation of the mechanical energy of a system is equal to the work of exterior forces acting on the system.

c) *Consequence*

An isolated system, i.e., which is not being acted upon by any exterior force, keeps a constant mechanical energy. The kinetic energy and the potential energy may vary separately but their sum remains constant. This makes conservation of energy a very simple way to solve many different types of physics problems.

5.5.1 Conservation of Energy Problem (SI units)

A 6.8×10^3 kg frictionless roller coaster car starts at rest 30 meters above ground level. Determine the speed of the car at (a) 20 m above ground level; (b) at ground level.

$$E_T = E_k + E_p = 1/2mv^2 + mgh$$

Initially v = 0 since the car starts at rest, h = 30 m, and the constant g ≈ 10 m/s², thus

$$E_T = 0 + m(10)(30) = 300m \text{ joules.}$$

Situation (a) where h = 20 m:

$$E_T = 300m = 1/2mv^2 + mgh$$

m cancels, multiply through by 2, solve for *v*:

$$v = \sqrt{2(300) - 2(10)20} = \sqrt{2(100)}$$
$$= \sqrt{2(10)} = 14 \text{ m/s}$$

Situation (b) at ground level h = 0:

$$E_T = 300m = 1/2mv^2 + 0$$

m cancels, multiply through by 2, solve for *v*:

$$v = \sqrt{600} = \sqrt{6(100)} = 10\sqrt{6} = 24 \text{ m/s}$$

- Note: the mass of the roller coaster is irrelevant!
- Note: you must be able to quickly estimate square roots (PHY 1.1.2, 2.6.1).

5.6 Conservative Forces

The three definitions of a conservative force are: i) after a round trip the kinetic energy of a particle on which a force acts must return to its initial value; ii) after a round trip the work done on a particle by a force must be zero; iii) the work done by the force on a particle depends on the initial and final positions of the particle and not on the path taken.

Examples: Friction disobeys all three of the preceding criteria thus it is a non-conservative force. The force $F_s = -kx$ (Hooke's Law, PHY 7.2.1) of an ideal spring on a frictionless surface is a conservative force. Gravity is a conservative force. If you throw a ball vertically upward, it will return with the same kinetic energy it had when it left your hand (*neglect air resistance*).

5.7 Power

The power P applied during the work W performed by a force F is equal to the work divided by the time necessary to do the work. In other words, power is the rate of doing work:

$$P = \Delta W / \Delta t.$$

• The SI unit for power is the *watt* (W) which equals one *joule per second* (J/s).

• Power can also be expressed as the product of a force on an object and the object's velocity: $P = Fv$.

Go online to GAMSAT-prep.com for free chapter review Q&A and forum.

FLUIDS AND SOLIDS
Chapter 6

Memorize	Understand	Not Required*
* Equation: density * Density of water * Equations for pressure, pressure change	* Buoyancy force, SG and height immersed * Streamline, turbulent flow; continuity/ Bernouilli's equation * Fluid viscosity, Archimedes' principle, surface tension; vapor press., atmospheric press. * Elastic properties of solids; effect of temperature	* Knowledge beyond introductory-level (A-level/Leaving Certificate/Year 12) course * Memorizing all the equations for solids * Memorizing equations: Continuity, hydrostatic pressure, Bernouilli's

GAMSAT-Prep.com

Introduction

A fluid is a substance that flows (*deforms*) under shear stress. This includes all gases and liquids. It is important to understand the properties without movement (hydrostatic pressure, Archimedes' principle) and with movement (continuity, Bernoulli's). On the other hand, a solid *resists* being deformed or submitting to changes in volume. A basic understanding of this *elastic* property of solids is required.

Additional Resources

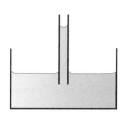

Free Online Q&A + Forum

GAMSAT-prep.com Videos

Flashcards

Special Guest

* The real GAMSAT may have advanced level information presented (ie. in a passage) but previous knowledge of said information is not required to answer the questions that would follow. Practice ACER and GS practice GAMSATs can help you clarify this point.

6.1 Fluids

6.1.1 Density, Specific Gravity

The *density* of an object is defined as the ratio of its mass to its volume.

$$density = mass / volume$$

This definition holds for solids, fluids and gases. From the definition, it is easy to see that solids are more dense than liquids which are in turn more dense than gases. This is true because for a given mass, the average distance between molecules of a given substance is bigger in the liquid state than in the solid state. Put simply, the substance occupies a bigger volume in the liquid state than in the solid state and a much bigger volume in gaseous state than in the liquid state.

At a given temperature, the *specific gravity* (SG) is defined as :

$$SG = \frac{density\ of\ a\ substance}{density\ of\ water}$$

The density of water is about 1 g/ml (= 1 g/cm^3 = 10^3 kg/m^3) over most common temperatures. So in most instances the specific gravity of a substance is the same as its density.

Note that the dimension of density is mass per unit volume, whereas the specific gravity is dimensionless. Density is one of the key properties of fluids (liquids or gases) and the other is pressure.

6.1.2 Hydrostatic Pressure, Buoyancy, Archimedes' Principle

Pressure (P) is defined as the force (F) per unit area (A):

$$P = F/A.$$

The force F is the normal (*perpendicular*) force to the area. The SI unit for pressure is the *pascal* (1 Pa = 1 N/m^2). Other units are: 1.00 atm = 1.01 × 10^5 Pa = 1.01 bar = 760 mmHg = 760 torr = 14.7 lb/in^2.

Pressure is also formulated as potential energy per unit volume as follows:

$$P = \frac{F}{A} = \frac{mg}{A} = \frac{(mg/A)}{(h/h)} = \frac{mgh}{v} = \rho gh$$

ρ = density and h = depth below surface; if the depth is changing we can write:

$$\Delta P = \rho g \Delta h.$$

Note: The physics in this section (PHY 6.1.2) can be used to solve ACER's GAMSAT Practice Test ('Green booklet') Q68-70, as well as Test 2 ('Purple booklet') Q29-32 and Q66-68.

We will now examine 6 key rules of incompressible fluids (liquids) that are not moving (*statics*).

1) In a fluid confined by solid boundaries, pressure acts perpendicular to the boundary – it is a <u>normal force</u>, sometimes called a *surface force*.

pipe or tube

dam

2) At any particular depth, the pressure of the fluid is the same in all directions.

3) The fluid or *hydrostatic pressure* depends on the density and the depth of the fluid. So it is easy to calculate the change in pressure in an open container, swimming pool, the ocean, etc.:

P_1 = atmospheric pressure
h_1 = surface = a depth of 0
$P_2 - P_1 = \Delta P$
$h_2 - h_1 = \Delta h$

$$\Delta P = \rho g \Delta h$$

<u>Vertical plane surfaces</u>

We can now combine rules 1, 2 and 3 about fluids to examine a special case which is that of a vertical plane surface like a vertical wall that is underwater.

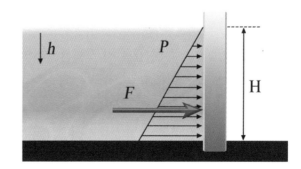

Of course pressure varies linearly with depth because $\Delta P = \rho g \Delta h$.

If the height of the vertical rectangular wall is H and the width W, with the help of calculus (which is *not* on the GAMSAT!), the equation for the force on the wall, or vertical plane, at any depth can be determined to be:

$$F = 1/2 \; \rho g W H^2$$

4) The size or shape of a container does not influence the pressure (= *hydrostatic paradox*). Note that the pressure is the same at the bottom of all 3 containers because the height h and fluid density are the same.

Hydraulic systems, like the brakes in a car, can multiply the force applied. For example, if a 50 N force is applied by the left piston in the diagram and if the right piston has an area five times greater, then the force out at F_2 is 250 N (thus the force vector F_2 is 5 times longer).

$$F_2 = A_2(F_1/A_1) = 5A_1(F_1/A_1) = 5(F_1)$$

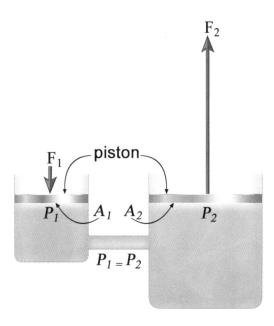

5) Pascal's Principle: If an external pressure is applied to a confined fluid, the pressure at every point within the fluid increases by that amount. This is the basis for hydraulic systems. Key points: (1) the pressure of the system is constant throughout and (2) by definition, P = F/A, so we get:

$$F_1/A_1 = F_2/A_2$$

6) An object which is completely or partially submerged in a fluid experiences an upward force equal to the weight of the fluid displaced (*Archimedes' principle*).

This buoyant force F_b is :

$$F_b = V\rho g = mg$$

where ρ is the density of the fluid displaced. An object that floats must displace at most its own weight.

Archimedes' principle can be used to calculate specific gravity. And in turn, specific gravity is equivalent to the fraction of the height of a buoyant object below the surface of the fluid. Thus if SG = 0.90, then 90% of the height of the object would be immersed in water. Therefore, less dense objects float.

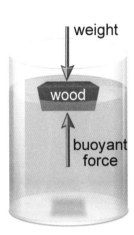

6.1.2.1 Atmospheric Pressure

Atmospheric pressure is the force per unit area exerted against a surface by the weight of the air above that surface. If the number of air molecules above a surface increases, there are more molecules to exert a force on that surface and thus, the pressure increases. On the other hand, a reduction in the number of air molecules above a surface will result in a decrease in pressure. Atmo-spheric pressure is measured with a "barome-ter", which is why atmospheric pressure is also referred to as *barometric* pressure.

Atmospheric pressure is often measured with a mercury (Hg) barometer, and a height of approximately 760 millimeters (30 in) of mer-cury represents atmospheric pressure at sea level (760 mmHg).

Unit	Definition or Relationship
SI Unit: 1 pascal (Pa)	$1 \text{ kg m}^{-1} \text{ s}^{-2} = 1 \text{ N/m}^2$
1 bar	1×10^5 Pa
1 atmosphere (atm)	101,325 Pa = 101.3 kPa
1 torr	1 / 760 atm
760 mmHg	1 atm
14.7 pounds per sq. in. (psi)	1 atm

Units of Pressure

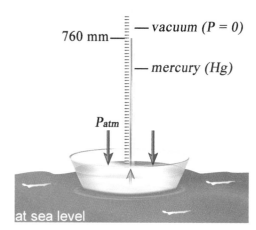

760 mm — vacuum (P = 0)

— mercury (Hg)

P_{atm}

at sea level

When the altitude or elevation increases, we get closer to "outer space" so there is less overlying atmospheric mass from gases, so that pressure decreases with increasing elevation.

elevation and atmospheric pressure

Figure III.B.6.0: Atmospheric pressure decreases with elevation. Mount Everest is about 8,800 meters (m) and a 747 can cruise at an altitude of 10,000 m but requires increased cabin pressure to prevent passengers from having altitude sickness and low oxygen (hypoxia).

6.1.2.2 Gauge Pressure

When you measure the pressure in your tires, you are measuring the pressure difference between the tires and atmospheric pressure, which is the *gauge* (or *gage*) pressure.

<u>Absolute pressure</u> is the pressure of a fluid relative to the pressure in a vacuum. The absolute pressure is then the sum of the gauge pressure, which is what you measure, and the atmospheric pressure.

$$P_{abs} = P_{atm} + P_{gauge}$$

Pressure can be measured in devices in which one or more columns of a liquid (i.e. mercury or water) are used to determine the pressure difference between two points (i.e. U-tube manometer, inclined-tube manometer).

Of course, electronic instruments for measurement are used more frequently.

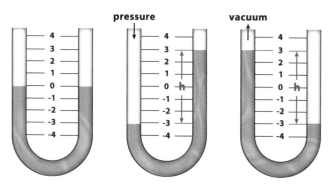

Figure III.B.6.0.0: When the U-tube has both ends open to the same pressure, the height of the liquid will be the same in each leg. If positive pressure is applied to one leg, it will force a difference in height h. When a vacuum (= *no pressure*) is applied to one leg, the liquid rises in that leg and falls in the other. The difference in pressure can be calculated: $\Delta P = \rho g \Delta h$ (PHY 6.1.2).

6.1.3 Fluids in Motion, Continuity Equation, Bernoulli's Equation

Fluids in motion are described by two equations, the continuity equation and Bernoulli's equation. Fluids are assumed to have <u>streamline</u> (= *laminar*) flow which means that the motion of every particle in the fluid follows the same path as the particle that preceded it. <u>Turbulent</u> flow occurs when that definition cannot be applied, resulting in molecular collisions, irregularly shaped whirlpools, energy is then dissipated and frictional drag is increased. The rate (R) of streamline flow is given by:

$$R = (volume\ past\ a\ point)/time = Avt\ /\ t = Av$$

volume = (cross-sectional area) (length) = (A) (vt) = Avt

length = distance = (velocity) (time) = vt

cross-sectional area of a tube = area of a circle = πr^2 where π can be estimated as 3.14 and r is the radius of the circle.

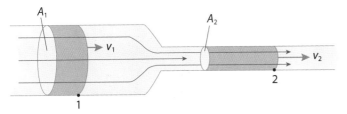

A_1 A_2 v_1 v_2 2   1

Figure III.B.6.0.1: Application of the continuity equation. When a tube narrows, the same volume occupies a greater length. For the same volume to pass points 1 and 2 in a given time, the speed must be greater at point 2.

• The equation can also be written as the **continuity equation**:

$$A_1v_1 = A_2v_2 = constant$$

where subscripts 1 and 2 refer to different points in the line of flow. The continuity equation can be used for an incompressible fluid flowing in an enclosed tube. For a compressible fluid:

$$\rho_1A_1v_1 = \rho_2A_2v_2 = constant$$

• **Bernoulli's equation** is an application of the law of conservation of energy and is:

$$P + \rho gh + 1/2\ \rho v^2 = constant$$

It follows:

$$P_1 + \rho gh_1 + 1/2\ \rho v_1^2 = P_2 + \rho gh_2 + 1/2\ \rho v_2^2$$

where subscripts 1 and 2 refer to different points in the flow.

A commonly encountered consequence of Bernoulli's equation is that where the height is relatively constant and the velocity of a fluid is high, the pressure is low, and vice versa.

{Various applications of the preceding equations will be explored in GS-1, the first practice test!}

6.1.4 Fluid Viscosity and Determining Turbulence

Viscosity is analogous to friction between moving solids. It may, therefore be viewed as the resistance to flow of layers of fluid (as in streamline or laminar flow) past each other. This also means that viscosity, as in friction, results in dissipation of mechanical energy. As one layer flows over another, its motion is transmitted to the second layer and causes this layer to be set in motion. Since a mass m of the second layer is set in motion and some of the energy of the first layer is lost, there is a transfer of momentum between the layers.

The greater the transfer of this momentum from one layer to another, the more energy that is lost and the slower the layers move.

The viscosity (η) is the measure of the efficiency of transfer of this momentum. Therefore the higher the viscosity coefficient, the greater the transfer of momentum and loss of mechanical energy, and thus loss of velocity. The reverse situation holds for a low viscosity coefficient.

Consequently, a high viscosity coefficient substance flows slowly (e.g. molasses), and a low viscosity coefficient substance flows relatively fast (e.g. water or, especially helium). Note that the transfer of momentum to adjacent layers is in essence, the exertion of a force upon these layers to set them in motion.

Whether flow is streamline or turbulent depends on a combination of factors already discussed. A convenient measure is Reynolds Number (R):

$$R = vd\rho / \eta$$

v = velocity of flow
d = diameter of the tube
ρ = density of the fluid
η = viscosity coefficient

In general, if R < 2000 the flow is streamline; if R > 2000 the flow is turbulent. Note that as v, d or ρ increases or η decreases, the flow becomes more turbulent.

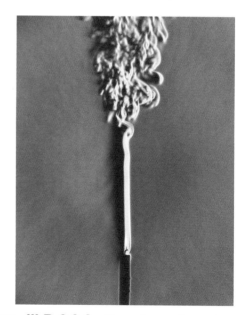

Figure III.B.6.0.2: The plume from this candle flame goes from laminar to turbulent in the upper 1/3 of the image. The Reynolds number can be used to predict where this transition takes place (Schlieren photograph of an ordinary candle in still air by Dr. Gary Settles).

6.1.5 Surface Tension

Molecules of a liquid exert attractive forces toward each other (cohesive forces), and exert attractive forces toward the surface they touch (adhesive forces). If a liquid is in a gravity free space without a surface, it will form a sphere (smallest area relative to volume).

If the liquid is lining an object, the liquid surface will contract (due to cohesive forces) to the lowest possible surface area. The forces between the molecules on this surface will create a membrane-like effect. Due to the contraction, a potential energy (PE) will present in the surface.

This PE is directly proportional to the surface area (A). An exact relation is formed as follows:

$$PE = \gamma A$$

γ = surface tension = PE/A = joules/m²

An alternative formulation for the surface tension (γ) is:

$$\gamma = F/l$$

F = force of contraction of surface
l = length along surface

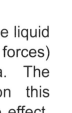
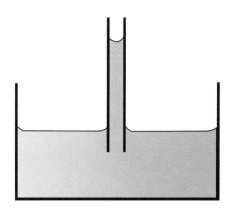

(a) cohesive > adhesive   (b) adhesive > cohesive

Figure III.B.6.1: Effects of adhesive and cohesive forces.
The distance the liquid rises or falls in the tube is directly proportional to the surface tension γ and inversely proportional to the liquid density and radius of the tube. Examples of 2 liquids consistent with the illustrations include: (a) mercury; (b) water.

Because of the contraction, a small object which would ordinarily sink in the liquid may float on the surface membrane. For example, a small insect like a "water strider."

The liquid will rise or fall on a wall or in a capillary tube if the adhesive forces are greater than cohesive or vice versa (*see* Figure III.B.6.1).

6.2   Solids

6.2.1   Elastic Properties of Solids

When a force acts on a solid, the solid is deformed. If the solid returns to its original shape, the solid is elastic. The effect of a force depends on the area over which it acts. Stress is defined as the ratio of the force to the area over which it acts. Strain is defined as the relative change in dimensions or shape of the object caused by the stress. This is embodied in the definition of the modulus of elasticity (ME) as:

$$ME = \frac{stress}{strain}$$

Some different types of stresses are tensile stress (equal and opposite forces

directed away from each other), compressive stress (equal and opposite forces directed towards each other), and shearing stress (equal and opposite forces which do not have the same line of action). There are two commonly used moduli of elasticity:

1) Young's Modulus (Y) for compressive or tensile stress:

$$Y = \frac{longitudinal \;\; stress}{longitudinal \;\; strain}$$

$$Y = \frac{(F/A)}{(\Delta l/l)} = \frac{F \times l}{A \Delta l}$$

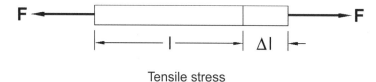

Tensile stress

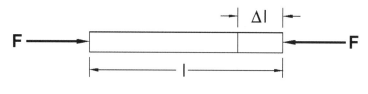

Compressive stress

Figure III.B.6.2: Compressive and Tensile Stress.

2) Shear modulus (S) or the modulus of rigidity is:

S = shearing stress / shearing strain

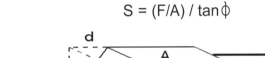

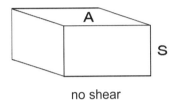

no shear

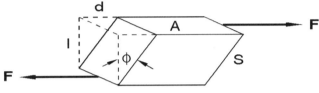

Figure III.B.6.3: Shear Stress. A is the area tangential to the force F.

6.3 The Effect of Temperature on Solids and Liquids

When substances gain or lose heat they usually undergo expansion or contraction.

Expansion or contraction can be by linear dimension, by area or by volume.

Table III.B.6.1: Substance thermal expansion.

Type	Final	Original	Change caused by heat
(1) *Linear*	L $L = L_0 + \alpha \Delta T L_0$ $L = L_0(1 + \alpha \Delta T)$ α = coefficient of linear thermal expansion ΔT = change in temperature	L_0	$\alpha \Delta T L_0$
(2) *Area*	A $A = A_0 + \gamma \Delta T A_0$ $A = A_0(1 + \gamma \Delta T)$ γ = coefficient of area thermal expansion = 2α	A_0	$\gamma \Delta T A_0$
(3) *Volume*	V $V = V_0 + \beta \Delta T V_0$ $V = V_0(1 + \beta \Delta T)$ β = coefficient of volume thermal expansion = 3α	V_0	$\beta \Delta T V_0$

Go online to GAMSAT-prep.com for free chapter review Q&A and forum.

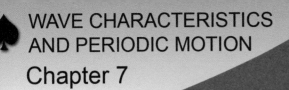
Memorize	Understand	Not Required*
fine: wavelength, frequency, velocity, ⏺plitude fine: intensity, constructive/destructive ⏺erference, beat freq. ⏺uation: relating velocity to frequency, ⏺velength ⏺uation: Hooke's Law, work (periodic motion)	* SHM, transverse vs. longitudinal waves, phase * Resonance, nodes, antinodes, pipes (standing waves) * Harmonics, overtones * Periodic motion: force, accel., vel., diplace., period * The simple pendulum, theory and calculations	* Knowledge beyond introductory-level (A-level/Leaving Certificate/Year 12) course * Memorizing displacement/elementary vibration equations * Memorizing equation for harmonics, simple pendulum

GAMSAT-Prep.com

Introduction ▮▮▮

Wave characteristics and periodic motion describe the motion of systems that vibrate. Topics include transverse and longitudinal waves, interference, resonance, Hooke's law and simple harmonic motion (SHM). Some basic equations must be memorized but for most of the material, you must seek a comfortable understanding.

Additional Resources

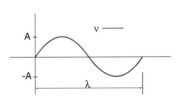

Free Online Q&A + Forum   GAMSAT-prep.com Videos   Flashcards   Special Guest

7.1 Wave Characteristics

7.1.1 Transverse and Longitudinal Motion

A wave is a disturbance in a medium such that each particle in the medium vibrates about an equilibrium point in a simple harmonic (*periodic*) motion. If the direction of vibration is perpendicular to the direction of propagation of the wave, it is called a <u>transverse wave</u> (e.g. light or an oscillating string under tension).

If the direction of vibration is in the same direction as the propagation of the wave, it is called a <u>longitudinal wave</u> (e.g. sound). Longitudinal waves are characterized by condensations (regions of crowding of particles) and rarefactions (regions where particles are far apart) along the wave in the medium.

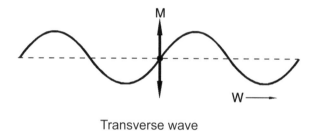

Transverse wave

Longitudinal wave

Figure III.B.7.1: Transverse and longitudinal waves.
W = wave propagation, R = rarefaction, C = condensation, M = motion of particle.

7.1.2 Wavelength, Frequency, Velocity, Amplitude, Intensity

The wavelength (λ) is the distance from crest to crest (or valley to valley) of a transverse wave. It may also be defined as the distance between two particles with the same displacement and direction of displacement. In a longitudinal wave, the wavelength is the distance from one rarefaction (or condensation) to another. The *amplitude* (A) is the maximum displacement of a particle in one direction from its equilibrium point. The *intensity* (I) of a wave is the square of the amplitude.

Frequency (*f*) is the number of cycles per unit time (per second = s^{-1} = hertz = Hz = SI unit). *Period* (*T*) is the duration of one cycle, it is the inverse of the frequency. *The velocity* (*v*) of a wave is the velocity of the propagation of the disturbance that forms the wave through the medium.

The velocity is inversely proportional to the inertia of the medium. The velocity can be calculated according to the following important equation:

$$v = \lambda f$$

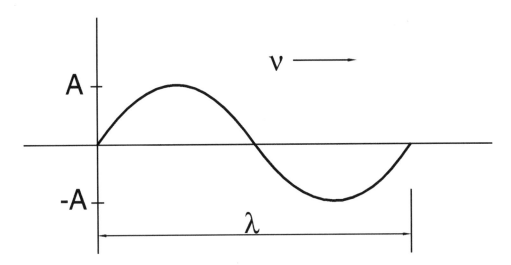

Figure III.B.7.2: Characteristics of waves.

7.1.3 Superposition of Waves, Phase, Interference, Addition

The superposition principle states that the effect of two or more waves on the displacement of a particle is independent. The final displacement of the particle is the resultant effect of all the waves added algebraically, thus the amplitude may increase or decrease. The *phase* of a particle under vibration is its displacement at the time of origin (t=0). The displacement can be calculated as follows:

$$x = A\sin(\omega t + \varphi)$$

where x is the displacement, A is the amplitude, ω is the angular velocity, t is the time, and φ is the phase.

Interference is the summation of the displacements of different waves in a medium. Certain criteria must first be established:

• *synchrony sources*: vibrations emitted by synchrony sources have the same phase.

• *coherent vibrations*: the phases of the vibrations are related, this means that the duration of the light impressions on the retina is much longer than the duration of a wave train between two emissions.

• *parallel vibrations*: the displacements of parallel vibrations keep parallel directions in space.

• *interference conditions*: two or more vibrations can interfere only when the are coherent, parallel and have the same period.

• *beat frequency*: the difference in frequency of two waves creates a new frequency (*see* Beats, PHY 8.4).

Given an elementary vibration $S_i = A_i\sin(w_t+\varphi_i)$ the composition of n vibrations that interfere is given by:

$$S_1 + S_2 + S_3 + ... + S_n = a_1\sin(wt+\varphi_1) + a_2\sin(wt+\varphi_2) + ...+ a_n\sin(wt+\varphi_n) = A\sin(wt+\Phi)$$

where A is the resultant amplitude and Φ the resultant phase. Constructive interference (*see Figure III.B.7.4*) is when the waves add to a larger resultant wave than either original.

This occurs maximally when the phase difference φ is a whole wavelength λ which corresponds to multiples of π.

This occurs at $\varphi = 0, 2\pi, 4\pi$, etc. Since $\varphi = 2\pi\Delta L/\lambda$, where ΔL equals the difference in path to a point of two waves of equal wavelength, these waves interfere constructively when $\Delta L= 0 , \lambda, 2\lambda, 3\lambda$, *etc.* See Figure III.B.7.3 for the definition of ΔL.

Destructive interference (*see Figure III.B.7.5*) is when the waves add to a smaller resultant wave than either original wave. This occurs maximally when $\varphi = \pi, 3\pi, 5\pi$, *etc.*, which are multiples of one-half of a wavelength where $180° = \pi$ which corresponds to ½λ. This occurs when $\Delta L = \lambda/2, 3\lambda/2, 5\lambda/2$, etc.

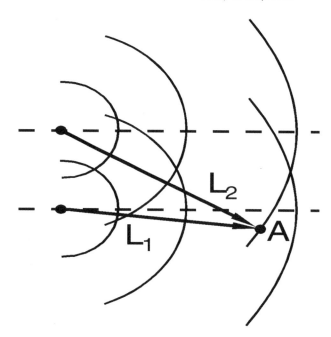

Figure III.B.7.3: Schematic for ΔL.
L_1 and L_2 are distances from the origins of the waves to point A. Thus $\Delta L = |L_2-L_1|$ (absolute value).

PHYSICS

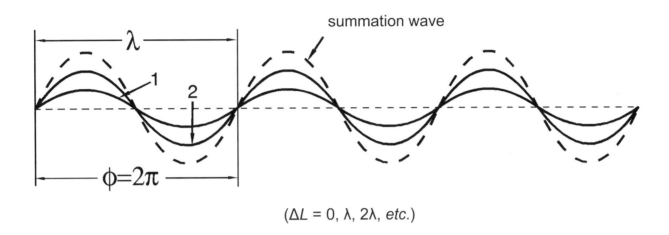

$(\Delta L = 0, \lambda, 2\lambda, etc.)$

Figure III.B.7.4: Maximal constructive interference.
Waves (1) and (2) begin at the points shown, have the same λ but different amplitudes. The summation wave is maximal (i.e. highest amplitude but same wavelength) since ΔL = λ *in this example.*

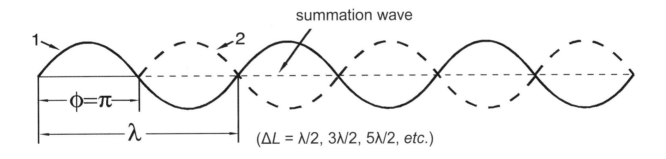

$(\Delta L = \lambda/2, 3\lambda/2, 5\lambda/2, etc.)$

Figure III.B.7.5: Maximal destructive interference.

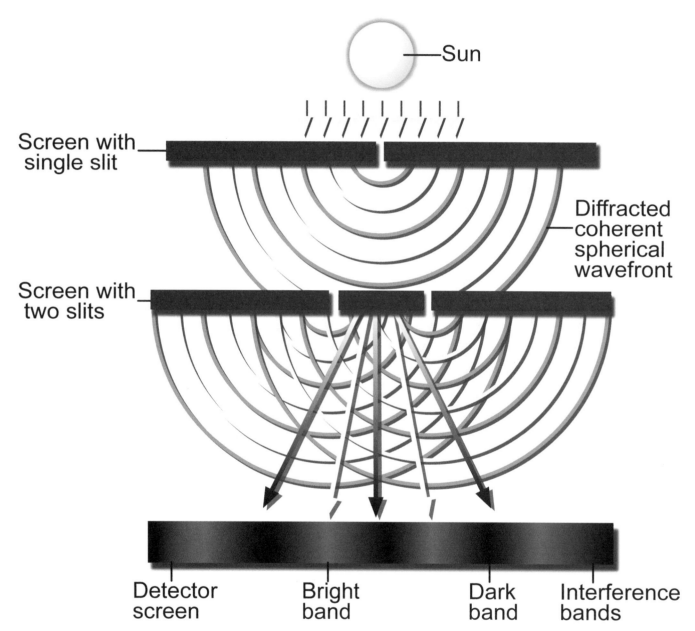

Figure III.B.7.5.1: Thomas Young's Double Slit Experiment Young's experiment demonstrates both the wave and particle natures of light. A coherent light source illuminates a thin plate with two parallel slits cut in it, and the light passing through the slits strikes a screen behind them. The wave nature of light causes the light waves passing through both slits to interfere, creating an interference pattern of bright and dark bands on the screen. However, at the screen, the light is always found to be absorbed as though it were made of discrete particles (photons). The double slit experiment can also be performed (using different apparatus) with particles of matter such as electrons with the same results. Again, this provides an additional circumstance demonstrating particle-wave duality. Diffraction is the apparent bending of a wave around a small obstacle. We see diffracted light waves through each of the slits above.

7.1.4 Resonance

Forced vibrations occur when a series of waves impinge upon an object and cause it to vibrate. Natural frequencies are the intrinsic frequencies of vibration of a system. If the forced vibration causes the object to vibrate at one of its natural frequencies, the body will vibrate at maximal amplitude. This phenomenon is called *resonance*. Since energy and power are proportional to the amplitude squared, they also are at their maximum.

7.1.5 Standing Waves, Pipes and Strings

Standing waves result when waves are reflected off a stationary object back into the oncoming waves of the medium and super-position results. *Nodes* are points where there is no particle displacement, which are similar to points of maximal destructive inter-ference.

Nodes occur at fixed end points (points that cannot vibrate). Antinodes are points that undergo maximal displacements and are similar to points of maximal constructive interference. Antinodes occur at open or free end points (*see Figure III.B.7.6*).

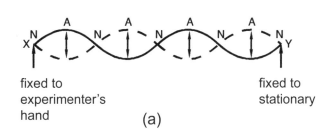

fixed to
experimenter's
hand

(a)

fixed to
stationary

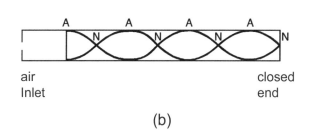

air
Inlet

closed
end

(b)

Figure III.B.7.6: Standing waves.
(a) <u>String</u>: Standing waves produced by an experimenter wiggling a string or rubber tube at point X towards a fixed point Y at the correct frequency. (b) <u>Pipe</u>: Standing wave produced in a pipe with a closed end point i.e. in a closed organ pipe where sound originates in a vibrating air column (A = *antinode* and N = *node*).

7.1.6 Harmonics

Consider a violin. A string is fixed at both ends and is bowed, transverse vibrations travel along the string; these disturbances are reflected at both ends producing a standing wave. The vibrations of the string give rise to longitudinal vibrations in the air which transmits the sound to our ears.

A string of length l, fixed at both ends, can resonate at frequencies f given by:

$$f_n = nv/(2l)$$

where the velocity v is the same for all frequencies and the number of antinodes $n = 1, 2, 3, ...$

The lowest frequency, $f_1 = v/(2l)$, is the *fundamental* frequency, and the others are called *overtones*. The fundamental is the first *harmonic*, the second harmonic $2f_1$ is the first overtone, the third harmonic $3f_1$ is the second overtone, etc. Overtones whose frequencies are integral multiples of the fundamental are called *harmonic series*.

7.2 Periodic Motion

7.2.1 Hooke's Law

The particles that are undergoing displacement when a wave passes through a medium undergo motion called simple harmonic motion (SHM) and are acted upon by a force described by Hooke's Law. SHM is caused by an inconstant force (called a *restoring force*) and as a result has an inconstant acceleration. The force is proportional to the displacement (*distance from the equilibrium point*) but opposite in direction,

$$F = -kx \text{ (Hooke's Law)}$$

where k = the spring constant, x = displacement from the equilibrium. The work W can be determined according to $W = \frac{1}{2}kx^2$.

Notice that the equation for the work done by the spring is identical to the potential energy of a spring (PHY 5.4). This is because when an external force stretches the spring, this work is stored in the force field, which is said to be stored as potential energy. If the external force is removed, the force field acts on the body to perform the work as it moves the body back to the initial position, reducing the stretch of the spring. For example, an archer applies human force over a distance (= work; PHY 5.1) to pull an arrow back in the bow, elastic potential energy is now stored in the stretched bow, when the arrow leaves the bow, the potential energy turns into kinetic energy.

Examples of objects that have elastic potential energy include stretched or compressed elastic bands, springs, bungee cords, shock absorbers (cars, trucks, bicycles), trampolines, etc.

The work done in compressing or stretching a spring can be determined by taking the area under a Force vs. Displacement graph for the spring (the latter is because work is force times displacement; PHY 5.1).

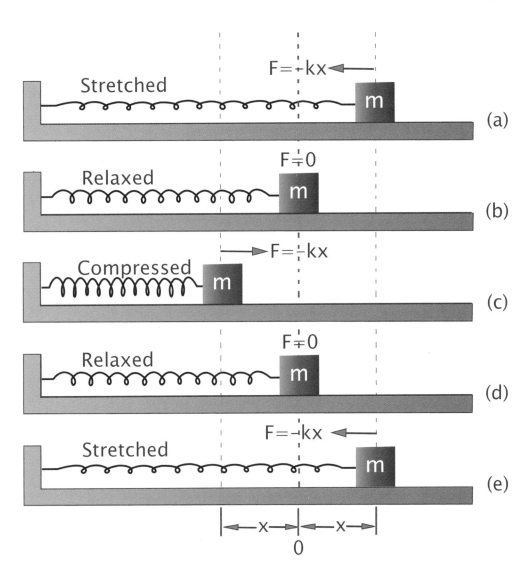

Figure III.B.7.7: Simple harmonic motion.

A block of mass m exhibiting SHM. The force F exerted by the spring on the block is shown in each case. Notice that the restoring force F is always pointing in the opposite direction to the direction of the displacement x. Because these two vectors are always opposite to each other, there is a negative sign built into the equation $F = -kx$.

7.2.2 Features of SHM and Hooke's Law

1) Force and acceleration are always in the same direction.

2) Force and acceleration are always in the opposite direction of the displacement (*this is why there is a negative sign in the equation for force*).

3) Force and acceleration have their maximal value at +A and -A; they are zero at the equilibrium point (*the amplitude A equals the maximum displacement x*).

4) Velocity direction has no constant relation to displacement and acceleration.

5) Velocity is maximum at equilibrium and zero at A and -A.

6) The period T can be calculated from the mass m of an oscillating particle:

$$T = 2\pi\sqrt{m/k}$$

where k is the spring constant. The frequency f is simply $1/T$.

7.2.3 SHM Problem: The Simple Pendulum

A simple pendulum consists of a point mass m suspended by a light inextensible cord of length l. When pulled to one side of its equilibrium position, the pendulum swings under the influence of gravity producing a periodic, oscillatory motion (= *SHM*). Given that the angle θ with the vertical is small, thus $\sin\theta \approx \theta$, determine the general equation for the period T.

The tangential component of mg is the restoring force since it returns the mass to its equilibrium position. Thus the restoring force is:

$$F = - mg\sin\theta.$$

Recall $\sin\theta \approx \theta$, $x = l\theta$, and for SHM $F = -kx$:

$$F = - mg\theta = - mgx/l = - (mg/l)x = - kx.$$

Hence $mg/l = k$, thus the equation for the period T becomes:

$$T = 2\pi\sqrt{\frac{m}{k}} = 2\pi\sqrt{\frac{m}{mg/l}} = 2\pi\sqrt{\frac{l}{g}}$$

The equation for the period in the simple pendulum is therefore independent of the mass of the particle.

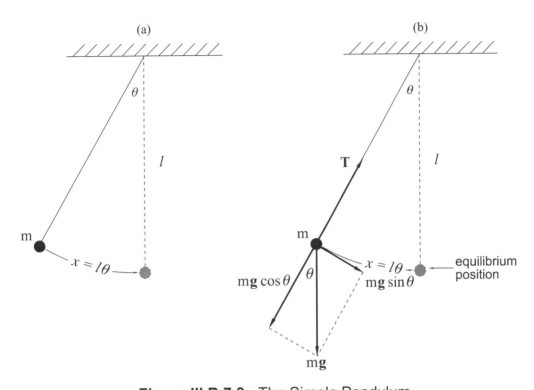

Figure III.B.7.8: The Simple Pendulum.
(a) The problem as it could be presented; the displacement x along the section of the circle (arc) is $l\theta$. (b) The vector components that should be drawn to solve the problem. The forces acting on a simple pendulum are the tension **T** in the string and the weight mg of the mass. The magnitude of the radial component of mg is $mg\cos\theta$ and the tangential component is $mg\sin\theta$.

A rough approximation of SHM would be a grandfather clock or a child on a swing. However, note that the *length l* in the equation of a simple pendulum refers to the length of the cord to the bob's or child's center of gravity (COG; PHY 2.1). For some common manipulations involving the equation for the period of a simple pendulum, *see* GM 1.5.6.

What do physicists enjoy doing the most at football games?
The 'wave'   :)

Go online to GAMSAT-prep.com for free chapter review Q&A and forum.

SOUND
Chapter 8

Memorize	Understand	Not Required*
* Sensory vs. physical correspondence of hearing	* Relative velocity of sound in solids, liquids and gases * The relation of intensity to P, area, f, amplitude * Calculation of the intensity level * Rules of logarithms * Doppler effect and calculations	* Knowledge beyond introductory-level (A-level/Leaving Certificate/Year 12) course * Memorizing specific frequencies, speed of sound, dB's

GAMSAT-Prep.com

Introduction ▮▮▮▮

Sound waves are longitudinal waves which can only be transmitted in a material, elastic medium. Speed, intensity, resonance (Chapter 7) and the Doppler effect help to describe the behavior of sound in different media. If the equations for sound intensity or the Doppler effect are required for the GAMSAT, they will be provided.

Additional Resources

Free Online Q&A + Forum

GAMSAT-prep.com Videos

Flashcards

Special Guest

8.1 Production of Sound

Sound is a longitudinal mechanical wave which travels through an elastic medium. Sound is thus produced by vibrating matter. There is no sound in a *vacuum* because it contains no matter (note: we have placed a table in PHY 11.6 comparing light and sound).

Compressions (condensations) are regions where particles of matter are close together; they are also high pressure regions. Rarefactions are regions where particles are sparse, they are low pressure regions of sound waves (PHY 7.1.1).

8.2 Relative Velocity of Sound in Solids, Liquids, and Gases

The velocity of sound is proportional to the square root of the elastic restoring force and inversely proportional to the square root of the inertia of the particles (e.g., density is a measure of inertia). Thus as a rule, the velocity of sound is higher in liquids as compared to gases, and highest in solids.

Furthermore, an increase in temperature increases the velocity of sound; conversely, a decrease in temperature decreases the velocity of sound in that medium.

8.3 Intensity, Pitch

Hearing is subjective but its characteristics are closely tied to physical characteristics of sound.

The quality depends on the number and relative intensity of the overtones of the waveform. Frequency, and therefore pitch are perceived by the ear from 20 to 20,000 Hz (hertz = cycles/second = s^{-1}). Frequencies below 20 Hz are called infrasonic. Frequencies above 20,000 Hz are called ultrasonic.

Sensory	Physical
loudness	intensity
pitch	frequency
quality	waveform

Table III.B.8.1:
Sensory and physical correspondence of hearing.

Sound intensity (I) is the rate of energy (power) propagation through space:

$I = (power/area)$ which is proportional to $(f^2 A^2)$

where f = frequency, A = amplitude.

The loudness varies with the frequency. The ears are most sensitive (hears sounds of lowest intensity) at approximately 2,000 to 4,000 Hz. I_o is taken to be 10^{-12} watts/cm², is barely audible and is assigned a value of 0 dB (zero *decibels*). Then intensity level (I) of a sound wave in dB is,

$$dB = 10\ \log_{10}(I/I_o)$$

where dB = the sound level, I = the intensity at a given level, I_o = the threshold intensity. {To calculate a change in the sound level or volume ΔV in units of dB, given two values for sound intensity, the given equation can be modified thus: $\Delta V = 10\log(I_{new}/I_{old})$}

Examples of some values of dB's are: whisper (20), normal conversation (60), subway car (100), pain threshold (120), and jet engine (160). Continual exposure to sound greater than 90 dB can lead to hearing impairment.

8.3.1 Calculation of the Intensity Level

What is the loudness or intensity level of Mr. Yell Alot's voice when he generates a sound wave ten million times as intense as I_o?

$I = (10\ 000\ 000)I_o = (10^7)I_o$

Thus
$$dB = 10\ \log_{10}(10^7 I_o/I_o)$$
$$= 10\ \log_{10} 10^7$$
$$= 70\ \log_{10} 10 = 70$$

{See GM 3.7 for rules of logarithms. Also, review log curves (GM 3.8) – especially the audiogram with GAMSAT-level MCQs, Fig. IV.3.6. Logs are common amongst ACER's GAMSAT materials.}

8.4 Beats

When sound of different frequencies are heard together, they interfere. Constructive interference results in beats. The number of beats per second is the absolute value of the difference of the frequencies ($|f_1 - f_2|$).

Hence, the new frequency heard includes the original frequencies and the absolute difference between them.

8.5 Doppler Effect

The Doppler effect is the effect upon the observed frequency caused by the relative motion of the observer (o) and the source (s). If the distance is decreasing between them, there is a shift to higher frequencies and shorter wavelengths (to higher pitch for sound and toward blue-violet for light, PHY 8.3 and 9.2.4). If the distance is increasing between them, there is a shift to longer wavelengths and lower frequencies (to lower pitch for sound and toward red for light). The summary equation of the above in terms of frequency (f) is :

$$f_o = f_s(V \pm v_o)/(V \pm v_s)$$

V = speed of the wave, v = speed of the observer (o) or the source (s).

Choose the sign such that the frequency varies consistently with the relative motion of the source and the observer. In other words, when the distance between the source and observer is *decreasing* use $+v_o$ and $-v_s$; if the distance is *increasing* use $-v_o$ and $+v_s$.

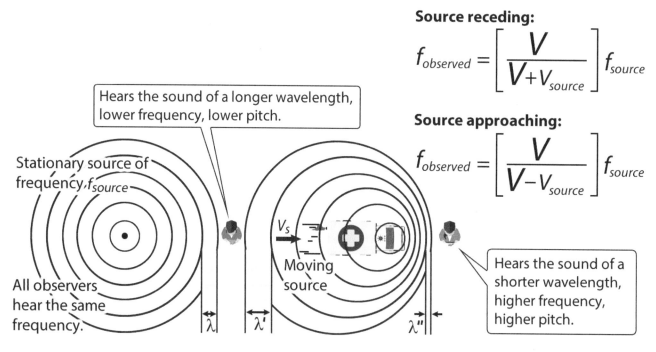

Source receding:

$$f_{observed} = \left[\frac{V}{V + V_{source}} \right] f_{source}$$

Source approaching:

$$f_{observed} = \left[\frac{V}{V - V_{source}} \right] f_{source}$$

Hears the sound of a longer wavelength, lower frequency, lower pitch.

Stationary source of frequency, f_{source}

All observers hear the same frequency.

V_s

Moving source

Hears the sound of a shorter wavelength, higher frequency, higher pitch.

Figure III.B.8.1: The Doppler Effect. When you hear the high pitch of a siren of an approaching emergency vehicle or ambulance, and notice that its pitch drops suddenly as it passes you: That is the Doppler effect. This occurs because the movement of the source alters the wavelength and the received frequency of the sound, even though the source frequency and wave velocity are unchanged.

Essentially, the approaching source moves closer during the period of the sound wave so the effective wavelength is shortened, giving a higher pitch since the velocity of the wave is unchanged. Similarly, the pitch of the receding sound source will be lowered. Note that the observers in the image are stationary so in each case $v_o = 0$. Adapted from HyperPhysics, Georgia State University.

8.5.1 Doppler Effect Problem (SI units)

A car drives towards a bus stop with its car stereo playing opera. The opera singer sings the note middle C (= 262 Hz) loudly; however, the people waiting at the bus stop hear C sharp (= 277 Hz). Given that the speed of sound V in air is 331 m/s, how fast is the car moving?

{*Remember the sign convention: since the distance between the source (the car) and the observer (people at the bus stop) is <u>decreasing</u> we use +v_o and -v_s*}

• the car (the *source* of the frequency) f_s = 262 Hz, v_s = unknown.

• the bus stop (where the *observers* are stationary) f_o = 277 Hz, v_o = 0 m/s.

$$f_o = f_s(V + v_o)/(V - v_s)$$
Thus
$$V - v_s = f_s (V + v_o)/f_o$$
Hence
$$v_s = - f_s (V + v_o)/f_o + V$$
Substitute

$$v_s = - 262(331 + 0)/277 + 331 = 17.9 \text{ m/s}.$$

• Note that the answer contains three significant figures.

The Doppler Effect is when stupid ideas seem smarter when you read them quickly

Go online to GAMSAT-prep.com for free chapter review Q&A and forum.

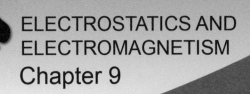

ELECTROSTATICS AND ELECTROMAGNETISM
Chapter 9

Memorize	Understand	Not Required*
...uations: for charge Q, Coulomb's law, ...ctric field ...uations: potential energy, absolute potential ...uation relating energy, planck's constant, ...quency	* Conservation of charge, use of Coulomb's law * Graphs/theory: electric field/potential lines, mag. induction * Potential difference, electric dipoles, mag. induction * Laplace's law, the right hand rule, magnetic field * Direction of F in magn. field; electromagnetism	* Knowledge beyond introductory-level (A-level/Leaving Certificate/Year 12) course * Memorizing coulomb's, permittivity or planck's constants * Memorizing equation with permittivity constant or dF * Calculus, derivatives, integrals, speed of light

GAMSAT-Prep.com

Introduction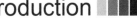

Electrostatics (statics = usu. at rest) refers to the science of stationary or slowly moving charges. Such charges can interact and behave in ways described by charge, electric force, electric field and potential difference. When a charge is in motion, it creates a magnetic field. Electromagnetism describes the relationship between electricity (moving electrical charge) and magnetism. The electromagnetic spectrum includes light and X-rays.

Additional Resources

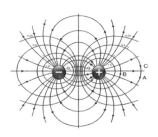

Free Online Q&A + Forum   GAMSAT-prep.com Videos   Flashcards   Special Guest

9.1 Electrostatics

9.1.1 Charge, Conductors, Insulators

By friction of matter we create between substances repulsive or attractive electric forces. These forces are due to two kinds of electric charges, distinguished by positive (+) and negative (−) signs. Each has a charge of 1.6×10^{-19} coulombs (= C = an SI derived unit; GM 2.1.3, Table 3) but differ in sign. The electron is the negative charge carrier, and the proton is the positive charge carrier. Substances with an excess of electrons have a net negative charge. Substances with a deficiency of electrons have a net positive charge. The total amount of charge Q of matter depends on the number of particles n and the charge e on each particle, thus $Q = ne$.

The conservation of charge states that a net charge cannot be created but that charge can be transfered from one object to another. One way of charging substances is by rubbing them (i.e., by contact).

For example, glass rubbed on fur becomes positive and rubber rubbed on fur becomes negative. Objects can also be charged by induction which occurs when one charged object is brought near to another uncharged object causing a charge redistribution in the latter to give net charge regions. Conductors transmit charge readily. Insulators resist the flow of charge.

9.1.2 Coulomb's Law, Electric Force

Charges exert forces upon each other. Like charges repel each other and unlike charges attract. For any two charges q_1 and q_2 the force F is given by Coulomb's Law:

$$F = k \frac{q_1 q_2}{r^2} = \frac{1}{4\pi\varepsilon_o} \left(\frac{q_1 q_2}{r^2} \right)$$

where k = coulomb's constant = 9.0×10^9 N-m²/C², ε_o = permittivity constant = 8.85×10^{-12} C²/N-m², and r = the distance between the charges. Note that the relationship of force and distance follows an inverse square law. Thus if the distance r is doubled [$(2r)^2 = 4r^2$], the new force is quartered ($F_{new} = F/4$). {cf. Law of Gravity: PHY 2.4}

A charge generates an electric field (E) in the space around it. Fields (force fields) are vectors. A field is generated by an object and it is that region of space around the object that will exert a force on a second object brought into that field. The field exists independently of that second object and is not altered by its presence. The force exerted on the second object depends upon that object and the field. The electric field E is given by:

$$E = F/q = k\ Q/r^2$$

where E and F are vectors, Q = the charge generating the field, and q = the charge placed in the field.

Charges exert forces upon each other through fields. The direction of a field is the direction <u>a positive charge would move if placed in it</u>. *Electric field lines* are imaginary lines which are in the same direction as E at that point. The direction is away from positive charges and toward negative charges, or put another way, the electric field is directed toward the decreasing potentials.

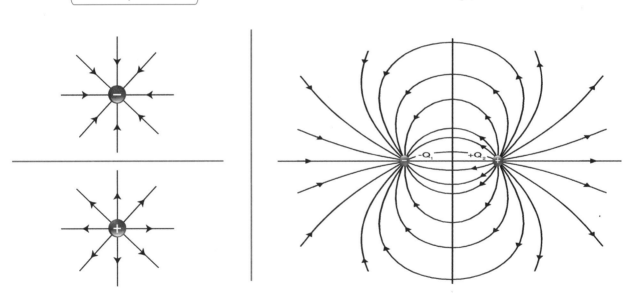

Figure III.B.9.1: Electric field lines.
The electric field is generated by the charges $-Q_1$ and $+Q_2$. The arrowheads show the direction of the electric field.

If an electric potential is applied between two plates in a vacuum (*in vacuo*), and an electron is introduced, the electron will experience an attractive force to the positive plate (*see Figure III.B.9.2*).

The force will cause the electron to accelerate towards the positive plate in a straight line. It suffers no collisions because the area between the plates is *in vacuo*. This effect is used in thermoionic valves.

If the electron is given some motion, and the electric field is applied perpendicular to the motion, interesting things happen (*see Figure III.B.9.3*). For example, a beam of electrons is emitted from a device called an electron gun. These electrons are moving in the *x* direction.

As the electrons pass between the plates they are accelerated in the *y* direction, as explained before, but their velocity in the *x* direction is unaltered. The electron beam is thus deflected as shown.

By varying the potential applied to the plates, the angle of deflection can be controlled. This effect is the basis of the cathode ray oscilloscope.

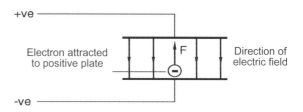

Figure III.B.9.2:
Electric field between parallel plates.

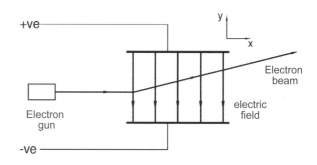

Figure III.B.9.3:
Electrostatic deflection of an electron beam.

9.1.4 Potential Energy, Absolute Potential

The *potential energy* (E_p) of a charged object in a field equals the work done on that object to bring it from infinity to a distance (r) from the charge setting up the electric field,

$$E_p = work = Fr = (qE)r = kQq/r$$

where Q = the charge setting up field, and q = the charge brought in to a distance r.

When a +q moves against E, its E_p increases. When a -q moves against the electric field E, its E_p decreases. If two positive or negative charges were brought together, work would have to be done to the system (and E_p would increase), and vice versa for charges of opposite charges.

The *absolute potential* (V) is a scalar, and it is defined at each distance (r) from a charge (Q) generating an electric field. It represents the negative of the work per unit charge in bringing a +q from infinity to r:

• $V = E_p/q = kQ/r$ in volts where 1 volt = 1 joule/coulomb.

• $V = Ed$ for a parallel plate capacitor where d = distance between the plates (PHY 10.4).

Equipotential lines are lines (and surfaces) of equal V and are *perpendicular* to electric field lines. Work can only be done when moving between surfaces of unequal V and is, therefore, independent of the path taken. No work is done when a charge (q) is moved along an equal potential (*equipotential*) surface (or line), because the component of force is zero along it. Potential (V) is defined in terms of positive charges such that V is positive when due to a +Q and negative when due a −Q. Potential (V) is added algebraically at a point (because it is a scalar).

See Figure III.B.9.4:

1) V_1, V_2 are two potentials perpendicular to the electric field E and the force F;
2) $V_2 - V_1$ is the potential difference (PD);
3)   charge (*q*) moved from A ($V_1 = 0.5$) to B ($V_2 = 1$) has work (*W*) done on it:

$$W = q(V_2 - V_1) = q(PD)$$

4)   charge (*q*) moved from A to C has no work done on it because this is along an equipotential surface ($V = 0.5$) and the non-zero component of force (*F*) is perpendicular to it;
5)   the lines of *F* are along the lines of *E*.

The *potential difference* (*PD*) is the difference in V between two points, or it is the work per unit positive charge done by electric forces moving a small test charge from the point of higher potential to the point of lower potential:

$$PD = V_a - V_b = volts = work/charge$$

$$work = q(V_a - V_b) = q(PD).$$

An *electric dipole* consists of two charges separated by some finite distance (d). Usually the charges are equal and opposite. The laws of forces, fields, etc., apply to dipoles. A dipole is characterized by its *dipole moment* which is the product of the charge (q) and d.

Dipoles tend to line up with the electric field (Fig. III.B.9.5). Motion of dipoles against an electric field requires energy as discussed above.

If you consider a single isolated point charge and the circular equipotential line produced, in 3 D, it is a sphere where each point on the surface of the sphere has the same potential because it is the same distance from the charge. This imaginary 3 D shape is called a *gaussian* surface.

dipole moment = *(charge)(distance) = qd*

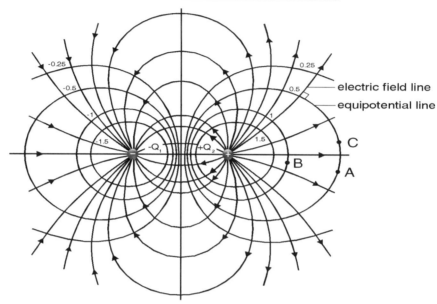

Figure III.B.9.4: Equipotential lines.

The circle-like curves around each charge $-Q_1$ and $+Q_2$ are the equipotential lines corresponding to each charge. The numbers represent the electric potential value (i.e. in millivolts) of the respective equipotential lines. Note the electric field lines as in Figure III.B.9.1.

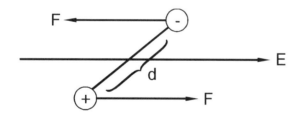

Dipole with equal and opposite charges

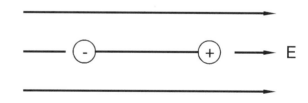

Alignment of dipole with E

Figure III.B.9.5: Dipole and electric field.

E = electric field, *F* = forces exerted by E on the dipole

9.2.1 Notion of Electromagnetic Induction

Coulomb's Law in electrostatics gives the nature of the forces acting upon electric charges at rest, but when the charges are moving, new forces appear.

They are not of the same nature as the electrostatic forces and they act differently on the electric charges. They are called electromagnetic forces.

9.2.2 Magnetic Induction Vector

Experiments have shown that two straight conductors (e.g. copper wires) traversed by electric currents of intensities I and I′ in the same direction are acted upon by an attractive force proportional to the product of the intensities and inversely proportional to the distance between the two conductors. It can be demonstrated that when the electric current in one of the conductors disappears, the force also disappears.

Therefore, the force is due to the motion of the electric charges in both conductors.

We decompose the phenomenon by introducing a new physical quantity: the magnetic induction vector B, also created by magnets.

The SI unit for B is the tesla where 1 T = 1 N/(A·m) = 10^4 gauss.

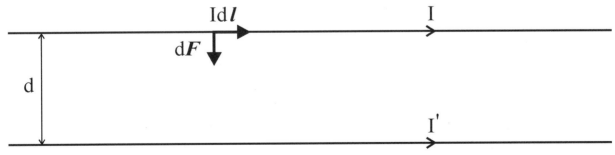

Figure III.B.9.6: Magnetic induction.
Two conductors a distance d apart; the current element *Idl* and the perpendicular force *dF* associated with the magnetic induction vector *B* are both shown. Vector B, which is not shown, has a direction perpendicular to both Idl and dF, pointing out of the page.

Thus, two effects have been shown by the preceding experiment:

1) a moving charge produces a magnetic induction.

2) a magnetic induction exerts a force on any nearby moving charge.

9.2.3 Laplace's Law

A test particle with charge dq moving at a velocity v in a magnetic induction field B is acted upon by a force dF given by the following formula:

$$dF = dq\ v \times B = dq\ v(B\sin\alpha)$$

where α is the angle formed by the direction of v with that of B (= the cross product).

The force dF is perpendicular to the magnetic induction vector and also to the displacement velocity vector of the charge (*see Figure III.B.9.6*).

When many charges are in motion so as to produce an electric current of intensity $I = dq/dt$ the force acting upon an elemental length of conductor dl traversed by that electric current is :

$$dF = I\ dl \times B = I\ dl(B\sin\alpha)$$

where α is the angle formed by the direction of the current element of conductor with that of B (= the cross product).

In order to determine the direction of a cross (= *vector*) product we can use the right-hand rule. If $c = a \times b$ then the right hand is held so that the curled fingers follow the rotation of a to b, the extended right thumb will point in the direction of c (dF in the preceding example). {Student's trick: "Grab the Wire!" Examine Fig. III.B.9.6. Turn the book around such that with your right hand open and thumb extended, the fingers point in the direction of dF and your thumb points in the direction Idl. As you begin to grab the wire, the initial direction of the tips of your fingers move perpendicular to both dF and Idl. Now the tips of your fingers make a circular motion around the wire. Those fingers have just described the direction of the magnetic induction vector B!}

An electromagnetic field is described as having at every point of the field, two perpendicular vectors: *the electric field* vector *E* and the magnetic induction field vector *B*.

Radar (= *radio detection* and ranging) is an example of a radio wave.

Visible light can be broken down into colors remembered by the mnemonic (*from highest to lowest wavelength*), Roy G. BIV: Red, Orange, Yellow, Green, Blue, Indigo, Violet.

The separation of white light into these colors can occur as a result of refraction through a prism (PHY 11.4) or through water (i.e. mist or rain resulting in a rainbow).

Planck developed the relation between energy (*E*) and the frequency *f* of the electromagnetic radiation,

$$E = hf$$

where *h* = planck's constant. Thus high frequency or short wave length corresponds to high energy and vice versa.

The speed of light (= electromagnetic radiation), given by c, can be measured from the wavelength λ and the frequency f of an electromagnetic wave in a vacuum (= *in vacuo* = no pressure/no particles approximated by outer space). Recall that v = λf (PHY 7.1.2), and so we have the special case for the speed of light,

$$c = \lambda f$$

The result is the constant $c = 3 \times 10^8$ m/s which, if required to answer a question during the GAMSAT, would be given in the passage or question stem. The speed at which light propagates through transparent materials, such as glass, water or air, is less than c, given by the refractive index n of the material (n = c/v; PHY 9.2.4). The change in c in different materials (refraction) is responsible for the colors of a rainbow.

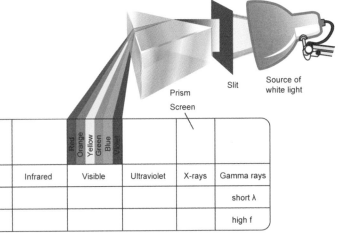

Figure III.B.9.6b: Right-hand rule.

Radio	Micro	Infrared	Visible	Ultraviolet	X-rays	Gamma rays
long λ						short λ
low f						high f

Figure III.B.9.7: The complete electromagnetic spectrum.

Go online to GAMSAT-prep.com for free chapter review Q&A and forum.

GOLD NOTES

Memorize	Understand	Not Required*
efinition/equation/units: current, resistance hm's law, resistors in series/parallel apacitance, capacitors in series/parallel irchoff's laws	* Battery, emf, voltage, terminal potential * Internal resistance of the battery, resistivity * Ohm's law, resistors in series/parallel * Parallel plate capacitor, series, parallel * Conductivity, power in circuits, Kirchoff's laws * Capacitor discharge curve (exponential decay)	* Knowledge beyond introductory-level (A-level/Leaving Certificate/Year 12) course * Complex/discrete/digital circuits * Transistors, FPGAs, microprocessors * Memorizing equations for rms voltage/current

GAMSAT-Prep.com

Introduction ▮▮▮▮

Electric circuits are closed paths which includes electronic components (i.e. resistors, capacitors, power supplies) through which a current can flow. There are 3 basic laws that govern the flow of current in an electrical circuit: Ohm's law and Kirchoff's first and second laws.

Additional Resources

Free Online Q&A + Forum

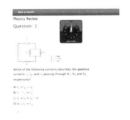

GAMSAT-prep.com Videos

Flashcards

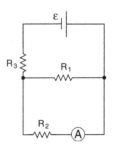

Special Guest

10.1 Current

The current (I) is the amount of charge (Q) that flows past a point in a given amount of time (t),

$$I = Q/t = amperes = coulombs/sec.$$

Current is caused by the movement of electrons between two points of significant potential difference of an electric circuit. Free electrons will accelerate towards the positive connection. As they move they will collide with atoms in the substance, losing energy which we observe as heat. The net effect is a drift of electrons at a roughly constant speed towards the positive connection. The motion of electrons is an *electric current*. As electrons are removed by the electric potential source at the positive connection, electrons are being injected at the negative connection. The potential can be considered as a form of *electron pump*.

This model explains many observed effects.

If the magnitude of the electric potential is increased, the electrons will accelerate faster and their mean velocity will be higher, i.e., the current is increased. The collisions between electrons and atoms transfer energy to the atoms. The collisions manifest themselves as heat. This effect is known as *Joule heating*. Materials such as these are termed ohmic conductors, since they obey the well-known Ohm's Law:

$$V = IR$$

where V is the voltage, I is the current, and R is the resistance.

The potential difference is maintained by a voltage source (emf). The direction of current is taken as the direction of <u>positive charge</u> movement, by convention. It is represented on a circuit diagram by arrows. Ammeters are used to measure the flow of current and are symbolized as in Figure III.B.10.1.

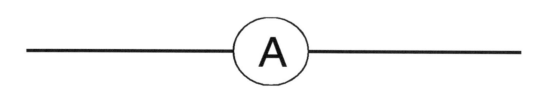

Figure III.B.10.1: Symbol of an ammeter.

Resistance (R) is the measure of opposition to the flow of electrons in a substance. Resistivity (ρ) is an inherent property of a substance. It varies with temperature. For example, the resistivity of metals increases with increasing temperature.

Resistance is directly proportional to resistivity and length *l* but inversely proportional to the cross-sectional area *A*.

$$R = \rho l/A$$

Resistance increases with temperature because the thermal motion of molecules increases with temperature and results in more collisions between electrons which impede their flow.

The units of resistance are ohms, symbolized by Ω (omega). From Ohm's Law, 1 ohm = 1 volt/ampere.

When a positive current flows across a resistor, there is a voltage decrease and an energy loss:

$$energy\ loss = Vq = VIt = joules$$

$$\boxed{power\ loss\ (P) = VIt/t = VI = watts}$$

$$watts = volts \times amperes = joules/sec.$$

The energy loss may be used to perform work. These relations hold for power (P),

$$P = VI = (IR)(I) = I^2R = V(V/R) = V^2/R.$$

constant (normal) resistance
"classic" image of resistor

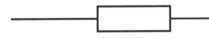

"modern" image of resistor

variable resistance (rheostat)

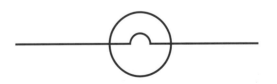

incandescent light bulb
treated like resistor

Figure III.B.10.2: Representations of resistors. Note that the filament inside of a light bulb (= *incandescent lamp* or *globe*) is a resistor. Because it resists the flow of current, it becomes hot and glows providing light. This is why a light bulb in a circuit is treated exactly like a resistor. The brightness of a light bulb depends on how much power it loses (= *dissipates*; P = VI). Consequently, when you are shopping to compare the brightness among similar types of light bulbs, the higher the number of watts, the brighter the bulb will be. Consider briefly reviewing SI units: GM 2.1.3.

Circuit elements are either in series or in parallel. Two components are in series when they have only one point in common; that is, the current travelling from one of them back to the emf source must pass through the other. In a complete series circuit, or for individual series loops of a larger mixed circuit, the current (I) is the same over each component and the total voltage drop in the circuit elements (resistors, capacitors, inductors, internal resistance of emf sources, etc.) is equal to the sum V_t of all the emf sources. The value of the equivalent resistance R_{eq} in a series circuit is:

$$R_{eq} = R_1 + R_2 + R_3 + . . .$$

Two components are in parallel when they are connected to two common points in the circuit; that is, the current travelling from one such element back to the emf source need not pass through the second element because there is an alternate path.

In a parallel circuit, the total current is the sum of currents for each path and the voltage is the same for all paths in parallel. The equivalent resistance in a parallel circuit is:

$$1/R_{eq} = 1/R_1 + 1/R_2 + 1/R_3 + . . .$$

10.2.1 Resistance Problem in Series and Parallel

Determine the equivalent resistance between points A and B in Figure III.B.10.3.

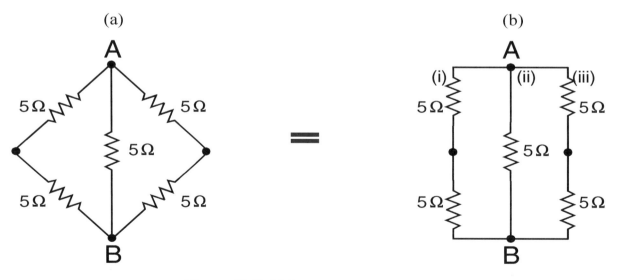

Figure III.B.10.3: Equivalent resistance.
(a) The problem as it could be presented; (b) the way you should interpret the problem.

• Wire (i) has two resistors in a row (*in series*): $R_{(i)} = 5 + 5 = 10\ \Omega$

• Wire (ii) has only one resistor: $R_{(ii)} = 5\ \Omega$

• Wire (iii) has two resistors in series: $R_{(iii)} = 5 + 5 = 10\ \Omega$

Between A and B we have three resistor systems in parallel: (i), (ii) and (iii), thus

$$1/R_{eq} = 1/R_{(i)} + 1/R_{(ii)} + 1/R_{(iii)}$$
$$= 1/10 + 1/5 + 1/10 = 4/10$$

multiply through by $10R_{eq}$ to get: $10 = 4R_{eq}$

thus $R_{eq} = 10/4 = 2.5\ \Omega$.

10.3 Batteries, Electromotive Force, Voltage, Internal Resistance

An *electromotive force (emf)* source maintains between its terminal points, a constant potential difference. The emf source replaces energy lost by moving electrons. Sources of emf are batteries (conversion of chemical energy to electrical energy) and generators (conversion of mechanical energy to electrical energy).

The source of emf does work on each charge to raise it from a lower potential to a higher potential.

Then as the charge flows around the circuit (naturally from higher to lower potential) it loses energy which is replaced by the emf source again.

energy supplied = energy lost

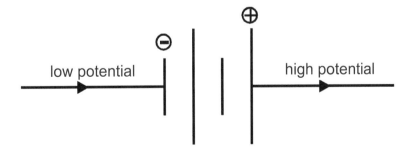

Figure III.B.10.4: Symbol of an emf source. Arrows show the normal direction of current.

Energy is lost whenever a charge (as current) passes through a resistor. The units of emf are volts. The actual voltage delivered to a circuit is not equal to the value of the source. This is reduced by an internal voltage lost which represents the voltage loss by the *internal resistance (r)* of the source itself. The net voltage is called the terminal voltage or *terminal potential* V_t.

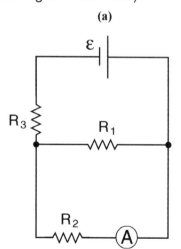

Figure III.B.10.5:
Simplified symbol of an emf source.

$$V_t = V - Ir = IR_t$$

I, R_t = totals for the circuit; V = maximal voltage output of the emf source.

When two emf sources are connected in opposition, (positive pole to positive pole) the charge loses energy when passing in the second emf source.

Therefore, if there is more than one emf source in a circuit, the total emf is the sum of the individual emf sources not in opposition reduced by the sum of individual sources in opposition in a given direction.

10.3.1 Kirchoff's Laws and a Multiloop Circuit Problem

Given that the emf of the battery ε = 12 volts and the resistors R_1 = 12 Ω, R_2 = 4.0 Ω, and R_3 = 6.0 Ω, determine the reading in the ammeter (*see Figure* III.B.10.6).

Ignore the internal resistance of the battery.

{*The ammeter will read the current which flows through it which is* i_2}

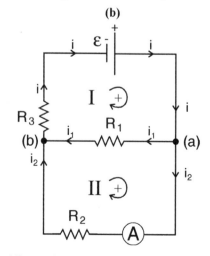

Figure III.B.10.6: A multiloop circuit.
(**a**) The problem as it could be presented; (**b**) the way you should label the diagram. Note that the current emanates from the positive terminal and is the same current i which returns to the emf source.

Kirchoff's Law I (*the junctional theorem*): when different currents arrive at a point (= *junction*, as in points (*a*) and (*b*) in the labelled diagram) the sum of current equals zero.

We can arbitrarily define all current *arriving* at the junction as <u>positive</u> and all current *leaving* as <u>negative</u>.

> Kirchoff's Law I $\qquad \Sigma i = 0$ at a junction

Thus at junction (a) $\qquad i - i_1 - i_2 = 0$

And for junction (b) $\qquad i_1 + i_2 - i = 0$

Both (a) and (b) reduce to equation (c):

$$i = i_1 + i_2$$

Kirchoff's Law II (*the loop theorem*): the sum of voltage changes in one continous loop of a circuit is zero. A single loop circuit is simple since the current is the same in all parts of the loop hence the loop theorem is applied only once.

In a multiloop circuit (loops *I* and *II* in the labelled diagram), there is more than one loop thus the current in general will not be the same in all parts of any given loop. We can arbitrarily define all voltage changes around the loop in the *clockwise* direction as <u>positive</u> and in the *counterclockwise* direction as <u>negative</u>.

Thus if by moving in the clockwise direction we can move from the battery's negative terminal (*low potential*) to its positive terminal (*high potential*), the value of the emf ε is negative.

> Kirchoff's Law II $\qquad \Sigma \Delta V = 0$ in a loop

Thus in loop *I* (*recall: V=IR*)

$$i_1 R_1 + i R_3 - \varepsilon = 0$$
And in loop II
$$i_2 R_2 - i_1 R_1 = 0$$

We now have simultaneous equations. There are three unknowns (i, i_1, i_2) and three equations (c, loop *I*, and loop *II*). We need only solve for the current i_2 which runs through the ammeter.

Substitute (c) into loop I

$$i_1 R_1 + (i_1 + i_2) R_3 - \varepsilon = 0$$
Thus
$$i_1 R_1 + i_1 R_3 + i_2 R_3 - \varepsilon = 0$$

Substitute i_1 from loop *II* where $i_1 = i_2 R_2/R_1$, hence
$$i_2 R_2 + i_2 R_2 R_3/R_1 + i_2 R_3 = \varepsilon$$
Begin isolating i_2
$$i_2(R_2 + R_2 R_3/R_1 + R_3) = \varepsilon$$
Isolate i_2
$$i_2 = \varepsilon(R_2 + R_2 R_3/R_1 + R_3)^{-1}$$
Substitute
$$i_2 = 12[4 + (4)(6)/(12) + 6]^{-1} = 12/12 = 1.0$$
ampere.

10.4 Capacitors and Dielectrics

Capacitors can store and separate charge. Capacitors can be filled with dielectrics which are materials which can increase capacitance. The capacitance (C) is an inherent property of a conductor and is formulated as:

C = charge/electric potential = Q/V = farad = coulomb/volt

The capacitance is the number of coulombs that must be transferred to a conductor to raise its potential by one volt.

The amount of charge that can be stored depends on the shape, size, surroundings and type of the conductor.

The higher the dielectric strength (i.e., the electric field strength at which a substance ceases to be an insulator and becomes a conductor) of the medium, the greater the capacitance of the conductor.

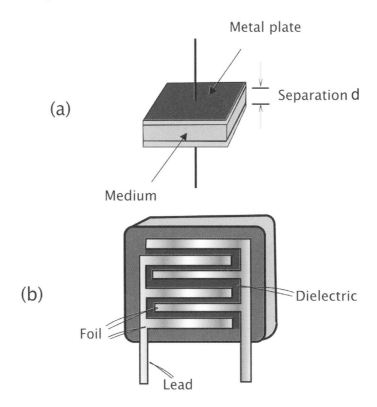

Figure III.B.10.7: (a) Parallel plate capacitor; (b) Ceramic capacitor.

A capacitor is made of two or more conductors with opposite but equal charges placed near each other.

A common example is the parallel plate capacitor. The important formulas for capacitors are:

1) C = Q/V where V = the potential between the plates
2) V = Ed where E = electric field strength, and d = distance between the plates
3) C is directly proportional to the surface area A of the plates and inversely proportional to the distance between the plates

$$C = \varepsilon_o A/d$$

for air as a medium between the plates. If the capacitor contains a dielectric, the above equation would by multiplied by the factor κ (= *dielectric constant*) whose value depends on the dielectric being used.

4) The equivalent capacitance C_{eq} for capacitors arranged in series and in parallel is:

$$\text{Series: } 1/C_{eq} = 1/C_1 + 1/C_2 + 1/C_3 \ldots$$

$$\text{Parallel: } C_{eq} = C_1 + C_2 + C_3 \ldots$$

The dielectric substances set up an opposing electric field to that of the capacitor which decreases the net electric field and allows the capacitance of the capacitor to increase ($C = Q/Ed$). The molecules of the dielectric are dipoles which line up in the electric field.

{cf. Fig. III.B.9.5 from PHY 9.1.4 and Fig. III.B.10.8 in this section}

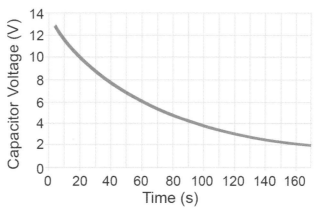

Figure III.B.10.7.1: Capacitor discharge curve. A capacitor is first charged by connecting it to a power supply. In this example, the capacitor is charged up to 14 volts. When the capacitor discharges through a resistor, the charge drains rapidly at first then decreases gradually. This pattern of decrease can be described as *exponential decay* and can be found in many areas of science (examples: first and second order reactions in General Chemistry, CHM 9.2; radioactive decay in Physics, PHY 12.4).

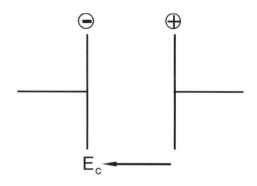

without dielectric

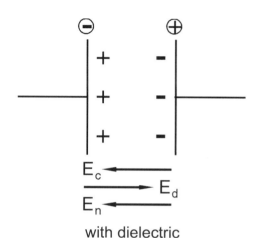

with dielectric

Figure III.B.10.8: Capacitors and dielectrics.
Note that the capacitor is symbolized by two parallel lines of equal length. The electric fields: E_c generated by the capacitor, E_d generated by the dielectric, and E_n is the resultant electric field.

The energy associated with each charged capacitor is:

Potential Energy $(PE) = W = (1/2V)(Q) = 1/2QV$

also

and

$$W = 1/2(CV)(V) = 1/2CV^2$$

$$W = 1/2Q(Q/C) = 1/2Q^2/C.$$

10.5 Root-Mean-Square Current and Voltage

DC (*direct current*) circuits contain a continuous current. Thus calculating power output is quite simple using $P = I^2R = IV$. However, AC (*alternating current*) circuits pulsate; consequently, we must discuss the <u>average</u> power output P_{av} where

$$P_{av} = (I_{rms})^2R = (I_{rms})(V_{rms})$$

which is true for a purely resistive load where the root-mean-square (*rms*) values are determined from their maximal (*max*) values:

$$I_{rms} = I_{max}/\sqrt{2} \quad \text{and} \quad V_{rms} = V_{max}/\sqrt{2}.$$

Thus by introducing the *rms* quantities the equations for DC and AC circuits have the same forms. AC circuit voltmeters and ammeters have their scales adjusted to read the *rms* values.

Go online to GAMSAT-prep.com for free chapter review Q&A and forum.

LIGHT AND GEOMETRICAL OPTICS
Chapter 11

Memorize	Understand	Not Required*
* Equations: PHY 11.3, 11.4, 11.5 * Rules for drawing ray diagrams	* Rules/equations: reflection, refraction, Snell's law * Dispersion, total internal reflection * Mirrors, lenses, real/virtual images * Ray diagrams * Lens strength, aberration	* Knowledge beyond introductory-level (A-level/Leaving Certificate/Year 12) course * Memorization of constants

GAMSAT-Prep.com

Introduction

Geometrical optics describes the propagation of light in terms of "rays." Rays are then bent at the interface of 2 rather different substances (i.e. air and glass) thus the ray may curve. A basic understanding of the equations and the geometry of light rays is necessary for solving problems in geometrical optics. Discrete questions regarding total internal reflection are frequent. Usually for the real GAMSAT, they will provide you with the optics equations to solve problems when needed. However, sometimes knowing the equation will give you an edge for "theoretical" questions and this is why we recommend that many optics equations be memorized.

Additional Resources

Free Online Q&A + Forum

GAMSAT-prep.com Videos

Flashcards

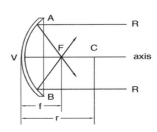

Special Guest

11.1 Visual Spectrum, Color

Geometrical optics is a first approximation of physical optics, which by its wavy nature, is part of the electromagnetic wave theory. The theory of light is dualistic:

• *particulate*: referring to a packet of energy called a photon when one wants, for example, to explain the photoelectric effect (= an experiment whereby light is shone onto a material resulting in the emission of electrons).

• *wavy*: when one wants to explain, for example, light interference and diffraction (PHY 7.1.3, Fig. III.B.7.5.1).

The optics domain of the electromagnetic wave theory corresponds to the following range of wavelengths of the electromagnetic spectrum (expressed in microns $1\mu = 10^{-6}\,m$):

$$0.4\mu < \lambda < 0.8\mu$$

or

$$0.4\mu < visible < 0.8\mu.$$

See PHY 9.2.4 for the colors in the visual spectrum. See PHY 9.2.4, 11.4 and 12.3 for the speed of light in a vacuum.

11.2 Polarization

An electromagnetic field is described as having at every point of the field two perpendicular vectors: *the electric field vector E and the magnetic induction field vector B.*

The electromagnetic wave front is polarized in a straight line when E and B are fixed at all times. Thus polarized light is light that has waves in only one plane.

11.3 Reflection, Mirrors

Reflection is the process by which light rays (= *imaginary lines drawn perpendicular to the advancing wave fronts*) bounce back into a medium from a surface with another medium (*versus being refracted or absorbed*). The ray that arrives is the *incident* ray while the ray that bounces back is the *reflected* ray. The laws of reflection are:

1) the angle of incidence (I) equals the angle of reflection (R) at the normal (*N*, the line perpendicular to the surface)
2) the I, R, N all lie in the same plane.

After a ray strikes a mirror or a lens it forms an image. A <u>virtual image</u> has no light rays passing through it and cannot be projected upon a screen.

A <u>real image</u> has light rays passing through it and can be projected upon a screen.

Mirrors have a plane surface, like an ordinary household mirror, or a non-plane surface. For a plane mirror, all incident light is reflected in parallel off the mirror and therefore all images seen are virtual, erect, left-right reversed and appear to be just as far (perpendicular distance) behind the mirror as the object is in front of the mirror.

In other words, the object (o) and the image (i) distances have the same magnitudes but have opposite directions ($i = -o$).

Spherical mirrors are non-plane mirrors which may have the reflecting surface convex (*diverges light*) or concave (*converges light*). We will see that the images formed by a converging mirror (concave) are like those for a converging lens (convex); and diverging mirrors (convex) and a diverging lens (concave) also form similar images.

The terminology for spherical mirrors is:

r = radius of curvature (distance from C to V)
C = center of curvature
F = focal point (AKA 'principal' focus)
V = vertex (center of the mirror itself)
axis = 'central' or 'optical' axis = line through C and V
f = focal length (distance from F to V)
i = image distance (distance from V to image along the axis)
o = object distance (distance from V to object along the axis)
AB = linear aperture (cord connecting the ends of the mirror; the larger the aperture, the better the resolution).

As a rule, capital letters refer to a point (*or position*) and small case letters refer to a distance.

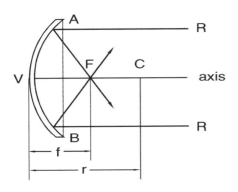

Concave (converging)

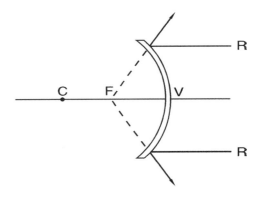

Convex (diverging)

Figure III.B.11.1: Reflection by spherical mirrors. R = the light rays.

With concave (spherical) mirrors the incident light is converged toward the axis. The path of light rays is as follows:

1)
if $o < f$, then the image is virtual and erect;
if $o > f$, then the image is real and inverted;
if $o = f$, then no image is formed;
2)
if $o < r$, then the image is enlarged in size;
if $o > r$, then the image is reduced in size;
if $o = r$, then the image is the same.

The relations are similar to those for a converging lens (convex). With convex (spherical) mirrors, the incident light is diverged from the axis after reflection. It is the backward extension (dotted lines in the diagram) that may pass through the focal point F. The path of light rays are as follows:

1) Incident rays parallel to the axis have backward extension of their reflections through F (*see Figure III.B.11.1*);
2) incident rays along a radius (that would pass C if extended) reflect back along themselves;
3) incident rays that pass through F (if extended) reflect parallel to the axis.

The image formed for a convex mirror is always virtual, erect and smaller than the object {Convex mirror = REV: Reduced, Erect, Virtual}. The mirror equation and the derivations from it allow the above relations between object and image to be calculated instead of memorized. The equation is valid for convex and concave mirrors:

$$1/i + 1/o = 1/f$$

$$f = r/2$$

$$M = magnification = -i/o.$$

Convention:
• for i and o, *positive* values mean <u>real</u>, *negative* values mean <u>virtual</u>;
• for r and f, *positive* values mean <u>converging</u>, *negative* values mean <u>diverging</u>;
• for M, a *positive* value means <u>erect</u>, *negative* is <u>inverted</u>;
• for M > 1 the image is <u>enlarged</u>, M < 1 the image is <u>diminished</u>.

Examples:
• concave mirror: headlights of a car, make-up mirror, the inside of a shiny spoon;
• convex mirror: car's side-view mirror, security mirrors, the outside of a shiny spoon.

11.4 Refraction, Dispersion, Refractive Index, Snell's Law

Refraction is the bending of light as it passes from one transparent medium to another and is caused by the different speeds of light in the two media.

If θ_1 is taken as the angle (to the normal) of the incident light and θ_2 is the angle (to the normal) of the refracted light, where 1 and 2 represent the two different media, the following relations hold (Snell's Law):

where v = velocity and λ = wavelength.

$$\frac{\sin \theta_1}{\sin \theta_2} = \frac{v_1}{v_2} = \frac{n_2}{n_1} = \frac{\lambda_1}{\lambda_2}$$

$$n = \frac{\text{speed of light in vacuum}}{\text{speed of light in medium}} = \frac{c}{v}$$

$c = 3 \times 10^8$ *m/sec* or 181,000 *mi/sec*
$n = 1.0$ for air, $n = 1.33$ for H_2O
$n = 1.5$ for glass (at $\lambda = 589$ *nm*)
n = *the refractive index which is a property of the medium*
n_1 = *refractive index of medium 1*
n_2 = *refractive index of medium 2*
N = *normal line to the surface*
S = *surface line, represents the separation between the two media (= interface = boundary)*
I = *incident light (= ray = beam)*
R = *refracted light (= ray = beam)*

The speed at which light propagates through transparent materials, such as glass, water or air, is less than c, as you can tell from index of refractions above.

The angle θ is smaller (closer to the normal, e.g. θ_1) in the more optically dense (higher n) medium.

Also the smaller wavelength of the incident light (i.e. toward the violet end), the closer θ_2 is to the normal (i.e. it is smaller than θ_1).

This means longer wavelengths travel faster in a medium than shorter wavelengths (i.e. shorter wavelengths are more subject to refraction).

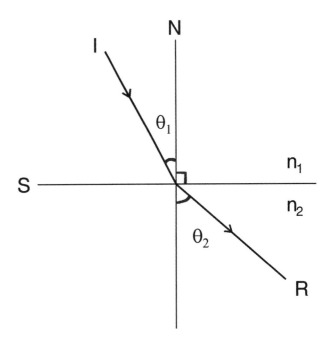

Figure III.B.11.2: Refraction.

This leads to *dispersion* which is the separation of white light (= *all colors together*) into individual colors by this differential refraction. For example, a prism disperses white light. See PHY 9.2.4.

The laws of refraction are:

1) The incident ray, the refracted ray and the normal ray all lie in the same plane.
2) The path of the ray (incident and refracted parts) is reversible.

When light passes from a more optically dense (higher n) medium into a less optically dense medium, there exists an angle of incidence such that the angle of refraction θ_2 is 90°.

This special angle of incidence is called the critical angle θ_c.

This is because when the angle of incidence is less then θ_c refraction occurs. If the angle of incidence is equal to θ_c, then neither refraction nor reflection occur.

And if $\theta_1 > \theta_c$, then <u>total internal reflection</u> (*ray is reflected back into the more optically dense medium*) occurs. The θ_c is found from Snell's Law:

$$n_1\sin\theta_c = n_2\sin\theta_2$$

$$\text{and } \theta_2 = 90° => \sin\theta_2 = 1$$

$$\text{giving } n_1\sin\theta_c = n_2 \times 1$$

$$\text{finally } \sin\theta_c = n_2/n_1$$

$$\text{where } n_2 < n_1.$$

When looking at an object under water from above the surface, the object appears closer than it actually is. This is due to refraction. In general:

apparent depth/actual depth = n_2/n_1

where n_2 = the medium of the observer, and n_1 = the medium of the object.

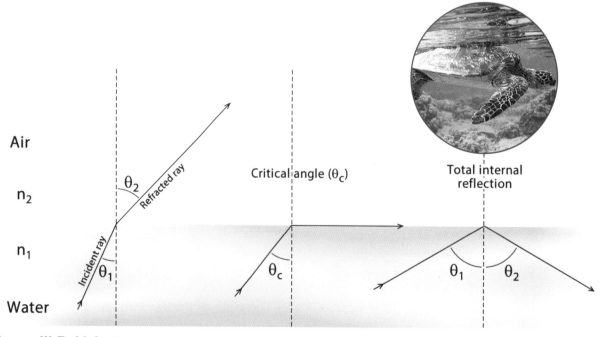

Air

n_2

θ_2

Refracted ray

Critical angle (θ_c)

Total internal reflection

n_1

Incident ray

θ_1

θ_c

θ_1

θ_2

Water

Figure III.B.11.3 The critical angle and total internal reflection. The inset shows the Green sea turtle, *Chelonia mydas*, and its reflection seen at the interface (boundary) where air and water meet.
Inset photo: TheBrockenInaGlory 2008, Wikimedia Commons.

11.5 Thin Lens, Diopters

A lens is a transparent material which refracts light. Converging lenses refract toward the axis, and diverging lenses refract the light away from the axis.

A converging lens is wider at the middle than at the ends, and the diverging lens is thinner at the middle than at the ends.

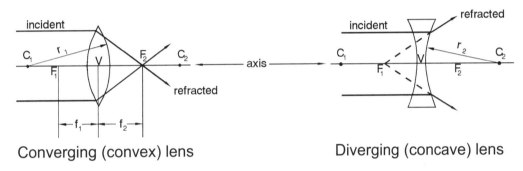

Figure III.B.11.4: Refraction by spherical lenses; r = the radius of curvature.

If the surface is convex, r is positive (e.g., r_1). If the surface is concave, r is negative (e.g., r_2).
Subscript 1 refers to the incident side, 2 refers to the refracted side.

C = center of curvature, F = focal point
V = the optical center of the lens or vertex
axis = line through C and V

f = focal length is the distance between V and F
i = image distance (from V to the image)
o = object distance (from V to the object).

The path rays through a lens are:

1) incident rays parallel to the axis refract through F_2 of the converging lens, and appear

to come from F_1 of a diverging lens (backward extensions of the refracted ray, see dotted line on diverging diagram);

2) an incident ray through F_1 of a converging lens or through F_2 of a diverging lens (if extended) are refracted parallel to the axis;

3) incident rays through V are not deviated (refracted).

For a converging lens (e.g., convex) the image formed depends on the object distance relative to the focal length (f). The relations (note similarity with a converging mirror) are:

1) if $o < f_1$, then image is virtual and erect;
if $o > f_1$, the image is real and inverted;
if $o = f_1$, then no image is formed;

2) if $o < 2f_1$, then the image is enlarged in size; if $o > 2f_1$, then the image is reduced in size; if $o = 2f_1$, then the image is the same; remember $2f_1 = r$.

For a diverging lens (e.g., concave), the image is always virtual, erect and reduced in size as for a diverging mirror (REV, cf. PHY 11.4).

The above relations can be calculated rather than memorized by use of the lens equation (similar to the mirror equation) and derivations from it,

1) $1/o + 1/i = 1/f$ (lens equation, same as mirror equation)

2) $D = 1/f = (n-1)(1/r_1 - 1/r_2)$, (lens maker's equation, n = index of refraction)

A <u>magnifying glass</u> (or "hand lens") is a convex lens that is used to produce a magnified image of an object. The lens is usually mounted in a frame with a handle. You can determine from the preceding rules that, in order to have an image that is erect (upright) and magnified for easier viewing, the object distance must be less than the focal length of the convex lens.

3) diopters $(D) = 1/f$ where f is in meters, measures the refractive *power* of the lens; the larger the diopters, the stronger the lens. The diopters has a positive value for a converging lens and a negative value for a diverging lens.

To get the refractive power (D) of lenses in series just add the diopters which can then be converted into focal length:

$$D_T = D_1 + D_2 = 1/f_T \; (T = total).$$

4) Note that you can add only inverses of focal lengths:

$$1/f_T = 1/f_1 + 1/f_2 \; . . .$$

5) $M = Magnification = -i/o = M_1 M_2$ for lenses in series.

Convention:
- for i and o, positive values mean real, negative values mean virtual;
- for r and f, positive values mean converging, negative values mean diverging;
- for M, a positive value means erect, negative is inverted.

The lens equation holds only for thin lenses (the thickness is small relative to other dimensions). For combination of lenses not in contact with each other, the image is found for the first lens (nearer the object) and then this image is used as the object of the second lens to find the image formed by it.

It should be noted that since concave lenses are concave on both sides they are sometimes called *biconcave*. Likewise, convex lenses may be called *biconvex*.

11.5.1 Lens Aberrations

In practice, the images formed by various refracting surfaces, as described in the previous section, fall short of theoretical perfection. Imperfections of image formation are due to several mechanisms or *aberrations.*

For example a nick or cut in a convex lens might create a microscopic area of concavity. Thus the light ray which strikes the aberration diverges instead of converging. Therefore the image will be less sharp or clear as the number or sizes of the aberrations increase.

11.6 Light vs. Sound

Property	Light	Sound
Type of wave	Transverse	Longitudinal
Travel through a vacuum?	Yes	No, can only pass through a solid, liquid or gas.
Velocity in air (approx.)	300 million m/s	340 m/s (notice that you can see lightning before you hear its sound, thunder)
Velocity in denser medium	Slower	Faster
Can they be reflected?	Yes	Yes
Can they be refracted?	Yes	Yes
Can they be diffracted?	Yes	Yes
Can they interfere?	Yes, e.g. bright vs dark	Yes, e.g. loud vs quiet
Variation in frequency from low to high	Red light to violet light	Low pitch (note) to high pitch

Table III.B.11.1: Comparing light and sound waves, GAMSAT Physics Chapters 7, 8 and 11. What about water waves like those you can see at the beach (after finishing your GAMSAT studies!)? Water waves are quite similar to sound waves (transverse, can be reflected, refracted and diffracted) but, of course, the velocity is not standard. Maximal destructive interference would create calm waters (for sound, similar to quiet), whereas maximal constructive interference could be caused by an earthquake (or other disturbance) and produce a tsunami (for sound, extremely loud similar to a volcanic eruption or standing right beside the speakers at a concert in a football stadium!).

Go online to GAMSAT-prep.com for free chapter review Q&A and forum.

Memorize	Understand	Not Required*
Basic atomic and nuclear structure Define 'isotopes' Equation for half-life	* Basic atomic structure, amu * Fission, fusion; the Bohr model of the atom * Isotopes and the calculation for weighted average * Problem solving for half-life * Quantized energy levels for electrons * Fluorescence	* Knowledge beyond introductory-level (A-level/Leaving Certificate/Year 12) course * Memorizing mass: neutrons/protons/electrons * Memorizing constants, conversions

GAMSAT-Prep.com

Introduction ▮▮▮

Atomic structure can be summarized as a nucleus orbited by electrons in different energy levels. Transition of electrons between energy levels and nuclear structure (i.e. protons, neutrons) are important characteristics of the atom. There is very little in this chapter that MUST be memorized for the GAMSAT.

Additional Resources

| Free Online Q&A + Forum | GAMSAT-prep.com Videos | Flashcards | Special Guest |

12.1 Protons, Neutrons, Electrons

Only recently, with high resolution electron microscopes, have large atoms been visualized. However, for years their existence and properties have been inferred by experiments. Experimental work on gas discharge effects suggested that an atom is not a single entity but is itself composed of smaller particles. These were termed elementary particles. A more encompassing expression would be "subatomic" particles.

The atom appears as a small solar system with a heavy nucleus composed of positive particles and neutral particles: *protons and neutrons*. Around this nucleus, there are clouds of negatively charged particles, called *electrons*. The mass of a neutron is slightly more than that of a proton (both ≈ 1.7×10^{-24} g); the mass of the electron is considerably less (9.1×10^{-28} g).

Since an atom is electrically neutral, the negative charge carried by the electrons must be equal in magnitude (but opposite in sign) to the positive charge carried by the protons.

Experiments with electrostatic charges have shown that **opposite charges attract (and like charges repel)**, so it can be considered that electrostatic forces hold an atom together. The difference between various atoms is therefore determined by their *composition*.

A hydrogen atom consists of one proton and one electron; a helium atom of two protons, two neutrons and two electrons. They are shown in diagram form in Figure III.B.12.1.

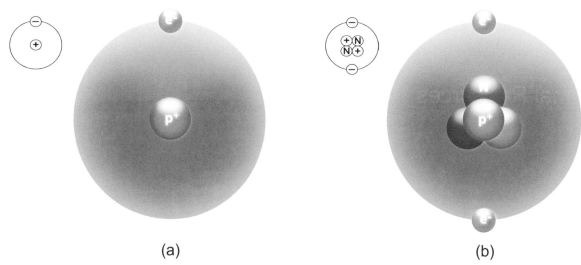

(a)   (b)

Figure III.B.12.1: Atomic structure simplified: (a) hydrogen atom; (b) helium atom. The images above are a summary of key features of the 2 simplest atoms. The insets (black and white) are basic sketches, while in color is essentially a cartoon for several reasons including: 1) the actual proportions cannot be drawn to scale because the space between the nucleus and electrons is too great and the electron itself is far smaller; 2) the actual position of an electron cannot be known (CHM 2.1; though the orange cloud is supposed to be a reminder); 3) subatomic particles do not have color in any traditional sense.

A proton has a mass of 1 a.m.u. (*atomic mass unit*) and a charge of +1, whereas, a neutron has a mass of 1 a.m.u. and no charge. The *atomic number* (*AN*) of an atom is the number of protons in the nucleus. In an atom of neutral charge, the atomic number (AN) is also equal to the number of electrons.

The atomic number is conventionally represented by the letter "Z". Each of the chemical elements has a unique number of protons which is identified by its own atomic number "Z". As an example, for the hydrogen H element, Z = 1 and for Na, Z = 11.

An *element* is a group of atoms with the same AN. *Isotopes* are elements which have the same atomic number (Z) but different number of neutrons and hence a different mass number (MN). As an example, the three carbon isotopes differ only in the number of neutrons and therefore have the same number of protons and electrons but differ in mass and are usually represented as follows: C-12, C-13 and C-14 or more specifically as follows: $^{12}_{6}C$, $^{13}_{6}C$ and $^{14}_{6}C$. It is therefore the number of protons that distinguishes elements from each other. The *weighted average* follows the natural abundance of the various isotopic compositions of an element.

The *mass number* (*MN*) of an atom is the number of protons and neutrons in an atom. The *atomic weight* (*AW*) is the weighted average of all naturally occurring isotopes of an element.

For example: Silicon is known to exist naturally as a mixture of three isotopes (Si-28, Si-29 and Si-30). The relative amount of each of the three different silicon isotopes is found to be 92.2297% with a mass of 27.97693, 4.6832% with a mass of 28.97649 and the remaining 3.0872% with a mass of 29.97377. The atomic weight of silicon is then determined as the weighted average (cf. GM 1.4.3 C) of each of the isotopes as follows:

$$\text{Si mass} = (27.97693 \times 0.922297)$$
$$+ (28.97649 \times 0.046832)$$
$$+ (29.97377 \times 0.030872)$$
$$= 28.0854 \text{ g/mol.}$$

It is also important to note that as the number of <u>protons</u> distinguishes *elements* from each other, it is their <u>electronic configuration</u> (CHM 2.1, 2.2, 2.3) that determines their *reactivity*.

The mass of a nucleus is always smaller than the combined mass of its constituent protons and neutrons. The difference in mass is converted to energy (E) which holds protons and neutrons together within the nuclear core.

Let's consider the number of protons and neutrons in two commonly discussed isotopes: carbon and hydrogen. Carbon C-12, C-13 and C-14 are isotopes with 12, 13 and 14 MN, respectively. The atomic number of carbon is 6 (this can be seen on a periodic table, CHM 2.4.1), which means that every carbon atom has 6 protons, so that the number of neutrons of these isotopes must be 6, 7 and 8, respectively. Likewise, hydrogen (AN = 1 = 1 proton) has 3 isotopes: H-1 (0 neutrons), H-2 (= deuterium, D; 1 neutron); and H-3 (= tritium, T; 2 neutrons).

12.3 Nuclear Forces, Nuclear Binding Energy, Stability, Radioactivity

Coulomb repulsive force (between protons) in the nuclei are overcome by nuclear forces. The nuclear force is a non-electrical type of force that binds nuclei together and is equal for protons and neutrons. The nuclear binding energy (E_b) is a result of the relation between energy and mass changes associated with nuclear reactions,

$$\Delta E = \Delta mc^2$$

in ergs in the CGS system, i.e. m = grams and c = cm/sec; ΔE = energy released or absorbed; Δm = mass lost or gained, respectively; c = velocity of light = 3.0×10^{10} cm/sec.

Conversions:
1 *gram* = 9×10^{20} *ergs*
1 *a.m.u.* = 931.4 *MeV* (*Mev* = 10^6 electron volts)
1 *a.m.u.* = 1/12 the mass of $_6C^{12}$.

The preceding equation is a statement of the law of conservation of mass and energy. The value of E_b depends upon the mass number (MN) as follows, (*see Figure III.A.11.2*):

The peak E_b/MN is at MN = 60. Also, E_b/MN is relatively constant after MN = 20. Fission is when a nucleus splits into smaller nuclei. Fusion is when smaller nuclei combine to form a larger nucleus. Energy is released from a nuclear reaction when nuclei with MN $\gg$ 60 undergo fission or nuclei with MN $\ll$ 60 undergo fusion. Both fusion and fission release energy because the mass difference between the initial and the final nuclear states is converted into energy.

Not all combinations of protons are stable. The most stable nuclei are those with an even number of protons and an even number of neutrons. The least stable nuclei are those with an odd number of protons and an odd number of neutrons. Also, as the atomic number (AN) increases, there are more neutrons (N) needed for the nuclei to be stable.

According to the *Baryon number conservation*, the total number of protons and neutrons remains the same in a nuclear reaction even with the inter-conversions occurring between protons and neutrons.

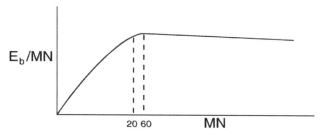

Figure III.A.11.2: Binding Energy per Nucleus. *E_b/MN = binding energy per nucleus; this is the energy released by the formation of a nucleus.*

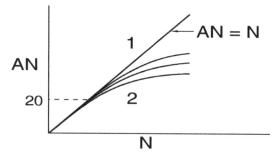

Figure III.A.11.3: Stability of Atoms. AN = atomic number and N = number of neutrons.

Up to AN = 20 (Calcium) the number of protons is equal to the number of neutrons, after this there are more neutrons. If an atom is in region #1 in Figure III.A.11.3, it has too many protons or too few neutrons and must decrease its protons or increase its neutrons to become stable. The reverse is true for region #2. All nuclei after AN = 84 (Polonium) are unstable.

Unstable nuclei become stable by fission to smaller nuclei or by absorption or emission of small particles. Spontaneous fission is rare. Spontaneous radioactivity (emission of particles) is common. The common particles are:

(1) alpha (α) particle = $_2He^4$ (helium nucleus);

(2) beta (β) particle = $_{-1}e^0$ (an electron);

(3) a positron $_{+1}e^0$ (same mass as an electron but opposite charge);

(4) gamma (γ) ray = no mass and no charge, just electromagnetic energy;

(5) orbital electron capture - nucleus takes electrons from K shell and converts a proton to a neutron. If there is a flux of particles such as neutrons ($_0n^1$), the nucleus can absorb these also.

> A neutron walks into a bar and asks the bartender: *"How much for a beer?"* The bartender answers: *"For you, no charge."* :)

12.4 Nuclear Reaction, Radioactive Decay, Half-Life

Nuclear reactions are reactions in which changes in nuclear composition occur. An example of a nuclear reaction which involves uranium and hydrogen:

$$_{92}U^{238} + _1H^2 \rightarrow _{93}Np^{238} + 2_0n^1$$

for $_{92}U^{238}$: 238 = mass number, 92 = atomic number. The sum of the lower (or higher) numbers on one side of the equation equals the sum of the lower (or higher) numbers on the other side of the equation. Another way of writing the preceding reaction is:

$_{92}U^{238}(_1H^2,2_0n^1)_{93}Np^{238}$. {# neutrons (i.e. $_{92}U^{238}$) = superscript (238) – subscript (92) = 146}

Radioactive decay is a naturally occurring spontaneous process in which the atomic nucleus of an unstable atom loses energy by the emission of ionizing particles. Such unstable nuclei are known to spontaneously decompose and emit minute atomic sections to essentially gain some stability. The radioactive decay fragments are categorized into alpha, beta and gamma-ray decays. The radioactive decay can result in a nuclear change (*trans-*

mutation) in which the parent and daughter nuclei are of different elements. For example, a C-14 atom may undergo a beta decay and emit radiation and as a result, transform into a N-14 daughter nucleus. It is also possible that radioactive decay does not result in transmutation but only decreases the energy of the parent nucleus. As an example, a Ni-28 atom undergoing a gamma decay will emit radiation and then transform to a lower energy Ni-28 nucleus. The following is a brief description of the three principle types of radioactive decay.

(1) **Alpha (α) decay:** Alpha decay is a type of radioactive decay in which an atomic nucleus emits an alpha particle. An alpha particle is composed of two protons and two neutrons which is identical to a helium-4 nucleus. An alpha particle is the most massive of all radioactive particles. Because of its relatively large mass, alpha particles tend to have the most potential to interact with other atoms and/or molecules and ionize them as well as lose energy. As such, these par-

ticles have the lowest penetrating power (= *least ability to go straight through matter, an object*). If an atomic nucleus of an element undergoes alpha decay, this leads to a transmutation of that element into another element as shown below for the transmutation of Uranium-238 to Thorium-234:

$$^{238}_{92}U \rightarrow {}^{234}_{90}Th + {}^{4}_{2}He^{2+}$$
$$^{238}U \rightarrow {}^{234}Th + \alpha$$

(2) **Beta (β) decay:** Beta decay is a type of decay in which an unstable nucleus emits an electron or a positron. A positron is the antiparticle of an electron and has the same mass as an electron but opposite in charge. The electron from a beta decay forms when a neutron of an unstable nucleus changes into a proton and in the process, an electron is then emitted. The electron in this case is referred to as a beta minus particle or β^-. In beta decays producing positron emissions, it is referred to as beta plus or β^+. For an

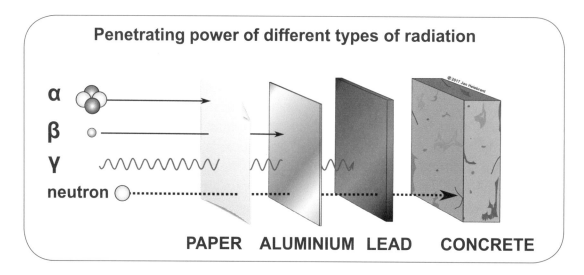

Penetrating power of different types of radiation

α

β

γ

neutron

PAPER   ALUMINIUM   LEAD   CONCRETE

atomic nucleus undergoing beta decay, the process leads to the transmutation of that element into another as shown for the transmutation of Cesium-137 for beta minus and Na-22 for beta plus emissions:

$$^{137}_{55}\text{Cs} \rightarrow {}^{137}_{56}\text{Ba} + \beta^-$$
$$^{22}_{11}\text{Na} \rightarrow {}^{22}_{10}\text{Ne} + \beta^+$$

(3) Gamma (γ) decay: Gamma decay is different from the other two types of decays. Gamma decay emits a form of electromagnetic radiation. Gamma rays are high energy photons known to penetrate matter very well and are symbolized by the Greek letter gamma (γ). A source of gamma decay could be a case in which an excited daughter nucleus - following an alpha or beta decay - lowers its energy state further by gamma-ray emission without a change in mass number or atomic number. The following is an example:

$$^{60}\text{Co} \rightarrow {}^{60}\text{Ni*} + \beta^-$$

Co-60 decays to an excited Ni*-60 via beta decay and subsequently, the excited Ni*-60 drops to ground state and emits gamma (γ) rays as follows:

$$^{60}\text{Ni*} \rightarrow {}^{60}\text{Ni} + \gamma$$

To summarize, a gamma ray has no charge and no mass since it is a form of electromagnetic radiation (PHY 9.2.4). As shown, gamma rays are usually emitted in conjunction with other radiation emissions.

Spontaneous radioactive decay is a first order process. This means that the rate of decay is *directly* proportional to the amount of material present:

$$\Delta m/\Delta t = \text{rate of decay}$$

where Δm = change in mass, Δt = change in time.

The preceding relation is equalized by adding a proportionality constant called the decay constant (k) as follows,

$$\Delta m/\Delta t = -km.$$

The minus sign indicates that the mass is decreasing. Also, $k = -(\Delta m/m)/\Delta t$ = fraction of the mass that decays with time.

The *half-life* ($T_{1/2}$) of a radioactive atom is the time required for one half of it to disintegrate. The half-life is related to k as follows,

$$T_{1/2} = 0.693/k.$$

Table III.A.11.1: Modes of Radioactive Decay

Decay Mode	Participating particles	Change in (A, Z)	Daughter Nucleus
Alpha decay	α	A = –4, Z = –2	(A – 4, Z – 2)
Beta decay	β^-	A = 0, Z = +1	(A, Z + 1)
Gamma decay	γ	A = 0, Z = 0	(A, Z)
Positron emission	β^+	A = 0, Z = –1	(A, Z – 1)

If the number of half-lives *n* are known we can calculate the percentage of a pure radioactive sample left after undergoing decay since the fraction remaining = $(1/2)^n$.

For example, given a pure radioactive substance X with $T_{1/2}$ = 9 years, calculating the percentage of substance X after 27 years is quite simple,

$$27 = 3 \times 9 = 3\ T_{1/2}$$

Thus

$$n = 3, (1/2)^n = (1/2)^3 = 1/8 \text{ or } 13\%.$$

After 27 years of disintegration, 13% of pure substance X remains. {Similarly, note that *doubling time* is given by $(2)^n$; see BIO 2.2}

12.5 Quantized Energy Levels For Electrons, Emission Spectrum

Work by Bohr and others in the early part of the last century demonstrated that the electron orbits are arranged in shells, and that each shell has a defined maximum number of electrons it can contain.

For example, the first shell can contain two electrons, the second eight electrons (see CHM 2.1, 2.2). The maximum number of electrons in each shell is given by:

$$N_{electrons} = 2n^2$$

$N_{electrons}$ designates the number of electrons in shell n.

The state of each electron is determined by the four quantum numbers:

- *principal quantum number n* determines the number of shells, possible values are: 1 (K), 2 (L), 3 (M), etc...
- *angular momentum quantum number l*, determines the subshell, possible values are: 0 (s), 1 (p), 2 (d), 3 (f), n-1, etc...

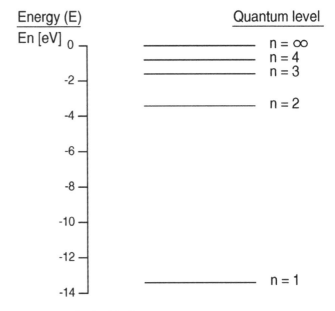

Figure III.A.11.4a: Energy levels. The energy E_n in each shell n is measured in electron volts.

- *magnetic momentum quantum number m_l*, possible values are: $\pm l, \dots, 0$
- *spin quantum number m_s*, determines the direction of rotation of the electron, possible values are: $\pm 1/2$.

Chemical reactions and electrical effects are all concerned with the behavior of electrons in the outer shell of any particular atom. If a shell is full, for example, the atom is unlikely to react with any other atom and is, in fact, one of the noble (inert) gases such as helium.

The energy that an electron contains is not continuous over the entire range of possible energy. Rather, electrons in a atom may contain only discrete energies as they occupy certain orbits or shells. Electrons of each atom are restricted to these discrete energy levels. These levels have an energy below zero.

This means energy is released when an electron moves from infinity into these energy levels.

If there is one electron in an atom, its ground state is n = 1, the lowest energy level available. Any other energy level, n = 2, n = 3, etc., is considered an excited state for that electron. The difference in energy (E) between the levels gives the absorbed (or emitted) energy when an electron moves to a higher orbit (or lower orbit, respectively) and therefore, the frequency (f) of light necessary to cause excitation.

$$E_2 - E_1 = hf$$

where E_1 = energy level one, E_2 = energy level two, h = planck's constant, and f = the frequency of light absorbed or emitted.

Therefore, if light is passed through a substance (e.g., gas), certain wavelengths will be absorbed, which correspond to the energy needed for the electron transition. An *absorption* spectrum will result that has dark lines against a light background. Multiple lines result because there are possible transitions from all quantum levels occupied by electrons to any unoccupied levels.

An *emission* spectrum results when an electron is excited to a higher level by another particle or by an electric discharge, for example. Then, as the electron falls from the

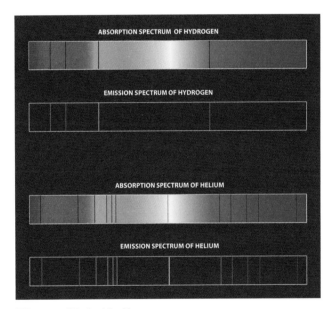

Figure III.A.11.4b: Absorption and emission spectra of the first two elements of the periodic table: hydrogen and helium. When electrons in an element become excited, for example by being heated, they enter higher energy orbits. When they return to their ground state, they release the extra energy as light radiation at a specific wavelength. The wavelengths emitted by an element are characteristic of that element. The dark lines within the absorption spectra show at what wavelengths light that passes through an element (when in its ground state) will be absorbed. As can be seen, the emission and absorption lines match. Credit: CARLOS CLARIVAN/SCIENCE PHOTO LIBRARY.

excited state to lower states, light is emitted that has a wavelength (which is related to frequency) corresponding to the energy difference between the levels since: $E_1 - E_2 = hf$. The resulting spectrum will have <u>light lines</u> against a <u>dark background</u>.

The total energy of the electrons in an atom, where KE is the kinetic energy, can be given by:

$$E_{total} = E_{emission} \text{ } (or \text{ } E_{ionization}) + KE$$

12.6 Fluorescence

Fluorescence is an <u>emission process</u> that occurs after light absorption excites electrons to higher electronic and vibrational levels. The electrons spontaneously lose excited vibrational energy to the electronic states. There are certain molecular types that possess this property, e.g., some amino acids (tryptophan).

The fluorescence process is as follows:
* **step 1** - absorption of light;

* **step 2** - spontaneous deactivation of vibrational levels to zero vibrational level for electronic state;
* **step 3** - fluorescence with light emission (longer wavelength than absorption).

Figure III.B.12.5 shows diagrammatically the steps described above. Step 2 which is not shown in the figure is the intermediate step between light absorption and light emission. See BIO 1.5.1 for fluorescence as applied to microscopy.

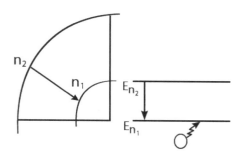

Step 1: light absorption   Step 3: light emission

Figure III.B.12.5: The fluorescence process. Represented is an atom with shells n_1, n_2 and their respective energy levels E_n.

If you have started from the beginning of the book then you are much more than half way finished! Don't worry about going back, it is best to complete all the associated online practice questions, take brief notes and then move on to the next section. And in closing this section, a quote from a pioneering atomic physicist:

"All of physics is either impossible or trivial. It is impossible until you understand it, and then it becomes trivial."
    – E. Rutherford

Good luck with your studies!

Go online to GAMSAT-prep.com for free chapter review Q&A and forum.

GAMSAT-Prep.com

GENERAL CHEMISTRY
PART III.A: PHYSICAL SCIENCES

IMPORTANT: The beginning of each science chapter provides guidelines as to what you should Memorize, Understand and what is Not Required. These are guides to get you a top score without getting lost in the details. Our guides have been determined from an analysis of all ACER materials plus student surveys. Additionally, the original owner of this book gets a full year access to many online features described in the Preface and Introduction including an online Forum where each chapter can be discussed.

STOICHIOMETRY

Chapter 1

Memorize	Understand	Not Required*
* Define: molecular weight * Define: empirical/molecular formula * Rules for oxidation numbers	* Composition by % mass * Mole concept, limiting reactants * Avogadro's number * Calculate theoretical yield * Basic types of reactions * Calculation of ox. numbers	* Knowledge beyond introductory-level (first year uni.) course * Balancing complex equations * Stoichiometric coefficients in competing reactions

GAMSAT-Prep.com

Introduction

Matter can be described as the substance that makes up all observable physical objects. Chemistry is the study of the composition, structure, properties and change of matter. This includes atoms (Physics Chapter 12) and molecules. The latter is characterized by chemical bonds formed between atoms to create chemical compounds. Stoichiometry is simply the math behind the chemistry involving products and reactants. The math is quite simple, in part, because of the law of conservation of mass that states that the mass of a closed system will remain constant throughout a chemical reaction.

Additional Resources

Free Online Q&A + Forum

GAMSAT-prep.com Videos

Flashcards

1.1 Generalities

Most substances known to us are <u>mixtures of pure compounds</u>. Air, for instance, contains the pure compounds nitrogen (~78%), oxygen (~21%), water vapor and many other gases (~1%). The <u>compositional</u> <u>ratio</u> of air or any other <u>mixture</u> may vary from one location to another. Each pure compound is made up of molecules which are composed of smaller units: the *atoms*. Atoms combine in very <u>specific</u> ratios to form

molecules. A molecule is the smallest unit of a compound presenting the properties of that compound. During a <u>chemical reaction</u> molecules break down into individual atoms which then recombine to form new compounds. <u>Stoichiometry</u> establishes relationships between the above-mentioned specific ratios for individual molecules (or moles) or for molecules involved in a given chemical reaction.

1.2 Empirical Formula vs. Molecular Formula

The molecules of oxygen (O_2) are made up of two atoms of the same <u>element</u>. Water molecules on the other hand are composed of two different elements: hydrogen and oxygen in the specific ratio 2:1. Note that water is not a mixture of hydrogen and oxygen since this ratio is specific and does not vary with the location or the experimental conditions. The *empirical formula* of a pure compound is the <u>simplest whole number ratio</u> between the numbers of atoms of the different elements

making up the compound. For instance, the empirical formula of water is H_2O (2:1 ratio) while the empirical formula of hydrogen peroxide is HO (1:1 ratio). The *molecular formula* of a given molecule states <u>the exact number</u> of the different atoms that make up this molecule. The empirical formula of water is identical to its molecular formula, i.e. H_2O; however, the molecular formula of hydrogen peroxide, H_2O_2, is different from its empirical formula (both correspond to a 1:1 ratio).

1.3 Mole - Atomic and Molecular Weights

Because of the small size of atoms and molecules chemists have to consider collections of a large number of these particles to bring chemical problems to our macroscopic scale. Collections of tens or dozens of atoms are still too small to achieve this practical purpose. For various reasons the number 6.02 × 10^{23} (<u>Avogadro's number:N_A</u>) was chosen.

It is the number of atoms in 12 grams of the most abundant *isotope* of carbon (isotopes are elements which are identical chemically since the number of protons are the same; their masses differ slightly since the number of neutrons differ). A <u>mole</u> of atoms or molecules (or in fact any particles in general) contains an Avogadro number of these particles. The weight in grams of a mole of atoms of a given element is the gram-atomic weight, GAW, of that element (sometimes weight is measured in atomic mass units - *see PHY 12.2, 12.3*). Along the same lines, the weight in grams of a mole of molecules of a given compound is its gram-molecular weight, GMW. Here are some equations relating these concepts in a way that will help you solve some of the stoichiometry problems:

For an element:
$$moles = \frac{weight\ of\ sample\ in\ grams}{GAW}$$

For a compound:
$$moles = \frac{weight\ of\ sample\ in\ grams}{GMW}$$

The GAW of a given element is not to be confused with the mass of a single atom of this element. For instance the mass of a single atom of carbon-12 (GAW = 12 g) is $12/N_A = 1.993 \times 10^{-23}$ grams. Atomic weights are dimensionless numbers based on carbon-12 as the reference standard isotope and are defined as follows:

$$\frac{mass\ of\ an\ atom\ of\ X}{mass\ of\ an\ atom\ of\ Y} = \frac{atomic\ weight\ of\ element\ X}{atomic\ weight\ of\ element\ Y}$$

Clearly if the reference element Y is chosen to be carbon-12 (which is the case in standard periodic tables) the GAW of any element X is numerically equal to its atomic weight. In the table of atomic weights, all the elements then have values in which are relative to the carbon-12 isotope. The molecular weight of a given molecule is equal to the sum of the atomic weights of the atoms that make up the molecule. For example, the molecular weight of H_2O is equal to 18.0 amu/molecule (H = 1.008 and O = 16.00). The molar weight (or molar mass) of H_2O is numerically equal to the molecular weight (18.0) however, the units are in grams/mol as the molar weight is based on a mole amount of substance. Thus, molecular weight and molar weight are numerically equivalent however, molecular weight is the weight (amu) per molecule and molar weight is based on the weight (grams) per mole (1 mol = 6.02×10^{23} molecules).

1.4 Composition of a Compound by Percent Mass

The percentage composition of a compound is the percent of the total mass of a given element in that compound. For instance, the chemical analysis of a 100 g sample of pure vitamin C demontrates that there are 40.9 g of carbon, 4.58 g of hydrogen and 54.5 g of oxygen. The percentage composition of pure vitamin C is:

%C = 40.9; %H = 4.58; %O = 54.5

The composition of a compound by percent mass is closely related to its empirical formula. For instance, in the case of vitamin

C, the determination of the number of moles of atoms of C, H or O in a 100 g of vitamin C is rather straightforward:

moles of atoms of C in a 100 g of vitamin C = 40.9/12.0 = 3.41

moles of atoms of H in a 100 g of vitamin C = 4.58/1.01 = 4.53

moles of atoms of O in a 100 g of vitamin C = 54.5/16.0 = 3.41

[GAW can be determined from the periodic table in Chapter 2]

To deduce the smallest ratio between the numbers above, one follows the simple procedure:

(i) divide each one of the previously obtained numbers of moles by the smallest one of them (3.41 in our case):

for C: 3.41 mol/3.41 mol = 1.00
for H: 4.53 mol/3.41 mol = 1.33
for O: 3.41 mol/ 3.41 mol = 1.00

(ii) multiply the numbers obtained in the previous step by a small number to obtain a whole number ratio. In our case we need to multiply by 3 (in most cases this factor is between 1 and 5) so that :

for C: $1.00 \times 3 = 3$
for H: $1.33 \times 3 = 4$ and
for O: $1.00 \times 3 = 3$

Therefore, in this example, the simplest whole number ratio is 3C:4H:3O and we conclude that the empirical formula for vitamin C is: $C_3H_4O_3$.

In the previous example, instead of giving the composition of vitamin C by percent weight we could have provided the raw chemical analysis data and asked for the determination of that composition.

For instance, this data would be that the burning of a 4.00 mg sample of pure vitamin C yields 6.00 mg of CO_2 and 1.632 mg of H_2O. Since there are 12.0 g of carbon in 44.0 g of CO_2 the number of milligrams of carbon in 6.00 mg of CO_2 (which corresponds to the number of mg of carbon in 4.00 mg of vitamin C) is simply:

6.00 mg $\times$ (12.0 g C/44.0 g CO_2) = 1.636 mg of C in 6.00 mg of CO_2 or 4.00 mg of vitamin C for further clarification.

To convert this number into a percent mass is then trivial (GM 1.4.3). Similarly, the percent mass of hydrogen is obtained from the previous data and bearing in mind that there are 2.02 g of hydrogen (and not 1.01 g) in 18.0 g of water.

Incidentally, "burning" means combustion (CHM 1.5.1, ORG 3.2.1) which takes place in the presence of excess oxygen and results in the production of heat (*exothermic*, CHM 8.2), the conversion of the chemical species (new products), and light can be produced (glowing or a flame).

The real GAMSAT does not usually provide a periodic table so the atomic weights (amu) will be given when required. Also, since calculators are not permitted, you should practice performing all calculations that you see in this textbook.

1.5 Description of Reactions by Chemical Equations

The convention for writing chemical equations is as follows: compounds which initially combine or <u>react</u> in a chemical reaction are called *reactants*; they are always written on the left-hand side of the chemical equation. The compounds which are <u>produced</u> during the same process are referred to as the *products* of the chemical reaction; they always appear on the right-hand side of the chemical equation. In the chemical equation:

$$2 \text{ BiCl}_3 + 3 \text{ H}_2\text{O} \rightarrow \text{Bi}_2\text{O}_3 + 6 \text{ HCl}$$

the coefficients represent the relative number of moles of reactants that combine to form the corresponding relative number of moles of products: they are the <u>stoichiometric coefficients</u> of the balanced chemical equation. The law of conservation of mass requires that the number of atoms of a given element remains constant during the process of a chemical reaction.

Balancing a chemical equation is putting this general principle into practice. Chemical equations must be balanced so that there are equal numbers of atoms of each element on both sides of the equation. Many equations are balanced by trial and error; however, caution must be practiced when balancing a chemical equation. It is always easier to balance elements that appear only in one compound on each side of the equation; therefore, as a general rule, always balance those elements first and then deal with those which appear in more than one compound last. Thus, a general suggestive procedure for balancing equations would be as follows: (1) count and compare the atoms on both sides of the chemical equation, (2) balance each element one at a time by placing whole number coefficients in front of the formulas resulting in the same number of atoms of each element on each side of the equation. Remember that a coefficient in front of a formula multiplies every atom in the formula (i.e., $2\text{BiCl}_3 = 2\text{Bi} + 6\text{Cl}$). It is best to leave pure elements or metals until the end. Therefore, balance the carbon atoms in both the reactant and product side first. (3) Balance hydrogens in both the reactant and products; and (4) finally, check if all elements are balanced with the smallest possible set of whole number coefficients.

Given the preceding chemical reaction, if H_2O is present in excessive quantity, then $BiCl_3$ would be considered the **limiting reactant.** In other words, since the amount of $BiCl_3$ is relatively small, it is the $BiCl_3$ which determines how much product will be formed. Thus if you were given 316 grams of $BiCl_3$ in *excess* H_2O and you needed to determine the quantity of HCl produced (theoretical yield), you would proceed as follows:

▶ Determine the number of moles of $BiCl_3$ (*see* CHM 1.3) given Bi = 209 g/mol and Cl = 35.5 g/mol, thus $BiCl_3$ = (1 × 209) + (3 × 35.5) = 315.5 or approximately 316 g/mol:

moles $BiCl_3$ = (316 g)/(316 g/mol)
= 1.0 mole of $BiCl_3$.

▶ From the stoichiometric coefficients of the balanced equation:

2 moles of $BiCl_3$: 6 moles of HCl; therefore, 1 mole of $BiCl_3$: 3 moles of HCl

▶ Given H = 1.00 g/mol, thus HCl = 36.5 g/mol, we get:

3 moles × 36.5 g/mol = 110 g of HCl (approx.).

Please note: The theoretical yield is the calculated amount of product that can be predicted from a balanced chemical reaction and is seldom obtained in the laboratory. The actual yield is the actual amount of product produced and recovered in the laboratory. The Percentage yield = Actual yield/Theoretical Yield × 100%.

1.5.1 Categories of Chemical Reactions

Throughout the chapters in General Chemistry we will explore many different types of chemicals and some of their associated reactions. The various chemical reactions may be classified generally as either a redox type (see section 1.6) or as a non-redox type reaction. The following chart is an overview of major chemical reaction classifications (categories) followed by examples (please confirm that all reactions are balanced). Follow the chart like a story that you should revisit but **do not memorize**.

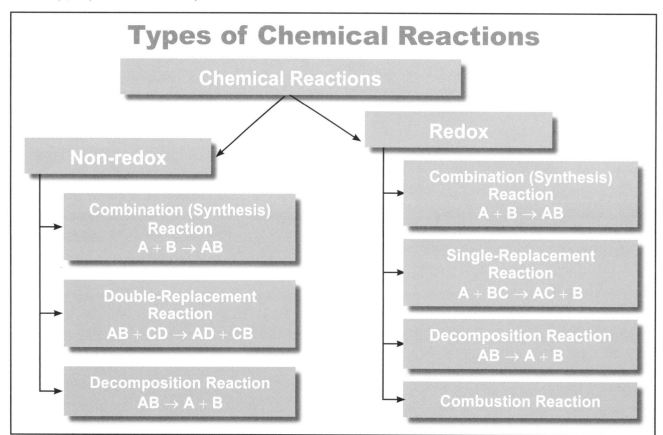

Non-redox

Combination (Synthesis) Reaction

General equation: $A + B \rightarrow AB$

Example: $SO_2(g) + H_2O(l) \rightarrow H_2SO_3 (aq)$

Double-Replacement Reaction (or Metathesis Reaction)

(a) Precipitation Type

General equation: $AB + CD \rightarrow AD + CB$

Example: $CaCl_2(aq) + Na_2CO_3(aq)$
$\rightarrow CaCO_3(s) + 2NaCl(aq)$

(b) Acid-Base Neutralization Type

General equation: $HA + BOH \rightarrow H_2O + BA$
(HA = any H^+ acid & BOH = any OH^- Base)

Example:
$2HCl(l) + Ba(OH)_2(aq) \rightarrow 2H_2O(l) + BaCl_2(aq)$

(c) Gas Evolution Type Reaction

General equation: $HA + B \rightarrow H_2O + BA$
($HA = H^+$ acid & B = special base salt $NaHCO_3$)

Example: $HCl(aq) + NaHCO_3(aq)$
$\rightarrow H_2CO_3(aq)* + NaCl(aq)$
$\rightarrow H_2O(l) + CO_2(g) + NaCl(aq)$
(*H_2CO_3 is carbonic acid, the "fizz" in sodas, which degrades to $CO_2(g)$ and $H_2O(l)$)

Decomposition Reaction (CHM 4.3.1)

General equation: $AB \rightarrow A + B$

Example: $H_2CO_3(aq) \rightarrow H_2O(l) + CO_2(g)$

Redox

Combination (Synthesis) Reaction

General equation: $A + B \rightarrow AB$

Example: $2H_2(g) + O_2(g) \rightarrow 2H_2O(l)$

Single-Replacement Reaction

General equation: $A + BC \rightarrow AC + B$

Example:
$Zn(s) + CuSO_4(aq) \rightarrow Cu(s) + ZnSO_4(aq)$

Decomposition Reaction

General equation: $AB \rightarrow A + B$

Example: $2NaCl(s) \rightarrow 2Na(l) + Cl_2(g)$
(electrolysis reaction, CHM 10.4)

Combustion Reaction

Example: $CH_4(g) + 2O_2(g) \rightarrow CO_2(g) + 2H_2O(g)$

Note that compounds in the preceding chart are identified as solid (s), liquid (l), gas (g) or solubilized in water which is an aqueous (aq) solution.

Combination (or synthesis) and decomposition type reactions are classified as both redox and non-redox reactions. Single replacement and combustion type reactions are classified as only redox type reactions; as the oxidation state of at least one atom species changes through electron transfer (oxidation/reduction) on either side of the chemical equation.

The double-replacement type reactions are basically known as precipitation (or solid forming) type reactions or acid-base (neutralization) type reactions. A double replacement type reaction involves ions (CHM 5.2) which exchange partners and may or may not form precipitates depending on the water solubility of the products formed (CHM 5.3). In acid-base (neutralization) type reactions, the usual products formed are both water and a salt (CHM 6.7). Certain acid-base type reactions however are known to form gas products otherwise known as "Gas Evolution type reactions" due to the instability of an intermediate salt product formed as a result of the acid-base reaction (see preceding chart).

When replacement reactions occur, often there are ions known as "spectator ions" that do not undergo any changes and remain ionized in aqueous solutions (cf. ORG 1.6). These ions can be left out of the end equation known as a "net ionic equation" because it does away with the spectator ions that are not consequential to the reaction. Net ionic equations are used to show the actual chemical reaction that occurs during a single or double-replacement type reaction. Thus, it is essential to recognize and familiarize oneself with the various categories of reactions to enable one to further understand chemical reactivity.

1.6 Oxidation Numbers, Redox Reactions, Oxidizing vs. Reducing Agents

The special class of reactions known as *redox* reactions are better balanced using the concept of oxidation state. In a redox reaction, oxidation and reduction must occur simultaneously. Oxidation is defined as either an increase in oxidation number or a loss of one or more electrons and reduction is defined as a decrease in oxidation number or a gain of one or more electrons. This section deals with these reactions in which electrons are transferred from one atom (or a group of atoms) to another.

First of all, it is very important to understand the difference between the ionic charge and the oxidation state of an element. For this let us consider the two compounds sodium chloride ($NaCl$) and water (H_2O). $NaCl$ is made up of the charged species or ions: Na^+

and Cl^-. During the formation of this ionic compound, one electron is transferred from the Na atom to the Cl atom. It is possible to verify this fact experimentally and determine that the charge of sodium in $NaCl$ is indeed $+1$ and that the one for chlorine is -1. The elements in the periodic table tend to lose (oxidation) or gain (reduction) electrons to different extents. Therefore, even in non-ionic compounds electrons are always transferred, to different degrees, from one atom to another during the formation of a molecule of the compound. The actual partial charges that result from these partial transfers of electrons can also be determined experimentally. The oxidation state is not equal to such partial charges. It is rather an artificial concept that is used to perform some kind of "electron bookkeeping."

In a molecule like H_2O, since oxygen tends to attract electrons more than hydrogen, one can predict that the electrons that allow bonding to occur between hydrogen and oxygen will be displaced towards the oxygen atom. For the sake of "electron bookkeeping" we assign these electrons to the oxygen atom. The charge that the oxygen atom would have in this artificial process would be -2: this defines the oxidation state of oxygen in the H_2O molecule. In the same line of reasoning one defines the oxidation state of hydrogen in the water molecule as $+1$. The actual partial charges of hydrogen and oxygen are in fact smaller; but, as we will see later, the concept of oxidation state is very useful in stoichiometry.

Here are the general rules one needs to follow to assign oxidation numbers (= oxidation states) to different elements in different compounds:

1. In elementary substances, the oxidation number of an uncombined element regardless of whether it is monatomic (1 atom), diatomic (2 atoms) or polyatomic (multiple atoms), is zero. This is, for instance, the case for N in N_2 or Na in sodium element, O in O_2, or S in S_8.

2. In monatomic ions the oxidation number of the element that make up this ion is equal to the charge of the ion. This is the case for Na in Na^+ (+1) or Cl in Cl^- (−1) or Fe in Fe^{3+} (+3). Clearly, monatomic ions are the only species for which atomic charges and oxidation numbers coincide.

3. In a neutral molecule the sum of the oxidation numbers of all the elements that make up the molecule is zero. In a polyatomic ion (e.g. SO_4^{2-}) the sum of the oxidation numbers of the elements that make up this ion is equal to the charge of the ion.

4. Some useful oxidation numbers to memorize:

For H: +1, except in metal hydrides (general formula XH where X is from the first two columns of the periodic table; CHM 2.4.1) where it is equal to −1.

For O: −2 in most compounds. In peroxides (e.g. in H_2O_2) the oxidation number for O is −1, it is +2 in OF_2 and −1/2 in superoxides (e.g. potassium superoxide: KO_2 which contains the O_2^- ion as opposed to the O^{2-} ion).

For alkali metals (first column in the periodic table): +1.

For alkaline earth metals (second column): +2.

Aluminium always has an oxidation number of +3 in all its compounds. (i.e. chlorides $AlCl_3$, nitrites $Al(NO_2)_3$, etc.)

The oxidation number of each Group VIIA element is −1; however, when it is combined with an element of higher electronegativity, the oxidation number is +1. For example, the oxidation number of Cl is −1 in HCl and the oxidation number of Cl is +1 in HClO.

An element is said to have been *reduced* during a reaction if its oxidation number decreased during this reaction, it is said to have been oxidized if its *oxidation* number increased. A simple example is:

$$Zn(s) \quad + \quad CuSO_4(aq) \longrightarrow$$
Oxid.#:   0   +2

$$ZnSO_4(aq) \quad + \quad Cu(s)$$
Oxid.#:   +2   0

During this reaction Cu is reduced (oxidation number decreases from +2 to 0) while Zn is oxidized (oxidation number increases from 0 to +2). Since, in a sense, Cu is reduced by Zn, Zn can be referred to as the reducing agent. Similarly, Cu is the oxidizing agent.

In chapters to come, we will discuss redox titrations (CHM 6.10) and more redox reactions in electrochemistry (CHM 10.1). Many of the redox agents in the table below will be explored in the chapters on Organic Chemistry.

Common Redox Agents	
Reducing Agents	**Oxidizing Agents**
* Lithium aluminium hydride ($LiAlH_4$) * Sodium borohydride ($NaBH_4$) * Metals * Ferrous ion (Fe^{2+})	* Iodine (I_2) and other halogens * Permanganate (MnO_4) salts * Peroxide compounds (i.e. H_2O_2) * Ozone (O_3); osmium tetroxide (OsO_4) * Nitric acid (HNO_3); nitrous oxide (N_2O)

How many moles are in guacamole?
Avocado's number.   :)

Reminder: Chapter review questions are available online for the original owner of this textbook. Doing practice questions will help clarify concepts and ensure that you study in a targeted way. First, register at gamsat-prep.com, then login and click on GAMSAT Textbook Owners in the right column so you can use your Online Access Card to have access to the Lessons section.

No science background? Consider watching the relevant videos at gamsat-prep.com and you have support at gamsat-prep.com/forum. Don't forget to check the Index at the beginning of this book to see which chapters are **HIGH**, **MEDIUM** and **LOW** relative importance for the GAMSAT.

Your online access continues for one full year from your online registration.

ELECTRONIC STRUCTURE AND THE PERIODIC TABLE
Chapter 2

Memorize	Understand	Not Required*
* Definitions of quantum numbers * The location of the first 20 elements in the periodic table	* Conventional notation, Pauli, Hund's * Box diagrams, IP, electronegativity * Valence, EA * Variation in shells, atomic size * Trends in the periodic table	* Knowledge beyond introductory-level (first year uni.) course * Memorizing Schroedinger's equation * IUPAC's systematic element names (gen. chem.)

GAMSAT-Prep.com

Introduction

The periodic table of the elements provides data and abbreviations for the names of elements in a tabular layout. The purpose of the table is to illustrate recurring (periodic) trends and to classify and compare the different types of chemical behavior. To do so, we must first better understand the atom. The periodic table is not usually provided in the real GAMSAT but you are still responsible for knowing the trends and relative locations of the most common atoms.

Additional Resources

Free Online Q&A + Forum

GAMSAT-prep.com Videos

Flashcards

Special Guest

2.1 Electronic Structure of an Atom

The modern view of the structure of atoms is based on a series of discoveries and complicated theories that were put forth at the turn of the twentieth century. The atom represents the smallest unit of a chemical element. It is composed of subatomic particles: protons, neutrons and electrons. At the center of the atom is the nucleus composed of protons and neutrons surrounded by electrons forming an electron cloud.

The protons and neutrons have nearly identical masses of approximately 1 amu whereas electrons, by contrast, have an almost negligible mass. Protons and electrons both have electrical charges equal in magnitude but opposite in sign. Protons consist of a single positive (+1) charge, electrons consist of a single negative charge (−1) and neutrons have no charge (Physics Chapter 12).

Atoms have equal numbers of protons and electrons unless ionization occurs in which ions are formed. Ions are defined as atoms with either a positive charge (cation) due to loss of one or more valence electrons or negative charge (anion) as a result of a gain in electron(s). An atom's valence electrons are electrons furthest from the nucleus and are responsible for an element's chemical properties and are instrumental in chemical bonding (See CHM 2.2 and 2.3 and Chapter 3).

Atoms of a given element all have an equal number of protons however, may vary in the number of neutrons. Atoms that differ only by neutron number are known as isotopes. Isotopes have the same atomic number but differ in atomic mass due to the differences in their neutron numbers. As they have the same atomic number, isotopes therefore exhibit the same chemical properties.

In the following paragraphs, we will only present the main ideas behind the findings that shaped our understanding of atomic structure. The first important idea is that electrons (as well as any subatomic particles) are in fact waves as well as particles; this concept is often referred to in textbooks as the "dual nature of matter" (cf. PHY 11.1).

Contrary to classical mechanics, in this modern view of matter, information on particles is not derived from the knowledge of their position and momentum at a given time but by the knowledge of the wave function (mathematical expression of the above-mentioned wave) and their energy. Mathematically, such information can be derived, in principle, by solving the master equation of quantum mechanics known as the Schrödinger equation. Moreover, the mathematical derivation of atomic orbitals and respective energies comes from solving the equation which includes the total energy profiles for the electrons as well as the wave function describing the wave-like nature of the electrons. Thus, the various solutions to the Schrödinger equation describes the atomic orbitals as complicated wave functions which may alternatively be graphically represented (See Figure III.A.2.1 and Figure III.A.2.2).

In the case of the hydrogen atom, this equation can be solved exactly. It yields the possible states of energy in which the electron can be found within the hydrogen atom and the wave functions associated with these states. The <u>square of the wave function</u> associated with a given state of energy <u>gives</u> the <u>probability to find the electron,</u> which is in that same state of energy, at any given point in space at any given time. These <u>wave functions</u> as well as their geometrical representations are referred to as the *atomic orbitals*. We shall explain further below the significance of these geometrical representations.

Atoms of any element tend to exist toward a minimal energy level (= ground state) unless subjected to an external environmental change. Even for a hydrogen atom there is a large number of possible states in which its single electron can be found (when it is subjected to different external perturbations). A labeling of these states is necessary. This is done using the quantum numbers. Hence, any orbital may be completely described by four quantum numbers; n, l, m_l and m_s. The position and energy of an electron and each of the orbitals are therefore described by its quantum number or energy state. The four quantum numbers are thus described as follows:

(i) n: *the principal quantum number*. This number takes the integer values 1, 2, 3, 4, 5... The higher the value of n the higher the energy of the state labelled by this n. This number defines the atomic shells K (n = 1), L (n = 2), M (n = 3) etc... or the size of an orbital.

(ii) l: *the angular momentum quantum number*. It defines the shape of the atomic orbital in a way which we will discuss further below. For a given electronic state of energy defined by n, l takes all possible integer values between 0 and n − 1. For instance for a state with n = 0 there is only one possible shape of orbital, it is defined by l = 0. For a state defined by n = 3 there are 3 possible orbital shapes with l = 0, 1 and 2.

All orbitals with l = 0 are called "s"-shaped, all with l = 1 are "p"-shaped, those with l = 2 or 3 are "d" or "f"-shaped orbitals respectively. The important shapes to remember are: i) s = spherical, and ii) p = 2 lobes or "dumbbell" (*see the following diagrams*). For values of l larger than 3, which occur with an n greater or equal to 4, the corresponding

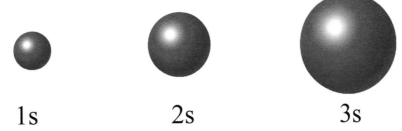

$1s$ $2s$ $3s$

Figure III.A.2.1: Atomic orbitals where l = 0. Notice that the orbitals do not reveal the precise location (position) or momentum of the fast moving electron at any point in time (Heisenberg's Uncertainty Principle). Instead, we are left with a 90% chance of finding the electron somewhere within the shapes described as orbitals.

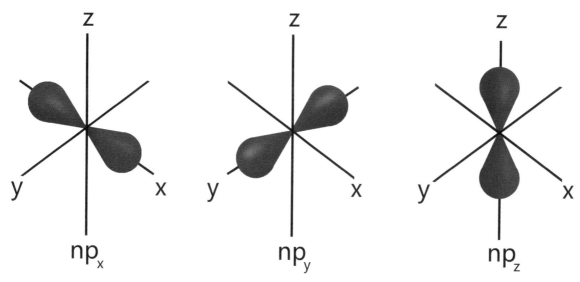

Figure III.A.2.2: Atomic orbitals where $l = 1$.

series of atomic orbitals follows the alphabetical order h, i, j, etc...

(iii) m_l: *the magnetic quantum number.* It defines the orientation of the orbital of a given shape. For a given value of l (given shape), m_l can take any of the $2l + 1$ integer values between $-l$ and $+l$. For instance for a state with $n = 3$ and $l = 1$ (3p orbital in notation explained in the previous paragraph) there are three possible values for m_l: -1, 0 and 1. These 3 orbitals are oriented along x, y or the z axis of a coordinate system with its origin on the nucleus of the atom: they are denoted as $3p_x$, $3p_y$ and $3p_z$. Figure III.A.2.2 shows the representation of an orbital corresponding to an electron in a state ns, np_x, np_y, and np_z. These are the 3D volumes where there is 90% chance to find an electron which is in a state ns, np_x, np_y, or np_z, respectively. This type of diagram constitutes the most common geometrical representation of the atomic orbitals (besides looking at the diagrams, consider watching one of the videos if you are having trouble visualizing these facts).

(iv) m_s: *the spin quantum number.* This number takes the values $+1/2$ or $-1/2$ for the electron. Some textbooks present the intuitive, albeit wrong, explanation that the spin angular momentum arises from the spinning of the electron around itself, the opposite signs for the spin quantum number would correspond to the two opposite rotational directions. We do have to resort to such an intuitive presentation because the spin angular moment has, in fact, no classical equivalent and, as a result, the physics behind the correct approach is too complex to be dealt with in introductory courses.

2.2 Conventional Notation for Electronic Structure

As described in the previous section, the state of an electron in an atom is completely defined by a set of four quantum numbers (n, l, m_l, m_s). If two electrons in an atom share the same n, l and m_l numbers their m_s have to be of opposite signs: this is known as the Pauli's exclusion principle which states that no two electrons in an atom can have the same four quantum numbers. This principle along with a rule known as Hund's rule which states that electrons fill orbital's singly first until all orbitals of the same energy are filled, constitutes the basis for the procedure that one needs to follow to assign the possible (n, l, m_l, m_s) quantum states to the electrons of a polyelectronic atom. Orbitals are "filled" in sequence, according to an example shown below. When filling a set of orbitals with the same n and l (e.g. the three 2p orbitals: $2p_x$, $2p_y$ and $2p_z$ which differ by their m_l's) electrons are assigned to orbitals with different m_l's first with parallel spins (same sign for their m_s), until each orbital of the given group is filled with one electron, then, electrons are paired in the same orbital with antiparallel spins (opposite signs for m_s). This procedure is illustrated in an example which follows. The electronic configuration which results from orbitals filled in accordance with the previous set of rules corresponds to the atom being in its lowest overall state of energy. This state of lowest energy is referred to as the ground state of the atom.

Note: There are 2 periodic tables at the end of this chapter which you may want to consult from time to time.

The restrictions related to the previous set of rules lead to the fact that only a certain number of electrons is allowed for each quantum number:

for a given n (given shell): the maximum number of electrons allowed is $2n^2$. The greater the value of n, the greater the energy level of the shell.

for a given l (s, p, d, f…): this number is $4l + 2$.

for a given m_l (given orbital orientation): a maximum of 2 electrons is allowed.

There is a **conventional notation** for the electronic structure of an atom:

(i)   orbitals are listed in the order they are filled (See Figure III.A.2.3)

(ii)   generally, in this conventional notation, no distinction is made between electrons in states defined by the same n and l but which do not share the same m_l.

For instance the ground state electronic configuration of oxygen is written as:

$$1s^2 \ 2s^2 \ 2p^4$$

When writing the electronic configuration of a polyelectronic atom orbitals are filled (with electrons denoted as the superscripts of the configurations) in order of increasing energy: 1s 2s 2p 3s 3p 4s 3d … according to the following figure:

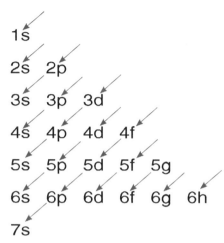

follow the direction of successive arrows moving from top to bottom

Figure III.A.2.3: The order for filling atomic orbitals.

Thus, the electronic configuration or the pattern of orbital filling of an atom generally abides by the following rules or principles:

1. Always fill the lowest energy (or ground state) orbitals first (Aufbau principle)

2. No two electrons in a single atom can have the same four quantum numbers; if n, l, and m_l are the same, m_s must be different such that the electrons have opposite spins. (Pauli exclusion principle) and

3. Degenerate orbitals of the subshell are each occupied singly with electrons of parallel spin before double occupation of the orbitals occurs (Hund's rule).

   An alternative way to write the aforementioned electronic configuration is based on the avoidance in writing out the inner core electrons. Moreover, this is an abbreviation of the previous longer configuration or otherwise known as a short hand electronic

configuration. Here, the core electrons are represented by a prior noble gas elemental symbol within brackets. As an example, calcium may be written in its expanded form or more commonly as a short hand notation represented as $[Ar]4s^2$ shown with the prior noble gas symbol for argon [Ar] written within brackets.

Another illustrative notation is also often used. In this alternate notation orbitals are represented by boxes (hence the referring to this representation as "box diagrams"). Orbitals with the same l are grouped together and electrons are represented by vertical ascending or descending arrows (for the two opposite signs of m_s).

For instance for the series H, He, Li, Be, B, C we have the following electronic configurations:

H: $1s^1$ box diagram: ↑

He: $1s^2$ box diagram: ↑↓ and not ↑↑
(rejected by Pauli's exclusion principle)

Li: $1s^2$ $2s^1$
↑↓ ↑

Be: $1s^2$ $2s^2$
↑↓ ↑↓

B: $1s^2$ $2s^2$ $2p^1$
↑↓ ↑↓ ↑ □ □

C: $1s^2$ $2s^2$ $2p^2$
↑↓ ↑↓ ↑ ↑ □

(to satisfy Hund's rule of maximum spin)

To satisfy Hund's rule the next electron is put into a separate 2p "box". The 4th 2p electron (for oxygen) is then put into the first box with an opposite spin.

O: $\boxed{\uparrow\downarrow}$ $\boxed{\uparrow\downarrow}$ $\boxed{\uparrow\downarrow \mid \uparrow \mid \uparrow}$

    $1s^2$ $2s^2$ $2p^4$

Within a given subshell l, orbitals are filled in such a way to maximize the number of half-filled orbitals with parallel spins. An unpaired electron generates a magnetic field due to its spin. Consequently, when a material is composed of atoms with unpaired electrons, it is said to be *paramagnetic* as it will be attracted to an applied external magnetic field (i.e. Li, Na, Cs). Alternatively, when the material's atoms have paired electrons, it is weakly repelled by an external magnetic field and it is said to be *diamagnetic* (i.e. Cu, molecular carbon, H_2, H_2O). Non-chemists simply call diamagnetic materials "not magnetic". The strongest form of magnetism is a permanent feature of materials like Fe, Ni and their alloys and is said to be *ferromagnetic* (i.e. a fridge magnet).

For the main group elements, the valence electrons of an atom are those that are involved in chemical bonding and are in the outermost principal energy level or shell. For example, for Group IA and Group IIA elements, only electrons from the s subshell are valence electrons. For Group IIIA through Group VIIIA elements, electrons from s and p subshell are valence electrons. Under certain circumstances, elements from Group IIIA through Group VIIA may accept electrons into its d subshell, leading to more than 8 valence electrons.

Finally, as previously mentioned, we should point out that electrons can be promoted to higher unoccupied (or partially occupied) orbitals when the atom is subjected to some external perturbation which inputs energy into the atom. The resulting electronic configuration is then called an <u>excited state configuration</u> (this concept was explored in PHY 12.5, 12.6).

2.3 Elements, Chemical Properties and The Periodic Table

Since most chemical properties of the atom are related to their outermost electrons (<u>valence electrons</u>), it is the orbital occupation of these electrons which is most relevant in the complete electronic configuration. The periodic table (there is one at the end of this chapter with a summary of trends) can be used to derive such information in the following way:

(i)   the row or <u>period</u> number gives the "n" of the valence electrons of any given element of the period.

(ii)   the first two columns or <u>groups</u> and helium (He) are referred to as the "s" block. The valence electrons of elements in these groups are "s" electrons.

(iii) groups 3A to 8A (13th to 18th columns) are the "p" group. Elements belonging to these groups have their ground state electronic configurations ending with "p" electrons.

(iv) Elements in groups 3B to 2B (columns 3 to 12) are called transition elements. Their electronic configurations end with $ns^2(n-1)d^x$ where n is the period number and $x = 1$ for column 3, 2 for column 4, 3 for column 5, etc... Note that these elements sometimes have unexpected or unusual valence shell electronic configurations.

This set of rules should make the writing of the ground-state valence shell electronic configuration very easy. For instance: Sc being an element of the "d" group on the 4th period should have a ground-state valence shell electronic configuration of the form: $4s^2 3d^x$. Since it belongs to group 3B (column 3) $x = 1$; therefore, the actual configuration is simply: $4s^2 3d^1$. However, half-filled (i.e. Cr) and filled (i.e. Cu, Ag, Au) d orbitals have remarkable stability. This stability behavior is essentially related to the closely spaced 3d and 4s energy levels with the stability associated with a half-filled (as in Cr) or completely filled (as in Cu) sublevel. Hence, this stability makes for unusual configurations (i.e. by the rules $Cr = 4s^2 3d^4$, but in reality $Cr = 4s^1 3d^5$ creating a half-filled d orbital). It can be noted that Cr therefore has an electronic configuration of $[Ar]4s^1 3d^5$, although four d electrons would be expected to be seen instead of five. This is because one electron from a s subshell jumps into the d orbital, giving the atom a half filled d subshell. As for Cu, it would have an electronic configuration of $[Ar]4s^2 3d^9$ by the rules. However, the Cu d shell is just one electron away from stability, and therefore, one electron from the s shell jumps into the d shell to convert it into $[Ar]4s^1 3d^{10}$.

Some metal ions form colored solutions due to the transition energies of the d-electrons.

A number of physical and chemical properties of the elements are periodic, i.e. they vary in a regular fashion with atomic numbers. We will define some of these properties and explain their trends:

(A) Ionization Energy

(i) The ionization energy (IE) is defined as the energy required to remove an electron from a gaseous atom or ion. The first ionization energy or potential (1st IE or IP) is the energy required to remove one of the outermost valence electrons from an atom in its gaseous state. The ionization potential increases from left to right within a period and decreases from the top to the bottom of a group or column of the periodic chart. The 1st IP drops sharply when we move from the last element of a period (inert gas) to the first element of the next period. These are general trends, elements located after an element with a half-filled shell, for instance, have a lower 1st IP than expected by these trends.

(ii) The second ionization is the energy or potential (2nd IE or IP) required to remove a second valence electron from the ion to form a divalent ion: the previous trends can be used if one remembers the relationship between 1st and 2nd ionization processes of an atom of element X:

$$X + energy \rightarrow X^+ + 1e^-$$
1st ionization of X
$$X^+ + energy \rightarrow X^{2+} + 1e^-$$
2nd ionization of X

The second ionization process of X can be viewed as the 1st ionization of X^+. With this in mind it is very easy to predict trends of 2nd IP's. For instance, let us compare the 2nd IP's of the elements Na and Al. This is equivalent to comparing the 1st IP's of Na^+ and Al^+. These, in turn, have the same valence shell electronic configurations as Ne and Mg, respectively. Applying the previous general principles on Ne and Mg we arrive at the following conclusions:

• the 1st IP of Ne is greater than the 1st IP of Mg

• the 1st IP of Na^+ is therefore expected to be greater than the 1st IP of Al^+

• the latter statement is equivalent to the final conclusion that the 2nd IP of Na is greater than the 2nd IP of Al.

(B) Electron Affinity
(iii) Electron affinity (EA) is the energy change that accompanies the following process for an atom of element X:

$$X(gas) + 1e^- \rightarrow X^-(gas)$$

This property measures the ability of an atom to accept an electron. The stronger the attraction of a nucleus for electrons, the greater the electron affinity (EA) will be. The electron affinity becomes more negative for non-metals than metals. Thus, halogen atoms (F, Cl, Br...) have a very negative EA because they have a great tendency to form negative ions. On the other hand, alkaline earth metals which tend to form positive rather than negative ions have very large positive EA's. The overall tendency is that EA's become more negative as we move from left to right across a period, they are more negative (less positive) for non-metals than for metals and they do not change considerably within a group or column.

(C) Atomic Radii
(iv) The atomic radius generally decreases from left to right across a period since the effective nuclear charge increases as the number of protons within an atom increases. The effective nuclear charge is the net charge experienced by the valence electrons as a result of the nucleus (ie, protons) and core electrons. Additionally, the atomic radius increases when we move down a group due to the shielding effect of the additional core electrons and the presence of another electron shell.

(D) Electronegativity
(v) Electronegativity is a parameter that measures the ability of an atom, when engaged in a molecular bond, to pull or repel the bond electrons. This parameter is determined from the 1st IE and the EA

of a given atom. Electronegativity follows the same general trends as the 1st IE. The greater the electronegativity of an atom, the greater its attraction for bonding electrons. In general, electronegativity is inversely related to atomic size. Moreover, the larger the atom, the less the ability for it to attract electrons to itself in chemical bonding.

In conclusion, as one moves to the right across a row in the periodic table, the atomic radii decreases, the ionization energy (IE) increases and the electronegativity increases. As one moves down along a column within the periodic table, the atomic radii increases, the ionization energy (IE) decreases and electronegativity decreases.

2.3.1 Bond Strength

When there is a big difference in electronegativity between two atoms sharing a covalent bond then the bond is generally weaker as compared to two atoms with little electronegativity difference. This is because in the latter case, the bond is shared more equally and is thus more stable.

Bond strength is inversely proportional to bond length. Thus, all things being equal, a stronger bond would be shorter. Bonds and bond strength is further discussed in ORG 1.3-1.5.1.

2.4 Metals, Nonmetals and Metalloids

The elements of the periodic table belong in three basic categories: metals, nonmetals and metalloids (or semimetals).

Metals – high melting points and densities characterize metals. They are excellent conductors of heat and electricity due to their valence electrons being able to move freely. This fact also accounts for the major characteristic properties of metals: large atomic radius, low ionization energy, high electron affinities and low electronegativity. Groups IA and IIA are the most reactive of all metal species.

Of course, metals tend to be shiny and solid (with the exception of mercury, Hg, a liquid at 'Standard Temperature and Pressure', STP). They are also *ductile* (they can be drawn into thin wires) and *malleable* (they can be easily hammered into very thin sheets).

Nonmetals – Nonmetals have high ionization energies and electronegativities. As opposed to metals, they do not conduct heat or electricity. They tend to gain electrons easily contrarily to metals that readily lose electrons when forming bonds.

Metalloids – The metalloids share properties with both metals and nonmetals. Their densities, boiling points and melting points do not follow any specific trends and are very unpredictable. Ionization energy and electronegativity values vary and can be found in between those of metals and non-metals. Examples of metalloids are boron, silicon, germanium, arsenic, antimony and tellurium.

Table III A.2.1

*General characteristics of metals, nonmetals and metalloids		
Metals	**Nonmetals**	**Metalloids**
• Hard and Shiny	• Gases or dull, brittle solids	• Appearence will vary
• 3 or less valence electrons	• 5 or more valence electrons	• 3 to 7 valence electrons
• Form + ions by losing e⁻	• Form – ions by gaining e⁻	• Form + and/or – ions
• Good conductors of heat and electricity	• Poor conductors of heat and electricity	• Conduct better than nonmetals but not as well as metals

*These are general characteristics. There are exceptions beyond the scope of the exam.

2.4.1 The Chemistry of Groups

Alkali metals – The alkali metals are found in Group IA and are different than other metals in that they only have one loosely bound electron in their outermost shell. This gives them the largest ionic radius of all the elements in their respective periods. They are also highly reactive (especially with halogens) due to their low ionization energies and low electronegativity and the relative ease with which they lose their valence electron.

Alkaline Earth metals – The alkaline earth metals are found in Group IIA and also tend to lose electrons quite readily. They have two electrons in their outer shell and experience a stronger effective nuclear charge than alkali metals. This gives them a smaller atomic radius as well as low electronegativity values.

Halogens – The halogens are found in Group VIIA and are highly reactive nonmetals with seven valence electrons in their outer shell. This gives them extremely high electronegativity values and makes them reactive towards alkali metals and alkaline earth metals that seek to donate electrons to form a complete octet. Some halogens are gaseous at Standard Temperature and Pressure (STP; CHM 4.1.1) (F_2 and Cl_2) while others are liquid (Br_2) or solid (I_2).

Noble gases – The noble gases (= 'inert gases') are found in the last group and are characterized by being a mostly nonreactive species due to their complete valence shell. This energetically favorable configuration of electrons gives them high ionization energies, low boiling points and no real electronegativities. They are all gaseous at room temperature.

Transition Elements – The transition elements are found in Groups IB to VIIIB and are characterized by high melting points and boiling points. Their key chemical characteristic is their ability to exist in a variety of different oxidation states. For the transition elements, the 4s shell gets filled prior to the 3d shell according to the Aufbau rule. However, electrons are lost from the 4s shell before the 3d shell. Thus, as the d electrons are held only loosely, this contributes to the high electrical conductivity and malleability of transition elements. This is because transition elements can lose electrons from both their s and d orbitals of their valence shell; the d electrons are held more loosely than the s electrons. They display low ionization energies and high electrical conductivities.

PERIODIC TABLE OF THE ELEMENTS

1 H 1.008																	2 He 4.003
3 Li 6.941	4 Be 9.012											5 B 10.81	6 C 12.011	7 N 14.007	8 O 15.999	9 F 18.998	10 Ne 20.179
11 Na 22.990	12 Mg 24.305											13 Al 26.982	14 Si 28.086	15 P 30.974	16 S 32.06	17 Cl 35.453	18 Ar 39.948
19 K 39.098	20 Ca 40.08	21 Sc 44.956	22 Ti 47.90	23 V 50.942	24 Cr 51.996	25 Mn 54.938	26 Fe 55.847	27 Co 58.933	28 Ni 58.70	29 Cu 63.546	30 Zn 65.38	31 Ga 69.72	32 Ge 72.59	33 As 74.922	34 Se 78.96	35 Br 79.904	36 Kr 83.80
37 Rb 85.468	38 Sr 87.62	39 Y 88.906	40 Zr 91.22	41 Nb 92.906	42 Mo 95.94	43 Tc (98)	44 Ru 101.07	45 Rh 102.906	46 Pd 106.4	47 Ag 107.868	48 Cd 112.41	49 In 114.82	50 Sn 118.69	51 Sb 121.75	52 Te 127.60	53 I 126.905	54 Xe 131.30
55 Cs 132.905	56 Ba 137.33	57 *La 138.906	72 Hf 178.49	73 Ta 180.948	74 W 183.85	75 Re 186.207	76 Os 190.2	77 Ir 192.22	78 Pt 195.09	79 Au 196.967	80 Hg 200.59	81 Tl 204.37	82 Pb 207.2	83 Bi 208.980	84 Po (209)	85 At (210)	86 Rn (222)
87 Fr (223)	88 Ra 226.025	89 **Ac 227.028	104 Unq (261)	105 Unp (262)	106 Unh (263)												

*	58 Ce 140.12	59 Pr 140.908	60 Nd 144.24	61 Pm (145)	62 Sm 150.4	63 Eu 151.96	64 Gd 157.25	65 Tb 158.925	66 Dy 162.50	67 Ho 164.930	68 Er 167.26	69 Tm 168.934	70 Yb 173.04	71 Lu 174.967
**	90 Th 232.038	91 Pa 231.036	92 U 238.029	93 Np 237.048	94 Pu (244)	95 Am (243)	96 Cm (247)	97 Bk (247)	98 Cf (251)	99 Es (254)	100 Fm (257)	101 Md (258)	102 No (259)	103 Lr (260)

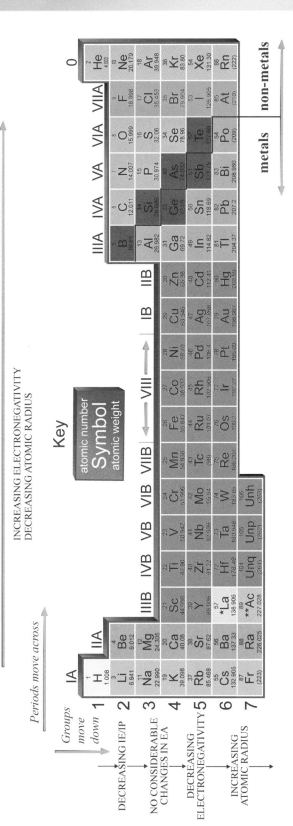

Element	Symbol	Atomic Number	Element	Symbol	Atomic Number
Actinium	Ac	89	Europium	Eu	63
Aluminum	Al	13	Fermium	Fm	100
Americium	Am	95	Fluorine	F	9
Antimony	Sb	51	Francium	Fr	87
Argon	Ar	18	Gadolinium	Gd	64
Arsenic	As	33	Gallium	Ga	31
Astatine	At	85	Germanium	Ge	32
Barium	Ba	56	Gold	Au	79
Berkelium	Bk	97	Hafnium	Hf	72
Beryllium	Be	4	Helium	He	2
Bismuth	Bi	83	Holmium	Ho	67
Boron	B	5	Hydrogen	H	1
Bromine	Br	35	Indium	In	49
Cadmium	Cd	48	Iodine	I	53
Calcium	Ca	20	Iridium	Ir	77
Californium	Cf	98	Iron	Fe	26
Carbon	C	6	Krypton	Kr	36
Cerium	Ce	58	Lanthanum	La	57
Cesium	Cs	55	Lawrencium	Lr	103
Chlorine	Cl	17	Lead	Pb	82
Chromium	Cr	24	Lithium	Li	3
Cobalt	Co	27	Lutetium	Lu	71
Copper	Cu	29	Magnesium	Mg	12
Curium	Cm	96	Manganese	Mn	25
Dysprosium	Dy	66	Mendelevium	Md	101
Einsteinium	Es	99	Mercury	Hg	80
Erbium	Er	68	Molybdenum	Mo	42

Element	Symbol	Atomic Number	Element	Symbol	Atomic Number
Neodymium	Nd	60	Selenium	Se	34
Neon	Ne	10	Silicon	Si	14
Neptunium	Np	93	Silver	Ag	47
Nickel	Ni	28	Sodium	Na	11
Niobium	Nb	41	Strontium	Sr	38
Nitrogen	N	7	Sulfur	S	16
Nobelium	No	102	Tantalum	Ta	73
Osmium	Os	76	Technetium	Tc	43
Oxygen	O	8	Tellurium	Te	52
Palladium	Pd	46	Terbium	Tb	65
Phosphorous	P	15	Thallium	Tl	81
Platinum	Pt	78	Thorium	Th	90
Plutonium	Pu	94	Thulium	Tm	69
Polonium	Po	84	Tin	Sn	50
Potassium	K	19	Titanium	Ti	22
Praseodymium	Pr	59	Tungsten	W	74
Promethium	Pm	61	(Unnilhexium)	(Unh)	106
Protactinium	Pa	91	(Unnilpentium)	(Unp)	105
Radium	Ra	88	(Unnilquadium)	(Unq)	104
Radon	Rn	86	Uranium	U	92
Rhenium	Re	75	Vanadium	V	23
Rhodium	Rh	45	Xenon	Xe	54
Rubidium	Rb	37	Ytterbium	Yb	70
Ruthenium	Ru	44	Yttrium	Y	39
Samarium	Sm	62	Zinc	Zn	30
Scandium	Sc	21	Zirconium	Zr	40

Go online to GAMSAT-prep.com for free chapter review Q&A and forum.

GOLD NOTES

BONDING

Chapter 3

Memorize	Understand	Not Required*
* Hybrid orbitals, shapes * Define Lewis: structure, acid, base * Define: octet rule, formal charge	* Ionic, covalent bonds * VSEPR, Resonance * Dipole, covalent polar bonds * Trends in the periodic table	* Knowledge beyond introductory-level (first year uni.) course * Details of VSEPR * Memorizing hybrids with d, f * Memorizing dipole moment equation

GAMSAT-Prep.com

Introduction

Attractive interactions between atoms and molecules involve a physical process called chemical bonding. In general, strong chemical bonding is associated with the sharing or transfer of electrons between atoms. Molecules, crystals and diatomic gases are held together by chemical bonds which makes up most of the matter around us.

Additional Resources

Free Online Q&A + Forum

GAMSAT-prep.com Videos

Flashcards

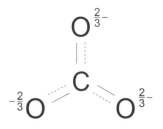

Special Guest

3.1 Generalities

Chemical bonds can form between atoms of the same element or between atoms of different elements. Chemical bonds are classified into three groups: ionic, covalent and metallic.

To summarize, if the electronegativity values of two atoms are:

- significantly different...
  - Ionic bonds are formed.
- similar...
  - Metallic bonds form between two metal atoms.
  - Covalent bonds form between two nonmetal atoms (or between metal and nonmetal atoms).
    - Non-polar covalent bonds form when the electronegativity values are very similar.

- Polar covalent bonds form when the electronegativity values are somewhat further apart.

We will also see in this chapter that many bonds are formed according to the octet rule, which states that an atom tends to form bonds with other atoms until the bonding atoms obtain a stable electron configuration of eight valence electrons in their outermost shells, similar to that of Group VIIIA (noble gas) elements. There are certain exceptions to the octet rule such as, hydrogen forming bonds with two valence electrons; beryllium, which can bond to attain four valence electrons; boron, which can bond to attain six; and elements such as phosphorus and sulfur, which can incorporate d orbital electrons to attain more than eight valence electrons.

3.1.1 The Ionic Bond

Ionic bonds form when there is a complete transfer of one or more electrons between a metal and a nonmetal atom. When an element X with a low ionization potential is combined with an element Y with a large negative electron affinity, one or more electrons are transferred from the atoms of X to the atoms of Y. This leads to the formation of cations X^{n+} and anions Y^{m-}. These ions of opposite charges are then attracted to each other through electrostatic forces which then aggregate to form large stable spatial arrangements of ions: crystalline solids. The bonds that hold these ions together are called ionic bonds.

There exists a large difference in electronegativity between ionically bonded atoms. Electronegativity is defined as the ability of an atom to attract electrons towards its nucleus in bonding and each atomic element is assigned a numerical electronegativity value with a greatest value of 4.0 assigned to the most electronegative element, fluorine. Ionic compounds are known to have high melting and boiling points and high electrical conductivity. In our general example, note that to maintain electrical neutrality the empirical formula of this ionic compound has to be of the general form: X_mY_n (the total positive charge: $n \times m$ is equal to the total negative charge: $m \times n$ in a unit formula).

For instance, since aluminium tends to form the cation Al^{3+} and oxygen the anion O^{2-} the empirical formula for aluminium oxide is Al_2O_3. Thus, the empirical or simplest formula is written for each of the formula units (Al_2O_3) which are part of a larger crystalline solid. The actual ionic solid lattice formed however, consists of a large and equal number of ions packed together in a manner to allow maximal attraction of all the oppositely charged ions.

H	2.1												
Li	1.0	Be	1.5	B	2.0	C	2.5	N	3.0	O	3.5	F	4.0
Na	0.9	Mg	1.2	Al	1.5	Si	1.8	P	2.1	S	2.5	Cl	3.0
K	0.8	Ca	1.0	Ga	1.6	Ge	1.8	As	2.0	Se	2.4	Br	2.8
Rb	0.8	Sr	1.0	In	1.7	Sn	1.8	Sb	1.9	Te	2.1	I	2.5
Cs	0.7	Ba	0.9	Tl	1.8	Pb	1.9	Bi	1.9	Po	2.0	At	2.2

Table III.A.3.0: Pauling's values for the electronegativity of some important elements. Note that elements in the upper right hand corner of the periodic table have high electronegativities and those in the bottom left hand corner of the table have low electronegativities (CHM 2.3, 2.4.1). Note that Pauling's electronegativity is dimensionless since it measures electron attracting ability on a relative scale. Of course, the numbers do not need to be memorized but understanding the trends is very important for both GAMSAT General and Organic Chemistry.

3.2 The Covalent Bond

Atoms are held together in non-ionic molecules by <u>covalent bonds</u>. In this type of bonding two valence electrons are shared between two atoms. Two atoms sharing one, two or three electron pairs form single, double or triple covalent bonds, respectively. As the number of shared electron pairs increases, the two atoms are pulled closer together, leading to a decrease in bond length and a simultaneous increase in bond strength. As opposed to ionic bonds, atoms in covalent bonds have similar electronegativity. Ionic and covalent bonding are thus considered as the two extremes in bonding types. Covalent bonding is further categorized into the following subclasses; non-polar, polar and coordinate types of covalent bonding.

Non-polar covalent bonding occurs when two bonding atoms have either equal or similar electronegativities or a calculated electronegativity difference of less than 0.4.

Polar covalent bonding occurs when there is a small difference in electronegativity between atoms in the range of approximately 0.4 up to 2.0. When the difference in electronegativity is greater than 2.0, ionic bonding is then known to occur between two atoms. The more electronegative atom will attract the bonding electrons to a larger extent. As a result, the more electronegative atom acquires a partial negative charge and the less electronegative atom acquires a partial positive charge.

Coordinate covalent bonding occurs when the shared electron pair comes from the lone pair of electrons of one of the atoms in the bonding component. Typically coordinate bonds form between Lewis acids (electron acceptors) and Lewis bases (electron donors) as shown below.

A$^+$ + $^-$B → A—B

Lewis Acid (Electron Acceptor)   Lewis Base (Electron Donor)   coordinate covalent bond

Al^{3+} Lewis Acid   H—Ö—H   Lewis Base   ⇌   Al with H$_2$O ligands

A <u>Lewis structure</u> is a representation of covalent bonding in which shared electrons are shown either as lines or as pairs of dots between two atoms. For instance, let us consider the H$_2$O molecule. The valence shell electronic configurations of the atoms that constitute this molecule are:

O: $2s^2 2p^4$
H: $1s^1$

Since hydrogen has only one electron to share with oxygen there is only one possible covalent bond that can be formed between the oxygen atom and each of the hydrogen atoms. Four of the valence electrons of the oxygen atom do not participate in this covalent bonding, these are called <u>non-bonding electrons or lone pairs</u>. The Lewis structure of

the water molecule is:

H:Ö:H or H-Ö-H

Lewis formulated the following general rule known as the <u>octet rule</u> concerning these representations: atoms tend to form covalent bonds until they are surrounded by 8 electrons (with few exceptions such as for hydrogen which can be surrounded by a maximum of only 2 electrons; see CHM 3.1). To satisfy this rule (and if there is a sufficient number of valence electrons), two atoms may share more than one pair of electrons thus forming more than one covalent bond at a time. In such instances the bond between these atoms is referred to as a double or a triple bond depending on whether there are two or three pairs of shared electrons, respectively.

Some molecules cannot fully be described by a single Lewis structure. For instance, for the carbonate ion: CO_3^{2-}, the octet rule is satisfied for the central carbon atom if one of the C...O bonds is double (see the following diagrams). While this leads us to thinking that the three C...O bonds are not equivalent, every piece of experimental evidence concerning this molecule shows that the three bonds are in fact the same (same length, same polarity, etc...). This suggests that in such instances a molecule cannot be described fully by a single Lewis structure. However, a molecule may in fact be represented by two or more valid Lewis structures. Indeed, since there is no particular reason to choose one oxygen atom over another we can write three equivalent Lewis structures for the carbonate ion. These three structures are called <u>resonance structures represented with a double-headed arrow between each resonance structure.</u> The carbonate ion (CO_3^{2-}) actually exists as a hybrid of the three equivalent structures. It is the full set of resonance structures that describe such a molecule. In this picture, the C...O bonds are neither double nor single, they are intermediate and have both a single and a double bonded character (see the following diagrams).

CO_3^{2-}

$$\left[\ddot{\ddot{O}}-C=\ddot{O}\atop |\atop :\ddot{O}:\right]^{2-} \leftrightarrow \left[\ddot{O}=C-\ddot{\ddot{O}}:\atop |\atop :\ddot{O}:\right]^{2-} \leftrightarrow \left[\ddot{\ddot{O}}-C-\ddot{\ddot{O}}:\atop ||\atop \ddot{O}:\right]^{2-}$$

The actual structure of the carbonate ion is therefore one which is intermediate between the three resonance structures and is known as a resonance hybrid as shown:

In many molecular structures, all of the respective resonance structures contribute equally to the hybridized representation. However, for some, resonance structures may not all contribute equally. Moreover, the more

stable the resonance structure, the more contribution of that structure to the true hybrid structure based on formal charges.

Thus, based on their stabilities, non-equivalent resonance structures may contribute differently to the true overall hybridized structure representation of a molecule.

It is often interesting to compare the number of valence electrons that an atom possesses when it is isolated and when it is engaged in a covalent bond within a given molecule. This is often quantitatively described by the concept of <u>formal charge</u>.

Generally, a formal charge is a calculated conjured charge assigned to each individual atom within a Lewis structure allowing one to distinguish amongst various possible Lewis structures. The formal charge on any individual atom is calculated based on the difference between the atom's actual number of valence electrons and the number of electrons the atom possesses as part of a Lewis structure.

Moreover, the number of electrons attributed to an atom within a Lewis structure (covalently bonded) is not necessarily the same as the number of valence electrons that would be isolated within that free atom, and the difference is thus referred to as the "formal charge" of that atom. This concept is defined as follows:

Formal charge (of atom X) = Total number of valence electrons in a free atom (V) – [(total number of nonbonding electrons

(N) + ½ total number of bonding electrons (B) in a Lewis structure)].

Where, V is the number of valence electrons of the atom in isolation (atom in ground state); N is the number of non-bonding valence electrons on this atom in the molecule; and B is the total number of bonding electrons shared in covalent bonds with other atoms in the molecule (see structure of CO_3^{2-} in the previous illustrations).

Let us apply this definition to the two previous examples: H_2O and CO_3^{2-}. This process is fairly straightforward in the case of the water molecule:

total # of valence e⁻'s in free O: 6
– total # of non-bonding e⁻'s on O in H_2O: 4
– 1/2 (total # of bonding e⁻'s) on O in H_2O: 2

Formal charge of O in $H_2O = 0$

In the case of the CO_3^{2-} ion, it is not as obvious. If we consider one of the three equivalent resonance forms, that of the oxygen with a double bond to carbon we have:

total # of valence e⁻'s in free O: 6
- total # of non-bonding e⁻'s on O in the ion: 4
- 1/2 (total # of bonding e⁻) on O in the ion: 2

Formal charge of O of C=O in the ion = 0

Similarly, the calculation of the formal charge for one of the two singly bonded oxygen's of C–O in the same ion leads to the following: $6 - 6 - 1/2(2) = -1$. Considering that CO_3^{2-} is represented by three resonance

forms, the actual formal charge of the oxygen atom is 1/3 (–1 –1 + 0) = –2/3. This value formally reflects the idea that the oxygen atoms are equivalent and that any one of them has a –1 charge in 2 out of three of the resonance forms of this ion. Here are some simple rules to remember about formal charges:

(i)   For neutral molecules, the formal charges of all the atoms should add up to zero.

(ii) For an ion, the sum of the formal charges must equal the ion's charge.

The following rules should help you select a plausible Lewis structure:

(i)   If you can write more than one Lewis structure for a given neutral molecule; the most plausible one is the one in which the formal charges of the individual atoms are zero.

(ii) Lewis structures with the smallest formal charges on each individual atom are more plausible than the ones that involve large formal charges.

(iii) Out of a range of possible Lewis structures for a given molecule, the most plausible ones are the ones in which negative formal charges are found on the most electronegative atoms and positive charges on the most electropositive ones.

In addition to these rules, remember that some elements have a tendency to form molecules that do not satisfy the octet rule:

(i) When sulfur is the central atom in a molecule or a polyatomic ion, it almost invariably does not fulfill the octet rule.

(ii) The number of electrons around S in these compounds is usually 12 (e.g. SF_6, SO_4^{2-}). This situation (<u>expanded octets</u>) also occurs in other elements in and beyond the third period.

(iii) Molecules that have an element from the 3A group (B, Al, etc...) as their central atom do not generally obey the octet rule. In these molecules there are less than 8 electrons around the central atom (e.g. AlI_3 and BF_3).

(iv) Some molecules with an odd number of electrons can clearly not obey the octet rule (e.g. NO and NO_2).

3.3 Partial Ionic Character

Except for <u>homonuclear molecules</u> (molecules made of atoms of the same element, e.g. H_2, O_3, etc...), bonding electrons are not equally shared by the bonded atoms. Thus a diatomic (= *two atoms*) compound like Cl_2 shares its bonding electrons equally; whereas, a binary (= *two <u>different</u> elements*) compound like CaO (calcium ox<u>ide</u>) or NaCl (sodium chloride) does not. Indeed, for the great majority of molecules, one of the two atoms between which the covalent bond occurs is necessarily more electronegative than the other. This atom will attract the bonding electrons to a larger extent (see CHM 3.2). Although this phenomenon does not lead to the formation of two separate ionic species, it does result in a molecule in which there are partial charges on these particular atoms: the corresponding covalent bond is said to <u>possess partial ionic character</u>. This polar bond will also have a dipole moment given by:

$$D = q \cdot d$$

where q is the absolute value of the partial charge on the most electronegative or the most electropositive bonded atom and d is the distance between these two atoms. To obtain the total dipole moment of a molecule one must add the individual dipole moment vectors present on each one of its bonds. Since this is a vector addition (see ORG 1.5), the overall result may be zero even if the individual dipole moment vectors are very large.

Non-polar bonds are generally stronger than polar covalent and ionic bonds, with ionic bonds being the weakest. However, in compounds with ionic bonding, there is generally a large number of bonds between molecules and this makes the compound as a whole very strong. For instance, although the ionic bonds in one compound are weaker than the non-polar covalent bonds in another compound, the ionic compound's melting point will be higher than the melting point of the covalent compound. Polar covalent bonds have a partially ionic character, and thus the bond strength is usually intermediate between that of ionic and that of non-polar covalent bonds. The strength of bonds generally decreases with increasing ionic character.

3.4 Lewis Acids and Lewis Bases

The Lewis model of acids and bases focuses on the transfer of an electron pair. Generally, a Lewis acid is defined as any substance that may accept an electron pair to form a covalent bond, while a Lewis base, is defined as any substance that donates an electron pair to form a respective covalent bond. Hence, as per the Lewis definition of an acid or base, a substance need not contain a hydrogen as defined by either Arrhenius or Bronsted-Lowry to be an acid, nor is a hydroxyl group (OH^-) needed to be a base (see CHM 6.1). A Lewis acid therefore generally has an empty electronic orbital that can accept an electron pair whereas a Lewis base will contain a full electronic orbital or lone pair of electrons ready to be donated.

In CHM 3.2, we pointed out some exceptions to the Lewis' octet rule. Among these were molecules that had a deficiency of electrons around the central atom as described previously (e.g. BF_3). When such a molecule is put into contact with a molecule with lone pairs (e.g. NH_3) a reaction occurs. Such a reaction can be interpreted as a donation of a pair of electrons from the second type of molecule (Lewis base) to the first type of molecule (Lewis acid), or alternately by an acceptance of a pair of electrons by the first type of molecule. Thus, as previously shown, molecules such as BF_3 are referred to as <u>Lewis acids</u> while molecules such as NH_3 are known as <u>Lewis bases</u>. Thus some examples of Lewis acids are: BF_3, H^+, Cu^{2+}, and Cr^{3+} and Lewis bases are: NH_3, OH^-, and H_2O. {l**E**wis **A**cids: **E**lectron pair **A**cceptors}.

The Lewis acid BF_3 and the Lewis base NH_3. Notice that the green arrows follow the flow of electron pairs.

3.5 Valence Shell Electronic Pair Repulsions (VSEPR Models)

One of the shortcomings of Lewis structures is that they cannot be used to predict molecular geometries. In this context a model known as the valence-shell electronic pair repulsion or VSEPR model is very useful. In this model, the geometrical arrangement of atoms or groups of atoms bound to a central atom A is determined by the number of pairs of valence electrons around A. VSEPR procedure is based on the principle that these electronic pairs around the central atom are arranged in such a way that the repulsions between them are minimized. The general VSEPR procedure starts with the determination of the number of electronic pairs around A:

# of valence electrons in a free atom of A
+ # of sigma (or single) bonds involving A
− # of pi (or double) bonds involving A

= (total # of electrons around A)

The division of this total number by 2 yields the total number of electron pairs around A. Note the following important points:

(i) A single bond counts for 1 sigma bond, a double bond for 1 sigma bond and 1 pi bond and a triple bond for 1 sigma and two pi bonds.

(ii) The general calculation that we have presented is performed for the purposes of VSEPR modeling; its result can be quite different from the one obtained in the corresponding Lewis structure.

(iii) For all practical purposes, one always assigns a double bond (i.e. 1 sigma bond and one pi bond) to a terminal oxygen (an oxygen which is not a central atom and is not attached to any other atom besides the central atom).

(iv) A terminal halogen is always assigned a single bond.

Once the number of pairs around the central atom is determined, the next step is to use Figure III.A.3.1 to predict the geometrical arrangement of these pairs around the central atom.

The next step is to consider the previous arrangement of the electronic pairs and place the atoms or groups of atoms that are attached to the central atom in accordance with such an arrangement. The pairs of electrons which are not involved in the bonding between these atoms and the central atom are known as lone pairs. If we subtract the number of lone pairs from the total number of pairs of electrons, we readily obtain the number of bonding electron pairs. It is the number of bonding electron pairs which ultimately determines the molecular geometry in the VSEPR model according to Table III.A.3.1.

On the other hand, as for the *electronic* geometrical arrangement of a molecule, one is also to consider the free lone pair(s) of electrons. Consequently, a simple molecule such as SO_2 (see Table III.A.3.1) will have a trigonal planar electronic geometry with a bent molecular geometry with the respective differences in geometrical arrangement based solely on the lone pair of the central sulfur atom. Thus, the electron and molecular geometry of a molecule may be different. (Note: electron geometry is based on the geometrical arrangement of electron pairs around a central atom, whereas, molecular geometry is based on the geometrical arrangement of the atoms surrounding a central atom). Let us consider three examples: CH_4, H_2O and CO_2.

1 – CH_4:

# of valence electrons on C:	4
+ # of sigma bonds:	+ 4
– # of pi bonds:	– 0

$$= 8/2 = 4 \text{ pairs}$$

According to Figure III.A.3.1 CH_4 corresponds to a tetrahedral arrangement. Each of these four pairs of electrons corresponds to a H atom bonded each to the central atom of carbon. Therefore, all 4 pairs of electrons are bonding pairs with a tetrahedral molecular and electronic geometry, respectively (due to a lack in lone pairs).

2 – H_2O:

# of valence electrons on O:	6
+ # of sigma bonds on the central O:	+ 2
- # of pi bonds on the central O:	– 0

$$= 8/2 = 4 \text{ pairs}$$

For the H_2O geometry, it also corresponds to a tetrahedral arrangement (i.e. 4 pairs). However, due to lone pairs surrounding each of the oxygen atoms, the molecular geometry is of a bent geometrical shape with a tetrahedral electronic geometrical configuration.

3 – CO_2:

# of valence electrons on C:	4
+ # of sigma bonds for terminal O's:	+ 2
- # of pi bonds for terminal O's:	– 2

$$= 4/2 = 2 \text{ pairs}$$

This total number of pairs corresponds to a linear arrangement. Since both of these electron pairs are used to connect the central C atom to the terminal O's there are no lone pairs left on C. Therefore, the number of bonding pairs is also 2 and both the molecular and electronic geometries are also linear.

Here are some additional rules when applying the VSEPR model:

(i) When dealing with a cation (<u>positive</u> ion) <u>subtract</u> the charge of the ion from the total number of electrons.

(ii) When dealing with an anion (<u>negative</u> ion) <u>add</u> the charge of the ion to the total number of electrons.

(iii) A lone pair repels another lone pair or a bonding pair very strongly. This causes some deformation in bond angles. For instance, the H–O–H angle is smaller than $109.5°$.

Table III.A.3.1: Geometry of simple molecules in which the central atom A has one or more lone pairs of electrons (= e^-).

Total number of e^- pairs	Number of lone pairs	Number of bonding pairs	Electron Geometry, Arrangement of e^- pairs	Molecular Geometry (Hybridization State)	Examples
3	1	2	Trigonal planar	Bent (sp^2)	SO_2
4	1	3	Tetrahedral	Trigonal pyramidal (sp^3)	NH_3
4	2	2	Tetrahedral	Bent (sp^3)	H_2O
5	1	4	Trigonal bipyramidal	Seesaw (sp^3d)	SF_4
5	2	3	Trigonal bipyramidal	T-shaped (sp^3d)	ClF_3

Note: dotted lines only represent the overall molecular shape and not molecular bonds. In brackets under "Molecular Geometry" is the hybridization, to be discussed in ORG 1.2.

(iv) The previous rule also holds for a double bond. Note that in one of our previous examples (CO_2), the angle is still 180° since there are two double bonds and no lone pairs. Indeed, in this geometry, the strong repulsions between the two double bonds are symmetrical.

(v) The VSEPR model can be applied to polyatomic molecules. The procedure is the same as above except that one can only determine the arrangements of groups of atoms around one given central atom at a time. For instance, you could apply the VSEPR model to determine the geometrical arrangements of atoms around C or around O in methanol (CH_3OH). In the first case the molecule is treated as $CH_3 - X$ (where $-X$ is $-OH$) and in the second it is treated as $HO-Y$ (where $-Y$ is $-CH_3$). The

linear arrangement of
2 electron pairs around
central atom A

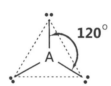

trigonal planar arrangement
of 3 electron pairs
around central atom A

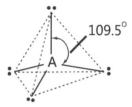

tetrahedral arrangement
of 4 electron pairs
around central atom A

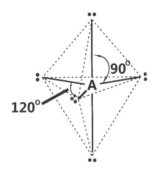

trigonal bipyramidal arrangement
of 5 electron pairs
around central atom A

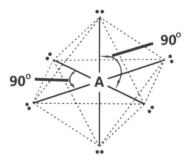

octahedral arrangement
of 6 electron pairs
around central atom A

Figure III.A.3.1: Molecular arrangement of electron pairs around a central atom A. Dotted lines only represent the overall molecular shape and not molecular bonds.

geometrical arrangement is tetrahedral in the first case which gives HCX or HCH angles close to 109°. The second case corresponds to a bent arrangement (with two lone pairs on the oxygen) and gives an HOY angle close to 109° as well. This also corresponds to a tetrahedral arrangement, however only two of these pairs are bonding pairs (connecting the H atoms to the central oxygen atom); therefore, the actual geometry according to Table III.A.3.1 is bent or V-shape geometry.

Go online to GAMSAT-prep.com for free chapter review Q&A and forum.

Memorize	Understand	Not Required*
* Define: temp. (°C, K), gas P and weight * Define: STP, ideal gas, deviation * Define: H bonds, dipole forces	* Kinetic molecular theory of gases * Maxwell distribution plot, H bonds, dipole F. * Deviation from ideal gas behavior * Equations: ideal gas/Charles'/Boyle's * Partial Press., mole fraction, Dalton's * Intermolecular forces, phase change/diagrams	* Knowledge beyond introductory-level (first year uni.) course * Memorizing Van der Waals' equation * Memorizing the gas constant R * Memorizing values: triple point of H_2O

GAMSAT-Prep.com

Introduction

A phase, or state of matter, is a uniform, distinct and usually separable region of material. For example, for a glass of water: the ice cubes are one phase (solid), the water is a second phase (liquid), and the humid air over the water is the third phase (gas = vapor). The temperature and pressure at which all 3 phases of a substance can coexist is called the triple point.

Additional Resources

| Free Online Q&A + Forum | GAMSAT-prep.com Videos | Flashcards | Special Guest |

* The real GAMSAT may have advanced level information presented (ie. in a passage) but previous knowledge of said information is not required to answer the questions that would follow. Practice ACER and GS practice GAMSATs can help you clarify this point.

Elements and compounds exist in one of three states: the gaseous state, the liquid state or the solid state.

4.1 The Gas Phase

A substance in the gaseous state has neither fixed volume nor fixed shape: it spreads itself uniformly throughout any container in which it is placed.

4.1.1 Standard Temperature and Pressure, Standard Molar Volume

Any given gas can be described in terms of four fundamental properties: mass, volume, temperature and pressure. To simplify comparisons, the volume of a gas is normally reported at 0°C (273.15 K) and 1.00 atm (101.33 kPa = 760 mmHg = 760 torr); these conditions are known as the standard temperature and pressure (STP). {Note: the SI unit of pressure is the pascal (Pa) and the old-fashioned Imperial unit is the pound per square inch because pressure is defined as force per unit area}

The volume occupied by one mole of any gas at STP is referred to as the standard molar volume and is equal to 22.4 L.

4.1.2 Kinetic Molecular Theory of Gases (A Model for Gases)

The kinetic molecular theory of gases describes the particulate behavior of matter in the gaseous state. A gas that fits this theory exactly is called an ideal gas. The essential points of the theory are as follows:

1. Gases are composed of extremely small particles (either molecules or atoms depending on the gas) separated by distances that are relatively large in comparison with the diameters of the particles.

2. Particles of gas are in constant motion, except when they collide with one another.

3. Particles of an ideal gas exert no attractive or repulsive force on one another.

4. The collisions experienced by gas particles do not, on the average, slow them down; rather, they cause a change in the direction in which the particles are moving. If one particle loses energy as a result of a collision, the energy is gained by the particle with which it collides. Collisions of the particles of an ideal gas with the walls of the container result in no loss of energy.

5. The <u>average kinetic energy</u> of the particles (KE = 1/2 mv²) <u>increases in direct proportion to the temperature</u> of the gas (KE = 3/2 kT) when the temperature is measured on an absolute scale (i.e. the Kelvin scale) and k is a constant (the Boltzmann constant). The typical speed of a gas particle is directly proportional to the square root of the absolute temperature.

The plot of the distribution of collision energies of gases is similar to that of liquids. However, molecules in liquids require a minimum escape kinetic energy in order to enter the vapor phase (see Figure III.A.4.1 in CHM 4.1.2).

The properties of gases can be explained in terms of the kinetic molecular theory of ideal gases.

Experimentally, we can measure four properties of a gas:

1. The <u>weight</u> of the gas, from which we can calculate the <u>number (N) of molecules or atoms</u> of the gas present;

2. The <u>pressure (P)</u>, exerted by the gas on the walls of the container in which this gas is placed (N.B.: a <u>vacuum</u> is completely devoid of particles and thus has *no* pressure);

3. The <u>volume (V)</u>, occupied by the gas;

4. The <u>temperature (T)</u> of the gas.

In fact, if we know any three of these properties, we can calculate the fourth. So the minimum number of these properties required to fully describe the state of an ideal gas is three.

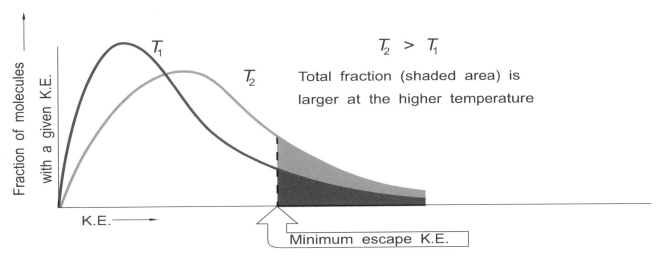

Figure III.A.4.1: The Maxwell Distribution Plot. At a higher temperature T_2, the curve peak is flattened, which means that gas particles within the sample are travelling at a wider range of velocities. Additionally, the larger shaded area at a temperature T_2 means that a greater proportion of molecules will possess the minimum escaping kinetic energy (KE) required to evaporate.

4.1.3 Graham's Law (Diffusion and Effusion of Gases)

Graham's law describes the mean (average) free path of any typical gas particle taken per unit volume. The process taken by such gas particles is known as *diffusion* and its related process *effusion* which are defined as follows:

Diffusion is the flow of gas particles spreading out evenly through random motion. Gas particles diffuse from regions of high concentration to regions of low concentration. The rate at which a gas diffuses is inversely proportional to the square root of its molar mass. The ratio of the diffusion rates of two different gases is inversely proportional to the square root of their respective molar masses. $Rate_1/Rate_2$ and

M_1/M_2 represents diffusion rates of gases 1 and 2 and the molar mass of gases 1 and 2. Lighter particles diffuse quicker than heavier particles.

Effusion is the movement of a gas through a small hole or pore into another gaseous region or into a vacuum. If the hole is large enough, the process may be considered diffusion instead of effusion. The rates at which two gases effuse are inversely proportional to the square root of their molar masses, the same as that for diffusion:

$$\frac{Rate_1}{Rate_2} = \sqrt{\frac{M_2}{M_1}}$$

4.1.4 Charles' Law

The volume (V) of a gas is directly proportional to the absolute temperature (expressed in Kelvins) when P and N are kept constant.

$$V = \text{Constant} \times T \quad \text{or} \quad V_1/V_2 = T_1/T_2$$

NOTE: For Charles' Law and all subsequent laws, the subscripts 1 and 2 refer to both initial and final values of all variables for the gas in question.

4.1.5 Boyle's Law

The volume (V) of a fixed weight of gas held at constant temperature (T) varies inversely with the pressure (P).

$$V = \text{Constant} \times 1/P \quad \text{or} \quad P_1V_1 = P_2V_2$$

4.1.6 Avogadro's Law

The volume (V) of a gas at constant temperature and pressure is directly proportional to the number of particles or moles (n) of the gas present.

$$V/n = \text{Constant} \quad \text{or} \quad V_1/n_1 = V_2/n_2$$

4.1.7 Combined Gas Law

For a given constant mass of any gas the product of its pressure and volume divided by its Kelvin temperature is equal to a constant (k). Therefore, by using the combined gas law, one may calculate any of the three variables of a gas exposed to two separate conditions as follows:

This relationship depicts how a change in pressure, volume, and/or temperature of any gas (at constant mass) will be affected as a function of the other quantities (P_2, V_2 or T_2).

$$\frac{P_1V_1}{T_1} = k = \frac{P_2V_2}{T_2} \quad \text{(at constant mass)}$$

4.1.8 Ideal Gas Law

The combination of Boyle's law, Charles' law and Avogadro's law yields the "ideal gas law":

$$PV = nRT$$

where R is the <u>universal gas constant</u> and n is the number of moles of gas particles.

R = 0.0821 L-atm/K-mole
= 8.31 kPa-dm^3/K-mole

A typical ideal gas problem is as follows: an ideal gas at 27 °C and 380 torr occupies a volume of 492 cm^3. What is the number of moles of gas?

Ideal Gas Law problems often amount to mere exercises of unit conversions. The easiest way to do them is to convert the units of the values given to the units of the R gas constant.

$$P = 380 \text{ torr} = \frac{380 \text{ torr}}{(760 \text{ torr/atm})} = 0.500 \text{ atm}$$

$$T = 27\,°C = 273 + 27\,°C = 300 \text{ K}$$

$$V = 492 \text{ cm}^3 = 492 \text{ cm}^3 \times (1 \text{ liter/1000cm}^3)$$
$$= 0.492 \text{ liter}$$

$$PV = nRT$$
$$n = PV/RT$$
$$n = \frac{(0.500 \text{ atm} \times 0.492 \text{ L})}{(0.0821 \text{ L-atm/K-mole} \times 300 \text{ K})}$$
$$n = 0.0100 \text{ mole}$$

Also note that the ideal gas law could be used in the following alternate ways (Mwt = molecular weight):

(i) since n = (mass m of gas sample)/(Mwt M of the gas)

$$PV = (m/M)RT$$

(ii) since m/V is the density (d) of the gas:

$$P = \frac{dRT}{M}$$

The calculations and variable manipulations in this section (CHM 4.1.8) are based on dimensional analysis (GM 2.2) which is of fundamental importance for all GAMSAT sciences.

4.1.9 Partial Pressure and Dalton's Law

In a mixture of unreactive gases, each gas distributes evenly throughout the container. All particles exert the same pressure on the walls of the container with equal force. If we consider a mixture of gases occupying a total volume (V) at a temperature (T) the term partial pressure is used to refer to the pressure exerted by one component of the gas mixture if it were occupying the entire volume (V) at the temperature (T).

Dalton's law states that the total pressure observed for a mixture of gases is equal to the sum of the pressures that each individual component would exert were it alone in the container.

$$P_T = P_1 + P_2 + \dots + P_i$$

where P_T is the total pressure and P_i is the partial pressure of any component (i).

The mole fraction (X_i) of any one gas present in a mixture is defined as follows:

$$X_i = n_i/n_{(total)}$$

where n_i = moles of that gas present in the mixture and $n_{(total)}$ = sum of the moles of all gases present in the mixture (see CHM 5.3.1).

Of course, the sum of all mole fractions in a mixture must equal one:

$$\Sigma X_i = 1$$

The partial pressure (P_i) of a component of a gas mixture is equal to:

$$\boxed{P_i = X_i P_T}$$

The ideal gas law applies to any component of the mixture:

$$P_i V = n_i R T$$

4.1.10 Deviation of Real Gas Behavior from the Ideal Gas Law

The particles of an ideal gas have zero volume and no intermolecular forces. It obeys the ideal gas law. Its particles behave as though they were moving points exerting no attraction on one another and occupying no space. Real gases deviate from ideal gas behavior particularly when the gas particles are forced into close proximity under high pressure and low temperature, as follows:

1. They do not obey $PV = nRT$. We can calculate n, P, V and T for a real gas on the assumption that it behaves like an ideal gas but the calculated values will not agree with the observed values.

2. Their particles are subject to intermolecular forces (i.e. forces of attraction between different molecules like Van der Waal forces; CHM 4.2) which are themselves independent of temperature. But the deviations they cause are more pronounced at low temperatures because they are less effectively opposed by the slower motion of particles at lower temperatures. Similarly, an increase in pressure

at constant temperature will crowd the particles closer together and reduce the average distance between them. This will increase the attractive force between the particles and the stronger these forces, the more the behavior of the real gas will deviate from that of an ideal gas. Thus, a real gas will act less like an ideal gas at higher pressures than at lower pressures. {Mnemonic: an ideal Plow and Thigh = an ideal gas exists when **Pressure** is **low** and **Temperature** is **high**}

3. The particles (i.e. molecules or atoms) occupy space. When a real gas is subjected to high pressures at ordinary temperatures, the fraction of the total volume occupied by the particles increases. At moderately high pressure, gas particles are pushed closer together and intermolecular attraction causes the gas to have a smaller volume than would be predicted by the ideal gas law. At extremely high pressure, gas particles are pushed even closer in such a way that the distance between them are becoming insignificant

compared to the size of the particles, therefore causing the gas to take up a smaller volume than would be predicted by the ideal gas law. Under these conditions, the real gas deviates appreciably from ideal gas behavior.

4. Their <u>size and mass</u> also affect the speed at which they move. At constant temperature, the kinetic energy (KE = 1/2 mv^2) of all particles – light or heavy – is nearly the same. This means that the heavier particles must be moving more slowly than the lighter ones and that the attractive forces between the heavier particles must be exercising a greater influence on their behavior. The greater speed of light

particles, however, tends to counteract the attractive forces between them, thus producing a slight deviation from ideal gas behavior. Thus, a heavier particle (molecule or atom) will deviate more widely from ideal gas behavior than a lighter particle. At low temperature, the average velocity of gas particles decreases and the intermolecular attraction becomes increasingly significant, causing the gas to have a smaller volume than would be predicted by the ideal gas law. {The preceding is given by Graham's law, where the rate of movement of a gas (*diffusion* or streaming through a fine hole – *effusion*) is inversely proportional to the square root of the molecular weight of the gas (see CHM 4.1.3)}

4.2 Liquid Phase (Intra- and Intermolecular Forces)

Liquids have the ability to mix with one another and with other phases to form solutions. The degree to which two liquids can mix is called their miscibility. Liquids have definite volume, but no definite shape. As we will discuss, molecules of liquids can be attracted to each other (*cohesion*) as they can be attracted to their surroundings (*adhesion*). The most striking properties of a liquid are its <u>viscosity</u> and <u>surface tension</u> (see CHM 4.2.1; PHY 6.1.4, 6.1.5). Liquids also distinguish themselves from gases in that they are relatively <u>incompressible</u>. The molecules of a liquid are also subject to forces strong enough to hold them together. These forces are intermolecular and they are weak attractive forces that is, they are effective over short

distances only. Molecules like methane (CH_4) are non-polar and so they are held together by weak intermolecular forces also known as Van der Waal forces (these include forces that are dipole-dipole, dipole-induced dipole and London forces). Whereas, molecules like water have much stronger intermolecular attractive forces because of the hydrogen bonding amongst the molecules. Hence, the most important forces are:

1. <u>Dipole-dipole forces</u> which depend on the orientation as well as on the distance between the molecules; they are inversely proportional to the fourth power of the distance. In addition to the forces between permanent dipoles, a dipolar

molecule induces in a neighboring molecule an electron distribution that results in another attractive force, the dipole-induced dipole force, which is inversely proportional to the seventh power of the distance and which is relatively independent of orientation.

2. London forces (or Dispersive forces) are attractive forces acting between nonpolar molecules. They are due to the unsymmetrical instantaneous electron distribution which induces a dipole in neighboring molecules with a resultant attractive force. This instantaneous unsymmetrical distribution of electrons causes rapid

polarization of the electrons and formation of short-lived dipoles. These dipoles then interact with neighboring molecules, inducing the formation of more dipoles. Dispersion forces are thus responsible for the liquefaction of noble gases to form liquids at low temperatures (and high pressures).

3. Hydrogen bonds occur whenever hydrogen is covalently bonded to an atom such as O, N or F that attract electrons strongly. Because of the differences in electronegativity between H and O or N or F, the electrons that constitute the covalent bond are closer to the O, N or F nucleus than

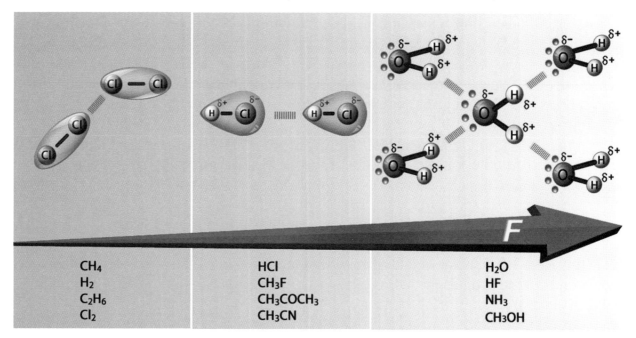

Table III.A.4.1: Van Der Waal's forces (weak) and hydrogen bonding (strong). London forces between Cl_2 molecules, dipole-dipole forces between HCl molecules and H-bonding between H_2O molecules. Note that a partial negative charge on an atom is indicated by δ^- (delta negative), while a partial positive charge is indicated by δ^+ (delta positive). Notice that one H_2O molecule can potentially form 4 H-bonds with surrounding molecules which is highly efficient. The preceding is one key reason that the boiling point of water is higher than that of ammonia, hydrogen fluoride or methanol.

to the H nucleus leaving the latter relatively unshielded. The unshielded proton is strongly attracted to the O, N or F atoms of neighboring molecules since these form the negative end of a strong dipole.

The slightly positive charge of the hydrogen atom will then be strongly attracted to the more electronegative atoms of nearby molecules. These forces are weaker than intramolecular bonds, but are much stronger than the other two types of intermolecular forces. Hydrogen bonding is a special case of dipole-dipole interaction. Hydrogen bonds are characterized by unusually strong interactions and high boiling points due to the vast amount of energy required (relative to other intermolecular forces) to break the hydrogen bonds. {Though the H-bonding atoms are often remembered by the mnemonic "Hydrogen is FON!", sulfur is also known to H-bond though far weaker than the more electronegative FON atoms.}

4.2.1 Viscosity

Viscosity is analogous to friction between moving solids. It may, therefore be viewed as the resistance to flow of layers of fluid or liquid past each other. This also means that viscosity, as in friction, results in dissipation of mechanical energy. As one layer flows over another, its motion is transmitted to the second layer and causes this layer to be set in motion. Since a mass m of the second layer is set in motion and some of the energy of the first layer is lost, there is a transfer of momentum between the layers.

The greater the transfer of this momentum from one layer to another, the more energy that is lost and the slower the layers move.

The viscosity (η) is the measure of the efficiency of transfer of this momentum. Therefore the higher the viscosity coefficient, the greater the transfer of momentum and loss of mechanical energy, and thus loss of velocity. The reverse situation holds for a low viscosity coefficient (see PHY 6.1.4).

Consequently, a high viscosity coefficient substance flows slowly (e.g. molasses), and a low viscosity coefficient substance flows relatively fast (e.g. water). Consider the following examples at room temperature and atmospheric pressure, from low to high viscosity: acetone (= nail polish remover, paint thinner) < water < motor oil < maple syrup < honey < molasses < fondue < toothpaste.

Note that the transfer of momentum to adjacent layers is in essence, the exertion of a force upon these layers to set them in motion.

4.3 Solid Phase

Solids have definite volume and shape and are incompressible under pressure. Intermolecular forces between molecules of molecular solids and electrostatic (i.e. coulombic or "opposite charges attract") interactive forces between ions of ionic solids are strong enough to hold them into a relatively rigid structure. A solid may be crystalline (ordered) or amorphous (disordered). A crystalline solid, such as table salt (NaCl) has a structure with an ordered geometric shape. Its atoms are arranged geometrically with a repeating pattern. It has a specific melting point. An amorphous solid, such as glass, has a molecular structure with no specific shape. It melts over a wide range of temperatures since the molecules require different amounts of energies to break bonds between them.

4.4 Phase Equilibria (Solids, Liquids and Gases)

4.4.1 Phase Changes

Elements and compounds can undergo transitions between the solid, liquid and gaseous states. They can exist in different phases and undergo phase changes which need not involve chemical reactions. Phase changes are reversible with an equilibrium existing between each of the phases. A phase is a homogeneous, physically distinct and mechanically separable part of a system. Each phase is separated from other phases by a physical boundary.

A few examples:

1. Ice/liquid water/water vapor (3 phases)

2. Any number of gases mix in all proportions and therefore constitute just one phase.

3. The system $CaCO_3(s) \rightarrow CaO(s) + CO_2(g)$ (2 phases, i.e. 2 solids: $CaCO_3$ and CaO and a gas: CO_2)

4. A saturated salt solution (3 phases: solution, undissolved salt, vapor)

An example of phase change is the vaporization of water into its vapor state. A system is considered homogeneous when it is uniform throughout its volume so that its properties are the same in all parts. This does not imply a single molecular species: a solution of sodium chloride is homogeneous provided its concentration is the same throughout.

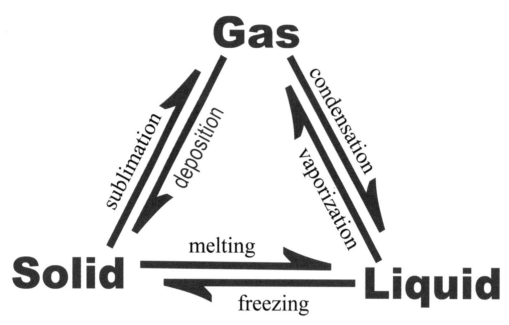

Figure III.A.4.2: Phase Changes

4.4.2 Freezing Point, Melting Point, Boiling Point

The conversion of a liquid to a gas is called <u>vaporization</u>. We can increase the rate of vaporization of a liquid by (i) increasing the temperature (ii) reducing the pressure, or (iii) both. Molecules escape from a liquid because, even though their average kinetic energy is constant, not all of them move at the same speed (*see Figure III.A.4.1*). A fast moving molecule can break away from the attraction of the others and pass into the vapor state. When a tight lid is placed on a vessel containing a liquid, the vapor molecules cannot escape and some revert back to the liquid state. The number of molecules leaving the liquid at any given time equals the number of molecules returning. Equilibrium is reached and the number of molecules in the fixed volume above the liquid remains constant. These molecules exert a constant pressure at a fixed temperature which is called the vapor pressure of the liquid. The vapor pressure is the partial pressure exerted by the gas molecules over the liquid formed by evaporation, when it is in equilibrium with the gas phase condensing back into the liquid phase. The vapor pressure of any liquid is dependent on the intermolecular forces that are present within the liquid and the temperature. Weak intermolecular forces result in volatile substances whereas strong intermolecular forces result in nonvolatile substances.

Boiling and evaporation are similar processes but they differ as follows: the vapor from a boiling liquid escapes with sufficient pressure to push back any other gas present, rather than diffusing through it. Vapor pressure increases as the temperature increases, as more molecules have sufficient energy to break the attraction between each other to escape into the gas phase. The boiling point is therefore the temperature at which the vapor pressure of the liquid equals to the opposing external pressure. Under a lower pressure, the boiling point is reached at a lower temperature. Increased intermolecular interactions (i.e. H_2O see CHM 4.2, alcohol see ORG 6.1, etc.) will decrease the vapor pressure thus raising the boiling point. Other factors being equal, as a molecule becomes heavier (increasing molecular weight), it becomes more difficult to push the molecule into the atmosphere thus the boiling point increases (i.e. alkanes see ORG 3.1.1).

The freezing point of a liquid is the temperature at which the vapor pressure of the solid equals the vapor pressure of the liquid. Increases in the prevailing atmospheric pressure decreases the melting point and increases the boiling point.

When a solid is heated, the kinetic energy of the components increases steadily. Finally, the kinetic energy becomes great enough to overcome the forces holding the components together and the solid changes to a liquid. For pure crystalline solids, there is a fixed temperature at which this transition from solid to liquid occurs. This temperature is called the melting point. Pure solids melt completely at one temperature. Impure solids begin to melt at one temperature but become completely liquid at a higher temperature.

4.4.3 Phase Diagrams

Figure III.A.4.3 shows the temperature of ice as heat is added. Temperature increases linearly with heat until the melting point is reached. At this point, the heat energy added does not change the temperature. Instead, it is used to break intermolecular bonds and convert ice into water. There is a mixture of both ice and water at the melting point. After all of the complete conversion of ice into water, the temperature rises again linearly with heat addition. At the boiling point, the heat added does not change the temperature because the energy is again used to break the intermolecular bonds. After complete

conversion of water into gas, the temperature will rise linearly again with heat addition.

Thus, during a phase change, there is no change in temperature. The energy that is added into the system is being used to weaken/break intermolecular forces; in other words, there is an increase in the potential energy of molecules rather than an increase in the average kinetic energy of molecules. The amount of energy to change one mole of substance from solid to liquid or from liquid to gas is called the molar *heat of fusion* and the molar *heat of vaporization* (CHM 8.7) Each

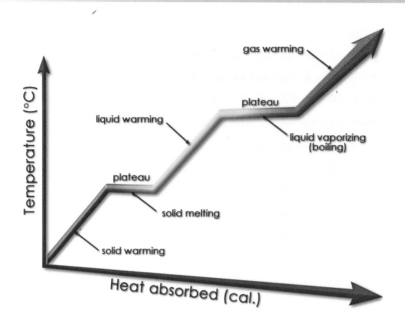

Figure III.A.4.3 Heating curve for H_2O

phase has its own specific heat. Enthalpy of vaporization is greater than that of fusion because more energy is required to break intermolecular bonds (from liquid phase to gas phase) than just to weaken intermolecular bonds (from solid phase to liquid phase).

The temperatures at which phase transitions occur are functions of the pressure of the system. The behavior of a given substance over a wide range of temperature and pressure can be summarized in a <u>phase diagram</u>, such as the one shown for the water system (Fig.III.A.4.4). The diagram is divided into three areas labeled **solid** (ice), **liquid** (water) and **vapor** in each of which only one phase exists. In these areas, P and T can be independently varied without a second phase appearing. These areas are bounded by curves AC, AD and AB. Line AB represents

sublimation/deposition (sublimation curve). Line AC represents evaporation/condensation (vaporization curve) and Line AD represents melting/freezing (fusion curve). At triple point A, all three phases are known to coexist. At any point on these curves, two phases are in equilibrium. Thus on AC, at a given T, the saturated vapor pressure of water has a fixed value. The boiling point of water (N) can be found on this curve, 100 °C at 760 mmHg pressure. The curve only extends as far as C, the <u>critical point</u>, where the vapor and liquid are indistinguishable. In general, the gas phase is found at high temperature and low pressure; the solid phase is found at low temperatures and high pressure; and the liquid phase is found at high temperatures and high pressure. The temperature at which a substance boils when the pressure is 1 atm is called the normal boiling point.

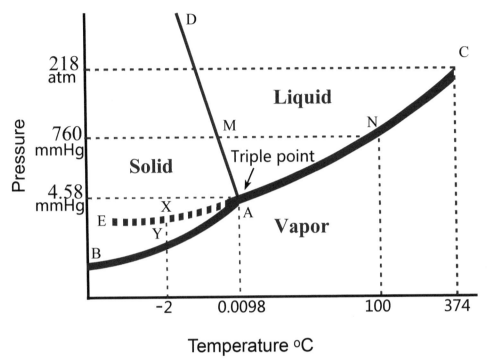

Figure III.A.4.4: Phase diagram for H_2O.

The extension of the curve CA to E represents the <u>metastable equilibrium</u> (*meta* = beyond) between supercooled water and its vapor. If the temperature is slightly raised at point X, a little of the liquid will vaporize until a new equilibrium is established at that higher temperature. Curve AB is the vapor pressure curve for ice. Its equilibria are of lower energy than those of AE and thus more stable.

The slope of line AD shows that an increase in P will lower the melting point of ice. This property is almost unique to water. Because of the negative slope of line AD, an isothermal increase in pressure will compress the solid (ice) into liquid (water). Thus H_2O is unique in that its liquid form is denser than its solid form. The high density of liquid water is due mainly to the cohesive nature of the hydrogen-bonded network of water molecules (see Table III.A.4.1 in CHM 4.2).

Most substances *increase* their melting points with increased pressure. Thus the line AD slants to the right for almost all substances. Point M represents the true melting point of ice, 0.0023 °C at 760 mmHg of pressure. (The 0 °C standard refers to the freezing point of water saturated with air at 760 mmHg). At point A, solid, liquid and vapor are in equilibrium. At this one temperature, ice and water have the same fixed vapor pressure. This is the <u>triple point</u>, 0.0098 °C at 4.58 mmHg pressure.

Go online to GAMSAT-prep.com for free chapter review Q&A and forum.

SOLUTION CHEMISTRY

Chapter 5

Memorize	Understand	Not Required*
• Define saturated, supersatured, nonvolatile • Common anions and cations in solution • Units of concentration • Define electrolytes with examples	* Colligative properties, Raoult's law * Phase diagram change due to coll. properties * Bp elevation, fp depression * Osmotic press, equation * Solubility product, common-ion effect * Solubility rules	* Knowledge beyond introductory-level (first year uni.) course * % solubility of glucose in water

GAMSAT-Prep.com

Introduction

A solution is a homogeneous mixture composed of two or more substances. For example, a solute (salt) dissolved in a solvent (water) making a solution (salt water). Solutions can involve gases in liquids (i.e. oxygen in water) or even solids in solids (i.e. alloys). Two substances are immiscible if they can't mix to make a solution. Solutions can be distinguished from non-homogeneous mixtures like colloids and suspensions.

Additional Resources

Free Online Q&A + Forum

GAMSAT-prep.com Videos

Flashcards

Special Guest

5.1 Solutions and Colligative Properties

Water (H_2O) is a universal solvent known as a pure substance or a one component system. Pure substances are often mixed together to form solutions. A solution is a sample of matter that is homogeneous but, unlike a pure substance, the composition of a solution can vary within relatively wide limits. Ethanol (= ethyl alcohol = "alcohol"; ORG 6.1) and water are each pure substances and each have a fixed composition, C_2H_5OH and H_2O, but mixtures of the two can vary continuously in composition from almost 100% ethanol to almost 100% water. Solutions of sucrose in water, however, are limited to a maximum percentage of sucrose - the solubility - which is 67% at 20°C, thus the solution is saturated. If the solution is heated, a higher concentration of sucrose can be achieved (i.e. 70%). Slowly cooling down to 20°C creates a supersaturated solution which may precipitate with any perturbation.

Intermolecular forces (see CHM 4.2) amongst various other parameters may either promote or may prevent the formation of a solution. The formation of solutions primarily involves the breaking of intermolecular forces between solutes and between solvents and the subsequent reformation of new intermolecular interactions amongst the solute and solvent. The initial step in solution formation (i.e. breakage of intermolecular forces amongst the solutes and solvent separately) is endothermic and the second step (i.e. reformation of intermolecular interactions between solute-solvent) is exothermic. If an overall reaction in solution formation is exothermic, the new intermolecular bonds between solute and solvent are more stable and a solution is

formed. {Note: "endothermic" - absorbs heat, "exothermic" - releases heat; "enthalpy" is a measure of the total energy; see CHM chapters 7 and 8 for details}

In the energetic requirements of solution formation, the formation of a solution may result in either an increase or a decrease in the enthalpy of solution dependant on the magnitude of interactions between the solute and solvent. Hence, energy changes do occur when a solution forms (i.e exothermic or endothermic). An increase in enthalpy, a positive heat of solution, results in more energy in a system i.e. less stable and weaker bonds. Whereas a decrease in enthalpy, a negative heat of solution, results in less energy in a system i.e. more stable and stronger bonds and thus the respective drive to the formation of a solution.

Lastly, the formation of a solution always results in an increase in entropy or disorder due to the insidious tendency for energy to disperse.

Generally the component of a solution that is stable in the same phase as the solution is called the solvent. If two components of a solution are in the same phase, the component present in the larger amount is called the solvent and the other is called the solute. Many properties of solutions are dependent only on the relative number of molecules (or ions) of the solute and of the solvent. Properties that depend **only** on the number of particles present and not the kind of particles are called colligative properties. For all colligative properties, a factor known as the Van't Hoff factor (i) is essentially required and defined as, the ratio of moles of particles or ions in a solution to the moles of all undissociated formula units (or molecules) within a solution. The factor (i) is therefore incorporated as a multiple of all the colligative properties equations, respectively (see below). Thus, for non-ionic solutions, the factor (i) is essentially equal to 1 as the particles are undissociated such as for sugar solutions. However, for ionic solutions, the factor (i) is dependent on the number of ions dissociated in solution (i.e., $NaCl = 2$, $CaCl_2 = 3$, etc.). Hence, the most important colligative properties can be found in the following sections.

5.1.1 Vapor-Pressure Lowering (Raoult's Law)

The vapor pressure of the components of an <u>ideal</u> solution behaves as follows:

$$p_i = X_i \, (p_i)_{pure}$$

where p_i = vapor pressure of component i in equilibrium with the solution

$(p_i)_{pure}$ = vapor pressure of pure component i at the same T

X_i = mole fraction of component i in the liquid.

Thus the vapor pressure of any component of a mixture is lowered by the presence of the other components. Experimentally, it can be observed that when dissolving a solute which cannot evaporate (= *nonvolatile*) into a solvent, the vapor pressure of the resulting solution is lower than that of the pure solvent. The extent to which the vapor pressure is lowered is determined by the mole fraction of the solvent in solution ($X_{solvent}$):

$$P = P^\circ X_{solvent}$$

where P = vapor pressure of solution
P° = vapor pressure of pure solvent (at the same temperature as P).

When rearranged this way, the vapor pressure of a solution is quantified by <u>Raoult's law</u> which states that the lowering of the vapor pressure of the solvent is proportional to the mole fraction of solvent and independent of the chemical nature of the solute.

Hence, to show by how much a solution's vapor pressure is lowered by a solute, we can therefore define the vapor pressure lowering (ΔP) by the following equation; $\Delta P = X_{solute} \, P^\circ_{solvent}$. Where, $\Delta P = P^\circ_{solvent} - P_{solution}$ and rearranging the differences between the solvent and solution vapor pressures and substituting the solvent mole fraction ($X_{solvent}$) with the solute mole fraction as $X_{solvent} = 1 - X_{solute}$, results in Raoult's law which indicates that the lowering of the vapor pressure is directly proportional to the solute mole fraction as stated previously.

5.1.2 Boiling-Point Elevation and Freezing-Point Depression

When the vapor-pressure curve of a dilute solution and the vapor-pressure curve of the pure solvent are plotted on a phase diagram (see Figure III.A.5.1), it can be seen that a vapor pressure lowering of a solution occurs at all temperatures and that the freezing point and boiling point of a solution must therefore be different from those of the pure liquid.

The freezing point of a pure solvent (water) is lowered or depressed with the addition of another substance; meaning that a solution (solvent + solute) has a lower freezing point than a pure solvent, and this phenomenon is called a "freezing point depression". Alternatively, the boiling point of a pure solvent (water) is elevated when another substance is added; meaning that a solution

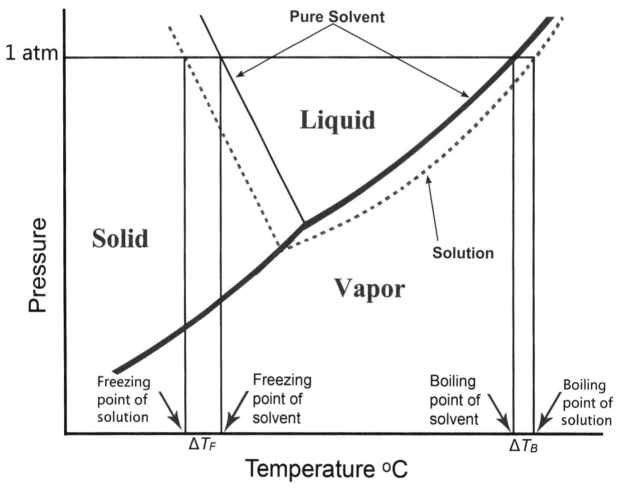

Figure III.A.5.1: Phase diagram of water demonstrating the effect of the addition of a solute.

has a higher boiling point than a pure solvent, and this phenomenon is called "boiling point elevation". The boiling point is therefore higher for the solution than for the pure liquid and the freezing point is lower for the solution than for the pure liquid. Since the decrease in vapor pressure is proportional to the mole fraction (see CHM 5.3.1) of solute, the boiling point elevation (ΔT_B) is also proportional to the mole fraction of solute and:

$$\Delta T_B = i\,K_B'X_B = i\,K_B m$$

where K_B' = boiling point elevation constant for the solvent

X_B = mole fraction of solute

m = *molality* (moles solute per kilogram of solvent; CHM 5.3.1)

i = Van't Hoff factor

K_B is related to K_B' through a change of units.

Similarly, for the freezing point depression (ΔT_F):

$$\Delta T_F = i\,K_F'X_B = i\,K_F m$$

where K_F' = freezing point depression constant for the solvent.

If K_F or K_B is known, it is then possible to determine the molality of a dilute solution simply by measuring the freezing point or the boiling point. These constants can be determined by measuring the freezing point and boiling point of a solution of known molality. If the mass concentration of a solute (in kg solute per kg of solvent) is known and the molality is determined from the freezing point of the solution, the mass of 1 mole of solute can be calculated.

It is important to recall that for a strong electrolyte solution such as NaCl which dissociates to positive and negative ions, the right hand side of the equation is multiplied by the Van't Hoff factor (i) equal to the number of ionic species generated per mole of solute. For NaCl n = 2 but for $MgCl_2$ n = 3. {Remember: colligative properties depend on the **number** of particles present}

5.1.3 Osmotic Pressure

The osmotic pressure (Π) of a solution describes the equilibrium distribution of solvent across semipermeable membranes separated by two compartments. When a solvent and solution are separated by a membrane permeable only to molecules of solvent (a semipermeable membrane), the solvent spontaneously migrates into the solution. The semipermeable membrane allows the solvent to pass but not the solute. Since pure solute cannot pass through the semipermeable membrane into the pure solvent side to equalize the concentrations, the pure solvent begins to then move into the solution side containing the solute. As it does so, the solution level rises and the pressure increases. Eventually a balance is achieved and the increased pressure difference on the solution side is the osmotic pressure. The solvent therefore migrates into the solution across the membrane until a sufficient hydrostatic pressure develops to prevent further migration of solvent. The pressure required to prevent migration of the solvent is therefore the osmotic pressure of the solution and is equal to:

$$\Pi = i\,MRT$$

where R = gas constant per mole
T = temperature in degrees K and
M = concentration of solute (mole/liter)
i = Van't Hoff factor

Note: molarity (M) is used in the osmotic pressure formulation in place of molality as is used for the other respective colligative properties as molarity is temperature dependent and molality is not temperature dependent.

Osmosis and osmotic pressure are also discussed in the context of biology in the following sections: BIO 1.1.1 and 7.5.2.

5.2 Ions in Solution

An important area of solution chemistry involves aqueous solutions. Water has a particular property that causes many substances to split apart into charged species, that is, to dissociate and form <u>ions</u>. Ions that are positively charged are called <u>cations</u> and negatively charged ions are called <u>anions</u>. {Mnemonic: <u>an</u>ions <u>a</u>re <u>n</u>egative <u>ions</u>} As a rule, highly charged species (i.e. $AlPO_4$, Al^{3+}/PO_4^{3-}) have a greater force of attraction thus are much less soluble in water than species with little charge (i.e. NaCl, Na^+/Cl^-). The word "aqueous" simply means containing or dissolved in water. All the following ions can form in water.

Common Anions					
F^-	Fluoride	OH^-	Hydroxide	ClO^-	Hypochlorite
Cl^-	Chloride	NO_3^-	Nitrate	ClO_2^-	Chlorite
Br^-	Bromide	NO_2^-	Nitrite	ClO_3^-	Chlorate
I^-	Iodide	CO_3^{2-}	Carbonate	ClO_4^-	Perchlorate
O^{2-}	Oxide	SO_4^{2-}	Sulfate	SO_3^{2-}	Sulfite
S^{2-}	Sulfide	PO_4^{3-}	Phosphate	CN^-	Cyanide
N^{3-}	Nitride	$CH_3CO_2^-$	Acetate	MnO_4^-	Permanganate

Common Cations			
Na$^+$	Sodium	H$^+$	Hydrogen
Li$^+$	Lithium	Ca^{2+}	Calcium
K$^+$	Potassium	Mg^{2+}	Magnesium
NH$_4^+$	Ammonium	Fe^{2+}	Iron (II)
H$_3$O$^+$	Hydronium	Fe^{3+}	Iron (III)

Table III.A.5.1: Common Anions and Cations.

As opposed to Organic Chemistry, the GAMSAT does not normally ask Inorganic Chemistry nomenclature (= *naming*) questions but it may be useful to have some background regarding the International Union of Pure and Applied Chemistry (IUPAC) standard suffixes: (1) Single atom anions are named with an *-ide* suffix (i.e. fluoride); (2) Oxyanions (*polyatomic* or "many atom" anions containing oxygen) are named with *-ite* or *-ate*, for a lesser or greater quantity of oxygen. For example, NO$_2^-$ is nitrite, while NO$_3^-$ is nitrate. The hypo- and per- prefixes can also indicate less oxygen and more oxygen, respectively (see hypochlorite and perchlorate among the Common Anions in Table III.A.5.1). (3) -ium is a very common ending of atoms in the periodic table (CHM 2.3) and it is also common among cations; (4) Compounds with cations: The name of the compound is simply the cation's name (usually the same as the element's), followed by the anion. For example, NaCl is *sodium chloride* and Ca$_3$N$_2$ is *calcium nitride*.

5.3 Solubility

The solubility of any substance is generally defined as the amount of the substance (solute) known to dissolve into a particular amount of solvent at a given temperature. The solubility of a solute into a solvent is dependent on the entropy change of solubilization as well as the types of intermolecular forces involved (see CHM 4.2 and 5.1). Solvation or dissolution is the process of interaction between solute and solvent molecules. This process occurs when the intermolecular forces between solute and solvent are stronger than those between solute particles themselves. Generally, ionic and polar solutes are soluble in polar solvents and nonpolar solutes are soluble in nonpolar solvents. Consequently, the expression "like dissolves like" is often used for predicting solubility.

In the following section, the definitions of the various solution concentration units are given with examples.

5.3.1 Units of Concentration

In the sections to follow, where possible, please try to complete the calculations as quickly as possible prior to looking at the solutions (i.e. apply dimensional analysis; GM 2.2).

There are a number of ways in which solution concentrations may be expressed.

Molarity (*M*): A one-molar solution is defined as one mole of substance in each liter of solution: M = moles of solute/liter of solution (solution = solute + solvent).

For example: If 55.0g of $CaCl_2$ is mixed with water to make 500.0 ml (0.5 L) of solution, what is the molarity (*M*) of the solution?

$$55.0g \text{ of } CaCl_2 = 55.0 \text{ g}/110.0 \text{ g/mol}$$
$$= 0.500 \text{ mol of } CaCl_2$$

Therefore, the Molarity = 0.500 mol $CaCl_2$/0.5L = 1.00 mol $CaCl_2$/L solution

Normality (*N*): A one-normal solution contains one equivalent per liter. An equivalent is a mole multiplied by the number of reacting units for each molecule or atom; the equivalent weight is the formula weight divided by the number of reacting units.

$$\# \text{ of Equiv.} = \text{mass (in g)/eq. wt. (in g/equiv.)}$$
$$= \text{Normality (in equiv./liter)}$$
$$\times \text{Volume (in liters)}$$

For example, sulfuric acid, H_2SO_4, has two reacting units of protons, that is, there are two equivalents of protons in each mole. Thus:

$$\text{eq. wt.} = 98.08 \text{ g/mole/2 equiv./mole}$$
$$= 49.04 \text{ g/equiv.}$$

and the normality of a sulfuric acid solution is twice its molarity. Generally speaking:

$$N = n\,M$$

where   *N* is the normality,
  M the molarity,
  n the number of equivalents per unit formula.

Thus for 1.2 M H_2SO_4:

1.2 moles/L × 2 eq/mole = 2.4 eq/L = 2.4 N.

Molality (*m*): A one-molal solution contains one mole/1000g of solvent.

m = moles of solute/kg of solvent.

For example: If 20.0g of NaOH is mixed into 500.0g (0.50 kg) of water, what is the molality of the solution?

$$20.0g \text{ of NaOH} = 20.0 \text{ g}/40.0 \text{ g/mol}$$
$$= 0.500 \text{ mol of NaOH}$$

Therefore, the Molality = 0.500 mol NaOH/0.50 kg water = 1.0 mol NaOH/kg water

Molal concentrations are not temperature-dependent as molar and normal concentrations are (since the solvent volume is temperature-dependent).

Density (ρ): Mass per unit volume at the specified temperature, usually g/ml or g/cm³ at 20°C.

Osmole (*Osm*): The number of moles of particles (molecules or ions) that contribute to the osmotic pressure of a solution.

Osmolarity: A one-osmolar solution is defined as one osmole in each liter of solution. Osmolarity is measured in osmoles/liter of solution (Osm/L).

For example, a 0.001 *M* solution of sodium chloride has an osmolarity of 0.002 Osm/L (twice the molarity), because each NaCl molecule ionizes in water to form two ions (Na^+ and Cl^-) that both contribute to the osmotic pressure.

Osmolality: A one-osmolal solution is defined as one osmole in each kilogram of solution. Osmolality is measured in osmoles/kilogram of solution (Osm/kg).

For example, the osmolality of a 0.01 molal solution of Na_2SO_4 is 0.03 Osm/kg because each molecule of Na_2SO_4 ionizes in water to give three ions (2 Na^+ and 1 SO_4^{2-}) that contribute to the osmotic pressure.

Mole Fraction: Is expressed as a mole ratio as the amount of solute (in moles) divided by the total amount of solvent and solute (in moles).

For example: If 110.0g of $CaCl_2$ is mixed with 72.0g water, what are the mole fractions of the two components?

$$72.0g \text{ of } H_2O = 72.0g/18.0 \text{ g/mol}$$
$$= 4 \text{ mol } H_2O$$

$$110.0g \text{ of } CaCl_2 = 110.0g/110 \text{ g/mol}$$
$$= 1 \text{ mol } CaCl_2$$

$$\text{Total mol} = 4 \text{ mol } H_2O + 1 \text{ mol } CaCl_2$$
$$= 5 \text{ mol } (H_2O \text{ and } CaCl_2)$$

Therefore,
$X(CaCl_2) = 1mol \, CaCl_2/5 \, mol \, CaCl_2 + H_2O = 0.2$
and
$X(water) = 4 \, mol \, H_2O/5 \, mol \, H_2O + CaCl_2 = 0.8$

Dilution: When solvent is added to a solution containing a certain concentration of solute it becomes diluted to produce a solution of a lower solute concentration. The equation representing this is:

$$\boxed{M_iV_i = M_fV_f}$$

Where M = molarity and
       V = volume with the initial (*i*) and final (*f*) concentrations being measured.

For example: How many ml of a 10.0 mol/L NaOH solution is needed to prepare 500 ml of a 2.00 mol/L NaOH solution?

Given: $M_iV_i = M_fV_f$, where M_i = 10.0 mol/L, M_f = 2.00 mol/L and V_f = 500 ml. Therefore, rearranging the equation gives $V_i = M_f \times V_f/M_i$ and so V_i = (2.00 mol/L)(0.5 L)/(10.0 moL) = 100 mL.

5.3.2 Solubility Product Constant, the Equilibrium Expression

Any solute that dissolves in water to give a solution that contains ions, and thus can conduct electricity, is an *electrolyte*. The solid (s) that dissociates into separate ions surrounded by water is <u>hydrated</u>, thus the ions are aqueous (*aq*).

If dissociation is extensive and irreversible, we have a <u>strong</u> electrolyte:

$$NaCl\ (s) \rightarrow Na^+\ (aq) + Cl^-\ (aq)$$

If dissociation is incomplete and reversible, we have a <u>weak</u> electrolyte:

$$CH_3COOH\ (aq) \rightleftharpoons CH_3COO^-\ (aq) + H^+\ (aq)$$

If dissociation does not occur, we have a nonelectrolyte:

$C_6H_{12}O_6$ (aq) or glucose sugar does NOT dissociate.

<u>Strong electrolytes</u>: salts (NaCl), strong acids (HCl), strong bases (NaOH).

<u>Weak electrolytes</u>: weak acids (CH_3COOH), weak bases (NH_3), complexes ($Fe[CN]_6$), tap water, certain soluble organic compounds, highly charged species (CHM 5.2; $AlPO_4$, $BaSO_4$, exception: AgCl as it is a precipitate in aqueous solutions).

<u>Nonelectrolytes</u>: deionized water, soluble organic compounds (sugars).

The solubility of a solute substance is the maximum amount of solute that can be dissolved in an appropriate solvent at a particular temperature. It can be expressed in units of concentration such as molarity, molality and so on (see CHM 5.3.1). When a maximum amount of solute has been dissolved, the solution is in equilibrium and is said to be saturated. As temperature increases, the solubility of most salts generally increases. However, it is the opposite for gases, as the solubility of gases is known to generally decrease as temperature increases.

When substances have limited solubility and their solubility is exceeded, the ions of the dissolved portion exist in equilibrium with the solid material. When a compound is referred to as insoluble, it is not completely insoluble, but is slightly soluble.

For example, if solid AgCl is added to water, a small portion will dissolve:

$$AgCl\ (s) \rightleftharpoons Ag^+\ (aq) + Cl^-\ (aq)$$

The precipitate will have a definite solubility (i.e. a definite amount in g/liter) or molar solubility (in moles/ liter) that will dissolve at a given temperature.

An overall equilibrium constant can be written for the preceding equilibrium, called the <u>solubility product</u>, K_{sp}, given by the following equilibrium expression:

$$K_{sp} = [Ag^+][Cl^-]$$

The preceding relationship holds regardless of the presence of any undissociated intermediate. In general, each concentration must be raised to the power of that ion's coefficient in the dissolving equation (in our example = 1). A different example would be Ag_2S which would have the following solubility product expression: $K_{sp}= [Ag^+]^2[S^{2-}]$. The calculation of molar solubility s in mol/L for AgCl would simply be: $K_{sp} = [s][s] = s^2$. On the other hand, the expression for Ag_2S would become: $K_{sp} = [2s]^2[s] = 4s^3$.

Knowing K_{sp} at a specified temperature, the molar solubility of compounds can be calculated under various conditions. The amount of slightly soluble salt that dissolves does not depend on the amount of the solid in equilibrium with the solution, as long as there is enough to saturate the solution. Rather, it depends on the volume of solvent. {Note: a low K_{sp} value means little product therefore low solubility and vice-versa}.

The following are examples of problems on solubility product constant and solubility calculations given one or the other.

Another example: The molar solubility of $PbCl_2$ in an aqueous solution is 0.0159 M. What is the K_{sp} for $PbCl_2$?

$$PbCl_2(s) \rightleftharpoons Pb^{2+}(aq) + 2Cl^-(aq)$$
$$K_{sp} = [Pb^{2+}][Cl^-]^2$$

For every mol of $PbCl_2$ that dissociates, one mol of Pb^{2+} and two mol of Cl^- are produced. Since the molar solubility is 0.0159M, $[Pb^{2+}] = 0.0159M$ and $[Cl^-] = 0.0159 \times 2 = 0.0318M$

Therefore,

$$K_{sp} = [0.0159][0.0318]^2 = 1.61 \times 10^{-5}$$

Another example: What are the concentrations of each of the ions in a saturated solution of Ag_2CrO_4 given that solubility product constant K_{sp} is 1.1×10^{-12}?

$$Ag_2CrO_4(s) \rightleftharpoons 2Ag^+(aq) + CrO_4^{2-}(aq)$$
$$K_{sp} = [Ag^+]^2[CrO_4^{2-}]$$

For every Ag_2CrO_4 that dissociates, two mol of Ag^+ ion and one mol of CrO_4^{2-} ion are produced.

Let x = concentration of CrO_4^{2-}, then 2x = concentration of Ag^+

Therefore,
$$K_{sp} = [2x]^2[x]$$
$$1.1 \times 10^{-12} = [2x]^2[x]$$
solving for x gives; $x = 6.50 \times 10^{-5}$ M

so,
$$[Ag^+] = 1.3 \times 10^{-4} \text{ M and}$$
$$[CrO_4^{2-}] = 6.5 \times 10^{-5} \text{ M}$$

"If you're not part of the solution, you're part of the precipitate!"   :)

5.3.3 Common-ion Effect on Solubility

If there is an excess of one ion over the other, the concentration of the other is suppressed. This is called the common ion effect. The solubility of the precipitate is decreased and the concentration can still be calculated from the K_{sp}.

For example, Cl^- ion can be precipitated out of a solution of AgCl by adding a slight excess of $AgNO_3$. If a stoichiometric amount of $AgNO_3$ is added, $[Ag^+] = [Cl^-]$. If excess $AgNO_3$ is added, $[Ag^+] > [Cl^-]$ but K_{sp} remains constant. Therefore, $[Cl^-]$ decreases if $[Ag^+]$ is increased. Because the K_{sp} product always holds, precipitation will not take place unless the product of $[Ag^+]$ and $[Cl^-]$ exceeds the K_{sp}. If the product is just equal to K_{sp}, all the Ag^+ and Cl^- ions would remain in solution. Thus, the solubility of an ionic compound in solution containing a common ion is decreased in comparison to the same compound's solubility in water. As another example, the solubility of CaF_2 in water at 25°C would be much larger in comparison to the solubility of the same CaF_2 compound in a solution containing a common ion such as NaF. This decrease in solubility of CaF_2 in a solution containing NaF would be due to the common fluoride (F^-) ion effect on the solubility of CaF_2.

5.3.4 Solubility Product Constant (K_{sp}) vs. Reaction Quotient (Q_{sp})

Solubility product constants are used to describe saturated solutions of ionic compounds of relatively low solubility. A saturated solution is in a state of dynamic equilibrium described by the equilibrium constant (K_{sp}).

$$M_xA_y(s) \leftrightarrow x\ M^{y+}(aq) + y\ A^{x-}(aq)$$

The solubility product constant $K_{sp} = [M^{y+}]^x [A^{x-}]^y$ in a solution at equilibrium (saturated solution). Note that "M" is meant to symbolize the metal and "A" represents the anion.

A reaction quotient is defined by the same formula: $Q_{sp} = [M^{y+}]^x [A^{x-}]^y$ in a solution at any point, not just equilibrium.

K_{sp} therefore represents the ion product at equilibrium while Q_{sp} represents the ion product at any point, not just at equilibrium; and in fact, equilibrium is just a special case of the reaction coefficient as we will see below:

If $Q_{sp} < K_{sp}$, the solution is unsaturated and no precipitate will form.

If $Q_{sp} = K_{sp}$, the solution is saturated and at equilibrium.

If $Q_{sp} > K_{sp}$, the solution is supersaturated and unstable. A solid salt will precipitate until ion product once again equals to K_{sp}.

5.3.5 Solubility Rules

The chemistry of aqueous solutions is such that solubility rules can be established:

1. All salts of alkali metals are soluble.

2. All salts of the ammonium ion are soluble.

3. All chlorides, bromides and iodides are water soluble, with the exception of Ag^+, Pb^{2+}, and Hg_2^{2+}.

4. All salts of the sulfate ion (SO_4^{2-}) are water soluble with the exception of Ca^{2+}, Sr^{2+}, Ba^{2+}, and Pb^{2+}.

5. All metal oxides are insoluble with the exception of the alkali metals and CaO, SrO and BaO.

6. All hydroxides are insoluble with the exception of the alkali metals and Ca^{2+}, Sr^{2+}, Ba^{2+}

7. All carbonates (CO_3^{2-}), phosphates (PO_4^{3-}), sulfides (S^{2-}) and sulfites (SO_3^{2-}) are insoluble, with the exception of the alkali metals and ammonium.

We do not suggest that you memorize the solubility rules. The rules should, however, confirm what you have been seeing regarding the common substances that have been presented in this chapter like sodium chloride, calcium chloride, sodium sulfate, sodium hydroxide, silver chloride, strong vs. weak electrolytes, etc. It is expected that you are familiar with the solubility of the common substances and, if reminded of the rules during an exam (or practice), that you can apply those rules to more unfamiliar substances.

Dear GAMSAT Chemistry,

If I understand correctly, alcohol *is* a solution?

Go online to GAMSAT-prep.com for free chapter review Q&A and forum.

Memorize	Understand	Not Required*
Define: Bronsted acid, base, pH Examples of strong/weak acids/bases K_w at STP, neutral H_2O pH, conjugate acid/base, zwitterions Equations: K_a, K_b, pK_a, pK_b, K_w, pH, pOH Equivalence point, indicator, rules of logarithms	* Calculation of K_a, K_b, pK_a, pK_b, K_w, pH, pOH * Calculations involving strong/weak acids/bases * Salts of weak acids/bases, buffers; indicators * Acid-Base titration/curve, redox titration	* Knowledge beyond introductory-level (first year uni.) course * Specific values for K_a and/or K_b * Memorizing Henderson-Hasselback equation

GAMSAT-Prep.com

Introduction ▮▮▮▮

Acids are compounds that, when dissolved in water, give a solution with a hydrogen ion concentration greater than that of pure water. Acids turn litmus paper (an indicator) red. Examples include acetic acid (in vinegar) and sulfuric acid (in car batteries). Bases may have [H^+] less than pure water and turns litmus blue. Examples include sodium hydroxide (= lye, caustic soda) and ammonia (used in many cleaning products).

Additional Resources

LOW pH = LOTS of H^+ LOTS OF OH^- = HIGH pH

| Free Online Q&A + Forum | GAMSAT-prep.com Videos | Flashcards | Special Guest |

* The real GAMSAT may have advanced level information presented (ie. in a passage) but previous knowledge of said information is not required to answer the questions that would follow. Practice ACER and GS practice GAMSATs can help you clarify this point.

6.1 Acids

A useful definition is given by Bronsted and Lowry: an acid is a proton (i.e. hydrogen ion) donor (cf. Lewis acids and bases, *see* CHM 3.4). A substance such as HF is an acid because it can donate a proton to a substance capable of accepting it. In aqueous solution, water is always available as a proton acceptor, so that the ionization of an acid, HA, can be written as:

$$HA + H_2O \rightleftharpoons H_3O^+ + A^-$$

or: $$HA \rightleftharpoons H^+ + A^-$$

The equilibrium constant is:

$$K_a = [H^+][A^-]/[HA]$$

Examples of the ionization of acids are:

$$HCl \rightleftharpoons H^+ + Cl^- \qquad K_a = \text{infinity}$$
$$HF \rightleftharpoons H^+ + F^- \qquad K_a = 6.7 \times 10^{-4}$$
$$HCN \rightleftharpoons H^+ + CN^- \qquad K_a = 7.2 \times 10^{-10}$$

Acids are generally divided into two categories known as binary acids and oxyacids. The first category is that of acids composed of hydrogen and a nonmetal such as chlorine (HCl). For the halogen containing binary acids, the acid strength increases as a function of the halogen size. Moreover, as the halogen size increases, its bond length increases while its bond strength decreases and as such, its acidity increases. Thus, the acidity of HI > HBr > HCl > HF.

The second category of acids form from oxyanions (anions containing a nonmetal and oxygen such as the hydroxide or nitrate ions, see CHM 5.2) are known as the oxyacids. The oxyacids contain a hydrogen atom covalently bonded to an oxygen atom which is bonded to another central atom X (H-O-X-etc). The more oxygen atoms that are bounded to the central atom, the more acidic the oxyacids (e.g. HClO vs $HClO_4$). Some examples of oxyacids are listed in Table III.A.6.1.

Note: a diprotic acid (*two protons*, i.e. H_2SO_4) would have K_a values for each of its two ionizable protons: K_{a1} for the first and K_{a2} for the second. Diprotic or any polyprotic acids are known to ionize in successive steps in which each of the steps contain their own dissociation or ionization acid constant, K_a. The first ionization constant (K_{a1}) is typically much larger than the subsequent ionization constants ($K_{a1} > K_{a2} > K_{a3}$, etc...).

Table III.A.6.1: Examples of acids that dissociate (CHM 5.2) completely (*strong*) and only partially (*weak*).

STRONG	WEAK	STRONG	WEAK
Perchloric $HClO_4$ Chloric $HClO_3$ Nitric HNO_3 Hydrochloric HCl	Hydrocyanic HCN Hypochlorous HClO Nitrous HNO_2 Hydrofluoric HF	Sulfuric H_2SO_4 Hydrobromic HBr Hydriodic HI Hydronium Ion H_3O^+	Sulfurous H_2SO_3 Hydrogen Sulfide H_2S Phosphoric H_3PO_4 Benzoic, Acetic and other Carboxylic acids

6.2 Bases

A base is defined as a proton acceptor. In aqueous solution, water is always available to donate a proton to a base, so the ionization of a base B, can be written as:

$$B + H_2O \rightleftharpoons HB^+ + OH^-$$

The equilibrium constant is:

$$K_b = [HB^+][OH^-]/[B]$$

Examples of the ionization of bases are:

$$CN^- + H_2O \rightleftharpoons HCN + OH^- \quad K_b = 1.4 \times 10^{-5}$$

$$NH_3 + H_2O \rightleftharpoons NH_4^+ + OH^- \quad K_b = 1.8 \times 10^{-5}$$

$$F^- + H_2O \rightleftharpoons HF + OH^- \quad K_b = 1.5 \times 10^{-11}$$

Strong bases include any hydroxide of the group 1A and 2A metals (e.g. NaOH, Ca(OH)$_2$). The most common weak bases are ammonia (NH$_3$) and any organic amine (ORG 11.1.1).

6.3 Conjugate Acid-Base Pairs

The strength of an acid or base is related to the extent that the dissociation proceeds to the right, or to the magnitude of K$_a$ or K$_b$; the larger the dissociation constant, the stronger the acid or the base. From the preceding K$_a$ values (CHM 6.1), we see that HCl is the strongest acid (almost 100% ionized), followed by HF and HCN. From the K$_b$'s given, NH$_3$ is the strongest base listed, followed by CN$^-$ and F$^-$. Clearly, when an acid ionizes, it produces a base. The acid, HA, and the base produced when it ionizes, A$^-$, are called a conjugate acid-base pair, so that the couples HF/F$^-$ and HCN/CN$^-$ are conjugate acids and bases.

Thus, an acid that has donated a proton becomes a conjugate base and a base that has accepted a proton becomes a conjugate acid of that base. For example, HCO$_3^-$/ CO$_3^{2-}$ are a conjugate acid/base pair, wherein

HCO$_3^-$ is the acid and CO$_3^{2-}$ is the conjugate base. Both dissociate partially in water and reach equilibrium.

A strong acid (HCl) has a weak conjugate base (Cl$^-$) and a strong base (NaOH) has a weak conjugate acid (OH$^-$). Whereas, a weak acid (CH$_3$COOH) has a strong conjugate base (CH$_3$COO$^-$) and a weak base (NH$_3$) has a related strong conjugate acid (NH$_4^+$).

Another example of conjugate acid-base pairs is amino acids (ORG 12.1). Amino acids bear at least 2 ionizable weak acid groups, a carboxyl (–COOH) and an amino (–NH$_3^+$) which act as follows:

$$R–COOH \rightleftharpoons R–COO^- + H^+$$

$$R–NH_3^+ \rightleftharpoons R–NH_2 + H^+$$

R–COO⁻ and R–NH₂ are the conjugate bases (i.e. proton acceptors) of the corresponding acids. The carboxyl group is thousands of times more acidic than the amino group. Thus in blood plasma (pH ≈ 7.4) the predominant forms are the carboxylate anions (R–COO⁻) and the protonated amino group (R–NH₃⁺). This form is called a *zwitterion* as demonstrated by the amino acid alanine at a pH near 7:

$$CH_3\text{-}CH\text{-}COO^-$$
$$|$$
$$NH_3^+$$
Alanine

The zwitterion bears no net charge.

6.4 Water Dissociation

Water itself can ionize:

$$H_2O + H_2O \rightleftharpoons H_3O^+ + OH^-$$

or:

$$H_2O \rightleftharpoons H^+ + OH^-$$

At STP, $K_w = [H^+][OH^-] = 1.0 \times 10^{-14} =$ <u>ion product constant</u> for water. It increases with temperature and in a neutral solution, $[H^+] = [OH^-] = 10^{-7}$ M. Note that $[H_2O]$ is not included in the equilibrium expression because it is a pure liquid and it is a large constant ($[H_2O]$ is incorporated in K_w).

6.5 The pH Scale

The <u>pH</u> of a solution is a convenient way of expressing the concentration of hydrogen ions $[H^+]$ in solution, to avoid the use of large negative powers of 10. It is defined as:

$$pH = -\log_{10}[H^+]$$

Thus, the pH of a neutral solution of pure water where $[H^+] = 10^{-7}$ is 7.

A similar definition is used for the hydroxyl ion concentration:

$$pOH = -\log_{10}[OH^-]$$

Since, $K_w = [H^+][OH^-]$

And so, $1.0 \times 10^{-14} = [H^+][OH^-]$

And taking the $-\log$ of both sides gives $-\log [1.0 \times 10^{-14}] = -\log[H^+][OH^-]$

So, $14.0 = -\log[H^+] + -\log[OH^-]$

Therefore, $14.0 = pH + pOH$

Finally, at 25°C, $pH + pOH = 14.0$

A pH of 7 is neutral. Values of pH that are greater than 7 are <u>alkaline</u> (basic) and values that are lower are <u>acidic</u>. The pH can be measured precisely with a pH meter (quantitative) or globally with an indicator which will have a different color over different pH ranges (qualitative). For example, *litmus paper* (very common) becomes blue in basic solutions and red in acidic solutions; whereas, *phenolphthalein* is colorless in acid and pink in base.

We will see in CHM 6.9 that a weak acid or base can serve as a visual (qualitative) indicator of a pH range. Usually, only a small quantity (i.e. drops) of the indicator is added to the solution as to minimize the risk of any side reactions.

6.5.1 Properties of Logarithms

Many GAMSAT problems every year rely on a basic understanding of logarithms (GM 3.7, 3.8) for one or more of: pH problems, reaction rates (CHM 9.5), Gibbs Free Energy (CHM 9.10), the Nernst equation (CHM 10.3), and decibels/sound (PHY 8.3). Here are the rules you must know:

1) $\log_a a = 1$
2) $\log_a M^k = k \log_a M$
3) $\log_a(MN) = \log_a M + \log_a N$
4) $\log_a(M/N) = \log_a M - \log_a N$
5) $10^{\log_{10} M} = M$

For example, let us calculate the pH of 0.001 M HCl. Since HCl is a strong acid, it will completely dissociate into H^+ and Cl^-, thus :

$$[H^+] = 0.001$$
$$-\log[H^+] = -\log (0.001)$$
$$pH = -\log(10^{-3})$$
$$pH = 3 \log 10 \qquad \text{(rule \#2)}$$
$$pH = 3 \qquad \text{(rule \#1, a = 10)}$$

Reminder: We worked out the shape of the graph for pH vs. hydrogen ion concentration in GM chapter 3, review question 15.

6.6 Weak Acids and Bases

Weak acids (HA) and bases (B) partially dissociate in aqueous solutions reaching equilibrium following their dissociation. The following is the generic reaction of any weak acid (HA) dissociation in an aqueous solution.

$$HA + H_2O \rightleftharpoons A^- + H_3O^+$$

Now let us begin by taking a closer look at the development of the acid and base equilibrium constants. Like all equilibrium, acid/base dissociation will have a particular equilibrium constant (K_a or K_b) which

will determine the extent of the dissociation (CHM 6.3). Thus, from the preceding equation for any generic acid (HA), the acid dissociation constant $K = [H_3O^+][A^-]/[H_2O][HA]$.

Very little water actually reacts and thus the concentration of water during the reaction is constant and can therefore be excluded from the expression for K. Therefore, this gives rise to the acid dissociation constant known as K_a.

Where, $K_a = K[H_2O] = [H_3O^+][A^-]/[HA]$

Likewise for a weak base dissociation in equilibrium,

$$B + H_2O \rightleftharpoons OH^- + BH^+$$

This gives rise to the base dissociation constant known as K_b.

Where, $K_b = K[H_2O] = [OH^-][BH^+]/[B]$

Weak acids and bases are only <u>partially ionized</u>. The ionization constant can be used to calculate the amount ionized, and from this, the pH.

Since weak acids are not completely dissociated, one needs to find the $[H^+]$ from the acid dissociation and then use a method known in most textbooks as the "ICE method". ICE is an acronym used in which, I = Initial acid $[H^+]$ concentration, C = Change in acid $[H^+]$ concentration and E = acid $[H^+]$ concentration at equilibrium. Thus, the acid concentration $[H^+]$ also represented as (x) at equilibrium is then used to calculate the pH. NOTE: the equilibrium concentration x is usually very small as the acid (or base) is weak and partially dissociated (or ionized). The following is an example of the application of the ICE method in solving for the $[H^+] = x$ at equilibrium and subsequently determining the pH of a weak acid solution.

Example: Calculate the pH and pOH of a 10^{-2} M solution of acetic acid (HOAc). K_a of acetic acid at 25°C = 1.75×10^{-5}.

$$HOAc \rightleftharpoons H^+ + OAc^-$$

The concentrations are:

	[HOAc]	[H⁺]	[OAc⁻]
Initial	10^{-2}	0	0
Change	$-x$	$+x$	$+x$
Equilibrium	$10^{-2} - x$	x	x

$$K_a = [H^+][OAc^-]/[HOAc] = 1.75 \times 10^{-5}$$
$$= (x)(x)/(10^{-2} - x)$$

The solution is a quadratic equation which may be simplified if <u>less than 5%</u> of the acid is ionized by neglecting x compared to the concentration (10^{-2} M in this case). We then have:

$$x^2/10^{-2} = 1.75 \times 10^{-5}$$
$$x = 4.18 \times 10^{-4} = [H^+]$$

And
$$pH = -\log (4.18 \times 10^{-4}) = 3.38$$
$$pOH = 14.00 - 3.38 = 10.62$$

To confirm the 5% criterion one needs to calculate as follows: $(4.18 \times 10^{-4})/(1.00 \times 10^{-2}) \times 100 = 4.18\%$ which is less than 5% and therefore justifies the usage of the 5% criterion.

Similar calculations hold for weak bases. Note that all the preceding can be estimated without a calculator once you know the squares of all numbers between 1 and 15 (GM 1.5.6). The root of 1.69 (a fair estimate of 1.75) is thus 1.3 (also *see* CHM 6.6.1 to see how to estimate an answer without a calculator). If you are struggling with the math, join the discussion "6.6 Weak Acids and Bases - log calculations" at gamsat-prep.com/forum.

6.6.1 Determining pH with the Quadratic Formula

If you need to calculate pH on the GAMSAT, it is very unlikely that you would need to use the quadratic equation; however, you are expected to be familiar with the different ways to calculate pH and that is why it is presented here.

The solutions of the quadratic equation

$$ax^2 + bx + c = 0$$

are given by the formula (do not memorize):

$$x = [-b \pm (b^2 - 4ac)^{1/2}]/2a$$

The problem in CHM 6.6 can be reduced to

$$K_a = (x)(x)/(10^{-2} - x) = 1.75 \times 10^{-5}$$
or

$$x^2 + (1.75 \times 10^{-5})x + (-1.75 \times 10^{-7}) = 0$$

Using the quadratic equation where $a = 1$, $b = 1.75 \times 10^{-5}$ and $c = -1.75 \times 10^{-7}$, and doing the appropriate multiplications we get:

$$x = [-1.75 \times 10^{-5} \pm (3.06 \times 10^{-10} + 7.0 \times 10^{-7})^{1/2}]/2$$

Thus $x = [-1.75 \times 10^{-5} \pm (7.00 \times 10^{-7})^{1/2}]/2$
$$= [-1.75 \times 10^{-5} \pm 8.37 \times 10^{-4}]/2$$

Hence the two possible solutions are

$$x = [-1.75 \times 10^{-5} - 8.37 \times 10^{-4}]/2 = -4.27 \times 10^{-4}$$

Or

$$x = [-1.75 \times 10^{-5} + 8.37 \times 10^{-4}]/2$$
$$= 4.10 \times 10^{-4}$$

The first solution is a negative number which is physically impossible for [H⁺], therefore pH = $-\log(4.10 \times 10^{-4}) = 3.39$.

Our estimate in CHM 6.6 (pH = 3.38) was valid as it is less than 1% different from the more precise calculation using the quadratic formula.

Given a multiple choice question with the following choices: 2.5, 3.4, 4.3 and 6.8 – the answer can be easily deduced.

$$-\log (4.10 \times 10^{-4}) = -\log 4.10 - \log 10^{-4}$$
$$= 4 - \log 4.10$$

however

$$0 = \log 10^0 = \log 1 < \log 4.10 << \log 10 = 1$$

Thus a number slightly greater than 0 but significantly less than 1 is substracted from 4. The answer could only be 3.4.

6.7 Salts of Weak Acids and Bases

A *salt* is an ionic compound in which the anion is not OH^- or O^{2-} and the cation is not H^+.

Acids and bases react with each other, forming a salt and water in a reaction known as a neutralization reaction. Salts are compounds composed of both a cation and anion (i.e. Na_2SO_4). As salts contain both a cation and anion, salts may therefore form acidic, basic or neutral solutions when dissolved into water. Hence, a salt can react with water to give back an acid or base in a reaction known as salt hydrolysis and thus affect the solution's pH. Moreover, a salt composed of an anion from a weak acid (CH_3COO^-) and a cation from a strong base (Na^+) dissociates and reacts in water to give rise to OH^- ions (a basic solution). Whereas, a salt composed of an anion from a strong acid (Cl^-) and a cation from a weak base (NH_4^+) dissociates and reacts in water to give rise to H^+ (an acidic solution).

Examples:

NaClO dissociates in water:

$$ClO^- + H_2O \rightleftharpoons HClO + OH^- \text{ (Basic)}$$

NH_4NO_3 dissociates in water:

$$NH_4^+ + H_2O \rightleftharpoons H_3O^+ + NH_3 \text{ (Acidic)}$$

The salt of a weak acid is a Bronsted base, which will accept protons. For example,

$$Na^+ OAc^- + H_2O \rightleftharpoons HOAc + Na^+ OH^-$$

The HOAc here is undissociated and therefore does not contribute to the pH. Because it hydrolyzes, sodium acetate is a weak base (the conjugate base of acetic acid). The ionization constant is equal to the basicity constant of the salt. The weaker the conjugate acid, the stronger the conjugate base, that is, the more strongly the salt will combine with a proton.

$$K_H = K_b = [HOAc][OH^-]/[OAc^-]$$

K_H is the hydrolysis constant of the salt. The product of K_a of any weak acid and K_b of its conjugate base is always equal to K_w.

$$K_a \times K_b = K_w$$

For any salt of a weak acid, HA, that ionizes in water:

$$A^- + H_2O \rightleftharpoons HA + OH^-$$
$$[HA][OH^-]/[A^-] = K_w/K_a.$$

The pH of such a salt is calculated in the same manner as for any other weak base.

Similar equations are derived for the salts of weak bases. They hydrolyze in water as follows:

$$BH^+ + H_2O \rightleftharpoons B + H_3O^+$$

B is undissociated and does not contribute to the pH.

$$K_H = K_a = [B][H_3O^+]/[BH^+]$$

And

$$[B][H_3O^+]/[BH^+] = K_w/K_b.$$

In conclusion, there are four types of salts formed based on the reacting acid and base strengths as follows:

(1) Strong acid + strong base:

$HCl(aq) + NaOH(aq) \rightarrow NaCl(aq) + H_2O(l)$

Salts in which the cation and anion are both conjugates of a strong base and a strong acid form neutral solutions. Note the use of a one-sided arrow in the reaction above which implies that the reaction goes to completion (thus only product and no reactant remains). Note the two-sided arrows in the reactions below which imply equilibrium: a point where forward and reverse reactions occur at equal rates (CHM 9.8).

(2) Strong acid + weak base:

$HCl(aq) + NH_3(aq) \rightleftharpoons NH_4Cl\ (aq)$

Salts that are formed based on a strong acid reacting with a weak base form acidic solutions.

(3) Weak acid + strong base:

$HOAc(aq) + NaOH(aq) \rightleftharpoons NaOAc(aq) + H_2O(l)$
(note: HOAc = acetic acid = CH_3COOH)

A salt in which the cation is the counterion of a strong base and the anion is the conjugate base of a weak acid results in the formation of basic solutions.

(4) Weak acid + weak base:

$HOAc(aq) + NH_3(aq) \rightleftharpoons NH_4OAc(aq)$

A salt in which the cation is a conjugate acid of a weak base and the anion is the anion of a weak acid will form a solution in which the pH will be dependent on the relative strengths of the acid and base.

Note: Using the rules of logarithms (GM 3.7; CHM 6.5.1), we can change

$K_aK_b = K_w$ to $-\log(K_aK_b) = -\log K_w$

which is the same as

$(-\log K_a) + (-\log K_b) = -\log K_w.$

Thus $pK_a + pK_b = pK_w.$

6.8 Buffers

A buffer is defined as a solution that resists change in pH when a small amount of an acid or base is added or when a solution is diluted. A buffer solution consists of a mixture of a weak acid and its salt or of a weak base and its salt.

For example, consider the acetic acid-acetate buffer. The acid equilibrium that governs this system is:

$HOAc \rightleftharpoons H^+ + OAc^-$

Along with the acid equilibrium component of the buffer solution as shown above, the buffer solution must also contain a significant amount of the conjugate base of the acid as a salt. The following equation depicts the conjugate base salt dissociation of the acetic acid-acetate buffer solution:

$$NaOAc \rightarrow Na^+ + OAc^-.$$

Thus, the buffer is made up of two components (1) a weak acid (HOAc) and (2) the conjugate base of the weak acid as a salt (NaAOc) so that both components are part of the buffer system in apt concentrations to make for a fully functional buffer.

When a small amount of NaOH base is added to the acetic acid/acetate buffer solution, the OH^- ions from the base will react with the free H^+ ions present in the buffer solution from the acetic acid dissociation. This will shift the equilibrium of the buffer toward the right which means more dissociation of the acid (HOAc). Thus, an increase in $[OH^-]$ from the addition of base to the buffer solution does not change pH significantly due to the reaction of the basic OH^- ions with the free protons (H^+) in solution.

The resistance to pH change is also noted with the addition of an acid (H^+) to the acetic acid/acetate buffer solution. The addition of acidic H^+ from the acid will react with the acetate ions ($HOAc^-$) from the salt dissociation of the buffer and this will also allow for the buffering capacity of the solution. Thus, due to the presence of both a weak acid and a conjugate base from the salt (or common ion), the buffer solution thus is known to maintain a pH within a certain range known as the buffering capacity.

Buffers must contain a significant amount of both a weak acid or weak base and its conjugate salts. A strong acid or strong base would not have any buffering capacity or effect within a buffer system as the dissociation would be irreversible and so the buffer capacity would not be present. In addition, a weak acid or base in itself would also not be able to work as a buffer system regardless of the fact that there is the presence of their conjugates as the concentrations of the conjugate acid or base from the weak acids or bases would not be sufficient to neutralize the addition of acids (H^+) or bases (OH^-). Thus, buffers require the addition of a conjugate acid or base as a salt to the weak acid or base component so to increase the salt concentration of the buffer solution.

If we were to add acetate ions into the system (i.e. from the salt), the H^+ ion concentration is no longer equal to the acetate ion concentration. The hydrogen ion concentration is:

$$[H^+] = K_a ([HOAc]/[OAc^-])$$

Taking the negative logarithm of each side, where $-\log K_a = pK_a$, yields:

$$pH = pK_a - \log ([HOAc]/[OAc^-])$$
or
$$pH = pK_a + \log([OAc^-]/[HOAc])$$

This equation is referred to as the Henderson-Hasselbach equation. It is useful for calculating the pH of a weak acid solution containing its salt. A general form can be written for a weak acid, HA, that dissociates into its salt, A^- and H^+:

$$HA \rightleftharpoons H^+ + A^-$$

$$pH = pK_a + \log([salt]/[acid])$$

The buffering capacity of the solution is determined by the concentrations of HA and A^-. The higher their concentrations, the more acid or base the solution can tolerate. The buffering capacity is also governed by the ratios of HA to A^-. It is maximum when the ratio is equal to 1, i.e. when $pH = pK_a$.

Similar calculations can be made for mixtures of a weak base and its salt:

$$B + H_2O \rightleftharpoons BH^+ + OH^-$$

And

$$pOH = pK_b + \log([salt]/[base])$$

Many biological reactions of interest occur between pH 6 and 8. One useful series of buffers is that of phosphate buffers. By choosing appropriate mixtures of $H_3PO_4/H_2PO_4^-$, $H_2PO_4^-/HPO_4^{2-}$ or HPO_4^{2-}/PO_4^{3-}, buffer solutions covering a wide pH range can be prepared. Another useful clinical buffer is the one prepared from tris(hydroxymethyl) aminomethane and its conjugate acid, abbreviated Tris buffer.

Amphoteric Species: Some substances such as water can act as either an acid or a base (i.e. a dual property). These types of substances are known as amphoteric substances. Water behaves as an acid when reacted with a base (OH^-) and alternatively, water behaves as a base when reacted with an acid (H^+). Many metal oxides and hydroxides are also known to be amphoteric substances. Furthermore, molecules that contain both acidic and basic groups such as amino acids are considered to be amphoteric in nature as well (ORG 12.1.2). The following are examples of the amphoteric nature of HCO_3^- reacting with an acid and a base and water (H_2O) reacting with an acid and base.

In acids: $HCO_3^- + H_3O^+ \rightarrow H_2CO_3 + H_2O$
In bases: $HCO_3^- + OH^- \rightarrow CO_3^{2-} + H_2O$
In acids: $H_2O + HCl \rightarrow H_3O^+ + Cl^-$
In bases: $H_2O + NH_3 \rightarrow NH_4^+ + OH^-$

6.9 Acid-base Titrations

The purpose of a titration is usually the determination of concentration of a given sample of acid or base (the analyte) which is reacted with an equivalent amount of a strong base or acid of known concentration (the titrant). The end point or equivalence point is reached when a stoichiometric amount of titrant has been added. This end point is usually detected with the use of an indicator which changes color when this point is reached. Note: the end point is not exactly the same as the equivalence point. The equivalence point is where a reaction is theoretically complete whereas an end point is where a physical change in solution such as a color change is determined by indicators.

Regardless, the volume difference between an end point and an equivalence point can usually be ignored.

The end point is determined precisely by measuring the pH at different points of the titration. The curve pH = f(V) where V is the volume of titrant added is called a <u>titration curve</u>. While a strong acid/strong base titration will have an equivalence point at a neutralization pH of 7, the equivalence point of other titrations do not necessarily occur at pH 7. In fact, a weak acid/strong base titration will result in an equivalence point of a pH > 7 and a strong acid/weak base titration results in an equivalence point of a pH < 7. The differential pH effects at the relative equivalence points are due to the conjugate acids and/or bases formed. An indicator for an acid-base titration is a weak acid or base.

The weak acid and its conjugate base should have two different colors in solution. Most indicators require a <u>pH transition range</u> during the titration of about two pH units. An indicator is chosen so that its pK_a is close to the pH of the equivalence point.

6.9.1 Strong Acid versus Strong Base

In the case of a strong acid versus a strong base, both the titrant and the analyte are completely ionized. For example, the titration of hydrochloric acid with sodium hydroxide:

$$H^+ + Cl^- + Na^+ + OH^- \rightarrow H_2O + Na^+ + Cl^-$$

The H^+ and OH^- combine to form H_2O and the other ions remain unchanged, so the net result is the conversion of the HCl to a neutral solution of NaCl. A typical strong-acid-strong base titration curve is shown in Fig. III.A.6.1 (case where the titrant is a base).

If the analyte is an acid, the pH is initially acidic and increases very slowly. When the equivalent volume is reached the pH sharply increases. Midway between this transition jump is the equivalence point. In the case of strong acid-strong base titration the equivalence point corresponds to a neutral pH (because the salt formed does not react with water). If more titrant is added the pH increases and corresponds to the pH of a solution of gradually increasing concentration of the titrant base. This curve is simply reversed if the titrant is an acid.

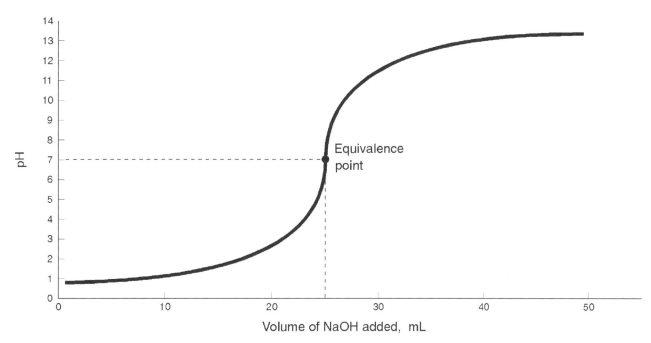

Figure III.A.6.1: The titration curve for a strong acid-strong base is a relatively smooth S-shaped curve with a very steep inclination close to the equivalence point. A small addition in titrant volume near the equivalence point will result in a large change in pH.

6.9.2 Weak Acid versus Strong Base

The titration of acetic acid with sodium hydroxide involves the following reaction:

$$HOAc + Na^+ + OH^- \rightarrow H_2O + Na^+ + OAc^-$$

The acetic acid is only a few percent ionized. It is neutralized to water and an equivalent amount of the salt, sodium acetate. Before the titration is started, the pH is calculated as described for weak acids. As soon as the titration is started, some of the HOAc is converted to NaOAc and a buffer system is set up. As the titration proceeds, the pH slowly increases as the ratio [OAc⁻]/[HOAc] changes.

Halfway towards the equivalence point, [OAC⁻] = [HOAC] and the pH is equal to pKₐ. At the equivalence point, we have a solution of NaOAc. Since it hydrolyzes, the pH at the equivalence point will be alkaline. The pH will depend on the concentration of NaOAc. The greater the concentration, the higher the pH. As excess NaOH is added, the ionization of the base, OAc⁻, is suppressed and the pH is determined only by the concentration of excess OH⁻. Therefore, the titration curve beyond the equivalence point follows that for the titration of a strong acid. The typical titration curve in this case is illustrated in Figure III.A.6.2.

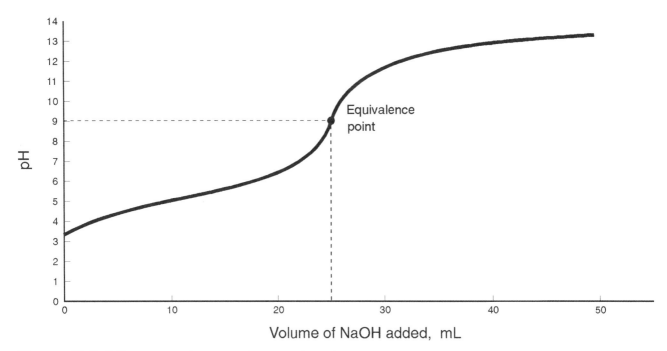

Figure III.A.6.2: The titration curve for a weak acid-strong base or alternatively a strong acid-weak base is somewhat irregular. The pH at the start of the titration prior to base addition is greater than that of a strong acid as the acid is a weak acid. The inclination close to the equivalence point is less significant due to the buffering effect of the solution prior to the equivalence point. A small addition in titrant volume near the equivalence point will therefore result in a small change in pH.

6.9.3 Weak Base versus Strong Acid

The titration of a weak base with a strong acid is analogous to the previous case except that the pH is initially basic and gradually decreases as the acid is added (curve in preceding diagram is reversed). Consider ammonia titrated with hydrochloric acid:

$$NH_3 + H^+ + Cl^- \rightarrow NH_4^+ + Cl^-$$

At the beginning, we have NH_3 and the pH is calculated as for weak bases. As soon as some acid is added, some of the NH_3 is converted to NH_4^+ and we are in the buffer region. At the <u>midpoint of the titration</u>, $[NH_4^+]$ = $[NH_3]$ and the pH is equal to $(14 - pK_b)$. <u>At the equivalence point</u>, we have a solution of NH_4Cl, a weak acid which hydrolyzes to give an acid solution. Again, the pH will depend on concentration: the greater the concentration, the lower the pH. Beyond the equivalence point, the free H^+ suppresses the ionization and the pH is determined by the concentration of H^+ added in excess. Therefore, the <u>titration curve beyond the</u>

equivalence point will be similar to that of the titration of a strong base. {The midpoint of the titration is considered to be halfway to the equivalence point of the titration curve.}

6.10 Redox Titrations

Redox titrations are based on a redox reaction or reduction-oxidation type reaction between an analyte (or sample) and a titrant. More specifically, redox titrations involve the reaction between an oxidizing agent, which accepts one or more electrons, and a reducing agent, which reduces the other substance by donating one or more electrons (CHM 1.6).

The most useful oxidizing agent for titrations is potassium permanganate - $KMnO_4$. Solutions of this salt are colorful since they contain the purple MnO_4^- ion. On the other hand, the more reduced form, Mn^{++}, is nearly colorless. So here is how this redox titration works: $KMnO_4$ is added to a reaction mixture with a reducing agent (i.e. Fe^{++}). MnO_4^- is quickly reduced to Mn^{++} so the color fades immediately. This will continue until there is no more reducing agent in the mixture. When the last bit of reducing agent has been oxidized (i.e. all the Fe^{++} is converted to Fe^{+3}), the next drop of $KMnO_4$ will make the solution colorful since the MnO_4^- will have nothing with which to react. Thus if the amount of reducing agent was unknown, it can be calculated using stoichiometry guided by the amount of potassium permanganate used in the reaction.

There are more questions on acids-bases in ACER's GAMSAT practice materials than any other General Chemistry subject. Though this fact does not guarantee what could be emphasized on any 1 new exam, it does underline the relative importance of this chapter. The best, next step would be to try some online chapter review practice questions – 'open book,' if necessary.

Go online to GAMSAT-prep.com for free chapter review Q&A and forum.

THERMODYNAMICS
Chapter 7

Memorize	Understand	Not Required*
* Define: state function	* System vs. surroundings * Law of conservation of energy * Heat transfer * Conduction, convection, radiation	* Knowledge beyond introductory-level (first year uni.) course * Memorizing: conversion between temperature scales or thermal units * Memorizing: 1st Law of Thermodynamics

GAMSAT-Prep.com

Introduction ▓▓■■

Thermodynamics, in chemistry, refers to the relationship of heat with chemical reactions or with the physical state. Thermodynamic processes can be analyzed by studying energy and topics we will review in the next chapter including entropy, volume, temperature and pressure.

Additional Resources

Free Online Q&A + Forum   GAMSAT-prep.com Videos   Flashcards   Special Guest

7.1 Generalities

Thermodynamics deals with fundamental questions concerning energy transfers. One difficulty you will have to overcome is the terminology used. For instance, remember that heat and temperature have more specific meanings than the ones attributed to them in every day life.

A thermodynamic transformation can be as simple as a gas leaking out of a tank or a piece of metal melting at high temperature or as complicated as the synthesis of proteins by a biological cell. To solve some problems in thermodynamics we need to define a "system" and its "surroundings." The system is simply the object experiencing the thermodynamic transformation. The gas would be considered as the system in the first example of transformations. Once the system is defined any part of the universe in direct contact with the system is considered as its surroundings. For instance, if the piece of metal is melted in a high temperature oven: the system is the piece of metal and the oven constitutes its surroundings.

In other instances, the limit between the system and its surroundings is more arbitrary, for example if one considers the energy exchanges when an ice cube melts in a thermos bottle filled with orange juice; the inside walls of the thermos bottle could be considered as part of "the system" or as part of the surroundings. In the first case, one would carry out all calculations as though the entire system (ice cube + orange juice + inside walls) is isolated from its surroundings (rest of the universe) and all the energy exchanges take place within the system. In the second case, the system (ice cube + orange juice) is not isolated from the surroundings (walls) unless we consider that the heat exchanges with the walls are negligible. There is also no need to include any other part of the universe in the latter case since all exchanges take place within the system or between the system and the inside walls of the thermos bottle.

Some systems may exchange both matter and energy with the surroundings. This is called an "open system". Alternatively, some systems may exchange energy only but not matter with the surroundings. This is called a "closed system". Finally, some systems do not exchange matter or energy with their surroundings. This is called an "isolated system". An isolated system therefore does not interact with its surroundings in any way.

7.2 The First Law of Thermodynamics

Heat, internal energy and work are the first concepts introduced in thermodynamics. Heat is thermal energy (a dynamic property defined during a transformation only), it is not to be confused with temperature (a static property defined for each state of the system). Internal energy is basically the average total mechanical energy (kinetic + potential) of the particles that make up the system. The first law of thermodynamics is often expressed as follows: when a system absorbs an amount of heat Q from the surroundings and does a quantity of work W on the same surroundings its internal energy changes by the amount:

$$\Delta E = Q - W$$

This law is basically the law of conservation of energy for an isolated system. Indeed, it states that if a system does not exchange any energy with its surroundings, its internal energy should not vary. If on the other hand a system does exchange energy with its surroundings, its internal energy should change by an amount corresponding to the energy it takes in from the surroundings.

The sign convention related to the previous mathematical expression of the first law of

thermodynamics is:

- heat absorbed by the system: $Q > 0$
- heat released by the system: $Q < 0$
- work done by the system on its surroundings: $W > 0$
- work done by the surroundings on the system: $W < 0$

Caution: Some textbooks prefer a different sign convention: any energy (Q or W) flowing from the system to the surroundings (lost by the system) is negative and any energy flowing from the surroundings to the system (gained by the system) is positive. Within such a sign convention the first law is expressed as:

$$\Delta E = Q + W$$

i.e. the negative sign in the previous equation is incorporated in W.

7.3 Equivalence of Mechanical, Chemical and Thermal Energy Units

The previous equation does more than express mathematically the law of conservation of energy, it establishes a relationship between thermal energy and mechanical energy. Historically thermal energy was always expressed in calories (abbreviated as cal.) defined as the amount of thermal energy required to raise the temperature of 1 g of water by 1 degree Celcius. The standard unit used for mechanical work is the "Joule" (J). This unit eventually became the standard unit

for any form of energy. The conversion factor between the two units is:

$$1 \text{ cal} = 4.184 \text{ J}$$

Chemists often refer to the amount of energies exchanged between the system and its surroundings to the mole, i.e., quantities of energy are expressed in J/mol or cal/mol. To obtain the energy per particle (atom or molecule), you should divide the energy expressed in J or cal by Avogadro's number.

7.4 Temperature Scales

There are three temperature scales in use in science textbooks: the Celsius scale, the absolute temperature or Kelvin scale, and the Farenheit scale. In the Celsius scale the freezing point and the boiling point of water are arbitrarily defined as 0 °C and 100 °C, respectively. The scale is then divided into equal 1/100th intervals to define the degree Celsius or centigrade (from latin centi = 100). The absolute temperature or Kelvin scale is derived from the centigrade scale, i.e., an interval of 1 degree Celsius is equal to an interval of 1 degree Kelvin. The difference between the two scales is in their definitions of the zero point:

$$0 \text{ K} = -273.13 \text{ °C.}$$

Theoretically, this temperature can be approached but never achieved (= the 'absolute zero'), it corresponds to the point where all motion is frozen and matter is destroyed.

The Farenheit scale has the disadvantage of not being divided into 100 degrees between its two reference points: the freezing point of water is 32 °F and its boiling point is 212 °F. To convert Farenheit degrees into Celsius degrees you have to perform the following transformation:

$$(X \text{ °F} - 32) \times 5/9 = Y \text{ °C}$$

or

$$\text{°F} = 9/5 \text{ °C} + 32.$$

7.5 Heat Transfer

There are three ways in which heat can be transferred between the system and its surroundings:

(a) heat transfer by conduction

(b) heat transfer by convection

(c) heat transfer by radiation

In the first case (a) there is an intimate contact between the system and its surroundings and heat propagates through the entire system from the heated part to the unheated parts. A good example is the heating of a metal rod

on a flame. Heat is initially transmitted directly from the flame to one end of the rod through the contact between the metal and the flame. When carrying out such an experiment you would notice at some point that the part of the rod which is not in direct contact with the flame becomes hot as well (please do not attempt!).

In the second case (b), heat is transferred to the entire system by the circulation of a hot liquid or a gas through it. The difference between this mode of transfer and the previous one, is that the entire system or a major part of it is heated up directly by the surroundings and not by propagation of the thermal energy from the parts of the system which are in direct contact with the heating source and the parts which are not.

In the third case (c) there is no contact between the heating source and the system. Heat is transported by radiation. The perfect example is the microwave oven where the water inside the food is heated by the

microwave source. Most heat transfers are carried out by at least two of the above processes at the same time.

Note that when a metal is heated it expands at a rate which is proportional to the change in temperature it experiences. {For a definition of the coefficient of expansion, *see* PHY 6.3.}

7.6 State Functions

As previously mentioned, the first law of thermodynamics introduces three fundamental energy functions, i.e., the internal energy E, heat Q, and work W. Let us consider a transformation that takes the system from an initial state (I) to a final state (F) (which can differ by a number of variables such as temperature, pressure and volume). The change in the internal energy during this transformation depends only on the properties of the initial state (I) and the final state (F). In other words, suppose that to go from (I) to (F) the system is first subjected to an intermediate transformation that temporarily takes it from state (I) to an intermediate state (Int.) and then to another transformation that brings it from (Int.) to (F), the change in internal energy between the initial state (I) and the final state (F) are

independent of the properties of the intermediate state (Int.). The internal energy is said to be a path-independent function or a state function. This is not the case for W and Q. In fact, this is quite conceivable since the amount of W or Q can be imposed by the external operator who subjects the system to a given transformation from (I) to (F). For instance, Q can be fixed at zero if the operator uses an appropriate thermal insulator between the system and its surroundings. In which case the change in the internal energy is due entirely to the work w ($\Delta E = -w$). It is easy to understand that the same result [transformation from (I) to (F)] could be achieved by supplying a small quantity of heat q while letting the system do more work W on the surroundings so that q − W is equal to −w. In which case we have:

	Work	Heat	Change in internal energy
1st transf.	w	0	$-w$
2nd transf.	$W = w + q$	q	$-w$

and yet in both cases the system is going from (I) to (F).

W and Q are not state functions. They depend on the path taken to go from (I) to (F). If you remember the exact definition of the internal energy you will understand that a system changes its internal energy to respond to an input of Q and W. In other words, contrary to Q and W, the internal energy cannot be directly imposed on the system.

The fact that the internal energy is a state function can be used in three other equivalent ways:

(i)   If the changes in the internal energy during the intermediate transformation are known, they can be used to calculate the change for the entire process from (I) to (F): the latter is equal to the sum of the changes in the internal energy for all the intermediate steps.

(ii) If the change in the internal energy to go from a state (I) to a state (F) is $E_{I \to F}$ the change in the internal energy for an opposite transformation that would take the system from (F) to (I) is:

$$\Delta E_{F \to I} = - \Delta E_{I \to F}$$

(iii) If we start from (I) and go back to (I) through a series of intermediate transformations the change in the internal energy for the entire process is zero.

W can be determined experimentally by calculating the area under a pressure-volume curve. The mathematical relation is presented in CHM 8.1.

Go online to GAMSAT-prep.com for free chapter review Q&A and forum.

ENTHALPY AND THERMOCHEMISTRY
Chapter 8

Memorize	Understand	Not Required*
* Define: endo/exothermic	* Area under curve: PV diagram * Equations for enthalpy, Hess's law, free E. * Calculation: Hess, calorimetry, Bond diss. E. * 2nd law of thermodynamics * Entropy, free E. and spontaneity	* Knowledge beyond introductory-level (first year uni.) course * Memorizing constants for latent heats * Memorizing equations

GAMSAT-Prep.com

Introduction

Thermochemistry is the study of energy absorbed or released in chemical reactions or in any physical transformation (i.e. phase change like melting and boiling). Thermochemistry for the GAMSAT includes understanding and/or calculating quantities such as enthalpy, heat capacity, heat of combustion, heat of formation, and free energy.

Additional Resources

$$\Delta G = \Delta H - T\,\Delta S$$

Free Online Q&A + Forum   GAMSAT-prep.com Videos   Flashcards   Special Guest

8.1 Enthalpy as a Measure of Heat

The application of the general laws of thermodynamics to chemistry lead to some simplifications and adaptations because of the specificities of the problems that are dealt with in this field. For instance, in chemistry it is critical, if only for safety reasons, to know in advance what amounts of heat are going to be generated or absorbed during a reaction. In contrast, chemists are generally not interested in generating mechanical work and carry out most of their chemical reactions at constant pressure. For these reasons, although internal energy is a fundamental function its use is not very adequate in thermochemistry. Instead, chemists prefer to use another function derived from the internal energy: the enthalpy (H). This function is mathematically defined as:

$$\Delta H = \Delta E + P \times (\Delta V)$$

where P and V are respectively the pressure and the volume of the system. Hence, the enthalpy change (ΔH) of any system is the sum of the change in its internal energy (ΔE) and the product of its pressure (P) and volume change (ΔV). As the three components, internal energy, pressure and volume are all state functions, the enthalpy (H) or enthalpy change (ΔH) of a system is therefore also a state function. Thus, enthalpy change depends only on the enthalpies of the initial and final states (ΔH) and not on the path and therefore it is an example of a state function itself. The enthalpy change of a reaction is defined by the following equation $\Delta H = H_{final} - H_{initial}$; where ΔH is the enthalpy change, H_{final} is the enthalpy of the products of a reaction, and $H_{initial}$ is the enthalpy of the reactants of a reaction. A positive enthalpy change ($+\Delta H$) would indicate the flow of heat into a system as a reaction occurs and is called an "endothermic reaction". A cold pack added over an arm swelling would provide for a good example of an endothermic reaction. A negative enthalpy change ($-\Delta H$) would be called an "exothermic reaction" which essentially gives heat energy off from a system into its surroundings. A bunsen burner flame (= a small adjustable gas burner used in chem. labs) would be an appropriate example of an exothermic reaction.

You may wonder about the use of artificially introducing another energy function when internal energy is well defined and directly related to kinetic and potential energy of the particles that make up the system. To answer this legitimate question you need to consider the case of the majority of the chemical reactions where P is constant and where the only type of work that can possibly be done by the system is of a mechanical nature. In this case, since a change in internal energy (ΔE) occurring during a chemical reaction is basically a measure of all the systems energy as heat and work (Q + W) exchange with the system's surroundings, therefore, $\Delta E = Q + W$ and since, $W = -P\Delta V$, then, the change in enthalpy during a chemical reaction reduces to: $\Delta H = \Delta E + P \times V = (Q + W) + P \times V = Q + W - W = Q$ In other words, the change in enthalpy during a chemical reaction reduces to:

$$\Delta H = \Delta E + P \times V = (Q + W) + P \times V = Q$$

In other words, the change of enthalpy is a direct measure of the heat that evolves or is absorbed during a reaction carried out at constant pressure.

8.1.1 The Standard Enthalpy of Formation or Standard Heat of Formation (ΔH_f°)

The standard enthalpy of formation, ΔH_f°, is defined as the change of enthalpy that would occur when one mole of a substance is formed from its constituent elements in a standard state reaction. All elements in their standard states (oxygen gas, solid carbon as graphite, etc., at 1 atm and 25°C) have a standard enthalpy of formation of zero, as there is no change involved in their formation. The calculated standard enthalpy of various compounds can then be used to find the standard enthalpy of a reaction. For example, the standard enthalpy of formation for methane (CH_4) gas at 25°C would be the enthalpy of the following reaction:

$$C(s, graphite) + 2H_2(g) \rightarrow CH_4(g),$$

where $\Delta H_f^\circ = -74.6$ KJ/mol. Thus, the chemical equation for the enthalpy of formation of any compound is always written with respect to the formation of 1 mole of the studied compound.

The standard enthalpy change for a reaction denoted as ΔH°_{rxn}, is the change of enthalpy that would occur if one mole of matter is transformed by a chemical reaction with all reactants and products under standard state. It can be expressed as follows:

$$\Delta H^\circ_{rxn} = (\text{sum of } n_f \Delta H^\circ_f \text{ of products}) - (\text{sum of } n_r \Delta H^\circ_f \text{ of reactants}),$$

where n_r represents the stoichiometric coefficients of the reactants and n_f the stoichiometric coefficients of the products. The ΔH°_f represents the standard enthalpies of formation.

8.2 Heat of Reaction: Basic Principles

As discussed, a reaction during which heat is released is said to be *exothermic* (ΔH is negative). If a reaction requires the supply of a certain amount of heat it is *endothermic* (ΔH is positive).

Besides the basic principle behind the introduction of enthalpy there is a more fundamental advantage for the use of this function in thermochemistry: it is a state function. This is a very practical property. For instance,

consider two chemical reactions related in the following way:

| reaction 1: | $A + B \rightarrow C$ |
| reaction 2: | $C \rightarrow D$ |

If these two reactions are carried out consecutively they lead to the same result as the following reaction:

| overall reaction: | $A + B \rightarrow D$ |

Because H is a state function we can apply the same arguments here as the ones we previously used for E. The initial state (I) corresponding to A + B , the intermediate state (Int.) to C, and the final state (F) to the final product D. If we know the changes in the enthalpy of the system for reactions 1 and 2, the change in the enthalpy during the overall reaction is:

$$\Delta H_{OVERALL} = \Delta H_1 + \Delta H_2$$

This is known as Hess's law. Remember that Hess's law is a simple application of the fact that H is a state function.

Thus, since the enthalpy change of a reaction is dependant only on the initial and final states, and not on the pathway that a reaction may follow, the sum of all the reaction step enthalpy changes must therefore be equivalent to the overall reaction enthalpy

change (ΔH). The enthalpy change for a reaction can then be calculated without any direct measurement by using previously determined enthalpies of formation values for each reaction step of an overall equation. Consequently, if the overall enthalpy change is determined to be negative ($\Delta H_{net} < 0$), the reaction is exothermic and is most likely to be of a spontaneous type of reaction and a positive ΔH value would correspond to an endothermic reaction. Thus, Hess's law claims that enthalpy changes are additive and thus the ΔH for any single reaction can be calculated from the difference between the heat of formation of the products and the heat of formation of the reactants as follows:

$$\Delta H^{\circ}_{reaction} = \Sigma \Delta H_f^{\circ}{}_{(products)} - \Sigma \Delta H_f^{\circ}{}_{(reactants)}$$

where the ° superscript indicates standard state values.

8.3 Hess's Law

Hess's law can be applied in several equivalent ways which we will illustrate with several examples…

Example: assume that we know the following enthalpy changes:

$$2H_2(g) + O_2(g) \rightarrow 2H_2O(l)$$
$$\Delta H_1 = -136.6 \text{ kcal} : R1$$
$$Ca(OH)_2(s) \rightarrow CaO(s) + H_2O(l)$$
$$\Delta H_2 = 15.3 \text{ kcal} : R2$$
$$2CaO(s) \rightarrow 2\,Ca(s) + O_2(g)$$
$$\Delta H_3 = +303.6 \text{ kcal} : R3$$

and are asked to compute the enthalpy change for the following reaction:

$$Ca(s) + H_2(g) + O_2(g) \rightarrow Ca(OH)_2(s) : R$$

It is easy to see that reaction (R) can be obtained by the combination of reactions (R₁), (R₂) and (R₃) in the following way:

$$- \tfrac{1}{2}(R3): \quad Ca(s) + \tfrac{1}{2}\,O_2(g) \rightarrow CaO(s)$$
$$+ \tfrac{1}{2}(R1): \quad H_2(g) + \tfrac{1}{2}\,O_2(g) \rightarrow H_2O(l)$$
$$- \quad (R2): \quad CaO(s) + H_2O(l) \rightarrow Ca(OH)_2(s)$$
$$\overline{\quad Ca(s) + H_2(g) + O_2(g) \rightarrow Ca(OH)_2(s)}$$

As we previously explained, since H is a state function the enthalpy change for (R) will be given by:

$$\Delta H = -1/2\Delta H_3 + 1/2\Delta H_1 - \Delta H_2$$

Example: assume that we have the following enthalpy changes as shown below:

R1: B_2O_3 (s) + $3H_2O$ (g) → $3O_2$ (g) + B_2H_6 (g)
$(\Delta H_1 = 2035\ kJ/mol)$

R2: H_2O (l) → H_2O (g) $(\Delta H_2 = 44\ kJ/mol)$

R3: H_2 (g) + $(1/2)O_2$ (g) → H_2O (l)
$(\Delta H_3 = -286\ kJ/mol)$

R4: $2B$ (s) + $3H_2$ (g) → B_2H_6 (g)
$(\Delta H_4 = 36\ kJ/mol)$

and are then asked to find the enthalpy change or ΔH_f of the following reaction (R):

R: $2B$ (s) + $(3/2)O_2$ (g) → B_2O_3 (s) $(\Delta H_f = ?)$

After the required multiplication and rearrangements of all step equations (and their respective enthalpy changes), the result is as follows:

$(-1) \times$ (R1) B_2H_6 (g) + $3O_2$ (g)
→ B_2O_3 (s) + $3H_2O$ (g)
$(\Delta H_1 = -2035\ kJ/mol)$

$(-3) \times$ (R2) $3H_2O$ (g) → $3H_2O$ (l)
$(\Delta H_2 = -132\ kJ/mol)$

$(-3) \times$ (R3) $3H_2O$ (l) → $3H_2$ (g) + $(3/2)O_2$ (g)
$(\Delta H_3 = 858\ kJ/mol)$

$(+1) \times$ (R4) $2B$ (s) + $3H_2$ (g) → B_2H_6 (g)
$(\Delta H_4 = 36\ kJ/mol)$

adding the equations while canceling out all common terms, we finally obtain:

$2B$ (s) + $(3/2)O_2$ (g) → B_2O_3 (s)
$(\Delta H_f = -1273\ kJ/mol)$

As noted in the initial example, it is shown that the enthalpy change (ΔH_f) for the final reaction is given by the following:

$$\Delta H_f = (-1)\Delta H_1 + (-3)\Delta H_2 + (-3)\Delta H_3 + (1)\Delta H_4$$

There are no general rules that would allow you to determine which reaction to use first and by what factor it needs to be multiplied. It is important to proceed systematically and follow some simple ground rules:

(i)   For instance, you could start by writing the overall reaction that you want to obtain through a series of reaction additions.

(ii) Number all your reactions.

(iii) Keep in mind as you go along that the reactants of the overall reaction should always appear on the left-hand side and that the products should always appear on the right-hand side.

(iv) Circle or underline the first reactant of the overall reaction. Find a reaction in your list that involves this reactant (as a reactant or a product). Use that reaction first and write it in such a way that this reactant appears on the left-hand side with the appropriate stoichiometric coefficient (i.e., if this reactant appears as a product of a reaction on your list you should reverse the reaction).

(v)   Suppose that in (iv) you had to use the second reaction on your list and that you had to reverse and multiply this reaction by a factor of 3 to satisfy the preceding rule. In your addition, next to this reaction or on top of the arrow write $-3 \times \Delta H_2$.

(vi) Repeat the process for the other reactants and products of the overall reaction

until your addition yields the overall reaction. As you continue this process, make sure to cross out the compounds that appear on the right and left-hand sides at the same time.

8.4 Standard Enthalpies

Hess's law has a very practical use in chemistry. Indeed, the enthalpy change for a given chemical reaction can be computed from simple combinations of known enthalpy changes of other reactions. Because enthalpy changes depend on the conditions under which reactions are carried out it is important to define standard conditions:

(i) Standard pressure: 1 atmosphere pressure (approx. = 1 bar).

(ii) Standard temperature for the purposes of the calculation of the standard enthalpy change: generally 25 °C. The convention is that if the temperature of the standard state is not mentioned then it is assumed to be 25 °C, the standard temperature needs to be specified in all other instances.

(iii) Standard physical state of an element: it is defined as the "natural" physical state of an element under the above standard pressure and temperature. For instance, the standard physical state of water under the standard temperature and pressure of 1 atm and 25 °C is the liquid state. Under the same conditions oxygen is a gas.

Naturally, the standard enthalpy change (notation: $\Delta H°$) for a given reaction is defined as the enthalpy change that accompanies the reaction when it is carried out under standard pressure and temperature with all reactants and products in their standard physical state.

Note that the standard temperature defined here is <u>different from the standard temperature for an ideal gas</u> which is: 0 °C.

8.5 Enthalpies of Formation

The enthalpy of formation of a given compound is defined as the enthalpy change that accompanies the formation of the compound from its constituting elements. For instance,

the enthalpy of formation of water is the $\Delta H_f°$ for the following reaction:

$$H_2 + 1/2\ O_2 \rightarrow H_2O$$

To be more specific the standard enthalpy of formation of water $\Delta H_f°$ is the enthalpy change during the reaction:

$$H_2(g) + 1/2 O_2(g) \xrightarrow[\text{1 atm}]{25°C} H_2O(l)$$

where the reactants are in their natural physical state under standard temperature and pressure.

Note that according to these definitions, several of the reactions considered in the previous sections were in fact examples of reactions of formation. For instance, in section 8.3 on Hess's law, reaction (R1) is the reaction of formation of two moles of water, if

reversed reaction (R3) would be the reaction of formation of two moles of CaO and the overall reaction (R) is the reaction of formation of 1 mole $Ca(OH)_2$. Also note that although one could use the reverse of reaction (R2) to form $Ca(OH)_2$, this reaction, even reversed, is not the reaction of formation of $Ca(OH)_2$. The reason is that the constitutive elements of this molecule are: calcium (Ca), hydrogen (H_2) and oxygen (O_2) and not CaO and H_2O. Enthalpies of formation are also referred to as heats of formation. As previously explained, if the reaction of formation is carried out at constant pressure, the change in the enthalpy represents the amount of heat released or absorbed during the reaction.

8.6 Bond Dissociation Energies and Heats of Formation

The bond dissociation energy, also known as the bond dissociation enthalpy, is a measure of bond strength within a particular molecule defined as a standard enthalpy change in the *homolytic* cleavage (= 2 free radicals formed; CHM 9.4) of any studied chemical bond. An example of bond dissociation energies would be the successive homolytic cleavage of each of the C-H bonds of methane (CH_4) to give, $CH_3\bullet + \bullet H$, $CH_2\bullet + \bullet H$, $CH\bullet + \bullet H$ and finally $C\bullet + \bullet H$. The bond dissociation energies for each of the homolytic CH bond cleavage of methane are determined to be as follows: 435 KJ/mol, 444 KJ/mol, 444 KJ/mol and 339 KJ/mol, respectively. The average of these four individual bond dissociation energies is known as the bond

energy of the CH bond and is 414 KJ/mol. Thus, with the exception of all diatomic molecules where only one chemical bond is involved so that bond energy and bond dissociation energy are in this case equivalent, the bond dissociation energy is not exactly the same as bond energy. Bond energy is more appropriately defined as the energy required to sever 1 mole of a chemical bond in a gas and not necessarily the measure of a chemical bond strength within a particular molecule. Bond energy is therefore a measure of bond strength. Moreover as just described, bond energy may be considered as an average energy calculated from the sum of bond dissociation energies of all bonds within a particular compound. Bond energies are always positive values as it always takes energy to break bonds apart.

The difficulty in defining bond dissociation energies in polyatomic molecules is that the amounts of energy required to break a given bond (say an O–H bond) in two different polyatomic molecules (H_2O and CH_3OH, for instance) are different. Bond dissociation energies in polyatomic molecules are approximated to an average value for molecules of the same nature. Within the framework of this commonly made approximation we can calculate the enthalpy change of any reaction using the *sum* of bond energies of the reactants and the products in the following way:

$$\Delta H^\circ_{(reaction)} = \Sigma BE_{(reactants)} - \Sigma BE_{(products)}$$

where BE stands for bond energies.

Standard enthalpy changes of chemical reactions can also be computed using enthalpies of formation in the following way:

$$\Delta H^\circ_{(reaction)} = \Sigma \Delta H_{(bonds\ broken)} + \Sigma \Delta H_{(bonds\ formed)}$$
$$= \Sigma BE_{(reactants)} - \Sigma BE_{(products)}$$

Note how this equation is similar but not identical to the one making use of bond energies. This comes from the fact that a bond energy is defined as the energy required to break (and not to form) a given bond. Also note that the standard enthalpy of formation of a mole of any **element** is zero.

8.7 Calorimetry

Measurements of changes of temperature within a reaction mixture allow the experimental determination of heat absorbed or released during the corresponding chemical reaction. Indeed the amount of heat required to change the temperature of any substance X from T_1 to T_2 is proportional to $(T_2 - T_1)$ and the quantity of X:

$$Q = mC(T_2 - T_1)$$

or

$$Q = nc(T_2 - T_1)$$

where m is the mass of X, n the number of moles. The constant C or c is called the heat capacity. The standard units for C and c are, respectively, the $Jkg^{-1}K^{-1}$ and the $Jmol^{-1}K^{-1}$. C which is the heat capacity per unit mass is also referred to as the specific heat capacity. If you refer back to the definition of the calorie (see CHM 7.3) you will understand that the specific heat of water is necessarily: 1 cal $g^{-1}\,^\circ C^{-1}$.

Note that heat can be absorbed or released without a change in temperature (CHM 4.3.3). In fact, this situation occurs whenever a phase change takes place for a pure compound. For instance, ice melts at a constant temperature of 0 °C in order to break the forces that keep the water molecules in a crystal of ice we need to supply an amount of heat of 6.01 kJ/mol. There is no direct way of calculating the heat corresponding to a phase change.

Heats of phase changes (heat of fusion, heat of vaporization, heat of sublimation) are generally tabulated and indirectly determined in calorimetric experiments. For instance, if a block of ice is allowed to melt in a bucket of warm water, we can determine the heat of fusion of ice by measuring the temperature drop in the bucket of water and applying the law of conservation of energy. The relevant equation is:

$$Q = m\,L$$

where L is the latent heat which is a constant.

Calorimetry is the science of measuring the heat evolved or exchanged due to a chemical reaction. The thermal energy of a reaction (defined as the system) is measured as a function of its surroundings by observing a temperature change (ΔT) on the surroundings due to the system. The magnitude in temperature change is essentially a measure of a system's or sample's energy content which is measured either while keeping a volume constant (bomb calorimetry) or while keeping a pressure constant (coffee-cup calorimetry).

In a constant volume calorimetry measurement, the bomb calorimeter is kept at a constant volume and there is essentially no heat exchange between the calorimeter and the surroundings and thus, the net heat exchange for the system is zero. The heat exchange for the reaction is then compensated for by the heat change for the water and bomb calorimeter material steel (or surroundings). Thus, $\Delta q_{system} = \Delta q_{reaction} + \Delta q_{water} + \Delta q_{steel} = 0$ in bomb calorimetry, and so $q_{cal} = -q_{reaction}$ in which the temperature change is related to the heat absorbed by the calorimeter (q_{cal}) and if no heat escapes the constant volume calorimeter, the amount of heat gained by the calorimeter then equals that released by the system and so, $q_{cal} = -q_{reaction}$ as stated previously. Note that since $Q = mc\Delta T$ as previously defined, and $q_{reaction} = -(q_{water} + q_{steel})$ therefore, $q_{reaction} = -(m_{water})(c_{water})\Delta T + (m_{steel})(c_{steel})\Delta T$.

For aqueous solutions, a coffee-cup calorimeter is usually used to measure the enthalpy change of the system. This is simply a polystyrene (Styrofoam) cup with a lid and a thermometer. The cup is partially filled with a known volume of water. When a chemical reaction occurs in the coffee-cup calorimeter, the heat of the reaction is absorbed by the water. The change in water temperature is used to calculate the amount of heat that has been absorbed (used to make products, so water temperature decreases) or evolved (lost to the water, so its temperature increases) in the reaction.

8.8 The Second Law of Thermodynamics

The first law of thermodynamics allows us to calculate energy transfers during a given transformation of the system. It does not allow us to predict whether a transformation can or cannot occur spontaneously. Yet our daily observations tell us that certain transformations always occur in a given direction. For instance, heat flows from a hot source to a cold source. We cannot spontaneously transfer heat in the other direction to make the hot source hotter and the cold source colder. The second law of thermodynamics states that entropy (S) of an isolated system will never decrease. In order for a reaction to proceed, the entropy of the system must increase. For any spontaneous process, the entropy of the universe increases which results in a greater dispersal or randomization of the energy ($\Delta S > 0$). The second law of thermodynamics allows the determination of the preferred direction of a given transformation. Transformations which require the smallest amount of energy and lead to the largest disorder of the system are the most spontaneous.

8.9 Entropy

Entropy is regarded as the main driving force behind all the chemical and physical changes known within the universe. All natural processes tend toward an increase in energy dispersal or, in other words, an entropy increase within our universe. Thus, a chemical system or reaction proceeds in a direction of universal entropy increase.

Entropy S is the state function which measures the degree of "disorder" in a system. For instance, the entropy of ice is lower than the entropy of liquid water since ice corresponds to an organized crystalline structure (virtually no disorder). In fact, generally speaking, the entropy increases as we go from a solid to a liquid to a gas. For similar reasons, the entropy decreases when an elastic band is stretched. Indeed, in the "unstretched" elastic band the molecules of the rubber polymer are coiled up and form a disorganized structure. As the rubber is stretched these molecules will tend to line up with each other and adopt a more organized structure.

Entropy has the dimension of energy as a function of temperature as J/K or cal/K. Entropy can therefore be related to temperature and is thus a measure of energy dispersal (in joules) per unit of temperature (in kelvins).

The second law of thermodynamics can be expressed in the alternative form: a spontaneous transformation corresponds to an increase of the entropy of the system plus its surroundings. Hence, a chemical system is known to proceed in a direction that increases the entropy of the universe. As a result, ΔS must be incorporated in an expression that includes both the system and its surroundings so that, $\Delta S_{universe} = \Delta S_{surroundings} + \Delta S_{system} > 0$. When a system reaches a certain temperature equilibrium, it then also reaches its maximal entropy and so, $\Delta S_{universe} = \Delta S_{surroundings} + \Delta S_{system} = 0$. The entropy of the thermodynamic system is therefore a measure of how far the equalization has progressed.

Entropy, like enthalpy, is a state function and is therefore path independent. Hence, a change in entropy depends only on the initial and final states ($\Delta S = S_{final} - S_{initial}$) and not on how the system arrived at that state. Under standard conditions, for any process or reaction, the entropy change for that reaction will be the difference between the entropies of products and reactants as follows:

$$\Delta S°_{reaction} = \Delta S°_{products} - \Delta S°_{reactants}$$

8.10 Free Energy

The Gibbs free energy G is another state function which can be used as a criterion for spontaneity. This function is defined as:

$$G = H - T \cdot S$$

where:

- H is the enthalpy of the system in a given state
- T is the absolute temperature and thus must always have a positive value (CHM 7.4)
- S is the entropy of the system.

Consequently, Gibbs free energy (G) also determines the direction of a spontaneous change for a chemical system. The derivation for the formulation thus incorporates both the entropy and enthalpy parameters studied in the previous sections. Following

various manipulations and derivations, one can then note that Gibbs free energy is an alternative form of both enthalpy and the entropy changes of a chemical process.

The standard Gibbs free energy of a reaction ($\Delta G°_{rxn}$), is determined at 25°C and a pressure of 1 atm. For a reaction carried out at constant temperature we can write that the change in the Gibbs free energy is:

$$\Delta G = \Delta H - T\,\Delta S$$

A reaction carried out at constant pressure is **spontaneous** if

$$\Delta G < 0, \textit{exergonic}$$

It is **not spontaneous** if:

$$\Delta G > 0, \textit{endergonic}$$

and it is in a **state of equilibrium** (reaction spontaneous in both directions) if:

$$\Delta G = 0.$$

As noted in the previous chapter, the study of thermodynamics generally describes the spontaneity or the direction and extent to which a reaction will proceed. It therefore enables one to predict if a reaction will occur spontaneously or not. Note that non spontaneous processes may turn into spontaneous processes if coupled to another spontaneous process or more specifically by the addition of some external energy.

Thermochemistry then can be used to essentially calculate how much work a system can do or require. Thermodynamics basically then deals with the relative potentials of both the reactants and products of a chemical system. The next chapter will describe the actual rate (or chemical kinetics or speed) of a chemical reaction. In chemical kinetics, the chemical potential of intermediate states of a chemical reaction may also be described and thus enabling one to determine why a reaction may be slow or fast.

Consider the summary of Gibbs free energy below. Note that the table should not to be committed to memory; however, you should be able to deduce the results in the fourth column. The GAMSAT often has 1-2 questions covering Gibbs free energy.

Enthalpy change	Entropy change	Gibbs free energy	Spontaneity
positive	positive	depends on T, may be + or −	yes, if the temperature is high enough
negative	positive	always negative	always spontaneous
negative	negative	depends on T, may be + or −	yes, if the temperature is low enough
positive	negative	always positive	never spontaneous

Go online to GAMSAT-prep.com for free chapter review Q&A and forum.

GOLD NOTES

RATE PROCESSES IN CHEMICAL REACTIONS
Chapter 9

Memorize	Understand	Not Required*
Reaction order Define: rate-determining step Generalized potential energy diagrams Define: activation energy, catalysis Define: saturation kinetics, substrate	* Reaction rates, rate law, determine exponents * Reaction mechanism for free radicals * Rate constant equation; apply Le Chatelier's * Kinetic vs. thermodynamic control * Law of mass action, equations for Gibbs free E., saturation kinetics, Keq	* Knowledge beyond introductory-level (first year uni.) course * Memorizing the rate constant equation

GAMSAT-Prep.com

Introduction ▖▌█

Rate processes involve the study of the velocity (speed) and mechanisms of chemical reactions. **Reaction rate** (= *velocity*) tells us how fast the concentrations of reactants change with time. **Reaction mechanisms** show the sequence of steps to get to the overall change. Experiments show that 4 important factors generally influence reaction rates: (1) the nature of the reactants, (2) their concentration, (3) temperature, and (4) catalysis.

Additional Resources

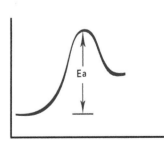

Free Online Q&A + Forum   GAMSAT-prep.com Videos   Flashcards   Special Guest

9.1 Reaction Rate

Consider a general reaction

$$2\,A + 3\,B \rightarrow C + D$$

The rate or the velocity at which this reaction proceeds can be expressed by one of the following:

(i) rate of disappearance of A: $-\Delta[A]/\Delta t$

(ii) rate of disappearance of B: $-\Delta[B]/\Delta t$

(iii) rate of appearance or formation of C: $\Delta[C]/\Delta t$

(iv) rate of appearance or formation of D: $\Delta[D]/\Delta t$

Where [ ] denotes the concentration of a reactant or a product in moles/liter. Thus, the reaction rate measure is usually expressed as a change in reactant or product concentration ($\Delta_{conc.}$) per unit change in time (Δt).

Since A and B are disappearing in this reaction, [A] and [B] are decreasing with time, i.e. $\Delta[A]/\Delta t$ and $\Delta[B]/\Delta t$ are negative quantities. On the other hand, the quantities $\Delta[C]/\Delta t$ and $\Delta[D]/\Delta t$ are positive since both C and D are being formed during the process of this reaction. By convention: rates of reactions are expressed as positive numbers; as a result, a negative sign is necessary in the first two expressions.

Suppose that A disappears at a rate of 6 (moles/liter)/s. In the same time interval (1s), in a total volume of 1L we have:

(3 mol B/2 mol A) × 6 mol A
= 9 moles of B disappearing
(1 mol C/2 mol A) × 6 mol A
= 3 moles of C being formed
(1 mol D/2 mol A) × 6 mol A
= 3 moles of D being formed

Therefore individual rates of formation or disappearance are not convenient ways to express the rate of a reaction. Indeed, depending on the reactant or product considered the rate will be given by a different numerical value unless the stoichiometric coefficients are equal (e.g. for C and D in our case).

A more convenient expression of the rate of a reaction is the overall rate. This rate is simply obtained by dividing the rate of formation or disappearance of a given reactant or product by the corresponding stoichiometric coefficient, i.e.:

overall rate = $-(1/2)\,\Delta[A]/\Delta t$, or $-(1/3)\,\Delta[B]/\Delta t$,

or $\Delta[C]/\Delta t$, or $\Delta[D]/\Delta t$.

A simple verification on our example will show you that these expressions all lead to the same numerical value for the overall rate: 3 (moles/L)/s. Therefore for a generic equation such as, $aA + bB \rightarrow cC + dD$, a generalization of the overall reaction rate would be as follows:

$$\text{Rate} = \frac{-1}{a}\frac{\Delta[A]}{\Delta t} = \frac{-1}{b}\frac{\Delta[B]}{\Delta t} = \frac{+1}{c}\frac{\Delta[C]}{\Delta t} = \frac{+1}{d}\frac{\Delta[D]}{\Delta t}$$

It can be seen from the preceding overall rate relationship that the rate is the same whether we use one of the reactants or one of the products to calculate the rates. Generally, one can see that knowing the rate of change in the concentration of any one reactant or product at a certain time point allows one to invariably determine the rate of change in the concentration of any other reactant or product at the same time point using the stoichiometrically balanced equation.

Whenever the term "rate" is used (with no other specification) it refers to the "overall rate" unless individual and overall rates are equal.

9.2 Dependence of Reaction Rates on Concentration of Reactants

The rate of a reaction (given in moles per liter per second) can be expressed as a function of the concentration of the reactants. In the previous chemical reaction we would have:

$$rate = k \, [A]^m \, [B]^n$$

where [ ] is the concentration of the corresponding reactant in moles per liter

k is referred to as the rate constant
m is the order of the reaction with respect to A
n is the order of the reaction with respect to B
m+n is the overall reaction order.

The rate constant k is reaction specific. It is directly proportional to the rate of a reaction. It increases with increasing temperature since the proportion of molecules with energies greater than the activation energy E_a of a reaction increases with higher temperatures.

According to the rate law above, the reaction is said to be an $(m + n)th$ order reaction, or, an mth order reaction with respect to A, or, an nth order reaction with respect to B.

The value of the m or nth rate orders of the reaction describes how the rate of the reaction depends on the concentration of the reactant(s).

For example, a zero rate order for reactant A (where $m = 0$), would indicate that the rate of the reaction is independent of the concentration of reactant A and therefore has a constant reaction rate (this is also applicable to reactant B). The rate equation can therefore be expressed as a rate constant k or the rate = k. The rate probably depends on temperature or other factors excluding concentration.

A first rate order for reactant A (where $m = 1$) would indicate that the rate of the reaction is directly proportional to the concentration of the reactant A (or B, where $n = 1$). Thus, the rate equation can be expressed as follows: $rate = k[A]^1$ or $rate = k[B]^1$.

A second rate order for reactant A ($m = 2$) would indicate that the rate is proportional to the square of the reactant concentration. The rate equation can thus be expressed as follows: rate = $k[A]^2$.

Hence, the rate orders or exponents in the rate law equation can be integers, fractions, or zeros and are not necessarily equal to the stoichiometric coefficients in the given reaction except when a reaction is the rate-determining step (or elementary step). Consequently, although there are other orders, including both higher and mixed orders or fractions that are possible as described, the three described orders (0, 1st and 2nd), are amongst the most common orders studied.

As shown by the graphical representation below, for the zero order reactant, as the concentration of reactant A decreases over time, the slope of the line is constant and thus the rate is constant. Moreover, the rate does not change regardless of the decrease in reactant A concentration over time and thus the zero order rate order. For the first order, the decrease in reactant A concentration is shown to affect the rate of reaction in direct proportion. Thus, as the concentration decreases, the rate decreases proportionally. Lastly, for the second order, the rate of the reaction is shown to decrease proportionally to the square of the reactant A concentration. In fact, the curves for 1st and 2nd order reactions resemble exponential decay.

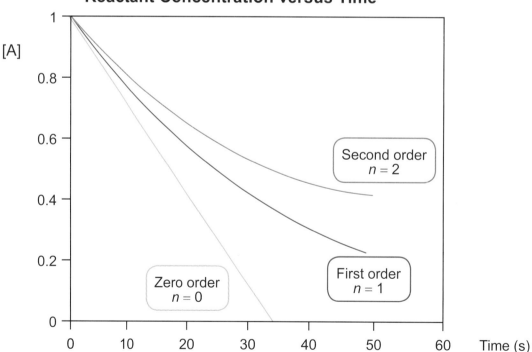

Reactant Concentration versus Time

Figure III.A.9.0: Reactant concentration vs. time curves. Notice that first and second order reactions have exponential decay curves (PHY 10.5) but, of course, second order reactions decay faster. It is expected that you can recognize the graphs above and those in the next section (CHM 9.2.1).

9.2.1 Differential Rate Law vs. Integrated Rate Law

Rate laws may be expressed as differential equations or as integrated rate laws. As differential equations, the relationship is shown between the rate of a reaction and the concentration of a reactant. Alternatively, the integrated rate law expresses a rate as a function of concentration of a reactant or reactants and time.

For example, for a zero order rate, Rate $= k[A]^0 = k$ and since Rate $= -\Delta[A]/\Delta t$, then $-\Delta[A]/\Delta t = k$ and following the integration of the differential function, the following zero-order integrated rate law is obtained: $[A]_t = -kt + [A]_0$, where $[A]_t =$ is the concentration of A at a particular time point t and $[A]_0$ is the initial concentration of A and k is the rate constant.

The following table summarizes the main rate laws of the 0, 1st and 2nd rate orders and their respective relationships.

Table 9.2.1: The graphs below do not need to be memorized but you may be expected to match any Integrated Rate Law equation with its graph since they follow the simple standard of y = mx + b (GM 3.4.4, 3.5.1).

Rate Law Summary					
Reaction Order	Rate Law	Units of k	Integrated Rate Law	Straight-Line Plot	Half-Life Equation
0	Rate $= k[A]^0$	$M \cdot s^{-1}$	$[A]_t = -kt + [A]_0$	y-intercept $= [A]_0$, slope $= -k$	$t_{1/2} = \dfrac{[A]_0}{2k} = \dfrac{1}{k}\dfrac{[A]_0}{2}$
1	Rate $= k[A]^1$	s^{-1}	$\ln[A]_t = -kt + \ln[A]_0$ $\ln\dfrac{[A]_t}{[A]_0} = -kt$	y-intercept $= \ln[A]_0$, slope $= -k$	$t_{1/2} = \dfrac{0.693}{k} = \dfrac{1}{k}(0.693)$
2	Rate $= k[A]^2$	$M^{-1} \cdot s^{-1}$	$\dfrac{1}{[A]_t} = kt + \dfrac{1}{[A]_0}$	slope $= k$, y-intercept $= 1/[A]_0$	$t_{1/2} = \dfrac{1}{k[A]_0} = \dfrac{1}{k}\dfrac{1}{[A]_0}$

As depicted by the table, the first and second order rate laws are also derived in a similar manner as the zero order rate law.

Included within the table is also the half-life's of the three described rate laws. The half-life of a reaction is defined as the time needed to decrease the concentration of the reactant to one-half of the original starting concentration (PHY 12.4). Each rate order has its own respective half-life (see graphs below).

The rate order of a reactant may be determined experimentally by either the isolation or initial rates method as described in the following section or by plotting concentration, or some function of concentration such as ln[ ] or 1/[ ] of reactant as a function of time. A linear relationship between the dependent concentration variable of reactant and the independent time variable will then delineate the actual order of the reactant. Moreover, if a linear curve is obtained when plotting [reactant] versus time, the order would be zero whereas, if a linear relationship is noted when plotting ln [reactant] versus time, this would be first order and second order would be for a linear relationship between 1/[reactant] versus time.

Therefore, the rate law of a reaction with a multi-step mechanism cannot be deduced from the stoichiometric coefficients of the overall reaction; it must be determined experimentally for a given reaction at a given temperature as will be described in the following section.

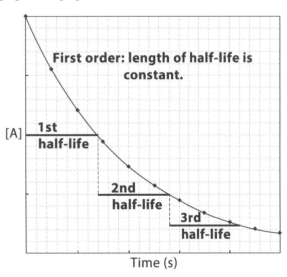

First order: length of half-life is constant.

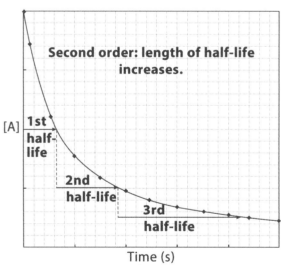

Second order: length of half-life increases.

9.3 Determining Exponents of the Rate Law

The only way to determine the exponents with certainty is via experimentation. The rate law for any reaction must therefore always be determined by experimentation, often by a method known as the "initial rates method or the isolation method".

Exp. #	Initial Concentration		Initial Rate $(mol\ L^{-1}\ s^{-1})$
	[A]	[B]	
1	0.10	0.10	0.20
2	0.20	0.10	0.40
3	0.30	0.10	0.60
4	0.30	0.20	2.40
5	0.30	0.30	5.40

In the initial rates method, if there are two or more reactants involved in the reaction, the reactant concentrations are usually varied independent of each other so that, for example, in a two reactant reaction, if one reactant concentration is altered the other reactant concentration would be kept constant and the effect on the initial rate of the reaction would be measured. Consider the following five experiments varying the concentrations of reactants A and B with resulting initial rates of reaction:

$$A + B \rightarrow \text{products}$$

In the first three experiments the concentration of A changes but B remains the same. Thus the resultant changes in rate only depend on the concentration of A. Note that when [A] doubles (Exp. 1, 2) the reaction rate doubles, and when [A] triples (Exp. 1, 3) the reaction rate triples. Because it is directly proportional, the exponent of [A] must be 1. Thus the rate of reaction is first order with respect to A.

In the final three sets of experiments, [B] changes while [A] remains the same. When [B] doubles (Exp. 3, 4) the rate increases by a factor of 4 ($= 2^2$). When [B] triples (Exp. 3, 5) the rate increases by a factor of 9 ($= 3^2$). Thus the relation is exponential where the exponent of [B] is 2. The rate of reaction is second order with respect to B.

$$\text{initial rate} = k[A]^1[B]^2$$

The overall rate of reaction (n+m) is third order. The value of the rate constant k can be easily calculated by substituting the results from any of the five experiments. For example, using experiment #1:

$$k = \frac{\text{initial rate}}{[A]^1\ [B]^2}$$

$$k = \frac{0.20\ mol\ L^{-1}\ s^{-1}}{(0.10\ mol\ L^{-1})\ (0.10\ mol\ L^{-1})^2}$$

$$= 2.0 \times 10^2\ L^2 mol^{-2} s^{-1}$$

k is the rate constant for the reaction which includes all five experiments.

Note: The units of the resultant rate constant "k" will differ depending on the overall rate order of a reaction.

9.4 Reaction Mechanism - Rate-determining Step

Chemical equations fail to describe the detailed process through which the reactants are transformed into the products. For instance, consider the reaction of formation of hydrogen chloride from hydrogen and chlorine:

$$Cl_2(g) + H_2(g) \rightarrow 2\ HCl(g)$$

The equation above fails to mention that in fact this reaction is the result of a chain of reactions proceeding in three steps:

Initiation step: formation of free chlorine radicals by photon irradiation or introduction of heat (= *radicals*, the mechanism will be discussed in organic chemistry):

$$1/2\ Cl_2 \rightleftharpoons Cl\cdot$$

The double arrow indicates that in fact some of the Cl free radicals recombine to form chlorine molecules, the whole process eventually reaches a state of equilibrium where the following ratio is constant:

$$K = [Cl\cdot]/[Cl_2]^{1/2}$$

The determination of such a constant will be dealt with in the sub-section on "equilibrium constants."

Propagation step: formation of reactive hydrogen free radicals and reaction between hydrogen free radicals and chlorine molecules:

$$Cl\cdot + H_2 \rightarrow HCl + H\cdot$$

$$H\cdot + Cl_2 \rightarrow HCl + Cl\cdot$$

Termination step: Formation of hydrogen chloride by reaction between hydrogen free radicals and chlorine free radicals.

$$H\cdot + Cl\cdot \rightarrow HCl$$

The detailed chain reaction process above is called the mechanism of the reaction. Each individual step in a detailed mechanism is called an elementary step. Any reaction proceeds through some mechanism which is generally impossible to predict from its chemical equation. Such mechanisms are usually determined through an experimental procedure. Generally speaking each step proceeds at its own rate.

The rate of the overall reaction is naturally limited by the slowest step; therefore, the rate-determining step in the mechanism of a reaction is the slowest step. In other words, the overall rate law of a reaction is basically equal to the rate law of the slowest step. The faster processes have an indirect influence on the rate: they regulate the concentrations of the reactants and products. The chemical equation of an elementary step reflects the exact molecular process that transforms its reactants into its products. For this reason its rate law can be predicted from its chemical equation: in an elementary process, the orders with respect to the reactants are equal to the corresponding stoichiometric coefficients.

In our example, experiments show that the rate-determining step is the reaction between chlorine radicals and hydrogen molecules, all the other steps are much faster. According to the principles stated, the rate law of the overall reaction is equal to the rate law of this rate-determining step. Therefore, the rate of the overall reaction is proportional to the concentration of hydrogen molecules and chlorine radicals but is not directly proportional to the concentration of chlorine molecules. However, since the ratio of concentrations of Cl and Cl_2 is regulated by the initiation step concentration, it can be shown that according to the mechanism provided the rate law is:

$$rate = k[H_2] \cdot [Cl_2]^{1/2}$$

It is important to note that the individual orders of a reaction are generally not equal to the stoichiometric coefficients.

9.5 Dependence of Reaction Rates upon Temperature

Rates of chemical reactions are generally very sensitive to temperature fluctuations. In particular, many reactions are known to slow down by decreasing the temperature or vise versa. How does one therefore explain the temperature dependence on reaction rates? The rate of a reaction is essentially equal to the reactant concentration raised to a reaction order (n) times the rate constant k or rate $= k[A]^x$. From the collision theory of chemical kinetics it was established that the rate constant of a reaction can be expressed as follows:

$$k = A\, e^{-Ea/RT}$$

- A is a constant referred to as the "Arrhenius constant" or the frequency factor which includes two separate components known as, the orientation factor (p) and the collision frequency (z). More specifically, the collision frequency (z) is defined as the number of collisions that molecules acquire per unit time and the orientation factor (p) is defined as the proper orientation reactant molecules require for product formation. Thus, the Arrhenius constant, A, is related to both the frequency of collisions (z) and the proper orientation (p) of the molecular collisions required for final product formation and so A = pz.
- e is the base of natural logarithms,
- E_a is the activation energy, it is the energy required to get a reaction started. For reactants to transform into products, the reactants must go through a high energy state or "transition state" which is the minimum energy (activation energy) required for reactants to transform into products. If two molecules of reactants collide with proper orientation and sufficient energy

or force in such a way that the molecules acquire a total energy content surpassing the activation energy, E_a, the collisions will result in a complete chemical reaction and the formation of products. Note: only a fraction of colliding reactant molecules will have sufficient kinetic energy to exceed an activation energy barrier.

- R is the ideal gas constant (1.99 cal mol^{-1} K^{-1})
- T is the absolute temperature.

It can therefore be seen that the rate constant, k, contains the temperature component as an exponent and thus, temperature affects a reaction rate by affecting the actual rate constant k. Note: A rate constant remains constant only when temperature remains constant. The rate constant equation otherwise known as the "Arrhenius equation"

thus describes the relationship between the rate constant (k) and temperature.

Either an increase in temperature or decrease in activation energy will result in an increase in the reaction constant k and thus an increase in the reaction rate. The species formed during an <u>efficient collision</u>, before the reactants transform into the final product(s) is called the <u>activated complex</u> or the <u>transition state</u>.

Within the framework of this theory, when a single step reaction proceeds, the potential energy of the system varies according to Figure III.A.9.1.

The change in enthalpy (ΔH) during the reaction is the difference between the total energy of the products and the reactants.

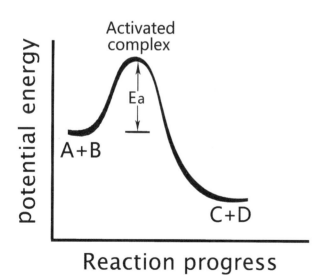

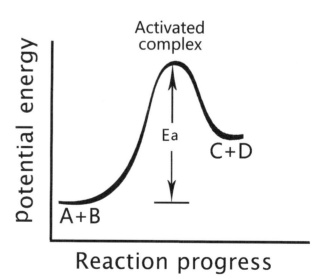

Figure III.A.9.1: Potential energy diagrams: exothermic vs. endothermic reactions.

The left curve of Figure III.A.9.1 shows that the total energy of the reactants is higher than the total energy of the products: this is obviously the case for an exothermic reaction. The right curve of Figure III.A.9.1, shows the profile of an endothermic reaction. A negative enthalpy change indicates an exothermic reaction and a positive enthalpy change depicts an endothermic reaction. The difference in potential energy between the reactant(s) and the activated complex is the activation energy of the forward reaction and the difference between the product(s) and the activated complex is the activation energy of the reverse reaction. Also note that the <u>bigger</u> the difference between the total energy of the reactants and the activated complex, i.e. the <u>activation energy E_a</u>, the <u>slower</u> the reaction.

If a reaction proceeds through several steps one can construct a diagram for each step and combine the single-step diagrams to obtain the energy profile of the overall reaction.

9.6 Kinetic Control vs. Thermodynamic Control

Consider the case where two molecules A and B can react to form either products C or D. Suppose that C has the lowest Gibbs free energy (i.e. the most thermodynamically stable product). Also suppose that product D requires the smallest activation energy and is therefore formed faster than C. If it is product C which is exclusively observed when the reaction is actually performed, the reaction is said to be <u>thermodynamically controlled</u> (i.e. out of a list of possible pathways the reactants choose the one leading to the most stable product). If on the other hand the reactants <u>choose</u> the pathway leading to the <u>product</u> which is <u>produced more quickly</u> it is said to be <u>kinetically controlled</u>.

9.7 Catalysis

A catalyst is a compound that does not directly participate in a reaction (the initial number of moles of this compound in the reaction mixture is equal to the number of moles of this compound once the reaction is completed). Catalysts work by providing an alternative mechanism for a reaction that involves a different transition state, one in which a lower activation energy occurs at the rate-determining step. Catalysts help lower the activation energy of a reaction and help the reaction to proceed. <u>Enzymes</u> are the typical <u>biological</u>

catalysts. They are protein molecules with very large molar masses containing one or more active sites (BIO 4.1-4.4). Enzymes are very specialized catalysts. They are generally specific and operate only on certain biological reactants called substrates. They also generally increase the rate of reactions by large factors. The general mechanism of operation of enzymes is as follows:

Enzyme (E) + Substrate (S) → ES (complex)

ES → Product (P) + Enzyme (E)

If we were to compare the energy profile of a reaction performed in the absence of an enzyme to that of the same reaction performed with the addition of an enzyme we would obtain Figure III.A.9.2.

As you can see from Figure III.A.9.2, the reaction from the substrate to the product is facilitated by the presence of the enzyme because the reaction proceeds in two fast steps (low E_a's). Generally, catalysts (or enzymes) stabilize the transition state of a reaction by lowering the energy barrier between reactants and the transition state. Catalysts (or enzymes) do not change the energy difference between reactants and products. Therefore, catalysts do not alter the extent of a reaction or the chemical equilibrium itself. Generally, the rate of an enzyme-catalysed reaction is:

rate = k[ES]

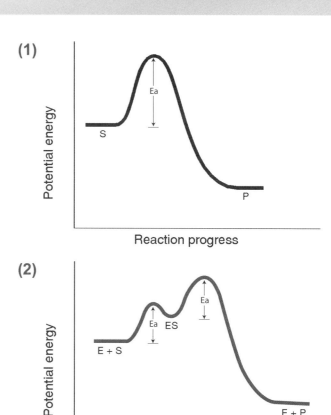

(1)

(2)

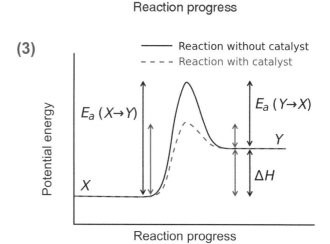

(3)

Figure III.A.9.2: Potential energy diagrams: **(1)** exothermic (CHM 9.5) without a catalyst; **(2)** exothermic with a catalyst; **(3)** showing both with and without a catalyst - the forward reaction being endothermic, thus the reverse reaction is exothermic.

The rate of formation of the product $\Delta[P]/\Delta t$ vs. the concentration of the substrate $[S]$ yields a plot as in Figure III.A.9.3.

When the concentration of the substrate is large enough for the substrate to occupy all the available active sites on the enzyme, any further increase would have no effect on the rate of the reaction. This is called *saturation kinetics* (BIO 1.1.2).

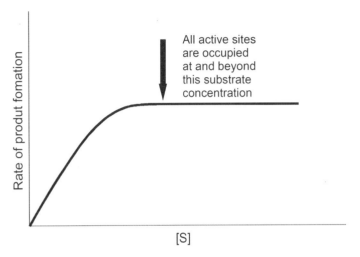

Figure III.A.9.3: Saturation kinetics.

9.8 Equilibrium in Reversible Chemical Reactions

In most chemical reactions once the product is formed, it reacts in such a way to yield back the initial reactants. Eventually, the system reaches a state where there are as many molecules of products being formed as there are molecules of reactants being generated through the reverse reaction. At equilibrium, the concentrations of reactants and products will not necessarily be equal, however, the concentrations remain the same. Hence, the relative concentrations of all components of the forward and reverse reactions become constant at equilibrium. This is called a state of "dynamic equilibrium". It is characterized by a constant K:

$$aA + bB \rightleftharpoons cC + dD$$

where a, b, c and d are the corresponding stoichiometric coefficients:

$$K = \frac{[C]^c \, [D]^d}{[A]^a \, [B]^b}$$

The equilibrium constant K (sometimes symbolized as K_{eq}) has a given value at a given temperature. If the temperature changes the value of K changes. At a given temperature, if we change the concentration of A, B, C or D, the system evolves in such a way as to re-establish the value of K. This is called the law of mass action. {Note: catalysts speed up the rate of reaction without affecting K_{eq}}

The following is an example of how an equilibrium constant K is calculated based on a chemical reaction at equilibrium. Remember that the equilibrium constant K can be directly calculated only when the equilibrium concentrations of reactants and products are known or obtained.

As an example, suppose that initially, 5 moles of reactant X are mixed with 12 moles of Y and both are added into an empty 1 liter container. Following their reaction, the system eventually reaches equilibrium with 4 moles of Z formed according to the following reaction:

$$X \text{ (g)} + 2Y \text{ (g)} \rightleftharpoons Z \text{ (g)}$$

For this gaseous, homogeneous mixture (CHM 1.7), what is the value of the equilibrium constant K?

At equilibrium, 4 moles of Z are formed and therefore, 4 moles of X and 8 moles of Y are consumed based on the mole:mole ratio of the balanced equation. Since 5 moles X and 12 moles Y were initially available prior to equilibrium, at equilibrium following the reaction, there remains 1 mol X and 4 moles Y. Since all of the reaction takes place in a 1 L volume, the equilibrium concentrations are therefore, 1 mol/L for X, 4 mol/L for Y and Z, respectively.

Thus, the equilibrium constant can then be calculated as follows:

$$K = [Z]/[X][Y]^2 = [4]/[1][4]^2 = 0.25.$$

The K value is an indication of where the equilibrium point of a reaction actually lies, either far to the right or far to the left or somewhere in between. The following is a summary of the significance of the magnitude of an equilibrium constant K and its meaning:

1. If K > 1, this means that the forward reaction is favored and thus, the reaction favors product formation. If K is very large, the equilibrium mixture will then contain very little reactant compared to product.

2. If K < 1, the reverse reaction is favored and so the reaction does not proceed very far towards product formation and thus very little product is formed.

3. If K = 1, neither forward nor reverse directions are favored.

Note: Pure solids and pure liquids do not appear in the equilibrium constant. Thus in heterogeneous equilibria, since the liquid and solid phases are not sensitive to pressure, their "concentrations" remain constant throughout the reaction and so, mathematically, their values are denoted as 1.

Naturally, H_2O is one of the most common liquids dealt with in reactions. Remember to set its activity equal to 1 when it is a liquid but, if H_2O is written as a gas, then its concentration must be considered.

9.8.1 The Reaction Quotient Q to Predict Reaction Direction

The reaction quotient Q is the same ratio as the equilibrium constant K (cf. CHM 5.3.4). Q defines all reaction progresses including the K value. In other words, the equilibrium constant K is a special case of the reaction quotient Q.

Thus, the Q ratio has many values dependent on where the reaction lies prior to or subsequent to the concentrations at equilibrium. One may therefore determine if a reaction is going towards an equilibrium by making more products or, alternatively, if a reaction is moving towards equilibrium by making more reactants. The following is a summary of what Q means in relation to K.

Consider the following reaction:

$$aA + bB \rightleftharpoons cC + dD,$$

$$Q = [C]^c[D]^d/[A]^a[B]^b$$

The reaction quotient Q relative to the equilibrium constant K is essentially a mea-

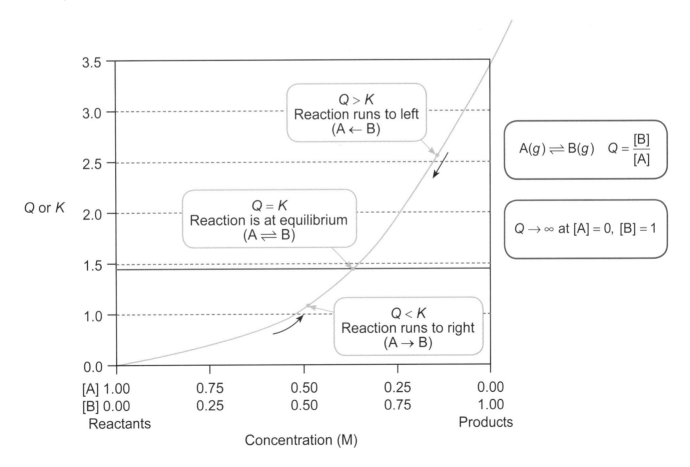

sure of the progress of a reaction toward equilibrium. The reaction quotient Q has many different values and changes continuously as a reaction progresses and depends on the current state of a reaction mixture. However, once all equilibrium concentrations have been reached, Q = K.

If Q = K, the reaction is at equilibrium and all concentrations are at equilibrium. If Q > K, there are more products initially than there are reactants so the reaction proceeds in reverse direction towards a decrease in product concentrations and a simultaneous increase in reactant concentrations until equilibrium is reached. If Q < K, there are more reactants then products and so the reaction proceeds forward towards product formation until equilibrium is reached.

9.9 Le Chatelier's Principle

Le Chatelier's principle states that whenever a perturbation is applied to a system at equilibrium, the system evolves in such a way as to compensate for the applied perturbation. For instance, consider the following equilibrium:

$$N_2 + 3H_2 \rightleftharpoons 2NH_3$$

If we introduce some more hydrogen in the reaction mixture at equilibrium, i.e. if we increase the concentration of hydrogen, the system will evolve in the direction that will decrease the concentration of hydrogen (from left to right). If more ammonia is introduced, the equilibrium shifts from the right-hand side to the left-hand side, while the removal of ammonia from the reaction vessel would do the opposite (i.e. shifts equilibrium from the left-hand side to the right-hand side).

In a similar fashion, an <u>increase in total pressure (decrease in volume)</u> favors the <u>direction which decreases the total number of compressible (i.e. gases) moles</u> (from the left-hand side where there are 4 moles to the right-hand side where there are 2 moles). It can also be said that when there are different forms of a gaseous substance, an increase in total pressure (decrease in volume) favors the form with the greatest density, and a decrease in total pressure (increase in volume) favors the form with the lowest density.

Finally, if the temperature of a reaction mixture at equilibrium is increased, the equilibrium evolves in the direction of the endothermic (heat-absorbing) reaction. For instance, the forward reaction of the equilibrium:

$$N_2O_4(g) \rightleftharpoons 2NO_2(g)$$

is endothermic; therefore, an increase in temperature favors the forward reaction over the backward reaction. In other words, the dissociation of N_2O_4 increases with temperature.

9.10 Relationship between the Equilibrium Constant and the Change in the Gibbs Free Energy

In the "thermodynamics" section we defined the Gibbs free energy (CHM 8.10). The *standard* Gibbs free energy ($G°$) is determined at 25 °C (298 K) and 1 atm. The change in the standard Gibbs free energy for a given reaction can be calculated from the change in the standard enthalpy and entropy of the reaction using:

$$\Delta G° = \Delta H - T \Delta S°$$

where T is the temperature at which the reaction is carried out. If this reaction happens to be the forward reaction of an equilibrium, the equilibrium constant associated with this equilibrium is simply given by:

$$\Delta G° = -R\,T \ln K_{eq}$$

where R is the ideal gas constant (1.99 cal mol^{-1} K^{-1}) and ln is the natural logarithm (i.e. log to the base e; see GM 3.7).

It is important to remember the sign for Gibbs free energy when the reaction is not spontaneous, spontaneous and at equilibrium (CHM 8.10).

After acid-bases, questions based on the information provided in this chapter (Chapter 9) would be the 2nd most frequently tested amongst ACER's practice materials for General Chemistry.

Go online to GAMSAT-prep.com for free chapter review Q&A and forum.

Memorize	Understand	Not Required*
Define: anode, cathode, anion, cation Define: standard half-cell potentials Define: strong/weak oxidizing/reducing agents	* Electrolytic cell, electrolysis * Calculation involving Faraday's law * Galvanic (voltaic) cell, purpose of salt bridge * Half reaction, reduction potentials * Direction of electron flow	* Knowledge beyond introductory-level (first year uni.) course * Memorizing the value of a faraday * Frost diagram

GAMSAT-Prep.com

Introduction

Electrochemistry links chemistry with electricity (the movement of electrons through a conductor). If a chemical reaction produces electricity (i.e. a battery or galvanic/voltaic cell) then it is an **electrochemical cell**. If electricity is applied externally to drive the chemical reaction then it is **electrolysis**. In general, oxidation/reduction reactions occur and are separated in space or time, connected by an external circuit. If you need to balance redox reactions using the "half-reaction method of balancing" (CHM 10.1) during the GAMSAT, you will be reminded of the rules (i.e. do not memorize them).

Additional Resources

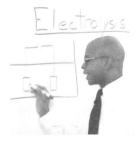

| Free Online Q & A | GAMSAT-prep.com Videos | Flashcards | Special Guest |

* The real GAMSAT may have advanced level information presented (ie. in a passage) but previous knowledge of said information is not required to answer the questions that would follow. Practice ACER and GS practice GAMSATs can help you clarify this point.

10.1 Generalities

Electrochemistry is based on oxidation-reduction or redox reactions in which one or more electrons are transferred from one ionic species to another. Recall that oxidation is defined as the loss of one or more electrons and reduction is defined as the gain in electron(s). In a redox reaction, reduction and oxidation must occur simultaneously. Before you read this section you should review the rules that allow the determination of the oxidation state of an element in a polyatomic molecule or ion and the definition of oxidation and reduction processes. We had previously applied the rules for the determination of oxidation numbers in the case of the following overall reaction (see CHM 1.6):

$$CuSO_4(aq) + Zn(s) \rightleftharpoons$$
Oxid.#: +2   0
$$Cu(s) + ZnSO_4(aq)$$
Oxid.#:   0   +2

The reduction and oxidation half-reactions of the forward process are:

reduction half-reaction:
$$Cu^{2+}(aq) + 2e^- \rightarrow Cu(s)$$

oxidation half-reaction:
$$Zn(s) \rightarrow Zn^{2+}(aq) + 2e^-$$

A half reaction does not occur on its own merit. Any reduction half reaction must be accompanied by an associated oxidation half reaction or vise versa, as electrons need to be transferred accordingly from one reactant to another. To determine the number and the side on which to put the electrons one follows the simple rules:

(i) The electrons are always on the left-hand side of a reduction half-reaction.

(ii) The electrons are always on the right-hand side of an oxidation half-reaction.

(iii) For a reduction half-reaction:

# of electrons required = initial oxidation #
                        – final oxidation #

(iv) For an oxidation half-reaction:
# of electrons required = final oxidation #
                        – initial oxidation #

The next step is to balance each half-reaction, i.e. the charges and the number of atoms of all the elements involved have to be equal on both sides. The preceding example is very simple since the number of electrons required in the two half-reactions is the same. Consider the following more complicated example:

reduction: $Sn^{2+}(aq) + 2e^- \rightarrow Sn(s)$
oxidation: $Al(s) \rightarrow Al^{3+}(aq) + 3e^-$

to balance the overall reaction you need to multiply the first half-reaction by a factor of 3 and the second by a factor of 2.

Balancing redox reactions in aqueous solutions may not always be as straight forward as balancing other types of chemical reactions. For redox type reactions, both the mass and the charge must be balanced. In addition, when looking at redox reactions occurring in aqueous solutions one must also consider at times if the solution is acidic or basic. The procedure used to balance redox reactions in acidic versus basic solutions is slightly different. Generally, the recommended steps used in balancing redox reactions is as follows and the method used is called the "*half-reaction method of balancing*":

1) Identify all the oxidation states of all elements within the redox reaction.

2) Identify the elements being oxidized and those being reduced.

3) Separate the overall redox reaction into its corresponding oxidation and reduction half reactions.

4) Balance all elements for each half reaction excluding hydrogen and oxygen.

5) Balance oxygen by the addition of water to the side missing the oxygen and balance the oxygen atoms by adding the appropriate coefficients in front of water.

6) Balance hydrogen by the addition of H^+ ion to the side missing the hydrogen atoms until hydrogen is balanced with the appropriate coefficients added. Note that the difference in balancing redox reactions in acidic versus basic aqueous solutions is at this step. In basic solutions, an additional step is required to neutralize the H^+ ions with the addition of OH^- ions so that both may then combine to form water.

7) Balance the half reactions with respect to charge by the addition of electrons on the appropriate side.

8) Balance the number of electrons for each half reaction by multiplying each of the half reactions (if required) with the appropriate coefficient.

9) Add the two half reactions making sure that all electrons are cancelled.

10) Finally, as a check: you should always verify that all elements and charges are balanced on both sides of the overall reaction and that the final overall reaction *never contains any free electrons.*

Example: In acidic solution, balance the following redox reaction:

$$Fe^{2+} (aq) + MnO_4^- (aq) \rightarrow Fe^{3+} (aq) + Mn^{2+} (aq)$$

Step 1:   +2   +7 –2   +3   +2

Step 2:
Fe is oxidized (+2 to +3)
Mn in MnO_4^- is reduced to Mn^{2+}
(+7 to +2, oxygen will be balanced with water)

Step 3:
Oxidation: $Fe^{2+} (aq) \rightarrow Fe^{3+} (aq)$
Reduction: $MnO_4^- (aq) \rightarrow Mn^{2+} (aq)$

Step 4, 5 and 6:
Oxidation: $Fe^{2+} (aq) \rightarrow Fe^{3+} (aq)$
Reduction: $8H^+ (aq) + MnO_4^- (aq)$
$\rightarrow Mn^{2+} (aq) + 4H_2O (l)$

Step 7:
Oxidation: $Fe^{2+} (aq) \rightarrow Fe^{3+} (aq) + 1e^-$
Reduction: $5e^- + 8H^+ (aq) + MnO_4^- (aq)$
$\rightarrow Mn^{2+} (aq) + 4H_2O (l)$

Step 8:
Oxidation: $5[Fe^{2+} (aq) \rightarrow Fe^{3+} (aq) + 1e^-]$
$5Fe^{2+} (aq) \rightarrow 5Fe^{3+} (aq) + 5e^-$
Reduction: $5e^- + 8H^+ (aq) + MnO_4^- (aq)$
$\rightarrow Mn^{2+} (aq) + 4H_2O (l)$

Step 9:
Overall: $5Fe^{2+} (aq) + 8H^+ (aq) + MnO_4^- (aq)$
$\rightarrow 5Fe^{3+} (aq) + Mn^{2+} (aq) + 4H_2O (l)$

Step 10:   Check if all is balanced.

The oxidation/reduction capabilities of substances are measured by their standard reduction half reaction potentials $E°(V)$. The reduction potential $E°(V)$ is a measure of the tendency of a chemical species to acquire electrons and thereby be reduced. The more positive the reduction potential, the more likely the species is to be reduced. Thus, the species would be regarded as a strong oxidizing agent. These potentials are relative. The reference half-cell electrode chosen to measure the relative potential of all other half cells is known as the **s**tandard **h**ydrogen **e**lectrode or SHE and it corresponds to the following half-reaction:

$$2H^+(1 \text{ molar}) + 2e^- \rightarrow H_2(1 \text{ atm}) \quad E° = 0.00 \text{ (V)}.$$

As the reference SHE cell potential is defined as 0.00 V, any half-cell system that accepts electrons from a SHE cell is reduced and therefore defined by a positive redox potential. Alternatively, any half-cell that donates electrons to a SHE cell is defined by a negative redox potential. Thus, the larger the reduction potential value of a half-cell, the greater the tendency for that half-cell to gain electrons and become reduced.

Standard half-cell potentials for other half-reactions have been tabulated and you will see examples to follow, and more in the online practice questions. They are defined for standard conditions, i.e., concentration of all ionic species equal to 1 molar and pressure of all gases involved, if any, equal to 1 atm. The standard temperature is taken as 25 °C. In the case of the Cu^{2+}/Zn reaction the relevant data is tabulated as reduction potentials as follows:

$$Zn^{2+}(aq) + 2e^- \rightarrow Zn(s) \quad E° = -0.76 \text{ volts}$$
$$Cu^{2+}(aq) + 2e^- \rightarrow Cu(s) \quad E° = +0.34 \text{ volts}$$

As shown, it can be seen that the Cu/Cu^{2+} electrode is positive relative to the SHE and that the Zn/Zn^{2+} is negative relative to the SHE. The more positive the $E°$ value, the more likely the reaction will occur spontaneously as written. The <u>strongest reducing agents</u> have <u>large negative $E°$ values</u>. The <u>strongest oxidizing agents</u> have <u>large positive $E°$ values</u>. Therefore, in our example Cu^{2+} is a stronger oxidizing agent than Zn^{2+}. This conclusion can be expressed in the following practical terms:

(i) If you put Zn in contact with a solution containing Cu^{2+} ions a spontaneous redox reaction will occur.

$$Zn(s) \rightarrow Zn^{2+} (aq) + 2e^-; \quad E°(V) = +0.76$$
$$Cu^{2+} (aq) + 2e^- \rightarrow Cu(s); \quad E°(V) = +0.34$$
$$E°_{cell} = E°_{red} + E°_{ox} = +0.34 + 0.76 = +1.10 \text{ V}.$$

(ii) If you put Cu directly in contact with a solution containing Zn^{2+} ions, no reaction takes place spontaneously.

$$Cu(s) \rightarrow Cu^{2+} (aq) + 2e^-; \quad E°(V) = -0.34$$
$$Zn^{2+} (aq) + 2e^- \rightarrow Zn(s); \quad E°(V) = -0.76$$
$$E°_{cell} = E°_{red} + E°_{ox} = -0.76 + (-0.34) = -1.10 \text{ V}.$$

Thus for the spontaneous reaction:

$$\textbf{(1)} \quad E° = E°_{red} - E°_{ox}$$
$$E° = E°_{red} - E°_{ox} = +0.34 - (-0.76) = 1.10 \text{ V}.$$
$$\text{or } \textbf{(2)} \; E°_{cell} = E°_{red} + E°_{ox} = +0.34 + 0.76 = 1.10 \text{ V}.$$

The positive value confirms the spontaneous nature of the reaction. {The theme of many exam questions: the oxidizing agent is *reduced*; the reducing agent is *oxidized*}

For a cell potential (E°) calculation, if one is to calculate it using the formula (1) should use the tabulated reduction potentials for both half cell reduction reactions. Alternatively, if one were to calculate the cell potential using the second formula (2), the half cell potential that has the lower potential value or the oxidized half cell (more negative value), needs to be reversed to have it in an oxidized format and therefore the electromotive (E°) potential sign itself is also inverted accordingly and the sum of the two half cells is then calculated. Also, note that the stoichiometric factors are <u>not</u> used if one is simply calculating the E° of the cell (because the concentrations are, of course, standard at 1 M).

10.2 Galvanic Cells

As a result of a redox reaction, one may harvest a substantial amount of energy and the energy generated is usually carried out in what is known as an electrochemical cell. There are two types of electrochemical cells: a galvanic (or voltaic) cell and an electrolytic cell. A galvanic cell produces electrical energy from a spontaneous chemical reaction that takes place within an electrochemical cell. On the other hand, an electrolytic cell induces a nonspontaneous chemical reaction within an electrochemical cell by the consumption of electrical energy.

Batteries are self-contained galvanic cells. A <u>galvanic cell</u> uses a <u>spontaneous redox reaction</u> to <u>produce electricity</u>. For instance, one can design a galvanic cell based on the spontaneous reaction:

$$Zn(s) + CuSO_4(aq) \rightarrow Cu(s) + ZnSO_4(aq)$$

An actual view of a galvanic cell is depicted in Figure III.A.10.1a. In addition, Figure III.A.10.1b shows a sketch of a line diagram of the same galvanic cell outlining all the different parts. Note that in Figure III.A.10.1b, Zn is not in direct contact with the Cu^{2+} solution; otherwise electrons will be directly transferred from Zn to Cu^{2+} and no electricity will be produced to an external circuit.

The half-reaction occurring in the left-hand (anode) compartment is the oxidation:

$$Zn(s) \rightarrow Zn^{2+}(aq) + 2e^-$$

The half-reaction occurring in the right-hand (cathode) compartment is the reduction:

$$Cu^{2+}(aq) + 2e^- \rightarrow Cu(s)$$

Therefore, <u>electrons flow</u> out of the compartment where the <u>oxidation</u> occurs to the compartment where the <u>reduction</u> takes place.

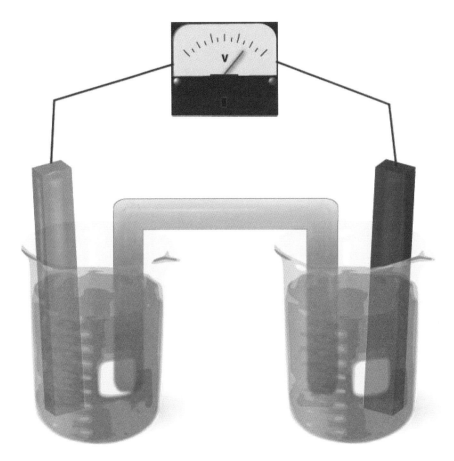

Figure III.A.10.1a: A galvanic (electrochemical) cell. As shown by the displacement in voltage via the volt-meter, the energy of a spontaneous redox reaction is essentially captured within the galvanic cell. A galvanic cell consists mainly of the following parts: **1)** Two separate half cells; **2)** Two solid element electrodes with differing redox potentials; **3)** Two opposing aqueous solutions each in contact with opposing solid electrodes; **4)** One salt bridge with an embedded salt solution; **5)** One ammeter or voltmeter and; **6)** An electrical solid element or wire to allow conductivity of electrons from anode to cathode.

The metallic parts (Cu(*s*) and Zn(*s*) in our example) of the galvanic cell which allow its connection to an external circuit are called <u>electrodes</u>. The electrode <u>out</u> of which <u>electrons flow</u> is the <u>anode</u>, the electrode <u>receiving</u> these <u>electrons</u> is the <u>cathode</u>. In a galvanic cell the <u>oxidation</u> occurs in the <u>anodic compartment</u> and the <u>reduction</u> in the <u>cathodic compartment</u>. The voltage difference between the two electrodes is called the <u>electromotive</u> force (*emf*) of the cell. The voltage is measured by the voltmeter.

All of the participants belonging to each of the half cells are included within their respective half cell. Consequently, one half of the electrochemical cell consists of an appropriate metal (Zn) immersed within a solution containing the ionic form of the same metal ($ZnSO_4$). The other half then contains the

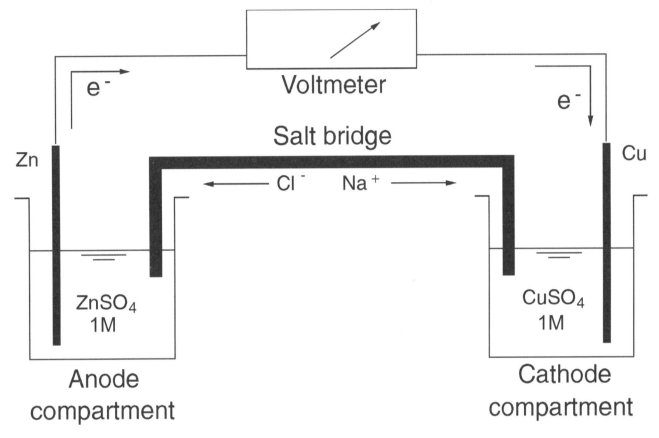

Figure III.A.10.1b: Line diagram of a galvanic (electrochemical) cell.

complementary metal (Cu) immersed into an aqueous solution consisting of its metal ion ($CuSO_4$) (Figure III.A.10.1b).

In certain cells, however, the participants involved in the reduction half reaction may all be part of the aqueous solution; in such a case, an inert electrode would replace the respective metal electrode. The inert electrode such as graphite or platinum would act as a conductive surface for electron transfer. An example of such a half-cell would be one where the reduction of manganese (Mn^{7+}) as MnO_4^- occurs in a solution which

also contains manganese as ions (Mn^{2+}). To complete the electrochemical circuit, the two half-cells are then connected with a conducting wire which provides a means for electron flow. Electrons always flow from the anode (oxidation half-cell) to the cathode (reduction half-cell). The electrical energy from the flow of electrons may then be harvested and transformed into some alternative form of energy or mechanical work (as required). In order to prevent an excessive charge build up within each of the half-cell solutions as a result of oxidation and reduction reactions at the anode and cathode, a salt bridge is constructed and used to connect both half-cell solutions.

> **Mnemonic:** LEO is A GERC
> - Lose Electrons Oxidation is Anode
> - Gain Electrons Reduction at Cathode

Electrochemical cells are usually represented as a cell diagram or a compact notation denoting all the parts of the cell. For example,

the cell diagram of the cell that was previously discussed in which Zn is oxidized and Cu reduced would be represented as follows:

$$Zn(s) \mid Zn^{2+}(aq) \parallel Cu^{2+}(aq) \mid Cu(s).$$

The oxidation half reaction is on the left and the reduction half reaction is on the right side of the cell diagram. The single vertical lines represent the substances of each half-cell in different phases (solid and aqueous) and the double vertical line represents the salt bridge.

10.2.1 The Salt Bridge

A salt bridge is a U-shaped tube with a strong electrolyte (CHM 5.3.2) suspended in a gel allowing the flow of the ions into the half-cell solutions. The salt bridge connects the two compartments chemically (for example, with Na^+ and Cl^-). It has two important functions:

1) Maintenance of Neutrality: As $Zn(s)$ becomes $Zn^{2+}(aq)$, the net charge in the anode compartment becomes positive. To maintain neutrality, Cl^- ions migrate to the anode compartment. The reverse occurs in the cathode compartment: positive ions are lost (Cu^{2+}), therefore positive ions must be gained (Na^+).

2) Completing the Circuit: Imagine the galvanic cell as a circuit. Negative charge leaves the anode compartment via *electrons* in a wire and then returns via *chemicals* (i.e. Cl^-) in the salt bridge. Thus the galvanic cell is an *electrochemical* cell.

As an alternative to a salt bridge, the solutions (i.e. $ZnSO_4$ and $CuSO_4$) can be placed in one container separated by a porous material which allows certain ions to cross (i.e. SO_4^{2-}, Zn^{2+}). Thus it would serve the same functions as the salt bridge.

10.3 Concentration Cell

If the concentration of the ions in one of the compartments of a galvanic cell is not 1 molar, the half-cell potential E is either higher or lower than E°. Therefore, in principle one could use the same substance in both compartments but with different concentrations to produce electricity.

Thus, one may construct a galvanic cell in which both half-cell reactions are the same however, the difference in concentration is the driving force for the flow of current. The emf is equal in this case to the difference between the two potentials E. Such a cell is called a concentration cell.

To determine the direction of electron flow the same rules as previously described are used. The cathodic compartment, in which the reduction takes place is the one corresponding to the largest positive (smallest negative) E.

The electromotive force varies with the differences in concentration of solutions in the half-cells. When the concentration of solution is not equal to 1M, the emf or E_{cell} can be determined by the use of the Nernst equation as follows:

$$E_{cell} = E°_{cell} - (RT/nF)(\ln Q)$$

or

$$E_{cell} = E°_{cell} - 0.0592V/n \, (\log Q)$$

where; $E°_{cell}$ is the standard electromotive force, R is the gas constant 8.314J/Kmol, T is the absolute temperature in K, F is the Faraday's constant (CHM 10.5), n is the number of moles of electrons exchanged or transferred in the redox reaction, and Q is the reaction quotient (CHM 9.8.1).

Under standard conditions, Q = 1.00 as all concentrations are at 1.00 M and since log 1 = 0, $E_{cell} = E°_{cell}$.

The police stopped a driver who had NaCl and a 9 volt. He was booked for a salt and battery.

10.4 Electrolytic Cell

There is a fundamental difference between a galvanic cell or a concentration cell and an <u>electrolytic cell</u>: in the first type of electrochemical cell a <u>spontaneous redox</u> reaction is used to produce a current, in the second type a current is actually imposed on the system to drive a <u>non-spontaneous redox reaction</u>. A cathode is defined as the electrode to which cations flow to and an anode is defined as the electrode to which anions flow. Thus, a similarity between the two cells is that the <u>cat</u>hode attracts <u>cat</u>ions, whereas the <u>an</u>ode attracts <u>an</u>ions. In both the galvanic cell and the electrolytic cell, reduction occurs always at the cathode and oxidation always occurs at the anode.

Remember the following key concepts:

(i) generally a battery is used to produce a current which is imposed on the electrolytic cell.

(ii) the battery acts as an electron pump: electrons flow into the electrolytic cell at the <u>cathode</u> and flow out of it at the <u>anode</u>.

(iii) the half-reaction occurring at the <u>cathode</u> is a <u>reduction</u> since it requires electrons.

(iv) the half-reaction occurring at the <u>anode</u> is an <u>oxidation</u> since it produces electrons.

In galvanic cells, a spontaneous oxidation reaction takes place at the cell's anode creating a source of electrons. For this reason, the anode is considered the negative electrode. However, in electrolytic cells, a non-spontaneous reduction reaction takes place at the cell's cathode using an external electrical energy as the source of electrons such as a battery. For this reason, the cathode is considered the negative electrode.

An electrolytic cell is composed of three parts: an electrolyte solution and two electrodes made from an inert material (i.e. platinum). The oxidation and reduction half reactions are usually placed in one container.

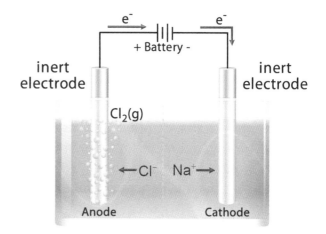

The diagram is a depiction of the electrolysis of molten NaCl. As such, the Na^+ and Cl^- ions are the only species that are present in the electrolytic cell. Thus, the chloride anion (Cl^-) cannot be reduced any further and so it is oxidized at the anode and the sodium cation (Na^+) is therefore reduced. The final products are sodium solid formation at the cathode and chlorine (Cl_2) gas formation at the anode.

Note: the flow of electrons is still from anode to cathode as is for galvanic cells.

10.5 Faraday's Law

Faraday's law relates the amount of elements deposited or gas liberated at an electrode due to current (PHY 9.1, 10.1).

We have seen that in a galvanic cell $Cu^{2+}(aq)$ can accept electrons to become $Cu(s)$ which will actually plate onto the electrode. Faraday's Law allows us to calculate the amount of $Cu(s)$. In fact, the law states that the weight of product formed at an electrode is proportional to the amount of electricity transferred at the electrode and to the equivalent weight of the material. Thus we can conclude that 1 mole of $Cu^{2+}(aq)$ + 2 moles of electrons will leave 1 mole of $Cu(s)$ at the electrode. One mole (= Avogadro's number) of electrons is called a *faraday* ($\mathcal{F}$). A faraday is equivalent to 96 500 coulombs. A coulomb is the amount of electricity that is transferred when a current of one ampere flows for one second ($1C = 1A \cdot s$).

10.5.1 Electrolysis Problem

How many grams of copper would be deposited on the cathode of an electrolytic cell if, for a period of 20 minutes, a current of 2.0 amperes is run through a solution of $CuSO_4$? {The molecular weight of copper is 63.5.}

Calculate the number of coulombs:

$$Q = It = 2.0\ A \times 20\ min \times 60\ sec/min$$
$$= 2400\ C$$

Thus

$$Faradays = 2400\ C \times 1\mathcal{F}/96\ 500\ C$$
$$= 0.025\mathcal{F}$$

Faradays can be related to moles of copper since

$$Cu^{2+} + 2e^- \rightarrow Cu$$

Since 1 mol Cu: 2 mol e⁻ we can write

$$0.025\mathcal{F} \times (1\ mol\ Cu/2\mathcal{F}) \times (63.5g\ Cu/mol\ Cu)$$
$$= 0.79g\ Cu$$

Electrolysis would deposit 0.79 g of copper at the cathode.

To do the previous problem, you must know the definition of current and charge (CHM 10.5) but the value of the constant (a Faraday) would be given on the exam. You should be able to perform the preceding calculation quickly and efficiently because it involves dimensional analysis (GM 2.2).

"A diamond is merely a lump of coal that did well under pressure." Another big step in your GAMSAT prep is behind you! Review your Gold Notes and practice, practice, practice! Good luck!

Go online to GAMSAT-prep.com for free chapter review Q&A and forum.

Common Root Words of Scientific Terms

The following is a list of root words, prefixes, and suffixes, which you may find helpful for your GAMSAT Section 3 review, problems and/or tests. Of course, a prefix is a group of letters added to the beginning of a word; a suffix is added to the end of a word.

Prefixes

A
aden- gland
adip- fat
aero- air
agri- field; soil
alb- white
alg-/algia- pain
alto- high
ambi- both
ameb- change; alternation
amni- fetal membrane
amphi-; ampho- both
amyl- starch
ana- up; back; again
andro- man; masculine
anemo- wind
angi- blood vessel; duct
ante- before; ahead of time
anter- front
antho- flower
anthropo- man; human
aqu- water
archaeo- primitive; ancient
arteri- artery
arthr- joint; articulation
aster-; astr- ; astro- star
ather- fatty deposit
atmo- vapor
audi- hear

aur- ear
auto- self

B
bacter-/bactr- bacterium; stick; club
baro- weight
bath- depth; height
bene- well; good
bi- (Latin) two; twice
bi-/bio- (Greek) life; living
brachi- arm
brachy- short
brady- slow
branchi- fin
bronch- windpipe

C
calor- heat
capill- hair
capit- head
carcin- cancer
cardi-/cardio- heart
carn- meat; flesh
carp- fruit
carpal- wrist
cata- breakdown; downward
caud- tail
cente- pierce
centi- hundredth

centr- center
cephal- head
cerat- horn
cerebr- brain
cervic- neck
chel- claw
chem- dealing with chemicals
chir- hand
chlor- green
chondr- cartilage
chrom-/chromo- color
chron- time
circa-; circum- around; about
cirru- hairlike curls
co- with; together
cocc- seed; berry
coel- hollow
coll- glue
coni- cone
contra- against
corp- body
cort-/cortic- outer layer
cosmo- world; order; form
cotyl- cup
counter- against
crani- skull
cresc-/cret- begin to grow
crypt- hidden; covered

Prefixes

cumul- heaped
cuti- skin
cyt- cell; hollow
   container

D
dactyl- finger
deca- ten
deci- tenth
deliquesc- become fluid
demi- half
dendr- tree
dent- tooth
derm- skin
di-/dipl- (Latin) two;
   double
di-/dia- (Greek) through;
   across; apart
dia- (Latin) day
digit- finger; toe
din- terrible
dis- apart; out
dorm- sleep
dors- back
du-/duo- two
dynam- power
dys- bad; abnormal;
   difficult

E
ec- out of; away from
echin- spiny; prickly
eco- house
ecto- outside of
en-/endo-/ent- in; into;
   within
encephal- brain
enter- intestine; gut
entom- insects
epi- upon; above; over

erythro- red
eso- inward; within;
   inner

F
ferro- iron
fibr- fiber; thread
fiss- split
flor- flower
flu-; fluct-; flux flow
foli- leaf
fract- break

G
gastr- stomach
geo- land; earth
gloss- tongue
gluc-/glyc- sweet; sugar
glut- buttock
gnath- jaw
gymno- naked; bare
gyn- female
gyr- ring; circle; spiral

H
halo- salt
hapl- simple
hecto- hundred
hem- blood
hemi- half
hepar/hepat- liver
herb- grass; plants
hetero- different; other
hex- six
hibern- winter
hidr- sweat
hipp- horse
hist- tissue
holo- entire; whole
homo- (Latin) man;

   human
homo- (Greek) same;
   alike
hort- garden
hydr- water
hygr- moist; wet
hyper- above; beyond;
   over
hyph- weaving; web
hypno- sleep
hypo- below; under; less
hyster- womb; uterus

I
ichthy- fish
infra- below; beneath
inter- between
intra- within; inside
iso- equal; same

K
kel- tumor; swelling
kerat- horn
kilo- thousand
kine- move

L
lachry- tear
lact- milk
lat- side
leio- smooth
leuc-/leuk- white; bright;
   light
lign- wood
lin- line
lingu- tongue
lip- fat
lith-; -lite stone;
   petrifying

Prefixes

loc- place
lumin- light

M
macr- large
malac- soft
malle- hammer
mamm- breast
marg- border; edge
mast- breast
med- middle
meg- million; great
mela-/melan- black;
    dark
mes- middle; half;
    intermediate
met-/meta- between;
    along; after
micro- small; millionth
milli- thousandth
mis- wrong; incorrect
mito- thread
mole- mass
mono- one; single
mort- death
morph- shape; form
multi- many
mut- change
my- muscle
myc- fungus
mycel- threadlike
myria- many
moll- soft

N
nas- nose
necr- corpse; dead
nemat- thread
neo- new; recent
nephro- kidney

neur- nerve
noct-/nox- night
non- not
not- back
nuc- center

O
ob- against
ocul- eye
oct- eight
odont- tooth
olf- smell
oligo- few; little
omni- all
onc- mass; tumor
opthalm- eye
opt- eye
orb- circle; round; ring
ornith- bird
orth- straight; correct;
    right
oscu- mouth
oste- bone
oto- ear
ov-/ovi- egg
oxy- sharp; acid; oxygen

P
pachy - thick
paleo- old; ancient
palm- broad; flat
pan- all
par-/para- beside; near;
    equal
path- disease; suffering
pent- five
per- through
peri- around
permea- pass; go
phag- eat

pheno- show
phon- sound
photo- light
phren- mind; diaphragm
phyc- seaweed; algae
phyl- related group
physi- nature; natural
    qualities
phyt- plant
pino- drink
pinni- feather
plan- roaming;
    wandering
plasm- formed into
platy- flat
pleur- lung; rib; side
pneumo- lungs; air
poly- many; several
por- opening
port- carry
post- after; behind
pom- fruit
pre- before; ahead of
    time
prim- first
pro- forward; favoring;
    before
proto- first; primary
pseudo- false; deceptive
psych- mind
pter- having wings or
    fins
pulmo- lung
puls- drive; push
pyr- heat; fire

Q
quadr- four
quin- five

Prefixes

R
radi- ray
ren- kidney
ret- net; made like a net
rhe- flow
rhin- nose
rhiz- root
rhodo- rose
roto- wheel
rubr- red

S
sacchar- sugar
sapr- rotten
sarc- flesh
saur- lizard
schis-/schiz- split; divide
sci- know
scler- hard
semi- half; partly
sept- partition; seven
sex- six
sol- sun
solv- loosen; free
som-/somat- body
somn- sleep
son- sound
spec-/spic- look at
spir- breathe

stat- standing; staying
stell- stars
sten- narrow
stern- chest; breast
stom- mouth
strat- layer
stereo- solid;
    3-dimensional
strict- drawn tight
styl- pillar
sub- under; below
super-/sur- over; above;
    on top
sym-/syn- together

T
tachy- quick; swift
tarso- ankle
tax- arrange; put in
order
tele- far off; distant
telo- end
terr- earth; land
tetr- four
thall- young shoot
toxico- poison
top- place
trache- windpipe
trans- across

tri- three
trich- hair
turb- whirl

U
ultra- beyond
uni- one
ur- urine

V
vas- vessel
vect- carry
ven-/vent- come
ventr- belly; underside
vig- strong
vit-/viv- life
volv- roll; wander

X
xanth- yellow
xero- dry
xyl- wood

Z
zo- animal
zyg- joined together
zym- yeast

Suffixes

A
-ap/-aph -touch
-ary/-arium -place for
    something
-ase -forms names of
    enzymes

B
-blast -sprout; germ;
    bud

C
-cell -chamber; small
    room

-chrome -color
-chym -juice
-cid/-cis -cut; kill; fall
-cul/-cule -small;
    diminutive
-cyst -sac; pouch;
    bladder

-cyte -cell; hollow
    container

D
-duct -lead

E
-elle -small
-emia -blood
-en -made of
-eous -nature of; like
-err -wander; go astray

F
-fer -bear; carry;
    produce
-fid -divided into
-flect/-flex -bend

G
-gam -marriage
-gene -origin; birth
-gest -carry; produce;
    bear
-glen -eyeball
-glob -ball; round
-gon -angle; corner

H
-hal/-hale -breathe;
    breath
-helminth -worm

I
-iac -person afflicted
    with disease
-iasis -disease;
    abnormal condition
-ism -a state or
    condition
-ist -person who deals
    with...
-itis -inflammation;
    disease

-ium -refers to a part of
    the body

K
-kary -cell nucleus

L
-less -without
-log -word; speech
-logist -one who
    studies...
-logy -study of...
-lys/-lyt/-lyst
    -decompose; split;
    dissolve

M
-mer -part
-meter/-metry
    measurement
-mot -move

N
-ner -moist; liquid
-node -knot
-nom/-nomy -ordered
    knowledge; law

O
-oid -form; appearance
-oma -abnormal
    condition; tumor
-orium/-ory -place for
    something
-osis -abnormal
    condition

P
-pathy -disease;
    suffering
-ped -foot
-ped -child
-phil -loving; fond of
-phone -sound

-phore; pher -bear;
    carry
-phyll -leaf
-phyte -plant
-plast -form
-pod -foot

R
-rrhage -burst forth
-rrhea -flow

S
-scop -look; device for
    seeing
-septic -infection;
    putrefaction
-sis -condition; state
-sperm -seed
-spher -ball; round
-spire -breathe
-spor -seed
-stasis -placed
-stome -mouth

T
-the/-thes -put
-thel -cover a surface
-therm -heat
-tom -cut; slice
-trop -turn; change
-troph -nourishment;
    one who feeds

U
-ul/-ule -diminutive;
    small
-ura -tail

V
-verge -turn; slant
-vor -devour; eat

Z
-zoa -animal

The Natural Order to Learn Science

This textbook is arranged such that each section presumes that you have completed your review of the previous section. The adventure begins with GAMSAT Math. Math provides the necessary basis for Physics and Chemistry and is invaluable for GAMSAT graph interpretation and analysis which is even more important than assumed knowledge for Biology.

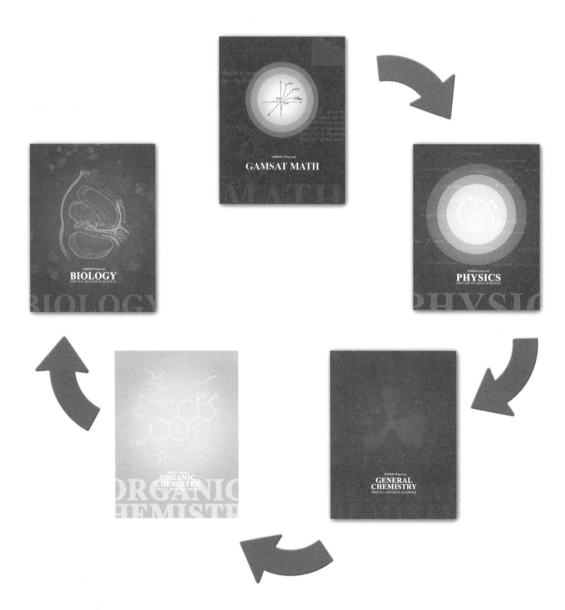